Confucian Iconoclasm

SUNY series in Chinese Philosophy and Culture

Roger T. Ames, editor

Confucian Iconoclasm

Textual Authority, Modern Confucianism,
and the Politics of Antitradition
in Republican China

PHILIPPE MAJOR

Cover Credit: Song Dynasty wooden statue in the Qingxu Daoist Temple in Pingyao (2007). Photograph by the author.

Open-access version of this text has been made possible due to the support of the Swiss National Science Foundation.

© 2023 State University of New York

All rights reserved

Printed in the United States of America

No part of this book may be used or reproduced in any manner whatsoever without written permission. No part of this book may be stored in a retrieval system or transmitted in any form or by any means including electronic, electrostatic, magnetic tape, mechanical, photocopying, recording, or otherwise without the prior permission in writing of the publisher.

For information, contact State University of New York Press, Albany, NY
www.sunypress.edu

Library of Congress Cataloging-in-Publication Data

Name: Major, Philippe, 1981– author.
Title: Confucian iconoclasm : textual authority, modern Confucianism, and the politics of antitradition in Republican China / Philippe Major.
Description: Albany : State University of New York Press, [2023] | Series: SUNY series in Chinese philosophy and culture | Includes bibliographical references and index.
Identifiers: LCCN 2023009059 | ISBN 9781438495484 (hardcover : alk. paper) | ISBN 9781438495507 (ebook) | ISBN 9781438495491 (pbk. : alk paper)
Subjects: LCSH: Confucianism—China—History—20th century.
Classification: LCC BL1840 .M333 2023 | DDC 299.5/12095105—dc23/eng/20230817
LC record available at https://lccn.loc.gov/2023009059

10 9 8 7 6 5 4 3 2 1

For Francesca

Contents

Acknowledgements	ix
Introduction	1
Chapter 1 Reviving the Spirit of Confucius	29
Chapter 2 Returning to the Origin	59
Interlude Contextualizing Teleological History and Individual Autonomy	83
Chapter 3 Performing Sagely Authority	97
Chapter 4 Subsuming the Truth of Former Masters and Sages	133
Conclusion Hegemony and the Politics of Antitradition	165
Notes	183
Bibliography	243
Index	263

Acknowledgments

If texts can indeed be described as textiles made of relatively novel patterns woven with the threads of tradition, as I suggest in the introduction, the present text is certainly no exception. Of the many threads that form the fabric of *Confucian Iconoclasm*, some are acknowledged in the references that crowd the endnotes. Others remain hidden from the view of the reader, however, as they were acquired from professional and personal relationships that informed and shaped both the text and its author.

Let me begin by acknowledging the relationships that molded a previous iteration of this text: my doctoral dissertation. First and foremost, I would like to thank my advisor, Professor Tan Sor-hoon, who provided invaluable comments and suggestions after tireless and prompt readings and rereadings of early drafts of the manuscript. Professor Tan's open-mindedness, her ability to adapt to my research pace and style, and her talent for steering me back on the right path whenever I erred are all remembered fondly.

I would also like to thank Professor Alan Cole, whose courses at the National University of Singapore on Chan Buddhism were a tremendous inspiration for the present project. Professor Cole's work on lineage-making, textual authority, and fetishizing tradition provided me with threads so fundamental that without them my dissertation would have taken an entirely different, and vastly impoverished, shape.

During the third year of my PhD, I spent two terms at KU Leuven, where I had the opportunity to meet Professor Carine Defoort, whose remarkable research, generosity, open-mindedness, friendliness, and fearless ability to question the status quo in academia were and still are an inspiration for me. It has been an honor to continue collaborating with Professor Defoort ever since. Her comments on earlier drafts of the introduction and conclusion were of great help in improving the manuscript. My work is also greatly indebted to Professor Nicolas Standaert, whose research, notably on the art of in-betweenness of Sinology, has been greatly inspiring to me. While living in Leuven, I also met with Professor Thierry Meynard, whose encouragement, support, and generosity were a great source of strength to pursue my research on Liang Shuming. I would also like to thank current and former PhDs of the Sinology Department of KU Leuven, who provided valuable feedback on the conclusion of the book and on an early draft of chapter 3: Chang Yao-Cheng 張堯程, Wang Xiaowei 王晓薇, Markus Haselbeck, Chen Yanrong 陈妍蓉, Wu Xiaoxin 吴晓欣, and Yang Hongfan 杨虹帆.

I would also like to express my sincere gratitude to the examiners of my doctoral dissertation. First, I would like to thank Professor Loy Hui Chieh, whose comments on the thesis but also on my work during the four years of the PhD program always challenged me to rethink and question my assumptions. I also thank Professor Huang Jianli for his encouraging comments on the thesis. And finally, I would like to express my deepest gratitude to Professor John Makeham, whose many comments and suggestions have brought to my attention numerous aspects of the thesis that required clarification and improvement. The thesis and the present book were both vastly improved and enriched thanks to Professor Makeham.

At the end of my PhD, I also spent six months at the Institute of Chinese Literature and Philosophy of Academia Sinica, where I received the generous support of Dr. Huang Kuan-min 黃冠閔. I had previously spent four years in Taiwan, three of which were devoted to the MA program in History at National Taiwan University. During this period, I learned tremendously from my advisor Professor Wu Chan-liang 吳展良, who introduced me to modern Chinese intellectual history and Liang Shuming.

While rewriting the thesis into the present book, I benefited from the tremendous support of, and inspiration from, my colleagues of the University of Basel research project *The Exterior of Philosophy: On the Practice of New Confucianism*. I cannot thank enough Professor Ralph Weber, whose comments on the book project and the terminologies that inform it were invaluable, as well as Chan Yim Fong 陳艷芳 and Milan Matthiesen, who tirelessly read through each chapter and provided innumerable comments and extremely valuable suggestions that contributed to making the book what it is.

Finally, I cannot thank my wife, Francesca Pierini, enough for her continuous love and support throughout the years—and her help with copyediting. Her strength, independence, and courage have been a source of inspiration from the first time we met in 2009 until today. Without her love, support, and friendship, this book would simply not exist. I would also like to thank my parents, Charles and Danielle, and my sister Isabelle for their continued support throughout the years.

I would also like to thank everyone at SUNY Press for their precious help during the review and editing processes, including Roger T. Ames, James Peltz, Ryan Morris, Laura Tendler, John Britch, and Aimee Harrison. I would also like to express my gratitude for the valuable comments and suggestions provided by the blind reviewers.

I would also like to acknowledge the many places that inspired this book and its previous iterations: Singapore, Koh Siboya, Sant'Elpidio a Mare, Scansano, Leuven, Wellington, Hong Kong, Ubud, Taipei, Basel, Nicotera, Piane Vecchie, and Las Palmas. I thank the following institutions and organizations for providing funding for the research that went into the present book: National University of Singapore, Academia Sinica, Nanyang Confucius Association, the Research Centre for Chinese Philosophy and Culture of the Chinese University of Hong Kong, and the Fonds de recherche du Québec–société et culture. I also thank the Swiss National Science Foundation for providing open access funding for the publication.

Finally, a short note about the cover. I took the picture at the Qingxu Daoist Temple (*Qingxu guan* 清虛觀) in Pingyao (平遙) in 2007. Built in the Tang dynasty, the temple includes more than twenty wooden statues produced during the Song period. It is unclear whether the missing section of the statue's head is time's doing or the result of human iconoclasm.

Introduction

Conventional wisdom has it that Confucians are, if not conservatives, at least traditionalists. Does the *Analects* (*Lunyu* 論語) not say that Confucius followed the Zhou; that he was a transmitter, not an innovator?[1] Is the history of Confucianism not marked by repeated attempts at returning to the source of tradition, whether this source be found in Old or New Texts, in the Five Classics or the Four Books? To be sure, a number of scholars have emphasized that Confucian traditionalism is not averse to change and innovation (despite what the Confucius of the *Analects* is recorded as having said), nor is it necessarily hostile to the idea that tradition must be adapted to new times, lest it loses its status of tradition and recedes into the ever-expanding dominion of the past.[2] But to think of Confucianism as iconoclastic seems inappropriate, oxymoronic. And yet in what follows it is argued that Confucian iconoclasm was the most important form, if judged in terms of its success, that the modern Confucian textual response to May Fourth took during the Republican period.

An alternative narrative

The predominant narrative of modern or New Confucianism has it that the movement—if movement there was—emerged in the 1920s as a reaction against May Fourth iconoclasm.[3] First and foremost, it gave itself the task of *preserving* tradition and pushing back against calls to bring about the wholesale modernization and westernization of China—the two being often equated in May Fourth parlance. Not that modern Confucians were entirely against modernization. They did recognize the value of science and democracy, and did acknowledge that to preserve tradition, they had to adapt it to the changing times. Preserving tradition did not entail a simple process whereby the contemporaries would passively inherit what was passed down onto them. It referred to a critical reappraisal of tradition that would abstract from it core values that could remain relevant in the modern period. That preservation left room for adaptation suggests that what the modern Confucians fought against was less modernization than its wholesale advocacy by the protagonists of the May Fourth Movement.[4]

In what follows, I present an alternative narrative, one that builds on the account presented above yet also diverts from it in important ways. Building on recent historiographical trends that have revealed important continuities between the so-called "conservative" and "progressive" intellectuals of the late Qing and early Republican periods,[5] the new narrative challenges the strict dichotomy between May Fourth iconoclasm and the modern Confucian "preservation" of tradition that forms a long-standing assumption of modern Chinese intellectual history. What was at stake, in the Confucian reaction to May Fourth during the Republican period, was much more complex than the term "preservation" suggests, as it involved, at its very core, questions of authority, of who has the right to speak in the name of tradition and to embody its essence in the changing times of the early twentieth century.[6] The alternative narrative proposed here pays greater attention to "Confucianism" and "modernity" as contested sites of power relations and to the manner in which "tradition" is reshaped by the discursive space in which it is inserted.

One of the major concerns of the most successful modern Confucian texts of this period is the question of how the authority of tradition can be reclaimed, adapted, and monopolized in textual formations. The resulting Confucianism is presented as an alternative to May Fourth, certainly, but by taking a closer look at the texts, we see that a number of May Fourth tropes were adopted by, and adapted to, the modern Confucian discourse to legitimize it within a discursive milieu significantly shaped by May Fourth assumptions. This does not entail that nothing of significance distinguishes this discourse from that of May Fourth, of course, but rather that both sides availed themselves of similar discursive means—first and foremost iconoclasm—to present their agenda as the only viable option in the context of Republican China.

Adopting a broad definition of "tradition" as "anything which is transmitted or handed down from the past to the present,"[7] the following chapters provide a close textual analysis of how the authority of the Confucian tradition, and of tradition more generally speaking, is portrayed and reclaimed by two Republican-period texts that oppose the May Fourth portrayal of Confucianism as an artifact of the past and enjoyed a significant amount of success after their publication, to the extent that both have been portrayed as foundational texts of modern or New Confucianism: Liang Shuming's (梁漱溟; 1893–1988) *Eastern and Western Cultures and Their Philosophies* (*Dongxi wenhua ji qi zhexue* 東西文化及其哲學; 1921; *Eastern and Western Cultures* hereafter)[8] and the classical Chinese edition of Xiong Shili's (熊十力; 1885–1968) *New Treatise on the Uniqueness of Consciousness* (*Xin weishi lun* 新唯識論; 1932; *New Treatise* hereafter).[9]

The following chapters pay particular attention to two interrelated aspects of the texts: their discourse on the role tradition plays in individual emancipation or in a modernization process teleologically oriented toward human liberty on the one hand, and the discursive techniques they employ to legitimize their discourse with the authority of tradition on the other. My central aim is to see which discursive tools were at the disposal of texts that endeavored to reactivate the authority of the Confucian *dao* (道) within the modern Chinese context, especially as one of their main objectives was to situate themselves within and against a discursive space hegemonized by the iconoclastic discourse of modernity advanced by the May Fourth protagonists.

Based on the close textual analysis that follows, I argue that the most successful modern Confucian texts of the Republican period are nearly as iconoclastic as the most radical of May Fourth intellectuals were, as on the one hand they deny that traditions can contribute to individual emancipation and to the modernization process, and on the other hand they conceptualize emancipation as a breaking free from the hold of tradition. There is an exception to this general rule, however. The Confucian tradition (as they define it) and to some extent the Buddhist one are singled out as traditions that can point the way to a liberation from tradition. Traditions are therefore valueless unless they represent what I call, following Edward Shils, "antitraditional traditions," or "antitraditions" for short: traditions that reject the value of all other traditions and show the way to a final liberation from the influences of the past.[10]

Confucian iconoclasm emerges as a reaction to May Fourth, but it does so less to "preserve" tradition than to subsume and monopolize it through the powerful means afforded by modern iconoclasm. At work in the texts studied is a dialectic whereby they salvage particular traditions that yield transhistorical truths from the dustbin of history before presenting themselves not only as contemporary representatives of such traditions, but also as their pinnacle: a pinnacle that sees the traditions entirely subsumed, clarified, finalized, and monopolized by the texts. It is by adapting the antitraditional discourse of modernity to its project that Confucian iconoclasm can present at least the discontinuous tradition of Confucianism, as it defines and subsumes it, as still relevant in the modern age.

The general picture that emerges from the close textual analysis that follows is that of texts engaged less in a politics of tradition than in what I call a "politics of antitradition," whereby different groups present their own project—May Fourth modernity or iconoclastic Confucianism—as the only one capable of freeing humanity from its situatedness in time and space. In doing so, Confucian iconoclasm reappropriates elements of the antitraditional discourse of modernity to its own ends, but in such a way as to challenge the Eurocentric conceptions of modernity promoted by May Fourth intellectuals and elevate its own Confucianism—in a way that is nearly as hegemonic, if not in actuality at least in its intent—into *the* universal culture capable of emancipating once and for all humanity from the shackles of tradition and history. What the texts propose is not an alternative to iconoclasm, but an alternative iconoclastic tradition to that of May Fourth—an antitradition subsumed under the banner of Confucianism.

The textual authority of tradition

The alternative narrative outlined above not only challenges accounts of the modern Confucian "preservation" of tradition by showing how authority and the monopolization of truth were central concerns of the modern Confucian response to May Fourth in the Republican period, but it also questions the appropriateness of adopting assumptions drawn from the field of classical Confucianism to study the modern period. Even if traditionalism forms one of the central assumptions underscoring a number of ancient texts classified as Confucian, we should nevertheless avoid reading modern Confucian texts through the lens of such assumptions. The emergence of Confucian iconoclasm in the Republican period is after all a new development, even if it is one that significantly borrows from the various sites of tradition, and notably that of the Wang Yangming (王陽明; 1472–1529) branch of Neo-Confucianism, which was better adapted, for reasons I hope will soon become clear, to the iconoclastic motives of the texts under study.[11] Yet until we establish, through a close analysis of the texts, which inclinations and intellectual predispositions they inherit from the past, we must be careful not to assume the presence of such inheritances in our approach toward them.

The alternative narrative presented here is also inscribed within a larger reconsideration of the heritage of modernity, one that challenges the assumption that within the modern context, unless they are protected and defended, traditions will inevitably and undoubtedly disappear at some point during the process of modernization.[12] The birth of the museum and the protection of national heritages, to name but two examples, speak to the rising significance of the language of *preservation* in the modern period. Whereas the modern Confucians might have shared at least some of the vocabulary of preservation in the aftermath of May Fourth—they did share with May Fourth thinkers the assumption that the disappearance of Chinese traditions was a potent possibility—the antithetical construal of the modern and the traditional underscored by such views should no longer be taken at face value for us who live in the twenty-first century.

The point is not to negate the fact that an important number of traditions were discontinued or significantly challenged during the modern period. Any historical period characterized by fast-pace transformations inevitably leads to changes in how contemporaries relate to the past (and vice versa). My main concern is rather with the discourse that sees in modernity a continuously renewed caesura with the past, to paraphrase Habermas,[13] and that makes of this caesura a precondition of human liberty and autonomy. It is important to understand this discourse as a significant component of the phenomenon of modernity rather than an accurate description of it. This discourse informs one of the most enduring discursive traditions of our times: the antitradition of modernity. This antitradition should not be conceptualized as an ex nihilo product of the moderns, however. It can perhaps best be described metaphorically as a textile[14] made of relatively novel patterns woven with the threads of tradition; as a reshaping and rearrangement of premodern traditions.[15]

While modernity is far from having produced a complete caesura with the premodern, the discourse that claims it did exactly that played a central role in reshaping the ways in which textual authority was performed in the modern period. Before the gradual advent of modernity, an idea could be sanctioned simply by tracing its origin back to an ancient text, or at least by claiming that it had such an origin.[16] The ancients and the classics formed zones of authority from which the contemporaries could draw, insofar as they were conceived as repositories of transhistorical truths passed down through the conduit of tradition.[17] By inserting oneself within such tradition, by learning its language and immersing oneself in its truths, and by commenting on the original meaning of the classics, one could partake in a ritual of social distinction setting apart an elite having access to transhistorical truths transmitted historically from masses regarded as entirely determined by the historical. For the happy few, transcending history could be transmitted along patriarchal lines of succession.

A complex hermeneutical relation between the ancients and the contemporaries regimented the ways in which the authority standing at the source of tradition could be reclaimed. This could be achieved through established codes of interpretation and commentary, or by claiming that one could build on the solid foundation laid by the ancients.[18] In both cases, what took place was often much more complex than a simple process of transmission or preservation of the originary truth of tradition. Rather, by "shaping the Ancients in authority figures," in Pascal Payen's words, one could "make of the temporal distance that separates us from them 'a transmission that is generative of meaning'" (and authority, I would add).[19] The ancients and the classics thus effectively functioned as means to translate ideas bound by the sociohistorical context of their emergence into transhistorical truths.

The purpose of this hermeneutical model was to mitigate the precariousness constitutive of any form of authority. In essence, authority is never truly "possessed" by anyone, as it is achieved through a social dialectic of recognition that continuously threatens to reverse the balance of power. While a ruler may claim to possess authority, his or her authority is but the result of the recognition of its legitimacy by the ruled.[20] To ensure consent and recognition, rulers have historically relied on a number of techniques, from rituals and speech acts aimed at presenting the instituting of the ruler in a position of power as something established independently of the ruled,[21] to discursive techniques projecting onto the origin of tradition or a transcendent Other the source of the ruler's authority.[22] The goal of such techniques is the naturalization of the authority of the ruler, thanks to which one could hide from the view of the ruled the fact that it is ultimately their recognition that institutes the ruler in a position of authority.

Of course, if their authority fails to be recognized by the ruled, rulers can always resort to coercion. While the unactualized but very real potential of coercion is a unique facet lurking in the background of political authority, resting on the monopoly of violence of the state, epistemic or textual authority has no other alternative but persuasion.[23] Whenever persuasion is insufficient or whenever it fails, the legitimacy of a text rests solely on the authority of its author, which precariously depends on the readers' willingness to recognize it. To be sure, there are a number of social factors, ranging from the reputation of the author to its affiliation with powerful institutions and historical figures, that impact the readership's inclination to recognize a text and its author as authoritative. Although such factors play a major role in the social dialectic of recognition, texts also have a vested interest, not unlike rulers, in presenting their positions as resting on grounds that are simply immune from contestation—grounds that cannot but be recognized as legitimate by the readers.

Two of the most important discursive techniques employed by texts to achieve this goal have been (1) that of portraying their own discourse as reactivating the originary, transhistorical truth of a tradition recognized as authoritative within a particular sociohistorical setting, and (2) that of claiming direct access to transhistorical truths, through a faculty (reason or *liangzhi* 良知, for example) expected to be recognized by the target readership as a universal and legitimate means of accessing such truths. Such techniques allow for the dialectic of social recognition to be mediated by a source of authority the legitimacy of which is socially embedded in the (Gadamerian) prejudices of a community.[24] By drawing from traditional and transhistorical sources of authority, texts can make it appear as if their authority was already established through socially accepted means, and thus hide from readers the fact that it is ultimately they who provide the authority of a text and its author with legitimacy.[25]

The antitradition of modernity

Although making the ancients into authority figures whose transhistorical truths could be passed down through the conduit of tradition was undoubtedly a powerful means to bolster the authority of the intellectual and social elite, especially before the advent of modernity, this model of authorization contained the seeds of its own demise. Insofar as one accepts that traditions have origins, that their transhistorical truths were once produced by the ancients in defiance of the historical traditions of their time, one must acknowledge the possibility that at least particularly gifted individuals, such as the ancients themselves, can access transhistorical truths independently of tradition. Within the very existence of the ancients resided the potential of challenging the necessity and authority of tradition.

While this is certainly not the place to provide a novel account of the rise of modernity, suffice it to point out, for the present purpose, that before the modern period, only semi-divine figures of an ancient past were normally portrayed as having the capacity to perceive truth in and of themselves, without and against tradition. What the moderns did, in a sense, is to claim they could reappropriate for themselves, in a Promethean fashion, the ability to access truths directly and autonomously, outside the dominion of tradition.[26] This could be done thanks to the universally shared faculty of reason, which allowed moderns access to the transhistorical without having to rely on the example set forth by the ancients. In sum, we see a gradual and incomplete displacement of the transhistorical, with the advent of modernity, from the originary sources of tradition to the inner core of the emancipated modern subject.

In the process, although the authority of tradition was never entirely eclipsed from the view of the moderns, it was certainly "amputated."[27] Its empire was challenged by the rise of the future, but also reason, autonomy, and the sciences, as the most important modern sources of authority.[28] Within what Wang Hui (汪暉) calls the new conception of historical time of modernity, which "moves linearly forward and cannot be repeated,"[29] oriented as it is toward a telos of emancipation and truth disclosure, tradition, as the Other of modernity, tends to be construed as lacking in value.[30] Or, more to the point, it tends to be regarded as a limitation imposed on the autonomous subject, hindering its apprehension of truth, given how tradition is the product of previous generations mired in the prejudices they themselves acquired from the past. Truth would remain at bay, in short, as long as humanity failed to free itself from prejudices inherited from traditions no longer conceived as emerging in transhistorical sources.

This is, of course, not the whole picture. After all, conservatism represents an important facet of the experience of modernity. But the *mainstream* discourse of modernity against which conservatism defined itself is an antitradition shaped around a new conception of historical time, one that fetishizes the "new" and the "present," the latter conceptualized less as the outcome of the past than the beginning of the future. As Jürgen Habermas notes in *The Philosophical Discourse of Modernity*:

> Because the new, the modern world is distinguished from the old by the fact that it opens itself to the future, the epochal new beginning is rendered constant with each moment that gives birth to the new. Thus, it is characteristic of the historical consciousness of modernity to set off "the most recent [*neuesten*] period" from the modern [*neu*] age: Within the horizon of the modern age, the present enjoys a prominent position as contemporary history [. . .]. A present that understands itself from the

horizon of the modern age as the actuality of the most recent period has to recapitulate the break brought about with the past as a *continuous renewal*.[31]

In other words, modernity presents itself as a dialectic between what-is and a what-ought-to-be no longer informed by the authority of what once was.[32]

The iconoclastic stance embedded in the new conception of time could be portrayed by its advocates as working against the monopolization of authority by the church, the aristocracy, and the ruling houses. Yet despite its avowed antipathy toward tradition, the discursive antitradition of modernity can nevertheless be regarded as a tradition in its own right, one that similarly served as a provider of ultimate sources of authority justifying the monopolization of truth by an elite (at a time of accentuated social mobility). Insofar as it could contribute to de-authorizing all other traditions by portraying them as limiting the potential for liberty inherent in human beings, the antitradition of modernity could serve, and has served, as a particularly powerful means through which authority could be monopolized by groups said to incarnate the spirit of all that is modern.

To be sure, a number of traditions presented themselves as purveying their followers with the ultimate truth before the advent of modernity (religions certainly did), and a good number of them did so while claiming all other traditions were either mistaken or inferior. What distinguishes the antitradition of modernity is its ability to hide the fact that it *is* a tradition (and a tradition among others). Instead of relying on the leap of faith central to religious attempts at monopolizing truth, the authority of the antitradition of modernity found solid ground in the belief that its own vision of the world was historically and scientifically proven. The antitraditional discourse of modernity could be employed by various groups seeking to hegemonize their position—be it communist, fascist, or (neo) liberal—by presenting it as the only possible outcome of history, as vetted by the modern tools of scientific historiography. The latter could serve as a new source of authority, one perfectly suited to hide the social dialectic of recognition from the view of those who accepted the metanarrative of modernity as objective and indisputable.

Apart from providing the discursive resources thanks to which members of the elite could present themselves as the incarnation, in the present, of the inevitable and emancipatory future, the new conception of time central to the antitradition of modernity could also be put to the task of sanctioning the enterprises of imperialism and colonialism. It could do so by presenting them as the only means to free the rest of humanity from its traditional shackles and introduce it in true History—that is, History oriented toward human liberty. Two discursive techniques central to this project of legitimation of the white man's burden are of particular importance for the present purpose, as they became underlying assumptions, as I hope will become clear in a moment, of May Fourth discourse.

First is the unilinear metanarrative of modernity, which proposed to taxonomize all world cultures within a single developmental model of history according to how far ahead in the progressive path toward the emancipatory telos they were. Insofar as within this metanarrative, the modern cultures of Europe represented the most advanced stage of modernization, they could be depicted as the universal future toward which all of humankind would inexorably evolve. This discourse effected a spatialization of time:[33] it accommodated all cultural spaces within a temporal narrative enabling Europe's self-portrayal as the emancipatory future of humanity.

Second is what Charles Taylor calls the "acultural understanding of modernity."[34] In such an understanding, modernity is construed not as a historical and cultural product defined by its situatedness in time and space, but as a gradual *discovery* of truth and human autonomy that took place *in spite of* the cultural background of its emergence. Modernity is said to have *naturally* emerged once moderns freed themselves from the prejudices and superstitions that plagued the premodern period. This entails that tradition and modernity stand in opposition to one another, and that they are incompatible and irreconcilable, an assumption that finds itself reflected in a number of dichotomies, between feudalism and freedom, object and subject of history, particularism and universalism, darkness and enlightenment, unreflective and self-conscious subjects, and so forth. Moreover, by naturalizing modernity, this discourse could establish its authority by pretending to be immune from contestation and above the social dialectic of recognition.

Allied to the unilinear metanarrative, the acultural understanding of modernity could provide colonialism with legitimacy. Non-European traditions, relegated to premodernity, could easily be portrayed as limitations imposed on their people's inherent potential for truth and liberty, a potential that could be realized only thanks to the impetus provided by the European colonial powers. This discourse reinforced the spatialization of time by depicting modern European cultures as inherently universal, while de-authorizing premodern, non-European locales as being held by irrational and servile traditions. Through the process of modernization, non-Europeans would be gradually uprooted from local cultures, a precondition to being introduced into the universal culture of modernity. Thus conceptualized, modernization involved a process of disembodiment, a passage from place to "placelessness."

The antitradition of May Fourth

The unilinear and acultural metanarrative of modernity was introduced into China at the end of the nineteenth century, most notably through the medium of social Darwinism. It soon became one of the most important paradigms of understanding the world and China's place in it during the early Republican period.[35] Facing a "crisis of meaning"[36] or "consciousness"[37] brought about by the disintegration of the sociopolitical order, as well as a sense that China had lost, after the first Sino-Japanese war, the privileged role of civilizational center that was traditionally ascribed to it, the May Fourth intellectual elite was drawn to the antitradition of modernity as an all-encompassing discourse that could make sense of China's predicament. This suggests that the remarkable translatability of the antitraditional discourse of modernity derives not from its inherent universality, as its proponents would have it, but from its ability (1) to serve as a powerful means to throw light on the historical condition in which the colonies and those subjected to European imperialism found themselves, and (2) to rally the nation-state—this newcomer—around the task of modernization to extricate it from the grasp of foreign powers and achieve the sovereignty promised by the project of modernity.

Besides allowing Chinese intellectuals to make sense of China's predicament and providing an all-encompassing means to solve it, the acultural and unilinear metanarrative of modernity served another purpose less frequently highlighted by historians. It enabled May Fourth intellectuals to produce a hegemonic discourse that reshaped the rules of intellectual distinction.[38] This was made possible by the fact that after the abolition of the imperial examination in 1905, the rules that codified the distribution of cultural and symbolic capital in the economy of the intellectual field had to be reinvented. Chinese intellectuals found themselves in a "conjuncture of organic crisis": a historical moment that sees the markers of transhistoricity and universality, as cultural commodities of high value, gradually emptied out of their content, notably because of the disintegration of former institutions that guaranteed a certain stability to the hegemonic order.[39] This was a crisis of "meaning" and "consciousness," but it was also an *institutional* crisis closely tied to a crisis of identity of the intellectual elite.

Before the twentieth century, the *shi* (士) class of scholar-officials had managed to achieve a relatively stable hegemonic position on the grounds that it alone could represent and incarnate traditional inheritances that conveyed transhistorical, universal truths. Although far from unchallenged,[40] the hegemonic success of the *shi* found support in the imperial court and the examination system—powerful institutions responsible for the production of social distinctions. After 1905, the university system replaced the imperial examination as the main institution through which cultural capital was acquired and transmitted. But in the early years of the Republic, the rules that codified access to the faculties were extremely diverse and porous.[41] Many of the professors filling in the ranks of the new universities were formally trained in the classics.[42] They competed against intellectuals who were self-taught, others who had received their education in Japan, and those who had been educated in North America or Western Europe.

Within such a conjuncture, the question remained open as to which group would replace the *shi* class by successfully presenting itself as the only social body capable of incarnating the universal in modern China. It is within this context that the May Fourth group deployed a powerful iconoclastic discourse that succeeded, around the turn of the 1920s, in recasting the May Fourth intellectuals as the only legitimate representatives of universality in modern China.[43]

The hegemonic success of May Fourth, in the intellectual field, was enabled by its adoption of the unilinear and acultural discourse of modernity. The spatial distinction between China and the West was reconceptualized, in this discourse, as a temporal divide within a single, unilinear model of historical development.[44] Because within this model "feudal" China was behind the "modern" West, by a thousand years on Chen Duxiu's (陳獨秀; 1879–1942) account,[45] the West could be presented as the inexorable—and universal—future toward which China had to evolve. Human autonomy and reason, incarnated by the modern West, would naturally emerge provided the Chinese could free themselves from the shackles of feudal traditions. In the social Darwinian terminology of Chen, unless the Chinese recognized the objective tide of history and contributed to bring about its ineluctable end, the Chinese "race" would become unfit for the times and be brought to extinction.[46] Although Chen depicts the present as a watershed historical moment in which the Chinese have to choose between the modern and feudal paths,⁴⁷ it is clear that, in his view, the choice is ultimately made by History.

Insofar as the future had already happened in the West, the equation between the universal future and the particular West in May Fourth discourse could be described as indisputably proven by History. May Fourth members could then proceed to suture the modern West, as the new incarnation of the universal, with contents particular to their own agenda. That few readers of *New Youth* (*Xin qingnian* 新青年; changed from *Qingnian* 青年 after the first volume; also known by its French name *La Jeunesse*) and other radical journals of the time had had the opportunity of traveling to the West and seeing it firsthand meant that the May Fourth group could use the "West" as a screen on which to project its own utopian imaginings of the future. As representatives of this future, "Mr. Science" (*sai xiansheng* 賽先生) and "Mr. Democracy" (*de xiansheng* 德先生) could be filled in with the utopian hopes of the May Fourth group.⁴⁸ Through a complex discourse that naturalized their agenda by presenting it as a *descriptive* account of a universal future that had already happened in the West, May Fourth members managed to portray themselves as the new incarnation of the universal.

The antitradition of modernity became, in May Fourth hands, a powerful hegemonic tool to monopolize authority and reject any alternative to the dual empires of science and democracy (as defined by the May Fourth intellectuals). By dressing the "modern West" and "feudal China" into the gowns of universality and particularism, respectively, the May Fourth group proposed a radical iconoclastic discourse in which all discursive positions, except that of May Fourth itself, could be depicted as remnants of the feudal past. Any intellectual who upheld the value of at least certain Chinese traditions, in short anyone who did not agree with May Fourth's radical iconoclasm, could be presented as the handmaiden of feudalism, patriarchy, and despotism. Chen Duxiu was particularly successful in deploying iconoclastic discursive techniques (reinforced by his unilinear conception of history) in opposition not only to Kang Youwei (康有為; 1858–1927), one of the main objects of his criticism in the second half of the 1910s,⁴⁹ but also to intellectuals who were much more moderate in their appreciation of the past, such as Du Yaquan (杜亞泉; 1873–1933).⁵⁰

Although a number of researchers have rightfully pointed out that the May Fourth attacks on tradition were in fact rather limited in scope, focusing particularly on the Confucian family system and the three bonds (*sangang* 三綱),⁵¹ this should not blind us to the fact that Chen Duxiu and other May Fourth iconoclasts presented their account of Confucianism as emblematic of the entirety of "feudal China."[52] Opposing any form of accommodation between the cultures of China and the modern West, Chen presented the two as essentially antithetical. One had to renounce Confucianism wholesale if one wished to introduce China into the modern age.[53] Scientism further strengthened this antitraditional discourse by enabling the rejection of previous forms of knowledge as "superstitious" (*mixin* 迷信).[54] In an article titled "1916" ("Yijiuyiliu nian" 一九一六年), Chen went so far as to declare that the year 1916 would split history into a before and an after, bringing about a thorough renewal of the individual, the state, society, the family, and the nation.[55] The introduction of modernity into China, in other words, would proceed from a freeing caesura with the past.

Enabled by the rise of print capitalism, the May Fourth politics of antitradition created a chain of equivalence[56] uniting, around the magazine *New Youth* and its modernizing agenda, the emerging "westernized" intellectuals and students in their shared opposition to the conservative other constructed in May Fourth discourse. This was May Fourth's answer to the conjuncture of organic crisis that followed the abolition of the imperial examination in 1905 and the fall of the Qing empire in 1911. Faced with the impressive diversity of the professorial body of the newly established universities and the plethora of voices represented in the growing number of magazines and newspapers published at the beginning of the Republic,[57] the May Fourth group deployed a politics of antitradition that "sowed the seeds of monologic hegemony that eventually dominated the literary, cultural, and political discourse of modern China."[58]

Although in the 1920s May Fourth members splintered into different groups—anarchists, liberals, Marxists—they continued to share a common opposition to the so-called traditionalists and conservatives for many years to come. Modernization discourse and the politics of antitradition could be put to the task of legitimizing both liberalism, as represented by the modern West, and Marxism, incarnated by the Bolshevik revolution. Both could be characterized as the only true content filling in the universal future of humanity, but only insofar as the shackles of tradition could be removed from the mind of the new Chinese subject. In this context, intellectuals seeking to reauthorize some form of tradition had to do so in opposition to the modernization metanarratives of liberals and Marxists, as well as to the claim that their program had been vetted by science and the modern rational subject.

The success of May Fourth hegemonic operations should therefore not be thought of in terms of the production of a single and unified discourse that filled in the universal projected onto the end of unilinear history and embedded in the autonomous subject emancipated from tradition. Different contents of the universal future and the autonomous subject were proposed by the different groups that emerged out of the May Fourth Movement. The hegemonic success of May Fourth discourse should be attributed rather to its ability to set new discursive rules, centered on its politics of antitradition, that both enabled and limited what one could legitimately argue and, equally importantly, on what grounds one could argue it. In short, May Fourth redefined the rules that codified what a legitimate claim to the universal, as cultural capital, ought to look like.[59]

The hegemonic success of May Fourth can be judged by the extent to which discursive positions opposed to it had to comply with its rules in their very attempt at decentering it. It is within this context that Confucian iconoclasm emerged as a *counter-hegemonic project* aimed at opening a discursive space for its Confucian alternative to the hegemonic universalism of May Fourth. This leads us to the following question: within a context that saw the emergence of the unilinear and acultural discourse of modernity, employed by May Fourth protagonists as a means to reshape the rules of intellectual distinction around their agenda, which discursive tools were at the disposal of texts that wished to reappropriate for themselves the authority of a tradition decried as feudal and unfit for modern times?

Confucian iconoclasm

While the relation between textual authority and tradition in classical and Song-Ming Confucianisms has been under study for quite some time,[60] this topic has not been sufficiently addressed when it comes to modern Confucianism. To be sure, a number of works have dealt with the question of the genealogy of the way (*daotong* 道統), especially in Mou Zongsan's (牟宗三; 1909–1995) discourse,[61] and Yü Ying-shih (余英時) has provided an important critique of the *daotong* logic lending authority to a claimed lineage between Xiong Shili and members of the so-called "second generation" of "New Confucianism."[62] But perhaps because the genealogical discourse of the modern Confucian texts of the Republican period, at least certainly those under study here, tends to remain implicit, scholars have tended to neglect the important question of how textual authority is constructed in them.[63]

Yet the question of how modern Confucian texts attempt to buttress their claims by appealing to the authority of tradition is of utmost importance, especially since such claims must find an answer to the May Fourth challenge not to appear as partaking in the outdated, feudal tradition decried by the May Fourth group. Attempting to monopolize the authority of the Confucian tradition with some measure of success within a historical context that sees the rise of iconoclastic rejections of that authority represents a novel challenge. Before one can ascribe to oneself the authority of the Confucian tradition within such context, one must first find a way to argue that this tradition is still of value, and do so both *within* and *against* a discursive milieu hegemonized by the antitraditional discourse of May Fourth. Studying how modern Confucian texts responded to May Fourth iconoclasm in their hope to present themselves as reactivating the *dao* thus appears to call for a closer scrutiny of the modes of textual authorization employed by such texts.

In this context, what could be presented, within the Confucian tradition, as valuable with a certain amount of success was greatly constrained by the May Fourth portrayal of Confucianism as supporting a sociopolitical order centered on feudal hierarchies. To escape May Fourth criticism, Confucian iconoclasm had to cleanse itself of the historical manifestations of Confucianism denounced as feudal. To do so, it drew a sharp distinction between what I call *tradition-as-history* and *tradition-as-value*, which made it possible to reject Confucianism's historical manifestations (tradition-as-history) and its enmeshment in state power as a deviation from the true spirit of the tradition, while simultaneously abstracting from the past a number of values purified from history (tradition-as-value).[64] Confucian iconoclastic texts could thus dissociate *their* Confucianism from that of May Fourth, but in a manner that significantly limited what could be valued of the past. Their rejection of tradition-as-history, for example, explains why their Confucianism is rather depoliticized, and why notions such as those of the three bonds and five relationships (*sangang wuchang* 三綱五常), of ritual (*li* 禮), and of statecraft (*jingshi* 經世), to name but a few, are conspicuously absent from the texts or only briefly mentioned in passing. It also explains why "Confucianism" denotes, in their discourse, a series of ideas rather than social practices, or, in the case of *Eastern and Western Cultures*, a series of ideas that inevitably must become social practices in the future.

The philosophical method played a significant role in enabling Confucian iconoclasm to abstract and immunize Confucianism-as-value from Confucianism-as-history, an essential prerequisite for presenting certain values as transhistorical. Through philosophical means, Confucian iconoclasm sought to answer the May Fourth challenge, first by admitting the Confucian defeat on the battlefield of history, but only to subsequently win the war on the battlefield of value. Philosophy could help reshape Confucianism into an ahistorical spirit, but in a manner that presumed a strongly iconoclastic stance toward traditions-as-history, given that they had deviated from the ahistorical values abstracted from the past.[65]

The iconoclastic stance toward tradition-as-history of the most successful modern Confucian texts of the Republican period was a product of their attempt at escaping the criticism of their opponents. Their iconoclastic verve, however, extends beyond tradition-as-history and reaches the very tradition-as-value they wish to reactivate. This puzzling conclusion—why would anyone devalue a tradition they claim to represent?—can best be explained by taking a closer look at the texts' discourse on tradition on the one hand, and at the way they legitimize their discourse with the authority of tradition on the other. While the following chapters provide a detailed analysis of these two layers of the texts, it is worth providing a short outline of the argument that unfolds to clarify the scope of Confucian iconoclasm, both in terms of its discursive content and form.

In terms of their discursive content, both texts deny, as noted above, that traditions can contribute to individual emancipation (in the *New Treatise*) or bring about the historical telos of human liberty (in *Eastern and Western Cultures*), with the exception of the Confucian tradition as they define it, and to some extent the Yogācāra one. Yet insofar as they conceive tradition as a limitation imposed on the autonomous subject, the Confucian tradition can be useful only insofar as it leads to its antithetical end: to a form of experience ultimately freed from the hold of the past. It is of value, in other words, only to the extent that it can be made into an *antitradition*.

Moreover, what the texts regard as worth saving of Confucianism are not values manifested in history, but ideals imagined and lived by a single sage (Confucius) or by a handful of individuals who directly intuited transhistorical values autonomously and in isolation from tradition. This entails that in and of themselves, Confucian values are not strictly speaking "traditional," given that they were never transmitted from one generation to the next. What *was* transmitted, however, are a number of canonical texts believed to encompass, in a hidden form, the transhistorical values of the sage(s) (and worthies). In sum, not only are traditions-as-history valueless in the texts' envisioning of emancipatory processes—they are portrayed as limitations in both cases—but tradition-as-value (their Confucianism) can be construed as a tradition in its own right, according to the discourse of the texts, only insofar as one speaks of the canonical texts that were transmitted through history. Apart from a limited number of canonical works, in short, the entirety of tradition is of no value.

In terms of their discursive form—of the methods of textual authorization they employ—both texts sanction their version of Confucianism by appealing to the authority of tradition. This is achieved through a complex hermeneutical process that ties the canon with its modern interpreter. To better understand this process, one must keep in mind that strictly speaking, it is not the canonical texts themselves that are valuable, but the transhistorical values conveyed in them. The *New Treatise* and *Eastern and Western Cultures* do not share with the Qing tradition of *kaojuxue* (考據學) a concern with providing a philologically accurate account of the classics, and they show no interest in what the commentarial tradition has to say about the canon. One of the most important assumptions underscoring the texts' hermeneutics lies in the implicit claim that insofar as they have directly intuited transhistorical truths, the texts' authors can comprehend the classics without the help of the commentarial or philological traditions. Since implied in this discourse is the idea that Liang and Xiong have already apprehended the transhistorical truths lodged in the canon, the latter remains of value, within this hermeneutical model, only inasmuch as it provides a means to buttress the texts' claim to have access to the transhistorical by demonstrating that their authors' vision of emancipation is one and the same as that of the sages of old.

This hermeneutical model recognizes the authority of tradition-as-value only to then allow for its subsumption by the modern interpreter. Both texts present themselves as the very pinnacle of the Confucian tradition: as the locale in which tradition is made available to readers in its entirety, repackaged in a modern format that is clearer, more systematic, and more accessible than that of the classics. Given that Confucian iconoclasm sees value in canonical texts only insofar as transhistorical values discovered by former sages are encoded in them, once such values have been successfully decoded by the modern interpreters and explained to their contemporaries in a language that is more readily accessible to them, the significance and worth of the classics are, if not entirely lost, at least considerably reduced. After all, why read the classics if their message has been made clearer and more systematic in *Eastern and Western Cultures* and the *New Treatise*? What takes place, in this hermeneutical model, is a process whereby the modern text substitutes itself for the entirety of tradition-as-value, replacing the latter with a fetishized version of it that is made available to readers in its totality.

In sum, both at the levels of the discursive form and content of the texts, Confucianism is reshaped into an "iconoclastic tradition." By this, I do not mean, of course, that Liang and Xiong were engaged in, or called for, the destruction of idols in religious temples—although, remarkably enough, in his youth Xiong did go around in the nude (as he himself later recalled) smashing statues in Buddhist and Daoist temples, a practice he gave up in his adult age.[66] Nor do I mean by it that iconoclasm was the main *intention* behind the writing of the *New Treatise* and *Eastern and Western Cultures*. It is entirely possible that Xiong and Liang saw themselves as "preservers" of the past; not of an indiscriminate past, of course, but one that was carefully curated by the authors to serve their purposes. By calling the texts "iconoclastic," I am referring not to the intentions of their authors, but to the *consequences* of the texts' discourse on tradition and of the manner in which they authorize this discourse by equating it with the message of past sages. My use of the term "iconoclastic," in short, denotes a *textual* form of iconoclasm.[67]

To sum up, I refer to the Confucianism of the texts as "iconoclastic" and as an "antitradition" insofar as it is (1) a tradition that is presented as the only one capable of bringing about a thorough emancipation of the individual and community from the hold of the past, (2) a tradition that rejects the authority of historical traditions and of traditional values except for those expressed in a narrowly defined canon, and (3) a tradition that is, *at least in theory*,[68] ultimately iconoclastic even vis-à-vis itself—that is, vis-à-vis the tradition-as-value it rescues from the dustbin of history—insofar as its value is mediated by the modern texts in a manner that significantly de-authorizes the previous sources of tradition-as-value. Confucian iconoclasm represents what I would call an "ouroboric tradition": a tradition that births itself by killing itself, by subsuming itself, in its entirety, into a single object—a text—that, in and of itself, cannot be properly called a "tradition" in its own right.[69] (Or, more properly speaking, the texts cannot be seen as part of a "tradition" if one provides them with the social recognition they seek: the recognition that they are the products of authors no longer defined by their socio-temporal situatedness.)

The ouroboric dimension of Confucian iconoclasm effectively echoes Alan Cole's analysis of the ways various religious narratives, both Buddhist and Christian, attempt to fetishize and subsume the truth of tradition, only to then offer it to readers, provided they perform a leap of faith legitimizing the texts' claim to fully represent tradition. Cole describes this process as requiring "three mutually reliant zones":

1) a deep origin of truth in the form of a past sage, saint, deity, or Being; 2) a means for moving that truth forward in time, be it through memory, texts, ritual practices, relics, or the regular reincarnation of the primal source in some contemporary form or body; 3) a contemporary spokesperson for that primordial truth who is sanctioned to represent it in the present, interpret it, and distribute it to a believing public, who delegate to him just this power and legitimacy.[70]

Without entering the complex debate on whether (modern) Confucianism is a religion, suffice it to say, for the present purpose, that the manner in which textual authority is constituted in Confucian iconoclasm does indeed follow the model proposed by Cole. It does so insofar as it posits an ultimate source of authority in the past which is then subsumed by the author and his text thanks to the former's alleged access to transhistorical truths that are one and the same as those achieved by the sages of the past.

Historical antitraditions

Confucian iconoclasm's discourse on the past is thoroughly modern, insofar as it construes the relation between the contemporary and the ancients as one of *emulation* rather than *transmission*. The texts emulate the ability to directly access the transhistorical that characterizes the genius of those individuals standing at the fountainhead of tradition.[71] Yet as in the case of the antitradition of modernity, one must be careful not to reproduce the language of the actors when describing Confucian iconoclasm. It is crucial that we treat the texts' self-portrayal, according to which they are the product of authors no longer bound by time and space, as a central component of the historical phenomenon of Confucian iconoclasm, and not as an accurate description of it.

By taking a step back from the texts' self-portrayal, we can come to see that although the discursive content and form of the texts are thoroughly iconoclastic in their implications, we, as researchers, can nevertheless describe them as traditional, insofar as they draw discursive tropes from a wealth of historical resources. This includes, among others, discursive resources inherited from historical Confucianisms. Even if one allows that historical Confucianisms tended to betray traditionalist inclinations, one must be careful to distinguish between *continuous* traditionalism, leaning toward the preservation of traditions that still exist, and *discontinuous* traditionalism, dedicated to the revival of traditions no longer extant (regardless of whether such traditions are mere projections of the contemporaries or historically accurate ones).[72]

It is first and foremost from the discontinuous type of traditionalism that Confucian iconoclasm draws discursive resources, as this type makes it possible to reject all currently extant traditions.[73] The notion of the genealogy of the way (*daotong*), for example, allowed Zhu Xi (朱熹; 1130–1200) and others to present their message as reactivating the originary *dao* of tradition and argue that its transmission had been lost for centuries from the pre-Qin period until the Song dynasty. Confucian iconoclasm inherited much of its discourse on the Confucian tradition from such antitraditional resources, as well as from what Yü Ying-shih calls the "anti-intellectual" strand of Neo-Confucianism associated with Wang Yangming.[74] According to members of this "anti-intellectual" strand, the *dao* can be directly intuited instead of inherited through transmission (a claim already implied in the idea that the transmission had been single-handedly revived by Zhou Dunyi [周敦頤; 1017–1073] in Zhu Xi's *daotong* logic). Within Confucianism's discontinuous traditionalism lingered some of the seeds of modern Confucian iconoclasm—seeds that were transplanted into the fertile soil of the politics of antitradition of the Republican period.

The above resources drawn from Confucianism represent what I call "historical antitraditions": discursive traditions that possess a significant iconoclastic potential and that have been transmitted historically. (By contrast, "(anti)tradition-as-history" refers to discursive formations, i.e., traditions established *in the discourse of the texts*.) Although it is beyond the scope of the present work to provide an exhaustive list of the historical antitraditions from which Confucian iconoclasm draws, the chapters that follow highlight some of them to support the assertion that the iconoclastic discourse of the texts is in fact significantly traditional. This discourse can be likened to a relatively novel textile woven with the threads of Chinese antitraditions on the one hand, and of the discursive antitradition of modernity on the other. This explains why I describe the texts' portrayal of Confucianism as an anti*tradition*, despite the fact that their discourse is ultimately ouroboric: birthing itself through a process of swallowing whatever value tradition is still believed to have in its midst.

The above suggests that Confucian iconoclasm can be conceived as an alternative antitradition to that of May Fourth not only in terms of its discursive content, according to which its own brand of Confucianism and not Eurocentric modernity can bring about human emancipation, but also in terms of its discursive form, insofar as the authority it performs in writing draws significant resources from historical antitraditions. Chapters 3 and 4 argue that the texts partake in a politics of antitradition aimed at reshaping the intellectual field around new rules of discursivity. Such rules are incarnated by the figure of the Confucian sage, who is made to represent an alternative ideal of autonomy and universality to that of the modern subject constructed in May Fourth discourse. In appearance sufficiently similar to the modern autonomous subject so as to represent a viable alternative to it, the figure of the sage is also sufficiently different from it so as to allow the production of new rules that codify the manner in which contemporaries can present themselves as legitimate bearers of autonomy and universality.

The alternative rules around which the texts seek to reshape the discursive field are not merely traditional, however. They do not simply reproduce traditional tropes of performing sagehood in writing. They are hybrid rules inherited from Chinese sources (Confucian and Buddhist foremost) *and* from the discourse of modernity. To support its project, Confucian iconoclasm recycles a number of discursive tropes (teleological history, the modern figure of the autonomous subject, the philosophical system produced by a genius) from the antitradition of modernity, and it largely reproduces the iconoclastic discursive framework of its opponents. This shows the remarkable translatability of the discourse of modernity—through what Lydia Liu calls "translingual practice"[75]—and its adaptability to agendas that are situated at the opposite ends of the intellectual spectrum.

May Fourth and Confucian iconoclasm should therefore be regarded as belonging to one and the same discursive milieu.[76] This discursive milieu is characterized by a politics of antitradition having for goal the monopolization of intellectual commodities associated with universality, autonomy, and liberty. Each group differs in its construal of what, in final instance, constitutes true universality and liberty: the modern autonomous subject awaiting humanity at the end of history or the figure of the sage released from the trappings of the here and now. Insofar as Confucian iconoclasm aspires to be the sole legitimate incarnation of the universal, there is little doubt that it betrays hegemonic ambitions. Such ambitions, however, remain somewhat less hegemonic than those of the Eurocentric discourse of modernity. After all, Confucian iconoclasm does recognize the limited yet existing value of the scientific method as a legitimate means to achieve truths, although it ultimately subordinates such truths to its own.[77]

The main goal of Confucian iconoclasm is therefore not that of preserving, against May Fourth attacks, tradition *as a sociohistorical reality*. As noted above, the texts are in fact as iconoclastic as May Fourth members when it comes to traditions-as-history. Rather, Confucian iconoclasm aspires to reinstate the authority of *discursive* antitraditions. It does so in order first to subsume and monopolize this authority, and second to put such discursive antitraditions, and the figure of the sage in particular, to the task of redefining the rules of discursivity. Confucian iconoclasm could thus hope to replace the hegemon with an alternative antitradition that could potentially serve, as the May Fourth discourse did, as a tool to monopolize the means of intellectual distinction. The main issue it faced, however, is that insofar as it had to abide by the rules of the hegemon in its very attempt at challenging it, its alternative antitradition ran the risk of being continuously undermined by the traces of the May Fourth hegemon scattered in its discourse. Paying closer attention to the discursive techniques deployed by Confucian iconoclasm to hide such traces and legitimize its alternative antitradition can help us get a better sense of the limits of what could be said within and against a discursive milieu defined by the May Fourth politics of antitradition—and therefore also of the extent to which May Fourth had indeed achieved a hegemonic status.

Texts and contexts

"Confucian iconoclasm" refers to a discursive strategy and project, one that is shared by both *Eastern and Western Cultures* and the *New Treatise*. This does not mean, however, that the texts do not differ from each other in important ways. There is much that sets them apart from one another. One is a philosophy of culture, the other an ontology of the mind-universe. One is framed as a direct intervention in an ongoing debate, the other seems unconcerned with the main issues of the day. Yet both share a common strategy and project. This does not entail, however, that their authors belonged to a self-identified group of Confucian iconoclasts who deliberately formed an alliance in opposition to a common adversary. That the texts share a common discursive project can rather be accounted for by the effect the discursive field equally had on both of them, insofar as it limited the discursive means through which the authority of Confucianism could be successfully reclaimed (and monopolized) in textual form.

To be sure, Confucian iconoclasm was not the *only* Confucian discursive strategy proposed in response to May Fourth during the Republican period. There were undoubtedly others, but none of them were overall as successful as *Eastern and Western Cultures*[78] and the *New Treatise*.[79] As the following chapters make clear, the texts' relative success can be explained by their ability to adapt to the rules of discursivity set by the May Fourth group, and those inscribed in its politics of antitradition in particular.[80] That the texts were relatively successful and popular is of importance, as I am interested in what could be *authoritatively* said within the historical context of post-May Fourth China. While it is true that these texts, and particularly the *New Treatise*, which was written in classical Chinese, did not enjoy the same popularity as the journal *New Youth* did (especially from 1919 onwards), for example, we can still regard them as relatively popular, at least insofar as they led to some form of public debate. Moreover, as mentioned above, both *Eastern and Western Cultures*[81] and the *New Treatise*[82] went on to be retrospectively acclaimed as foundational texts of modern or New Confucianism. This goes to show how their discourse on tradition and their method of authorization have integrated the mainstream discourse of modern Confucianism, to the extent that they have become originary sources of authority themselves (clearly not to the extent of a text like the *Analects*, but they have become sources of authority nonetheless).

As may be clear by now, the objects of this study are not the thinkers Liang Shuming and Xiong Shili, but the texts *Eastern and Western Cultures* and the *New Treatise*. This is justified by my interest in the realm of discourse and textual authority, but also by the fact that I wish to avoid taking for granted that behind the tensions and contradictions of the texts stands a figure, the author, who would serve the function of unifying and homogenizing the discourse of the texts; who would serve as a "principle of a certain unity of writing."[83] By focusing on texts, however, my goal is not to do away with the notion of authorship altogether. I occasionally refer, in the following chapters, to Liang and Xiong as the authors of the texts.[84] Rather, my engagement with the controversial notion of the "death of the author" has three specific goals.

First, what I wish to reject is the idea of an *author-God*: of an author who is treated, insofar as it is regarded as the ultimate source of the texts, as a mirror image of the Judeo-Christian God qua ex nihilo creator.[85] By contrast, I am interested in texts as what Roland Barthes calls "new tissue[s] of quotations drawn from the innumerable centres of culture,"[86] but also as new textual tissues woven within, and shaped by, a sociohistorical setting characterized by the rise of the discourse of modernity. Emphasizing the sociohistorical, intertextual, and traditional dimensions of texts does not mean, however, that the notion of the author should be rejected entirely. If we rethink the author as a sociohistorically situated point of convergence of various and at times conflicting traditions (including discursive traditions), as formed through and by traditions that are never entirely one's own and are always to some extent shared, we can still appeal to the figure of the author, but understood, as it will be in what follows, as a medium or filter of various traditions that speak through him or her and through the texts he or she produces. Both author and text can be thought of as new tissues, new patterns woven with the threads of tradition and situated in sociohistorical contexts within which certain traditions are regarded as more authoritative than others.

Second, the notion of the death of the author can also help us rethink accounts that overemphasize the role of individual agency in the "manufacture" or "invention" of tradition. To be sure, traditions can at times be shaped by agents who relate to them as subjects do toward objects. Even when this is the case, however, they are shaped by agents who are themselves the product of the many traditions in which they partake, and not by ex nihilo creators who manufacture them out of the raw material of the past.[87] It is therefore not always clear, in the relation between agent and tradition, which of the two manufactures the other. Moreover, by emphasizing how the discursive project of Confucian iconoclasm is significantly shaped by the discursive milieu and the politics of antitradition that informs it, we can counterbalance the tendency, particularly in philosophical studies of modern Confucianism, to emphasize human agency at the expense of the sociohistorical context. This approach does not entail a repudiation of the notion of agency, however. It signifies that one's agency is negotiated through the sociohistorical context in which one evolves and through the various sites of tradition that inform one's experiences and that both limit and enable what one can say.

Finally, by rejecting the notion of the author-God, I wish to refrain from appealing to "the thought of Liang Shuming" and "the thought of Xiong Shili." Since the scope of my analysis is limited to the *New Treatise* and *Eastern and Western Cultures*, I avoid referring to other texts written by Xiong and Liang to make sense of these two works or do away with contradictions and tensions within them.[88] Moreover, my central focus remains the *discourse* of the texts. I therefore do not position myself as to whether their portrayal of Liang and Xiong as ultimate representatives of the Confucian tradition-as-value, as authors who have reached a complete and supra-linguistic understanding of it, has any validity. Even if Liang and Xiong had somehow gained a supra-linguistic and intuitive understanding of the Confucian truth, provided that such a thing is possible, this intuition would have had to be translated in a text whose truth claims had to be authorized textually.

I leave unanswered, for the present purpose, the question of whether the texts should be ultimately classified, *in terms of their philosophical contents*, as Confucian or Buddhist.[89] By calling the texts "modern Confucian,"[90] I simply mean that they *claim* to reactivate and subsume the *dao* of the Confucian tradition, and that they do so by incorporating significant elements of the antitraditional discourse of modernity. I refrain from positioning myself as to whether this claim is accurate or not, as this would require that I provide a strict definition of "Confucianism" by singling out its doctrinal core and/or its legitimate representatives. Doing so, however, would be to partake in the very relations of power, centered on the question of who has the right to speak in the name of tradition, I analyze.

To be clear, my portrayal of Confucian iconoclasm in no way suggests that its Confucianism is somewhat "inauthentic." This would be to assume that if we go sufficiently far back, we can retrieve a moment in history when the tradition was "authentic," and therefore not already contested and subject to competing claims to authority.[91] The language of authenticity, I suggest, should be an object of study, not a prism through which we can aspire to deepen our understanding of tradition. Letting go of the authentic/inauthentic distinction as an analytical tool, and with it of other contrasting pairs mapped onto the authentic/inauthentic model, such as those between Kongzi (孔子) and Confucius or *ru* (儒) and Confucianism,[92] does not entail that any account of tradition is equally valid, of course. What it means is that in order to strive for a more accurate account of tradition, we should be careful not to reproduce the language of the actors we study, especially when it comes to actors who have a vested interest in ascribing to themselves the symbolic and cultural capital associated with tradition.

By remaining at a distance from the language of authenticity of the texts, we can understand "Confucianism," as well as "modernity," as contested sites of power relations; as symbolic commodities over which various texts attempt to establish a monopoly. Coupled with my engagement with the notion of the death of the author, this entails that the two texts under study can reveal something of the intellectual and sociohistorical milieux of their emergence, and of what could and could not be *authoritatively* said within a discursive milieu hegemonized by the antitradition of May Fourth. Through a study of these texts, we can grasp something of the remarkable power of the antitradition of modernity, as it was translated into a different context and put to dissimilar uses by texts situated on both sides of the progressive/conservative divide as it has been commonly understood by historians. Emerging from this study is a sense that Confucian iconoclasm represents an alternative antitradition or an alternative (discourse of) modernity.[93]

In what follows, I first discuss the role (or lack thereof) tradition plays in the emancipatory discourse of *Eastern and Western Cultures* (chapter 1) and the *New Treatise* (chapter 2). After a brief interlude, which further contextualizes the texts' iconoclasm within the discursive milieu of their time, chapters 3 and 4 provide a detailed analysis of the various discursive techniques employed by *Eastern and Western Cultures* and the *New Treatise* to legitimize their discourse with the authority of tradition. Finally, the conclusion discusses at greater length the question of textual authority and the hegemonic struggle that characterizes the politics of antitradition in which May Fourth and Confucian iconoclasm are engaged.

1

Reviving the Spirit of Confucius

Shortly after its publication in 1921, *Eastern and Western Cultures* had the illustrious honor of becoming somewhat of a philosophy bestseller. Since then, the book and its author have been received in sharply contrasting ways. While most have emphasized the conservative or traditionalist stance of the work,[1] others have paid closer attention to its modern dimension,[2] while some have put forth the argument that Liang never saw the modern and the traditional in antithetical terms.[3] While each of these interpretations finds support in the complex metanarrative of history the text weaves together,[4] I argue in the following that ultimately this metanarrative strips tradition of its value almost entirely, with the notable (yet partial) exception of the ideals and spirits of two geniuses of the so-called "axial age."

Before addressing the implications the text's metanarrative of history, and its description of the driving force behind it, hold with regard to the value of tradition, it should be noted that *Eastern and Western Cultures* is a work deeply embedded in the time and place of its birth. The late 1910s saw the emergence of a debate on Eastern and Western cultures, fuelled by a sense of crisis of the intellectual elite that fashioned in many respects what was retrospectively baptized the New Culture Movement.[5] While the theme of the rapport between Eastern and Western cultures was hardly new—scholar-officials had dealt with the issue of the place the Qing empire should afford to borrowings from the West since the nineteenth century— intellectuals approached it from a new angle in the late 1910s. For one thing, the question was no longer merely that of assessing which aspects of Western civilization should be translated into the Chinese milieu. The 1911 Xinhai Revolution had not borne the expected political fruits, and attempts at reinstating the monarchy—first by Yuan Shikai (袁世凱; 1859–1916) in 1915–1916 and then by Zhang Xun (張勳; 1854–1923) in 1917—were answered by a growing sense, among the more radical intelligentsia, that China's problems were not primarily military or political in scope, but found their source in a culture diametrically opposed to the modern age.

Chen Duxiu was arguably the foremost representative of this position. In a number of articles published in *New Youth*, he repeatedly deployed biological metaphors to make the social Darwinist point that just like new cells replacing old ones, modern civilization had to replace the hierarchical, patriarchal, and despotic sociopolitical order inherited from the past, lest the Chinese should face the tragic fate of extinction.[6] His attacks were not directed at all aspects of Chinese culture, however. They singled out the Confucian family system and the hierarchical order it sanctioned as the main culprits responsible for China's backwardness. Yet Chen opined that because Chinese and Western cultures were entirely incompatible, China's entry into the modern age (equated in Chen with Western culture) necessitated an iconoclastic rejection of all of China's traditions.

Not everyone agreed with such a radical position, of course. Chen's colleague at Peking University, and the man who would later co-found the Communist Party with him, Li Dazhao (李大釗; 1889–1927), published in 1918 an article in which he agreed with Chen that Eastern and Western cultures were diametrically opposed, respectively representing passive and active types of civilization, but he concluded that a blending of the two was not only possible but also desirable.[7] Du Yaquan, the influential editor-in-chief of *Eastern Miscellaneous* (*Dongfang zazhi* 東方雜誌), also promoted a syncretic culture that would blend the best of both worlds. But after the events on May Fourth 1919, Chen Duxiu's views, as well as those of his colleague Hu Shi (胡適; 1891–1962), became the mainstream position against which alternative outlooks had to define themselves. The Chinese youth of the period were increasingly formed to think of the distinction between Eastern and Western cultures in temporal instead of spatial terms, as cultures behind and ahead of one and the same model of development.

Chen's relative victory in the elite discursive field was both propelled *and* mitigated by the May Fourth events. While his metanarrative of modernity temporalizing spatial distinctions became widespread, the positing of Western Europe and North America at the vanguard of history that had marked his discourse of the second half of the 1910s was challenged by the Treaty of Versailles, which had caused the May Fourth demonstrations. By ceding to Japan concessions in the Shandong province, which had formerly belonged to Germany, the allies betrayed the trust Chinese intellectuals like Chen had put in them, especially in view of the thousands of Chinese workers who died in support of the allies' cause. Within this context, the Bolshevik revolution of 1917 came to be viewed by a growing number of intellectuals, including Chen himself, as representative of a new vanguard in world history, one that could perhaps even be reached by China *before the West*.[8]

Moreover, news of the devastation wrought by the First World War certainly cast a long shadow on a modern Western civilization that had been taken, up until then, as a model to follow by Chen and other iconoclasts writing for his journal *New Youth*. This was the message brought home from Europe by Liang Qichao (梁啟超; 1873–1929), who had journeyed through Europe for most of 1919. In his *Records of My Travel Impressions in Europe* (*Ouyou xinying lu* 歐遊心影錄), Liang tells the tale of a Europe losing its faith in unilinear progress following the European model. This leads him to reevaluate his stance on Chinese civilization following the "moral bankruptcy" of Europe. Only China, he recalls an American journalist telling him, could save the West by producing a syncretism of the two civilizations.[9]

It is within this context, to which he directly alludes in the introduction of his work, that Liang Shuming found an interest in the topic of the differences between Eastern and Western cultures.[10] This led him to give a series of lectures on the topic, first at Peking University in the autumn of 1920, and then in Jinan in August 1921, under the auspices of a summer university organized by the teachers of Shandong. Based on notes taken during the Jinan lectures by Liang's student—and soon-to-be famous linguist—Luo Changpei (羅常培; 1899–1958), notes that he revised himself, Liang first published each chapter individually as his Jinan lectures were ongoing. In October of the same year, he had the chapters published together in a single volume,[11] to which he added a preface in which he professed he had undergone somewhat of a "conversion" to Confucianism.[12]

Liang's book, which made his name soon after its publication, sets out to resolve tensions not only between Eastern and Western cultures, but also between the radical *New Youth* group and those who upheld that Chinese culture still had value in the modern period. As Catherine Lynch notes, Liang felt an acute responsibility to defend Chinese culture against the attacks of the *New Youth* group he knew only too well, as its headquarters were situated at the very university where Liang taught from 1917 to 1924. But he felt most alienated from the university's Confucian scholars, who seemed "to have a peculiar ability to insulate themselves from the

New Culture movement."[13] Liang sought to position himself between the two groups—as an opponent of the May Fourth group, certainly, but as one who would not shy away from answering the group's most poignant criticisms of tradition.[14]

In an effort to forge a middle path between Chen Duxiu and Liang Qichao, *Eastern and Western Cultures* provides a new historical metanarrative that upholds the relative superiority of a "Chinese culture" capable of saving the "moral bankruptcy" of Western civilization, while simultaneously admitting to Chen the fact that *as of now*, the West was closer than China to the emancipatory telos of history. Yet Liang's acute concern with the May Fourth side of the debate on Eastern and Western cultures means that he framed his lectures as a direct answer to the May Fourth group, so much so that his portrayal of "Chinese culture" was significantly informed by the iconoclasm of the latter. What follows supports this interpretation by taking a closer look at the text's historical metanarrative and its portrayal of the driving force behind it.

Before doing so, however, a word on the terminologies used throughout this chapter and the subsequent ones is in order. First is an important distinction between "traditions" and "historical traditions." For the sake of clarity, I use the former to refer to traditions formulated *in the discourses I study* (e.g., Confucianism as construed by the texts), while the latter indicate *extra-discursive* traditions. This does not mean that such traditions are non-discursive—they can be either discursive or non-discursive. What it means is that they are situated *outside the discourses I study* (e.g., traditions, Confucian or not, that have shaped the texts but that are not discussed by them). In short, the latter denote traditions that I single out to make sense of the texts, while the former are traditions established by the texts themselves.[15]

Second is the distinction I draw between "traditions" and "antitraditions." While the former is a generic term that refers to "anything which is transmitted or handed down from the past to the present,"[16] the latter is a subcategory of traditions that oppose all other traditions and that show the way to a final liberation from the influences of the past. "Antitraditions" refer to those antitraditions within the discourse of the texts, while "historical antitraditions," discussed at greater length in the third chapter, denote antitraditions that are left undiscussed by the texts but that bear their mark on them.

I also distinguish, particularly in my discussion of *Eastern and Western Cultures*, between "traditions-as-history" and "traditions-as-value." The former indicate traditions as they took shape in history, while the latter denote traditions regarded as having transhistorical value, on the basis that they have managed to remain untainted by the exigencies of history. When the latter serve the purpose of discursively rejecting all other traditions, I call them "antitraditions-as-value." Of further note is that both "tradition-as-value" and "tradition-as-history" refer to traditions embedded *within the discourse of the texts*. I do not make such distinctions at the level of historical traditions, as this would be to partake in the very practices of orthodoxy and hegemony formation I analyze.

Finally, it is worth noting that all of the above terminologies are etic. What follows is not a conceptual history of "tradition" as construed by the texts. In fact, the texts rarely use the term "*chuantong*" (傳統) or any other term that might be read as a relatively straightforward counterpart to the English "tradition." Instead, this chapter and the next inquire into whether the texts regard any form of transmission from past to present as playing a positive and meaningful role in achieving their emancipatory goal.

Cultural pluralism

To get a better grasp of the role (or lack thereof) assigned to tradition in its metanarrative, a good place to start is the question *Eastern and Western Cultures* sets out to answer: "Must Eastern cultures be eradicated from their roots, or can they overturn their fate [*fanshen* 翻身]?"[17] This question is significant, as it assumes that Eastern cultures are gradually disappearing, and that their fate must be "overturned" if they are to have any hope of surviving the crisis that befell them. To overturn their fate, the text adds, Eastern cultures cannot simply survive in their homelands. They must become, like Western culture at the time (according to the text), *global* cultures. This shows the extent to which the text's portrayal of Eastern cultures—and the traditions that comprise them—partakes in a paradigm it shares with the protagonists of the May Fourth Movement. According to this paradigm, (1) the solution to China's problems is located in the cultural sphere, (2) Eastern cultures are in danger of extinction, and (3) the modern world is characterized by a process of homogenization of cultures, so that the very survival of Eastern cultures hinges on their ability to successfully navigate the passage from the local and the particular to the global and the universal.

Before attending to the difficult question of what "Eastern cultures" are and how they can become global, *Eastern and Western Cultures* first grounds its understanding of cultural differences in a complex metaphysics. The universe, the text proposes, is but a ceaseless process of living, meaning that "there is only life and no *thing* that lives," no substance that retains its self-same identity in the endless flux of change.[18] The constant transformations of the life-universe are the result of a process of demand and answer (*yi wen yi da* 一問一答). Human desires, which can never be fulfilled completely, keep on seeking satisfaction in the world, and in the process compel the universe to continuously arise and transform in order to answer the unquenchable thirst of human beings.[19] Human will or desire (*yiyu* 意欲) is thus the very stuff of which life and the universe are made.[20]

Based on this anthropocentric metaphysics, the text defines culture as "the way of life of a people."[21] As a way of life, each culture originates in the specific ways people seek satisfaction in the world. To explain cultural differences, the book distinguishes three types of "needs" or "demands" (*wen* 問), according to the extent to which they can be satisfied. While material needs can be fulfilled if we struggle hard enough to bend the material world to our will, needs or demands that involve other human beings are more complex, as one can never entirely control what another person thinks or feels. The satisfaction of such needs ultimately lies outside the realm of our control. Finally, demands that relate to the causal laws of the universe simply cannot be met, because such laws are entirely independent of our will.[22]

Having established this threefold typology, the text goes on to argue that each culture has gradually developed, over time, an attitude that can cope with one type of needs, but that is ill-equipped to face the other two. There are thus three types of cultures, of which the West, China, and India are paradigmatic representatives. Given that they adopted a will (*yiyu*) that is unique to them, each of the three cultures has evolved along a path or orientation (*luxiang* 路向) of its own.

The path adopted by Western culture finds its basis in a will that continuously seeks satisfaction externally. When confronted with a problem, those adopting this will attempt to modify the external circumstances responsible for the problem they face. This "forward-oriented will," as the text calls it, is precisely what allowed the West to dominate nature and give rise to science and democracy.[23] Chinese culture, by comparison, predominantly makes use of a will to "modify, mediate, and moderate one's desires."[24] When confronted with a problem, one who adopts this approach will not search for a solution by modifying the external circumstances, but "will try to find personal satisfaction within the circumstances" by "reconciling one's desires [with the circumstances]."[25] As to Indian culture, its will turns its back on desire altogether: "When facing a problem, those who have taken this path [. . .] will want to eradicate the issue or the need from its very roots. [. . .] All those who hold an ascetic attitude toward desire belong to this category."[26] Buddhism offers the paradigmatic example of such an attitude, although the text also associates Christianity, and the European Middle Ages, with it.

Eastern and Western Cultures' three-tiered cultural typology borrows from the May Fourth position in its very attempt at challenging it. For one thing, the text's cultural model relies on an anthropomorphization of cultures, in the sense that each culture possesses its own will that answers various issues by making use of a method unique to it.[27] The text thus tends to gloss over the many tensions and contradictions that inhere in the cultures it discusses to portray them as homogeneous organisms. Like determined individuals, cultures are of a single will. As such, there is no point in talking about the possibility of blending East and West by picking and choosing elements from both sides that could benefit the world of tomorrow. Given that it describes each facet of a culture as the direct product of the will on which it is based, Liang's cultural model precludes the possibility of adopting foreign cultural products while retaining one's own will. And since cultures cannot be of two wills, appropriating for oneself the culture of another is simply impossible without a drastic change at the level of one's will. The text thus shares Chen Duxiu's judgment that Eastern and Western cultures are ultimately incompatible and that cultural amalgams are impossible. It in fact congratulates Chen, in no uncertain terms, for having realized this point.[28]

Yet, although the text's conclusion on cultural blending resembles Chen's closely, their premises differ in important ways. In Chen's case, cultural incompatibility finds justification in a unilinear metanarrative that temporalizes Chinese culture and Western culture as feudal and modern, respectively, and that conceptualizes the modern as a process of emancipation from the feudal. In the case of *Eastern and Western Cultures*, it is because each culture relies on its own distinct will that the three cultures cannot be reconciled. In fact, because the three cultures have evolved along their own pathways in parallel to one another, the text maintains that without contact with the West, Chinese culture never would have given rise to science, democracy, or an industrial revolution comparable to that of Europe.[29] This position makes it possible for the text to reject Eurocentric models of unilinear history, such as that of Chen, according to which something resembling modern Western culture represents the inevitable telos toward which China would eventually evolve. Instead, *Eastern and Western Cultures* puts forth a cultural pluralism acknowledging that each of the three cultures it discusses possesses its own strengths and weaknesses.[30] This does not entail, however, that the text promotes a form of cultural relativism according to which there would be no objective standpoint from which to assess the merits and demerits of each culture. As we will see, the text introduces such an objective standpoint in the form of an alternative, non-Eurocentric historical metanarrative that makes room for the successive and accumulative development of the strengths of each culture.

Historical metanarrative

Humanity, according to *Eastern and Western Cultures*, faces issues on three fronts: the material, the interpersonal, and the existential. But it cannot resolve all of them at once. It must face them in order of priority.[31] In the first phase of history, humans deal with basic material needs, such as food, shelter, clothing, and so forth. Only the attitude of the Western will oriented forward can fulfill such needs by dominating nature and modifying the environment in which humans live to make it better adapted to satisfy their material needs. Western culture had not spread across the world in the nineteenth and early twentieth centuries by accident. It provided the only method suited to resolve the material issues emblematic of the first phase of history in which humanity found itself. Therein—and not in an inherent superiority—lies the strength of Western culture.[32] Its weakness, on the other hand, is that in dealing with interpersonal issues, it relies on the same forward-oriented will used to dominate nature. Colonialism and imperialism, but also rampant capitalism, industrialization, and mechanization, are the direct products, according to the text, of the misdirected appropriation of the Western will to dominate fellow human beings. Although Western culture allows humanity to fulfill its basic human needs and increase its livelihood, it is also responsible for the rise of unprecedented issues such as social alienation, exploitation, and the replacement of the emotional bond between people with mechanistic and calculative interpersonal relations.[33]

Once the basic needs of humanity become less and less of a pressing issue, humanity would gradually come to realize the significance of interpersonal issues—issues that the Western will oriented forward, because of its propensity toward control and domination, cannot but exacerbate further. At this point in history, humanity would gradually come to adopt the Chinese will, as only it was suited to resolve the difficult problems that pertain to interpersonal relations. Given that the other ultimately lies outside the realm of our control, interpersonal issues necessitate a willingness to adapt one's expectations and needs to the situation at hand. This is precisely what the Chinese will to "modify, mediate, and moderate one's desires" has to offer: a method to cope with the fact that human beings live in societies. Although the text readily admits that the Chinese will led to disastrous results on the front of material needs, this is because Chinese culture was too far ahead of its time. It provided the means to solve complex interpersonal issues before it had fulfilled the more basic material needs of humanity. As humanity entered the second phase of history, however, Chinese culture would experience a revival and would make it possible for humanity to develop harmonious interpersonal relations and establish a more symbiotic rapport with nature.[34]

Finally, as the problem of interpersonal relations gradually resolves itself, humanity would come to realize the deep-rooted issue of existence. By this, the text refers to the fact that human beings cannot escape suffering as long as they retain a dual attachment to world and self. *Saṃsāra* would be the last issue humanity faces. In this phase of history, "Indian culture," which the text reduces to Buddhism, would experience a revival, as the will at its basis, turning its back on desire as it is, would enable humanity to emancipate itself from the cycle of life, death, and rebirth. However, because humanity was still far from this historical stage, the text discourages the practice of Buddhism, at least for the time being.[35]

That Western culture was becoming global, at the time the book was published, entailed that humanity lived in the first phase of history. May Fourth iconoclasts were therefore very much of their time. Like them, Liang could see the need for westernization—the satisfaction of basic human needs hung in the balance—but, unlike them, he could also see what lay ahead: the "sinicization" of humanity. In fact, Liang did not have to look far ahead in the future to draw the contours of what awaited humanity, as he saw signs that the West was already slowly but surely moving toward adopting the Chinese will. Relying on rigid dichotomies, he maintained that Western philosophy was transitioning from an intellectualist and rationalist study of the absolute, the unchanging, and the external world (the Western approach) to an intuitive study of the relative, the constantly changing, and the living (the Chinese approach). Evidence of this passage could be detected in the works of Peter Kropotkin (1842–1921), William James (1842–1910), Rudolf Christoph Eucken (1846–1926), Henri Bergson (1859–1941), John Dewey (1859–1952), and, perhaps more surprisingly, Bertrand Russell (1872–1970). Moreover, Liang saw the emergence of psychology and socialism—especially guild socialism—as indications that the West had embarked on a "sinicization" of its culture (for reasons that will become clear in a moment).[36]

The modern world was thus heading toward a revival of the cultures of China and India. This did not mean, however, that the *contemporary* culture of China represented the future of humanity, in the same way the then-contemporary culture of the West represented an image of what the future held in store for China in May Fourth discourse. A subtle semantic shift occurs when the text discusses the Eastern cultures awaiting their revival. In such cases, "culture" refers not to the "way of life of a people," as the text itself defines the term, but to *ideals* Confucius and the Buddha had put forth in ancient times—ideals that were never realized historically, although the text's metanarrative made sure that history evolved toward precisely such a realization.

The ideal imagined by Confucius was centered on the creation of harmonious interpersonal relations and the fulfilment of the union of heaven and the human (*tianren heyi* 天人合一). Such ideals could be realized if humanity followed a natural way of life based on intuitions (*zhijue* 直覺), as opposed to an instrumental kind of rationality (*lizhi* 理智) rooted in the Western will.[37] This explains why the text presents Western cultural products such as guild socialism and psychology as manifestations of "Chinese culture," since the former seeks the harmonious kind of interpersonal relations Confucius advocated, while the latter's emphasis on the unconscious reminds Liang of the intuitive method set forth by Confucius. Any sign of intuition and harmonious interpersonal relations, regardless of the geographical and cultural contexts, is thus invariably associated with a "Chinese culture" that is "Chinese" only to the extent it was first imagined by Confucius. "Chinese" thus comes to signify "Confucius," while "culture" refers to the ideal envisioned by the sage more than 2000 years ago.

This semantic shift enables the text to imply that both the May Fourth iconoclasts and Liang are right, although what they are right about differs in important ways. *Eastern and Western Cultures* comes to this conclusion by dissociating what I call "tradition-as-value" from "tradition-as-history," thus allowing it to abstract something of universal value from the past.[38] While the ideal of Confucius (tradition-as-value) certainly needed to be salvaged from the attacks of the iconoclasts, the latter had it right when it came to the historical cultures of China (traditions-as-history). Insofar as they manifested a failure to implement the ideal of Confucius in practice, Chinese traditions-as-history had to be relegated to the dustbin of history.

According to the text, nobody had truly understood "the philosophy of human life" (*rensheng zhexue* 人生哲學) of Confucius, although some had come closer, such as Wang Yangming, the members of the Taizhou school (*Taizhou xuepai* 泰州學派), especially Wang Gen (王艮; 1483–1541), and Dai Zhen (戴震; 1723–1777).[39] But even they had been unable to infuse history with the philosophy of life of the great sage, since Confucius's vision was too far ahead of his time, too precocious (*zaoshou* 早熟) for his followers to put in practice.[40]

The precociousness of the Confucian ideal explains why China tried to deal with the problem of human interactions pertaining to the second stage of history before it had fulfilled the basic human needs of the first. Because the problems of the second stage cannot be solved until one has successfully completed the first stage, however, China could not evolve along the path of the universal historical model proposed by the text. This explains why China had no proper history, according to the text, and no progress at all from the Warring States period until the modern era.[41] This goes to show the extent to which the text's construal of Chinese traditions-as-history is informed by the most iconoclastic of May Fourth discourses, which often reproduced Eurocentric conceptions of China as historically stagnant or altogether devoid of progress. In *Eastern and Western Cultures*, however, China's lack of proper history—that is, *progressive* history—serves the purpose of first conceding to May Fourth iconoclasts that the *historical manifestations* of Confucianism were of no value in the modern period, before claiming that the *spirit* of Confucius, insofar as it remained uncontaminated by history, retained value and would soon be revived.

Modernity as caesura

Eastern and Western Cultures manages to channel the spirit of the May Fourth iconoclasts in rejecting the value of Chinese traditions-as-history and in reiterating the myth of an unchanging China. Its discourse also reproduces mainstream conceptions of modernity as a caesura allowing humanity to break free from the hold of the past and move forward in history's ineluctable drive toward human emancipation. As we saw, in order to oppose Eurocentric models of unilinear history, the text asserts, regarding the *actual histories* of the West, China, and India, that they had embarked on unique historical trajectories that evolved in parallel to one another. However, when it comes to the modern period and the future of humankind, the text proposes a new model of unilinear development that reauthorizes Eastern traditions-as-value by projecting them onto the telos of history.

By distinguishing sharply between history as it should be and history as it was, the text produces a gap between the modern and the premodern. Premodernity was the time of plural and synchronic cultures: a time when a plurality of cultures, each having its own strengths (at least when it came to the *ideals* they had produced), developed along unique pathways, cohabiting in geographically distinct locales at one and the same time. But with the advent of modernity, culture becomes diachronic and homogeneous: the three cultures now succeed one another in three phases that take place homogeneously across the globe. By temporalizing spatial distinctions, modernity is able to provide a segue from cultural plurality to homogeneity, from particularism to universalism.[42] This explains why, according to the text, "Chinese culture" can survive in modern times only if it becomes global.[43]

The premodern period is devoid of progress, as the three cultures are yet to embark on the evolutionary scheme devised by *Eastern and Western Cultures*. While the precociousness of China and India led to their historical stagnation, the West did not embark on the path of teleological history—the marker of all that is modern—until the Renaissance, when humanity's bid to take its destiny into its own hands began. The West thus functions as the birthplace of teleological history.[44] This explains why the text often reproduces a Kantian construal of the Enlightenment as liberating humanity from its "self-imposed tutelage." "How did democracy come about?," the text asks. "It did so by an awakening of humanity—an awakening to humanity's nature [*benxing* 本性]—and a liberation from the tutelage of the church, the pope, and feudal lords."[45] The text also invokes the commonplace that during the Renaissance, Europe "awoke from the darkness" of the Middle Ages.[46]

As we saw above, Liang remains highly critical of important dimensions of "Western culture," such as the lack of harmony he sees in its social order and the alienation of the modern individual incapable of relating to others emotionally. This should not blind us to the fact, however, that the text also regards Western culture as thoroughly freeing in its ability to introduce the East into teleological history. In fact, the text often makes use of a discursive technique recurrent in May Fourth literature, whereby the "modern West" functions as a partially imagined other allowing one to denounce various aspects of Chinese culture. It is from the perspective of Western democracy, for example, that the text provides a critique of "oriental despotism." The despotic dimension of Chinese culture, the text argues, not only rid the subjects of the emperor of any agency, but it also impeded the development of an egalitarian society along the Western model.⁴⁷

Democracy provides the text with an outside from which to condemn Chinese traditions-as-history, often in terms that are oddly reminiscent of May Fourth iconoclasm:

> For thousands of years, [the ethical code *said* to be Confucian] has made us impotent in any attempt to liberate ourselves from various authorities, and so individuality could not develop and sociality could not flourish either. This is our biggest point of inferiority compared to the West.
>
> 數千年以來使吾人不能從種種在上的威權解放出來而得自由；個性不得伸展，社會性亦不得發達，這是我們人生上一個最大的不及西洋之處。⁴⁸

By blaming "Confucian" social hierarchies—such as that of the three bonds (*sangang* 三綱)—and the patriarchal family system (*you zuzhang jiazhang de zhidu* 有族長家長的制度) for prohibiting the rise of the individual in China,⁴⁹ the text sides with the May Fourth group, which had successfully managed to portray the autonomous modern individual as the very antithesis of a Confucian social order characterized by the dependence of the individual on the family and the group.⁵⁰

Eastern and Western Cultures' criticism of tradition-as-history also echoes May Fourth iconoclasm at another level. Reviewing the differences between Chinese and Western medicine, as well as between Western science and Chinese metaphysics (*xuanxue* 玄學), the text provides a critique of the notions of *yinyang* (陰陽) and *wuxing* (五行) that is reminiscent of the May Fourth attack on superstitions (*mixin* 迷信). After decrying the Chinese tendency to explain various phenomena, such as thunder, wind, or long life, by appealing to spirits, ghosts, or predetermination, the text comments that the Chinese,

> due to their lack of knowledge, fail to understand the reason for these phenomena, and thus inevitably inherit the thought of their primitive forebearers. Add to this their habit of giving complete approbation to what has not yet been properly examined to get to the truth, and there remains only one step before they start believing in things like spirits and ghosts.

> 前者［中國人］因為知識既缺乏不明白這些現象的所以然，不免為初民思想之遺留，又加以他的夙養，總愛於尚未檢驗得實的予以十分之肯定，於是就進一步而為有神有鬼等等思想了。[51]

The text then goes on to contrast the Chinese attitude, which it qualifies as unscientific (*wu kexue* 無科學) or non-scientific (*fei kexue* 非科學), with Western knowledge, which is presented as thoroughly scientific. To be sure, elsewhere the text holds a positive attitude toward Chinese metaphysics, and the notion of constant changes elaborated in the *Changes* (*Yijing* 易經) in particular, as long as such an intuitive metaphysics is not confused with physics.[52] But overall, the text does not find any scientific value in Chinese culture. While Liang does not use the term "superstition" (*mixin*), which was widely employed to attack Chinese traditions during the May Fourth period, his contrast between Western science and Chinese metaphysics bears striking similarities with dichotomies advanced by Chen Duxiu and other *New Youth* writers.[53]

By contrast, whenever Chinese traditions-as-history managed to make manifest Confucius's ideal, however imperfectly, *Eastern and Western Cultures* does commend them. Although the "Confucian" ethical code prevented the rise of individuality, as we saw above, the text praises its emphasis on affectionate bonds between family members.

> Although since the spiritual ideal of Confucius was never realized, these were but a few ancient rituals (*lifa* 禮法), inflexible dogmas that led to prejudices and dark injustices, so that affliction was considerable, families and society could still achieve a certain contentment, not of the apathetic, antagonistic, and calculative type, but [of the type] that contributed to fostering the vitality of people's lives and that cannot but be considered a strength and a success.

> 雖因孔子的精神理想沒有實現，而只是些古代禮法，呆板教條以致偏欹一方，黑暗冤抑，苦痛不少，然而家庭裏，社會上，處處都能得到一種情趣，不是冷漠、敵對、算帳的樣子，於人生的活氣有不少的培養，不能不算一種優長與勝利。[54]

Chinese traditions-as-history are therefore of value only to the extent that they managed to imperfectly embody Confucius's ideal. Ultimately, however, the historical embodiments of Confucius's ideal remained entangled in, and polluted by, customs and dogmas that were greatly detrimental to Chinese society. Overall, the text admits, "the Chinese were rarely able to put to use Confucius's ideas," so that "from thousands of years ago until now," Chinese culture "was shaped by the dregs history had left behind and was formed by inflexible rules of conduct."⁵⁵ The ideal of Confucius could thus truly manifest itself in history only after China freed itself from the dregs of its past, and only after it satisfied the basic needs of its people under the impetus of the West.

Although the text explicitly rejects the characterization of the East/West divide in terms of cultures that are behind and ahead of the same process of evolution, its repudiation of Eastern traditions-as-history and its valorization of the emancipatory features of the modern West lead it back to a temporalization of the spatial divide.⁵⁶ After reviewing the gap between Eastern and Western cultures at the levels of spiritual, social, and material life, the text concludes with the following comments:

> Looking at Eastern cultures and their philosophies, we see that they are all at a standstill, remaining the same through the ages, so that thousands of years later [their] cultures and philosophies are still the same as they were thousands of years ago. Given that everything we have is what the ancients left behind, and that everything later generations do is but the leftovers of the ancients, [we can say that] Eastern cultures are ancient cultures. Western culture is not like this: it continuously adapts to the changing times, its thought being renewed daily. Given that in it the new surpasses the old, and there is no revival of the old ways, [we can say that] Western culture is a new culture.
>
> 我們看東方文化和哲學，都是一成不變的，歷久如一的，所有幾千年後的文化和哲學，還是幾千年前的文化，幾千年前的哲學。一切今人所有的，都是古人之遺；一切後人所作，都是古人之餘；然則東方化⁵⁷即古化。西方化便不然；思想逐日的翻新，文化隨時闢創，一切都是後來居上，非復舊有，然則西方化就是新化。⁵⁸

This passage refrains from portraying Eastern and Western cultures as partaking in the same evolutionary scheme. As such, the above comments could be read as meaning that *within their own unique historical trajectories*, Eastern cultures are ancient while Western culture is new and modern. Yet ultimately, the historical metanarrative proposed by the text cannot avoid depicting Eastern traditions-as-history as *behind* Western culture. Judging the three traditions-as-history from the normative standard of the text's historical metanarrative, only the West had truly engaged in the race of teleological history. China and India were simply unable to leave the starting line because of their untimely and precocious fixation on the finish line.[59] In a manner that recalls the discursive trope of the white man's burden, only the West, in the text's discourse, possesses the ability to introduce Eastern cultures in teleological history and free them from the passivity and stagnancy of their past.

The above goes to show the extent to which the text reproduces the May Fourth idea that the modern age was birthed in a radical act of emancipation from the past. The text also recycles well-worn dichotomies along the lines of a stagnant and passive East on the one hand and an active, progressive, and agency-driven West on the other. And it shares with the May Fourth iconoclasts an optimistic belief in the emancipatory power of teleological history, which it associates, not unlike them, with science and democracy. While science liberated humanity from "all kinds of concepts and beliefs handed down from the past,"[60] the text maintains, democracy enabled its awakening and its affirmation of the individual.[61]

Despite such close ties with the discourse of May Fourth, the text charts its own course when it comes to abstracting a spirit from the distant past and claiming that history evolves toward its concrete realization. Yet this means that what is still valuable of the past is not a tradition that is passed down from generation to generation, however, but the spirit of an ancient genius who was able to transcend his time to produce, if not in reality at least in ideality, an image of what the future should be. As we will see by looking at the text's metaphysics, it is precisely the ability of the ancient geniuses to transcend the limitations of their time that the text seeks to revive.

The struggle between spirit and matter

Although the text presumes that history follows a predetermined course, it also assumes that humans have the ability to free themselves from the tyranny and determinism of the past. Disentangling this tension opens up another perspective on the text's construal of the relation the contemporary living in the teleological phase of history entertains with the past.

Even though the work does not explicitly address the issue of determinism and agency, its comments on the notion of the mandate of heaven (*tianming* 天命) and its discussion of the metaphysical flow of a universe in constant transformation give us some clues as to how the individual relates or *should* relate to the past. Regarding the mandate of heaven, the text has the following to say:

> What we call the "mandate of heaven" is difficult to discuss. Roughly speaking, it denotes the process of evolution of nature. The origin of this great process of the universe goes far back, which explains why its power is so great. This process is difficult to redirect since its power continuously manifests itself in the production of every moment. Apart from my action at this very moment which is not determined [by it], all other aspects of the environment surrounding this action escape me and belong to what is already decided [*yicheng* 已成]. These aspects of the environment which have already been decided can be called "determining circumstances" [*jihui* 機會 or *jiyuan* 機緣], regardless of whether they are favorable or unfavorable to my action at this moment.
>
> 所謂天命原很難講，大概說去就是指那造化流行而言。這個宇宙大的流行，他的來路非常之遠；惟其遠，其力量亦非常之大，一直貫注下來，成功這個局面，很難轉的。除了我當下這一動是未定的，其餘周圍種種方面情形都在我之外而屬於已成。這周圍已成的局面都可以叫做機會，或機緣——不拘他對於我這一動為順為逆。[62]

As this discussion of the mandate of heaven shows, human freedom is limited by objective conditions. After all, the text makes it clear that the fulfilment of some of our desires, such as the desire to change the other or escape suffering and death, is out of our hands.

Although the above excerpt does not address the issue of historical determinism, its portrayal of human agency and evolution does have significant implications for history. Overall, evolution possesses a direction that can be studied, and this can help predict its future course. This is precisely what the text does: it deduces the inevitable direction human civilization must take through a study of the wills at the basis of the cultures of the

West, China, and India. This suggests that the overall evolution of humankind simply cannot be altered. After all, even geniuses such as Confucius and the Buddha, who could freely imagine the culture of the future, were not able to amend the historical model in order to skip the early phase(s) of history and enter a more advanced stage directly. Humanity can thus oppose the natural process of evolution, but this opposition will merely delay the inevitable; will merely halt human civilization on its course to destiny. This explains why the text claims it is better to rejoice in heaven's mandate (*letian* 樂天) than to try opposing it.[63]

Although the text admits history follows a predetermined course, it rejects historical materialism, insofar as the latter treats "the culture of humanity as a mere passive reaction to the environment, rejecting the possibility of creative action."[64] While Liang agrees with most Marxists that consciousness (*yishi* 意識) has no bearing on the economic base, he condemns historical materialism for failing to take into account the notion of spirit (*jingshen* 精神).[65] Although valuable to explain material causal relations in history (*yuan* 緣), historical materialism ultimately ignores deeper causes (*yin* 因) found at the level of spirit. It is spirit that provides human beings with the potential—fully activated only in extremely rare cases—to transcend historical determinism in order to produce transhistorical values. This is precisely what Confucius and the Buddha did when imagining the cultures of the future. The text in fact goes so far as to suggest that "what we call culture is in all aspects the creation of geniuses."[66]

The relation the text establishes between determinism and agency can be further elucidated by looking at its discussion of the constant transformations of the universe. As we saw at the beginning of this chapter, the text portrays the universe as a constant flux that arises in answer to human needs, following the analogy of a question that requires an answer. The text associates the endless process of question and answer with a continuous struggle that takes place between what it calls—borrowing from Yogācāra—the "previous self" (*qianci de wo* 前此的我 or *yicheng de wo* 已成的我) and the "present self" (*xianzai de wo* 現在的我):

> What we call life is a struggle of the present self against the previous self [. . .]. Every present self, when hoping to act in an outward manner, meets the obstruction of the previous self. For example, if there is a rock in front of me which obstructs my way, and I need to use force in order to remove it, this is of course considered an obstacle. If I want to walk, or if I want

to drink tea, at this moment my limbs and the teacup can all be considered obstacles. Because my limbs and the teacup all belong to the material world [*qi shijian* 器世間][67]—the previous self—they are unwieldy things. In order to satisfy a need and move my limbs or raise the teacup to my lips, I must strive to alter the situation of the previous self, otherwise I will not be able to satisfy [this need]. This striving to alter the situation of the previous self in order to obtain some result is what is called "struggle." All use of force is a struggle. And since in our lives we are at all times using force, we are also constantly struggling.

所謂生活就是用現在的我對於前此的我之奮鬥……。因為凡是「現在的我」要求向前活動，都有「前此的我」為我當前的「礙」，譬如我前面有塊石頭，擋著我過不去，我須用力將他搬開固然算是礙，就是我要走路，我要喝茶，這時我的肢體，同茶碗都算是礙；因為我的肢體，或茶碗都是所謂「器世間」——「前此的我」——是很笨重的東西，我如果要求如我的願，使我肢體運動或將茶碗端到嘴邊，必須努力變換這種「前此的我」的局面，否則是絕不會滿意的；這種努力去改變「前此的我」的局面而結果有所取得，就是所謂奮鬥。所以凡是一個用力都算是奮鬥；我們的生活無時不用力，即是無時不奮鬥。[68]

Following this passage, the text goes on to explicitly associate the previous self with matter and the present self with spirit,[69] thus conceptualizing the material world as the solidification, or materialization, of the spirit of elapsed selves. Although the above passage bears on the metaphysics of the text and not its take on history, we can see how the two are intricately linked, insofar as the spirit of the present self is the element missing in historical materialism—the source of humanity's ability to transcend the limitations of matter and the past.

Although *Eastern and Western Cultures* remains rather vague on the specifics of how this process of transcendence works, it is fair to assume that its views are highly indebted to Yogācāra, in which cognitive objects are interpreted as the manifestation of the potentiality inherent in seeds stored in the eighth consciousness—seeds that are the direct product of previous cravings and desires.[70] In Yogācāra, however, this process applies to consciousness, while in *Eastern and Western Cultures*, it informs a metaphysics of constant transformations, whereby spirit continuously solidifies into matter. Insofar as it represents the physical manifestation of the past in the present, matter is closely associated with the notion of tradition, and can even be understood as one of the many shapes traditions take. Agency, within this context, is redefined in terms of a constant struggle by spirit to emancipate itself from the limiting and restricting power of both matter and tradition.

We can leave aside for the present purpose the issue that by presenting the body as an obstacle to the spirit of the present self thirsting for tea, the text overlooks the obvious fact that without embodiment, the spirit would never feel thirsty in the first place, and without limbs to bring the teacup to "its" lips, and without lips at all, thirst could simply not be satisfied. Such issues highlight the rigidity of the text's dichotomies, as well as its strong tendency toward idealism. What matters for our purpose is the text's intriguing conflation of the idealist struggle against matter with the (modern) theme of transcendence from the limitations of the past, which helps us get a better sense of the inner dynamics at work in the historical metanarrative set forth by the text.

It has become clear that history is a stage on which a struggle between spirit and matter, and between the present (self) and the past, is waged. In the ancient period, the spirits of two geniuses were able to transcend, to varying degrees, the limitations imposed on them by matter and the past to produce transhistorical ideals entirely untainted by traditions-as-history. But until the modern age, issues related to the material condition of humanity prevented the historical realization of their ideals. The value of Western culture thus precisely resides in its ability to fulfill material needs so that humanity can then focus on "spiritualizing" the world, on making spirit manifest in the world of matter. By this, I mean that in the second phase of history, the external world is gradually reshaped in the image of an ideal that is purely spiritual, being the product of a genius no longer defined by his embodiment.

Whereas history and spirit (or value) were estranged in the premodern period, the second phase of teleological history witnesses a gradual merging of the two. Unlike the first phase of history, in which humanity relates to the world and others as means to satisfy needs and wants that have their origin in the body, the second phase sees human beings gradually learn to emancipate themselves from such selfish predispositions. The kind of emotionally grounded interpersonal relationships Confucius urges us to adopt should in fact help us halt our tendency to relate to the world and other human beings as subjects relate to objects. One can then come to realize that the universe, others, and oneself are part of a single holistic process of living, so that the boundary between self and non-self progressively fades. "The self and the universe merge into one," the text alleges, "as the mode of thinking [of the West] that seeks an [utilitarian] estimation of costs and benefits dissolves, fundamentally causing problems to stop arising."[71]

Since those living during the second phase of teleological history will no longer be experiencing the kind of distress that calculating reason had brought about in the first phase, there will no longer be any need for religions to exist. Their sole purpose, in the past, had been to console human beings experiencing such distress. There is an exception to this rule, however. Buddhism represents the only true religion capable of bringing about humanity's ultimate emancipation from suffering. Unlike Confucianism, what Buddhism seeks, according to *Eastern and Western Cultures*, is not a fusion with the world but an ultimate transcendence or extrication (*chaotuo* 超脫 or *tuoli* 脫離) from it. This can be achieved by renouncing what functions as the very motor of history: desire or will. Through this renunciation, the universe ceases to arise, as the present self, having rid itself of desire, no longer produces the kind of demands or needs that requires an answer from the universe. The goal of Buddhism is therefore to exit the world (*chushi* 出世), to break the spirit free from its dependence on the body, matter, and the universe of constant transformations.[72] And given how the text conceives of matter as the physical manifestation of our past, by breaking free from matter at the end of history, the present self—spirit—also emancipates itself from the past.

Understood as spirit's ultimate emancipation from matter and tradition, the telos of history can only take place if matter has been previously "spiritualized" in the second phase of teleological history, just like this second phase can only take place once the limitations matter imposes on spirit are curtailed by satisfying humanity's basic material needs. This explains why Thierry Meynard argues that Confucianism and "Chinese culture" effectively function, in this metanarrative, as historicized skillful means enabling humanity's final enlightenment.[73] Liang, in this reading, can be interpreted as a modern Bodhisattva who employs the tools of modernity to achieve a traditional goal. Although Meynard is right in emphasizing that the ultimate goal of history is Buddhist in nature, I doubt whether Confucianism can be described as a skillful means in the context of Liang's metanarrative, however, insofar as the spiritualization of the world taking place in the second phase of history has value in and of itself. Perhaps Western culture might also at first sight appear like a skillful means to better ends, although overall the text does find intrinsic value in the fulfillment of basic human needs. Ultimately, however, the ideals of Confucianism and Buddhism, one this-worldly and one other-worldly, are certainly loftier.

It is of particular interest that the text should posit Buddhism as the emancipatory end of history, particularly given Liang's tendency, in texts written from the 1930s to the 1960s, to depict the evolution of his own thought in terms of a progression from utilitarianism (Western culture) to Buddhism and *finally* Confucianism.[74] When describing this personal evolution, Liang portrays utilitarianism and Buddhism as extreme poles around which his life was shaped: between action and thought, between participation in the world (*rushi* 入世) and withdrawal from it (*chushi*), and between national and existential issues—the first pole of each being represented by utilitarianism, the second by Buddhism. As to Confucianism, Liang presents it as a middle path enabling him to reach a proper balance between the two extremes.

It is clear, from this short outline of Liang's "self-narratives," as Thierry Meynard calls them,[75] that he finds theoretical resources for his historical metanarrative in his personal experiences, or at least in the narrative he builds around such experiences. It is of interest, however, that in its historical metanarrative, the text modifies the sequential order to present the end of history as a Buddhist emancipation rather than a Confucian middle path. By translating the Western telos of modernity understood as an ideal of freedom from authority into a Buddhist radical emancipation from matter and desire, what the text can oppose is the Eurocentric dimension of the metanarrative of modernity, but not the framework of the metanarrative itself, that is, the idea that modernity leads to absolute liberation. Had the text portrayed the historical process as a search for equilibrium among extreme poles of existence, replacing the ideal of liberation with one of balance, its criticism would have extended to the historical *framework* of modernity itself.[76] Instead, the text elects to co-opt the metanarrative framework to project its own interpretation of ancient ideals onto the telos of history and reauthorize them in the process.

The Spirit of Confucius

Although the text conceives of history as predetermined in its general course, deterministic history ultimately leads to its own opposite: the spirit's transcendence from causality once and for all. Progress is thus reconceptualized as a passage from determinism to freedom, although, as the cases of Confucius and the Buddha show, transcendence from determinism, matter, and the past is possible, during any time period, albeit only for geniuses. In the teleological phase of history, the spirit of transcendence of the two geniuses is reappropriated by humanity in a way that echoes how in the modern period contemporaries begin to see themselves not as inheritors of the ancients, but as individuals who can channel the creative act of the ancients in the present.[77]

That the text seeks to reshape the moderns in the image of ancient geniuses can be exemplified by taking a look at the solution to China's predicament that *Eastern and Western Cultures* proposes. Without going into too many details, suffice it to say, for our purpose, that Liang finds himself between a rock and a hard place toward the end of his book, and doubly so. The first issue he faces is that of China's precociousness. Because of it, China could neither go back to the first phase of teleological history, as it was, in a sense, too advanced to do so, nor could it go forward, since it had not yet satisfied the material needs of its citizens and still needed to run the full course of the first phase of teleological history.[78]

The ideal of "Chinese culture" could thus be implemented only if "Western culture" was first adopted. Yet although the text remains unequivocal that the spirits of democracy and science have to be accepted unconditionally,[79] it also identifies a number of issues that befell Western civilization, because of its excessive use of rationality, and that should be avoided at all costs by the Chinese.[80] But how could the text recommend the adoption of the positive aspects of Western culture (science and democracy) while avoiding its dark side, given how it conceives culture as the holistic expression of the way of life of a people and rejects the possibility of any synthesis between Eastern and Western cultures?

The solution proposed by the text is to argue that China should "accept Western culture wholesale, but change it from its roots up" by "modifying its attitude" toward life.[81] It did not escape Liang's contemporaries that this amounted to a cultural synthesis the possibility of which had been denied in the text's introduction.[82] Others argued that this solution entailed a revival of the late-Qing discourse that called for the synthesis of "Chinese culture as essence and Western culture for practical application" (*zhongti xiyong* 中體西用).[83] The text, after all, hoped to import certain aspects of modern Western culture while "retaining" the Chinese attitude. Although what the text sought to do, in effect, was to revive an attitude that had never been fully manifested in history: that of resoluteness (*gang* 剛).

Resoluteness is defined by the text as "an extremely rich internal strength" that can "sum up the whole philosophy of Confucius."[84] To make this point, the text quotes from *Analects* 5:11, in which Confucius judges that Shen Cheng (申枨) cannot be *gang* given that he is "full of desires."[85] On this basis, the text concludes that while desire and *gang* "both appear to be forces that lead forward fiercely, one is full of an internal strength, while the other is false—it lacks fullness and its strength is illusory." This is due to the fact that "the drive of one is internal while that of the other is external," meaning that while *gang* finds its source in spirit, desire is motivated by material needs and wants.[86] This entails that while Western culture rests on a will to satisfy the material needs of the body, Confucian resoluteness can serve as a forward-oriented will, but one led by the inner spirit of the self rather than its bodily needs.

By adopting Confucian resoluteness, modern China can import cultural elements, such as science and democracy, that are predicated on the Western will oriented forward, while avoiding societal ills that arise from an overemphasis on the satisfaction of material desires. The text's approach toward the modern West is thus similar to its attitude toward premodern China: traditions-as-value have to be salvaged and abstracted from their failed or highly imperfect manifestations in history. After all, the text finds interest in the *spirits* of science and democracy. Their manifestations in modern Western history, however, have brought about a dissection of nature's unity because of an exaggerated use of scientific rationality and a focus on selfish individual rights and litigious relations between human beings regarding each other as enemies. The text is clear on the fact that the goal of its discussion of resoluteness is "to promote an attitude of striving forward, while at the same time rejecting the undesirable trend of externally pursuing material things."[87] Only this Confucian type of inner strength or resoluteness would "make up for the ingrained shortcomings of the Chinese, rescue the Chinese from their actual predicament, and avoid the negative aspects of the West."[88]

What is of value of Confucius, apart from the ideal of harmonious interpersonal relations he advocated, is therefore also the ability to provide the moderns with a spirit of resoluteness that can help them refocus on the internal, spiritual domain. This can in turn encourage them to transcend the limitations associated with the historicity and materiality of the human condition. Looking back in time, those who adopt the spirit of resoluteness can distinguish between tradition-as-value and tradition-as-history, proceed to filter value out from history, and in the process repeatedly produce a caesura with the past; with a history that failed to channel the genius of the ancients. Confucius himself, after all, had been able to transcend the limitations of his time to judge, from a purely spiritual perspective, what should be preserved of the past before producing an ideal unpolluted by history. The text mentions, in one instance, that Confucius was able to gather, in his ideal, all that was still of value of the past.[89]

It is far from a coincidence that Liang's portrayal of the spirit of resoluteness of Confucius offers a mirror image of his own effort to purify tradition-as-value from traditions-as-history.[90] Liang's own relationship to the past is meant to find legitimacy in the fact that Confucius himself performed the historical role of filtering out value from history in the past. The notion of *gang*, which in itself does not properly *denote* this spirit as much as it *implies* it, plays a pivotal role in this process, insofar as it refers to a turn inward that allows the very kind of filtering of value from history that Confucius is said to have performed to produce his ideal. The figure of Confucius thus serves as a source of authority onto which the text projects its own agenda.

While I have characterized Confucius's rapport with the past, and Liang's, as one of transcendence, I should clarify that this does not entail a radical departure from the world (this goal is reserved for the revival of Buddhism in the last phase of history). Rather, the kind of transcendence associated with the spirit of Confucius involves a freeing of the self from matter, history, and tradition. What these three share is a static, congealed, and unyielding nature that impedes the self as it attempts to freely adapt to the transforming flow of the universe and merge with it. It is by becoming one with the universe that one continuously frees oneself from the static anchor and determinism the past and matter both represent. Once freed from the determinism of the past, however, one is reinserted in a different type of determinism, one that is future-centric and teleologically oriented toward humanity's final emancipation from any form of determinism. If a tradition at all, in sum, the spirit of Confucius is an antitradition that leads to a state of absolute autonomy from the dominion of the traditional.

Conclusion

How can the place of tradition in the historical metanarrative of the text be best conceptualized? On the one hand, it is clear that *Eastern and Western Cultures* is written in opposition to May Fourth iconoclasts—the introduction of the book makes this explicit. On the face of it, we can say that the text's goal is to produce a new metanarrative that affords space to reauthorize certain traditions against the iconoclasm that was gaining ground at Peking University at the time. Liang's promotion of tradition differs from that of Confucius in the *Analects*, however, in that he does not promote a return to an idealized sociopolitical order of the past, insofar as for him the ideal of Confucius had never been realized in practice. The text manages to integrate a Confucian nostalgic call for a return to the ancients within a modern metanarrative positing liberation onto the telos of history. Despite the irrevocably modern nature of this metanarrative, it is put to the task of reauthorizing the text's own take on tradition. This explains why many have interpreted this discourse as conservative, in the sense that it aims at conserving some form of tradition by integrating it within a modern historical framework.

Although there is some truth to this, one must also ask whether what the discourse sets out to "preserve" can be adequately called a "tradition" in its own right. By this, I do not mean that we should ask whether its portrayal of Confucianism, as revolving around interpersonal harmony, intuition, and resoluteness (*gang*), adequately reflects Confucianism as expressed in the classics. I am not interested, in this context, in whether Liang should be deemed a "real" Confucian or not, given the role Buddhism plays in his teleological model of history or given that one might think he has deviated from the *original* meaning of Confucianism (whatever that may be). Rather, what interests me is the question of how the text's metanarrative itself makes room or not for tradition, understood broadly as "anything which is transmitted or handed down from the past to the present."[91]

To answer this question, one might begin by pointing out the traditions that the metanarrative of *Eastern and Western Cultures* excludes. For one thing, the cultural pluralism upheld by the text, although undeniably more diverse than the cultural monism promoted by Eurocentric metanarratives of modernity, nevertheless excludes all traditions outside of the three civilizational centers on which the text focuses. Given how it is meant to be both universal and homogeneous, the teleological historiographical model of the text relegates African, Latin American, Middle Eastern, Southeast Asian, and Polynesian traditions, to name but a few, to the dustbin of history.

Moreover, by appealing to a single will to explain the existence of cultural units essentially independent from one another, and by associating this will to a *particular* tradition, such as Confucianism or Buddhism, the text essentializes such cultural units and rejects the role played by other traditions in their development. In doing so, the text inherits the May Fourth tendency to synecdochically equate Confucianism with China and neglect the significant roles Daoism, Buddhism, Legalism, and popular cultures played in the historical development of Chinese *cultures*.[92] The same holds true of "Indian culture," which the text reduces to Buddhism.

On this front, it is significant that the lectures Liang gave and the book that followed belong to the genre of philosophy of culture.[93] Approaches that give more room to empirical research would have made it impossible for the text to deploy its synecdochical discursive technique. The text, after all, would have had to pay closer attention to the heterodox traditions it condemns to the dustbin of history as well as to the tensions that inhere in Buddhism and Confucianism. By contrast, philosophy is well equipped to the task of abstracting a single spirit from the flow of history and making it representative of an entire culture.

It remains to be seen, however, whether Confucianism and Buddhism could be properly called "traditions" in the context of *Eastern and Western Cultures*. Not only does the text reduce "Chinese culture" to "Confucianism," as we have seen, but it also reduces the latter to Confucius's ideal (the type of interpersonal relations he promoted) and spirit (his ability to transcend the limitations of his time) and rejects the history of Confucianism as a failure to live up to them. As such, the spirit and ideal of the sage are in no way "transmitted or handed down from the past to the present." To be sure, the text does admit that some aspects of Confucius's ideal were put in practice historically, but this was done in a highly imperfect and incomplete manner. What is of value to the moderns is the ideal of Confucius, not its incomplete manifestations in history. This entails that the ideal must be *revived* rather than *inherited* or *preserved*. On this basis, it would be more accurate to label the text as "revivalist" rather than "traditionalist" or "conservative," given that there is not much the text wants to *conserve* of the then-current state of affairs, except for certain aspects of Western culture (I doubt this is what scholars have in mind when calling Liang a "conservative," however).[94] This is significant, as revivalism, unlike conservatism, allows for the opening of a gap between the production of an ideal and its revival, and thus leaves room for an iconoclastic rejection of the historical period separating the two (as the Renaissance discourse on the Middle or Dark Ages exemplifies).

Although Confucius's spirit and ideal cannot be conceived as transmitted in themselves, the classical texts in which they were concealed (so well that no Confucian before Liang was able to truly unveil them) can, insofar as they were handed down from generation to generation. How else but through the help of the classics would Liang have been able to comprehend and revive the ideal and spirit of Confucius? The only traditions still valuable, within this complex metanarrative, are therefore textual. This is significant, as texts tend to entertain an ambiguous relation with the spatio-temporal. Although texts are physically written down at a particular time in history, we are nevertheless inclined to stress their eternal dimension, especially given that they cannot be reduced to their physical manifestations (as *Fahrenheit 451* reminds us).[95] As such, it is little surprising that texts tend to be associated with the possibility of transcending the limitations of embodiment and historical context, as *Eastern and Western Cultures*' observations on the classical canon (discussed at greater length in the third chapter) imply.

Apart from the specific metanarrative it sets forth, the text's depiction of the workings of history also suggests tradition can only impede history's progression toward the emancipatory telos. It is important to note that the text does not portray the relation between spirit and history as dialectical. Spirit (tradition-as-value) is *the* undeniable force behind history, but history does not necessarily affect spirit, insofar as spirit possesses, in and of itself, the potential to extricate itself from the grasp of the historical. This explains why Confucius and the Buddha were able to produce ideals that were not of their time. As such, while culture is entirely the product of geniuses, geniuses are in no way the product of culture and history.

One of the implicit goals of the text is to symbolically reappropriate the spirit of Confucius and reshape the moderns into geniuses who can transcend the limitations of matter and the past. This entails that teleological history, at least from the second phase onward, is entirely the product of agents who transcend the limitations of the past. This was not the case in premodern history, however. At that point in time, individuals were entirely defined by traditions that did not possess any real potential to emancipate humanity from the determinism of the past. Before the modern period, the Chinese were imprisoned in a culture incapable of producing any change. While this culture did have some positive effects, as we have seen, overall it limited the human potential to directly manifest spirit without the impediment of matter and the past. Only with the advent of modernity can humanity put in practice the spirit of transcendence of the ancient geniuses, and thus repeat in the present the historical caesura they had produced in their own time.

The assumption that modern individuals can transcend the sociohistorical conditions of their existence informs much of the discourse of *Eastern and Western Cultures*. Following the discourse of May Fourth iconoclasts, the text never asks whether it is *possible* at all to completely reject Chinese culture or whether it is possible to accept the Western tradition wholesale.

The question the text asks—should Eastern cultures be revived or rejected?—assumes the possibility of emancipating the individual, and the whole nation, from the traditions to which they belong. This question takes for granted that standing in a subject-object relation to tradition, individuals can freely decide, from the outside, the fate of tradition. To borrow Lu Xun's metaphor, it assumes that the process whereby Chinese culture devours those raised in its midst *can* be (and ultimately *should* be) halted.[96]

It is true that in elaborating its recommendation for the attitude that should be assumed toward both Western and Chinese cultures, the text admits that the Chinese cannot reject their will and simply adopt that of the West. But this is due to the fact that China found itself, because of the precociousness of its culture, in a position that prevented it from both returning to the first phase of teleological history *and* advancing forward. If not for this issue, which is precisely the reason why the Chinese could not emancipate themselves from the determinism of the past, China could have in theory adopted the Western will. The metanarrative of history upheld by the text allows for cultures to modify their will—after all, the text suggests that the West was in the process of adopting the Chinese will. China's inability to transcend the limitations of history is therefore due to the fact that it had not yet properly entered the teleological phase of history. Once in this phase, China and the rest of the world could, if not modify the universal sequence of history described by the text, at least find in this universal history the resources to gradually and increasingly transcend the limitations of the past.

This goes to show how, at the levels of both the text's metanarrative of history and its description of what drives teleological history, tradition plays no role except that of a limitation, the very existence of which will gradually disappear as humanity moves along the historical process. Of the entire scope of Chinese traditions, only the spirit and ideal of Confucius are of value in bringing about the desired telos of history. They can do so insofar as the text refashions them into an antitradition. Being an *anti*tradition insofar as it allows humanity's transcendence from the dominion of the past, Confucianism remains an anti*tradition*, in the discourse of the text itself,[97] only to the extent that one speaks of the *classical texts* in which the spirit of Confucius is embedded, as only these have been historically transmitted. But insofar as the spirit they convey has been elucidated by Liang in a manner that is both clearer and better attuned to history's ineluctable course, the classical canon itself cannot but lose at least some of its appeal, as least in the eyes of readers who are in agreement with *Eastern and Western Cultures*' portrayal of the past.

2

Returning to the Origin

The previous chapter introduced *Eastern and Western Cultures* as a work explicitly bearing the mark of the place and time of its birth. By comparison, the *New Treatise* appears to look for the erasure of any sign that would situate it temporally or spatially. This might be due to differences intrinsic in the philosophical subgenres in which the two works are engaged. While philosophy of culture must retain one foot in the empirical and one out, the ontology of the mind-universe proposed by the *New Treatise* is meant to be valid for anyone, anywhere, and at any time. This explains, at least in part, the atemporal and aspatial tonality of the work.

Nevertheless, the *New Treatise* was not created in a historical vacuum. Xiong regarded the book as the result of a lengthy process of revision of his ideas on Yogācāra. In 1923, he published the first edition of a work he retrospectively considered an early draft of the *New Treatise*. Named *A General Account of Consciousness-Only Learning* (*Weishixue gailun* 唯識學概論), it aimed at introducing Yogācāra to its readers, for the most part without engaging in much criticism of the school. Three years later, Xiong published a revised edition of the same work. Amending it once more, Xiong published the new version under the name *Treatise on Consciousness-Only* (*Weishi lun* 唯識論).[1]

During this period, Xiong grew increasingly dissatisfied with key doctrines of Yogācāra. This led him to revise his work yet again and publish it, in 1932, under the title *New Treatise on the Uniqueness of Consciousness*.[2] Even though this work proposes an explicit denunciation of Yogācāra, based on Xiong's interpretation that the school promotes ontological dualism or pluralism,[3] it nevertheless claims that Confucian sages and Buddhist masters shared a similar insight into Reality. This might account for the fact that the language of the *New Treatise*, along with the resources from which it draws, are highly hybrid in character. While Xiong's notion of inherent mind (*benxin* 本心), central to his soteriological discourse, can be traced back to the *Mencius* (*Mengzi* 孟子), and his ontology of constant transformations to the *Changes*, his language certainly remains heavily reliant on Yogācāra terminology, and his monograph draws, as John Makeham argues, from a variety of other Buddhist resources, including Madhyamaka, *The Awakening of Mahāyāna Faith* (*Dasheng qixin lun* 大乘起信論), and the Huayan (華嚴) doctrine of nature origination (*xingqi* 性起).[4] This explains why Makeham describes Xiong's philosophical system as a form of "Confucio-Buddhist syncretism."[5]

Such syncretism is not without recalling *Eastern and Western Cultures*, which projects both Confucianism and Buddhism onto the telos of history in order to reauthorize them, while inscribing its reinterpretation of Confucianism within an epistemological framework derived from Yogācāra.[6] As such, both works could be interpreted, and have been interpreted,[7] as providing a "Confucio-Buddhist syncretism."

Unlike that of *Eastern and Western Cultures*, however, the *New Treatise*'s syncretism is not presented as an answer to the issues of the time. In fact, several aspects of the text make it appear relatively out of time. Although published in 1932, Xiong's magnus opus is written in classical Chinese, a written form that was gradually becoming obsolete at the time of its publication.[8] Moreover, the work hardly references any contemporary events or figures. Extremely few and far between are references to contemporary scholars,[9] and for a philosophical work of the Republican period, mentions or allusions to Western philosophers are strikingly rare.

Furthermore, the text makes no acknowledgment of the most debated philosophical issues that marked the 1920s, such as the debate between science and views of life, or the various debates surrounding the rise of Marxism and liberalism as contrasting options for the future of China. The many "-isms" that rose to fame in the 1910s and 1920s are also for the most part remarkably absent from the *New Treatise*—and not because Xiong agreed with Hu Shi that intellectuals ought to focus on concrete problems (the *New Treatise* is anything but concrete). The various political upheavals that marked the 1920s and the beginning of the 1930s—the disintegration of the first united front, the Northern Expedition, the survival of warlordism, the Japanese occupation of Manchuria, and so forth—are also left unmentioned in the *New Treatise*.

Be that as it may, Xiong did not live under a rock during the period he wrote what he considered early drafts of the *New Treatise*. In 1920, he entered the prestigious China Institute of Inner Learning (*Zhina neixue yuan* 支那內學院) to study Yogācāra under Ouyang Jingwu's (歐陽竟無; 1871–1943) guidance. He did so under the recommendation of Liang Shuming, who had come to know Xiong through an article the latter had written on Buddhism—an article of which Liang was highly critical.[10] Two years later, Xiong was hired, once again with the help of Liang's recommendation, to teach a course on Yogācāra in the Philosophy department of Peking University, where Liang himself had been teaching since 1917. Xiong taught at the university for two years, before taking some time away because of issues with his health. He then returned to the university in 1932, the year of the publication of the *New Treatise*.[11]

Xiong's association with Peking University, the most prestigious institution of higher learning at the time—and still today—implies that he must have been highly aware of the issues of his day, which were discussed at length by the faculty members and students of the university. The *New Treatise*'s apparent disinterestedness is therefore clearly not the result of its author's alienation from society. It appears to be a choice, conscious or not, made by Xiong to give the work an air of timelessness better suited to the eternal truths he sought to impart to his readers. At least this is one way to interpret the work's careful attempt at remaining "out of time" and "out of place."

Despite this careful attempt, however, the *New Treatise* can still be regarded as engaged in the issues of the day on at least two fronts. First is the front of Chinese philosophy. The introduction of the discipline of philosophy in the early twentieth century brought with it a number of assumptions regarding what proper philosophical work ought to look like.[12] One such assumption, introduced via Japan, was the idea that philosophy is the work of individuals presenting their views in the form of *philosophical systems*. Applying this criterion to the history of Chinese philosophy was not an easy task, however. This issue was directly linked to the problem of the legitimacy and survival of local traditions in the context of a purportedly universal modernity. It seemed that Chinese philosophy could survive in the modern period only in the form of a system. Highly aware of this problem, as John Makeham points out, Xiong took upon himself the task of producing precisely such a system by drawing from various resources—mainly Buddhist and Confucian, but also, to a lesser extent, Daoist.[13] By showing that even though it lacked systematicity in the past, Chinese philosophy nevertheless lent itself to a modern systematization, Xiong sought to challenge the May Fourth portrayal of Chinese philosophy as a thing of the past.

On a second front, the *New Treatise* was also written as an indirect answer to the national issues that plagued China at the time. Xiong's participation in revolutionary activities leading to the Xinhai revolution, during which he witnessed, like Liang Shuming after the revolution, what he considered the lax and immoral behavior of his fellow revolutionaries, had given him the sense that what China was in dire need of was not a new political system, but an ethical transformation of its people.[14] In adopting this view, Xiong was not particularly unconventional. Many before him had held similar positions. Since the late Qing dynasty, it had become somewhat commonplace for the intellectual elite to rather condescendingly blame China's issues on the low ethical standards and physical attributes of the Chinese, that "sick man of East Asia" (*dongya bingfu* 東亞病夫).[15] Liang Qichao, for example, had sought to renew the citizenry by instilling in them a new form of public morality that would supplement the private morality the Chinese already possessed. The goal, in doing so, was to save the nation by strengthening it (*jiuwang tuqiang* 救亡圖強) from the ground up, through a thorough refashioning of its citizens on the basis of a robust model of ethical conduct.[16]

May Fourth intellectuals inherited much of their program from their predecessors on this front. Their solutions to China's problems turned away from the narrowly defined political realm and focused on the reformation of the people through the adoption of a new culture better adapted to modern times. Ethical transformation was an integral part of this program. The goal was to produce a new citizenry that would embody the values of self-consciousness, autonomy, individualism, and active participation in society to counter the alleged passivity of the Chinese people.[17] The new ethics of individual autonomy would free the individual from the traditional family system, so that the newly formed citizens could directly participate in politics without the interference of family members.

Xiong had also come to the conclusion that China's salvation rested on an ethico-cultural remodeling of the people after his participation in revolution activities. This led him to the publication of *Book of the Mind* (*Xinshu* 心書) in 1918. In it, Xiong presents his attempt to "illuminate the fundamentals of humaneness [*ren* 仁] and righteousness [*yi* 義]" as a means to "stop the prevailing of heresy" and save both nation and race (*wuguo wuzhong* 吾國吾種) from extinction.[18] In a letter to Mou Zongsan published in May 1948, Xiong explains his composition of the *New Treatise* in terms that highlight his concern for the fate of the nation:

> Now again we are in a weak and dangerous situation. With the strong aggression of European culture, our authentic spirit has been extinct. People are accustomed to self-disregard, self-violence, self-abandonment. Everything is copied from the outside, with little self-establishment. Hence the *New Doctrine* must be written.

> 今當衰危之運，歐化侵凌，吾固有精神蕩然泯絕，人習於自卑、自暴、自棄，一切向外剿竊而無以自樹，新論固不得不出。[19]

Xiong's ontology of the mind-universe was therefore directly aimed at saving China by providing its people with the ethical means to do so.[20] To this extent, the *New Treatise* shares with May Fourth a common assumption, according to which saving China can and should be achieved through a top-down cultural/ethical reformation of its people.

Given Xiong's goal of national salvation, one might wonder why the *New Treatise* presents itself in such a timeless, unsituated manner. Could Xiong not have inserted in a more explicit manner his ontology of the mind-universe within the framework of his concerns for national salvation? The answer to this question, I argue, is to be found at the level of the soteriological discourse of the text, which is introduced in what follows. For now, suffice it to say that the *New Treatise* proposes a model of self-cultivation shaped around a process of atomization, whereby the mind gradually purifies itself from everything it regards as external to itself—the body, emotions, others, traditions, habits, and so forth. Once entirely freed from its outside, the mind can finally recover the pure form it originally held before the birth of the body. Within the context of this soteriological discourse, the timelessness and placelessness of the *New Treatise* can be interpreted as an attempt to embody the disinterested systematicity expected of a modern work of philosophical ontology, certainly, but also as an effort to put in practice and perform the kind of atomization and autonomy it espouses. It is the mind's purification from the markers of time (traditions, habits inherited from the past) and space (the body, matter) that the *New Treatise* enacts by cleansing itself of as many indicators of its situatedness as possible. The text's apparent disinterestedness thus provides it with the means to bring about an end that is far from disinterested.

The text can therefore be regarded as answering May Fourth on two fronts: by systematizing Chinese traditions into a philosophical ontology that fulfils criteria inherited from the hegemonic center of knowledge production and recognized as legitimate by May Fourth members on the one hand, and by endeavoring to transform the Chinese citizenry by appealing to national resources instead of Western cultural products on the other. The former goal is discussed at greater length in the fourth chapter, while the present chapter focuses on the latter. It does so by paying particular attention to the soteriological discourse of the text, which is meant to help readers progress toward the recovery of their inherent mind. I argue that in this process, traditions play no other role than that of a limitation from which the mind must be liberated. I conclude, however, that not unlike *Eastern and Western Cultures*, the *New Treatise* makes an exception for the writings of previous sages and masters, which form the only tradition capable of setting the readers on the path that leads to their final emancipation from the hold of the past.

To make this argument, I first look at the text's depiction of self-cultivation, which I then situate in the context of the *New Treatise*'s construal of the mind-universe as a process of instantaneous arising and ceasing negating the possibility of temporal continuity. Finally, I discuss the text's radical redefinition of "learning" as a process whereby one breaks free from everything one has acquired since birth.

The myth of the eternal return

The *New Treatise*'s characterization of self-cultivation follows a straightforward model of return to the origin. At birth, everyone is endowed with an inherent mind that forms the core of our human nature (*xing* 性). The inherent mind is "quiescent and perfectly bright, without an iota of imperfection," and it remains so throughout our lives, although gradually we become unaware of its existence.[21] This is due to our inclination to mistake what the text calls the "habituated mind" (*xixin* 習心) for our only true mind. The goal of self-cultivation is to progressively purify the mind from the afflictions that invariably arise along with the habituated mind, so that the inherent mind can slowly but surely resurface from its hidden source. Emancipation is thus construed as a reversal of the process that sees the growing alienation of the mind from the pure origin.

The *New Treatise* describes this process of alienation as one in which the mind loses its original communion with the endless flux of transformation of the universe. The text singles out the birth of the body as the triggering event initiating the fall[22] from inherent to habituated mind. This is because one tends to become attached to one's body as a "private possession" that is "one's own" (*si* 私), so that one ends up contrasting it with the myriad things that make up the universe.[23] Attachment to the physical self is reinforced by various desires or cravings that have their origin in the body: cravings for food, of course, but also for sex, romantic love, self-identity, a future existence, descendants, things enjoyed in the past, what one sees, and for craving itself.[24] Emotions also contribute to strengthening the process of dissociation between self and non-self.[25] As a result of one's attachment to embodied selfhood, one becomes unaware of the fact that body and universe are one, or, in words strongly echoing those of Liang Shuming, that the "great life force of the universe is an undifferentiated whole and so cannot be dissected and divided."[26]

By growing attached to the body and the subject/object divide it causes, one's mind is gradually transformed by external things until it becomes itself like a material object.[27] It is at this point that the mind comes to be habituated, which entails that it becomes as fragmented as the cognitive objects it mistakenly believes truly exist as entities separate from itself. By contrast, the inherent mind conceives the external world not as cognitive objects posited against a thinking subject, but as one and the same as the mind itself. The inherent mind, in short, follows human nature in believing that "things and me are the same whole/body."[28]

The process of the fall, whereby one gradually becomes alienated from one's nature and one's inherent mind, can be better understood by looking at two notions that play a central role in the soteriological discourse of the text: mental associates (*xinsuo* 心所) and habituated tendencies (*xiqi* 習氣). Since these two notions relate to the way the present is continuously shaped by the past, they are closely tied to the issue of tradition that concerns us here.

Habituated tendencies function similarly to the notion of "seeds" in Yogācāra. They are stored potentialities inherited from the past that can become active in the present. They originate in a process whereby "sentient beings store all past actions so as to aid future desires, thus leading all former actions to possess residual power that clearly forms a tendency, an uninterrupted flow of similarity [*dengliu* 等流]."[29] In other words, habituated tendencies are the means through which the past produces the various habits of the mind responsible for its deviation from its inherent purity. Given this understanding, the text relates habituated tendencies to the Buddhist notion of "karmic power" (*yeli* 業力).[30]

Habituated tendencies are deposited in our mind (in the eighth consciousness,[31] to be more precise), awaiting their activation. Once activated, they manifest themselves in the form of mental associates. Mental associates attach themselves to the mind, adding onto it various preconceptions, feelings, memories, and arbitrary preferences associated with what is mistakenly regarded as the various "objects" of cognition. Mental associates are directly responsible for causing the mind to posit a subject against which cognitive objects can be seen as external.

The text illustrates the workings of mental associates with the example of our perception of the color blue. While the inherent mind simply reflects the color as it is, without adding anything onto it, mental associates supplement other characteristics to the perceived color, such as an agreeable or disagreeable feeling.[32] One's experience of an agreeable feeling, upon seeing a blue object, can therefore be conceived as the effect of accumulated past experiences that manifest themselves in the present as mental associates. The issue Xiong has with this is that gradually, the agreeable feeling and the blue color become enmeshed in such a way that one is no longer capable of directly perceiving (*xianliang* 現量) blue, as the inherent mind does, without supplementing it with a number of biases inherited from past experiences. This causes the mind to be "transformed by things," in the sense that it comes to adhere to the various distinctions resulting from the operation of the mental associates as reflecting the reality of things, so much so that the mind itself becomes as fragmented as the cognitive objects it wrongly posits. At that point, the inherent mind—which never splits the perceptual field into different objects, and never generates a gulf between subject and object—comes to be hidden from the view of the "subject."

Following the birth of the body, to sum up, the mind gradually loses its connection with the origin (the inherent mind) because of the manifestation, in the present, of various tendencies accumulated from past experiences. The text's narration of this fall, as the birth of the body can be described, is thus predicated on a number of rather strict dichotomies, between the origin and the postnatal, between the innate and the acquired, between the pure and the impure, and between the one and the many, to name but a few.[33] Habituated tendencies belong to the latter pole of these dichotomies, insofar as they are accumulated through time after birth, and thus tend to obstruct the oneness of the inherent mind with which one was born.

The goal of self-cultivation is to reverse the process of alienation from the origin initiated by the birth of the body. While "people lose their nature" (*xing*) after "being enslaved to [bodily] form and imprisoned by afflictions,"[34] they never lose the latent potential to recover their nature (*fuxing* 復性) and reconnect with the inherent mind. They can achieve this goal by following a complex regime of cultivation of wholesome mental associates (*shanshu* 善數), which are the manifestation of pure habituated tendencies (*jingxi* 淨習). Although acquired from past experiences, pure habituated tendencies manage to preserve their bond with human nature, given that they retain the inherent virtue of the latter.[35]

The last section of the *New Treatise* is devoted to the classification of thirty-eight mental associates.[36] Some of them, such as craving, antipathy, and ignorance, are classified as "defiled" by the text, while others, such as contra-craving, contra-antipathy, and contra-ignorance, are described as "wholesome."[37] The latter three, as their names suggest, have the ability to counter the effects of the former three until they ultimately annihilate them. Once all defiled mental associates have been replaced by wholesome ones, one has completed the process of recovering one's nature, which also entails that the habituated mind, plagued by defiled mental associates, has been replaced by the purity of the inherent mind.[38]

Self-cultivation, in sum, is described as a process whereby one gradually frees oneself from the influence of one's own past. Before one achieves the final goal of the self-cultivation process—characterized as a state of wisdom (*zhi* 智) by the text—habituated tendencies are so pervasive in one's experience of the world that "the content of [human] life," Xiong bemoans, "is nothing but the totality of past actions."[39] It is precisely the fact that "past actions" are acquired through experience, and not inherited from birth, that makes of them obstacles in our path of recovering the inherent purity of the mind. Of the various inheritances of the past, only that which accords with the pure origin should be preserved. Once everything else is discarded, one can finally recover one's nature and fuse, once again, with the endless transformations of the universe.

The oneness of mind

As we saw, the birth of the body brings about various distinctions, between self and non-self as well as between various cognitive objects mistakenly regarded as having identities of their own. This process of fragmentation of reality finds itself reversed through the cultivation of wholesome mental associates. Gradually, the mind ceases to be transformed by things and recovers the original state of oneness with which it was originally endowed. Once one's nature is recovered and one's mind no longer posits itself against a variety of others, one realizes that "mind" and "universe" are signifiers of a single signified, which the *New Treatise* calls "Fundamental Reality" (*shiti* 實體) or simply "Reality" (*ti* 體).[40] Given the text's ontological equation of the inherent mind with the universe, it is worth paying closer attention to its metaphysical construal of the latter, as it gives us a sense of the functioning that allows the emancipated mind to perform an uninterrupted caesura with the past.

The text describes the ceaseless process of transformation that is the mind-universe by appealing to the *tiyong* (體用) polarity, which is put to rather idiosyncratic use. The metaphysics of the text is founded on the assumption that (Fundamental) Reality (*ti* 體) and the phenomenal realm of functions (*yong* 用), which are mapped onto the noumenal/phenomenal divide, are ultimately one and the same. Although they can be nominally distinguished, and although they might appear severed from one another to those the text calls "ordinary people," one who achieves wisdom comes to understand that they are ontologically undistinguishable. According to what is commonly referred to as Xiong's doctrine of nonduality of Reality and functions (*tiyong bu'er lun* 體用不二論),[41] one can nominally describe Reality as the Reality of functions, and depict functions as the manifestations of Reality, although ultimately even these distinctions are but nominal constructs aimed at helping readers recover their nature.[42]

Since the myriad of functions are but the manifestation of a single Fundamental Reality, the text characterizes its ontological views as monist. The oneness of Fundamental Reality, however, should not be construed as an unchanging substance underlying the constant changes of the myriad phenomena. Rather, the text proposes that we regard Reality itself as the constant transformation (*hengzhuan* 恆轉) or Supreme Change (*taiyi* 太易)[43] that manifests itself as functions through a complex process of contraction (*xi* 翕) and expansion (*pi* 闢).[44]

When contracting, transformations phenomenally appear to be solidifying and come close to becoming matter, as contracting is responsible for transforming what was originally formless into phenomenal forms. Contraction never leads to full materialization, however, since expansion prevents contraction from turning into materiality by ensuring that what was originally formless remains so. What we conventionally speak of as "matter" and "mind" are merely the *tendencies* of contraction and expansion, which never cease to transform and which are never fully brought to completion.[45]

Because it regards matter and mind as two tendencies of a single process of transformation, the *New Treatise* openly criticizes both idealists and materialists, since both are attached to the mistaken view that there are "real minds" or "real material objects."[46] Despite this claim, however, the text ultimately adopts an idealist position. Because it "never loses its self-nature of vigor through movement,"[47] the mind is never entirely deprived of its ability to adapt to the constant transformations of Reality. This is not the case with the tendency of contraction (matter). Although it never reaches the state of materialization, its tendency toward solidification makes contraction unable to continuously adapt to the constant transformations of Fundamental Reality. It is precisely for this reason that the birth of the body is presented by the text as a form of degeneration, as it obstructs the mind's ability to continuously transform with the endless flux of the universe.[48]

For these reasons, the text asserts that the tendency of expansion should be regarded as the ruler (*zhuzai* 主宰). As is often the case with the *New Treatise*, this claim is both prescriptive and descriptive—that is, it is prescriptive precisely because it describes ontological Reality. This explains why self-cultivation takes the form of a gradual training whereby the mind learns to control the body.[49] While defiled habituated tendencies allow matter and the body to transform the mind into a thing, as we saw above, the cultivation of wholesome mental associates reverses this process, so that the mind can "embody" all things, to the extent that "there is nothing in the whole world that it does not look upon as not being me."[50] It is when the "mind is definitely not transformed by things," when it has finally won over matter, that "it may also be said that the mind is not different from Fundamental Reality."[51] The text in fact redefines the cardinal Confucian concept of humaneness (*ren* 仁) to accord with this understanding of the relation between mind and matter: "If objects transform [according to the mind], one will be at ease, and that [. . .] is how one's humaneness [*ren*] can be realized with diligent sincerity [*dun* 敦]."[52]

Although the text maintains that ontologically, Fundamental Reality and the phenomenal realm of functions are one and the same, its soteriological description of how the mind must control matter and embody all things does rely on a strict distinction between the two. Undeniably, the text presents both the mind and matter as belonging to the phenomenal side of the divide, but this is only true for the habituated mind transformed into a fragmented thing. Once it recovers its original oneness, the mind merges with Fundamental Reality. As an iteration of the one-many polarity, the distinction between Fundamental Reality and functions serves to describe the soteriological passage to enlightenment as a fusion with the oneness of the universe. But precisely because the end result is a form of oneness described as escaping the grasp of language—after all, names cannot but dissect Reality into distinct objects[53]—the text must insist that ultimately, its own distinction between Fundamental Reality and functions does not hold. Yet this should not blind us to the fact that discursively speaking, this distinction plays an essential role in the soteriological message of the text.

I come back to this theme in chapter 4, as the tension between the ontological claim to oneness of the text and the strict dichotomies that sustain its soteriological discourse is closely related to the issue of textual authority. For now, suffice it to point out that the one-many polarity that underlies the discourse of the *New Treatise* does not merely refer to a metaphysical distinction between the noumenal and the phenomenal, but also purports to describe a soteriological (or epistemological) process of awakening, understood as a passage from fragmentation and alienation to oneness.[54]

Breaking free from the past

It might appear that we have now strayed from the path of our inquiry. What does the mind "embodying" all things in the universe have to do with the issue of the role tradition plays in the process of self-cultivation after all? To answer this question, we must remember that in the discourse of the *New Treatise*, matter and the body are intricately linked to the process whereby the residual power of the past, stored in our consciousness as habituated tendencies, is activated in the present through the manifestation of mental associates. As such, the text's call for the liberation of the mind from its enslavement to the body runs parallel to its discourse on the emancipation of the present from all it has inherited from the past, so that it can unceasingly regenerate the pure birth of the origin moment after moment. This will become clearer by taking a closer look at the text's description of the constant transformations of consciousness and the universe, which draws resources from the Buddhist notion of instantaneous arising and ceasing (*chana shengmie* 剎那生滅) and from the *Changes*, respectively.

From the perspective of the phenomenal realm of functions, the text finds the cause responsible for the continuous rise of consciousness in the process of self-animation (*zidong* 自動) of consciousness itself. By "self-animation," the text means that consciousness is continuously arising and ceasing; continuously renewing itself. It is but the flow of an endless series of thought-instants that cease as soon as they arise. One thought-instant arises as another ceases, although the previous thought-instant should not be regarded as the cause of the subsequent one.[55] Rather, each thought-instant is autonomous and independent, and the cause of each should be found in the process of self-animation itself.[56] Borrowing from the Buddhist notion of instantaneous arising and ceasing, the text explains that although consciousness appears continuous, this is only because like the reel of a film, one tends to build a narrative of causality and continuity where there ultimately is but a series of fixed images independent from one another.[57]

On this basis, the *New Treatise* negates the existence of movement, as nothing remains from one moment to the next that could be said to be moving.[58] Time itself, the text goes on to say, is illusory, and is but a transformed image of space. Because following the birth of the body there is attachment to objects, the concept of space arises, and because space is wrongly posited, the past, the present, and the future can be demarcated as if they were spatial locations. Without attachment to one's body and to objects—as well as to the subject, one could add, since the two are interdependent—one would come to realize that time and space are but false constructs.[59]

Xiong's portrayal of consciousness as continuously arising and ceasing finds echo in his construal of the universe. Presenting his views as borrowed from the *Changes*, he characterizes the process of transformation of the universe as a ceaseless flow of creativity (*chuang* 創). Life (*sheng* 生) itself is but the manifestation of creativity's endless stream:

> Days where there is life are all days of creation and regeneration. Not for an instant is there an absence of creativity due to momentary rest, or an absence of regeneration due to attachment to what has passed. If there were a moment in which there was no creation and no regeneration, then at that moment one would no longer be living.

> 故有生之日，皆創新之日，不容一息休歇而無創，守故而無新。使有一息而無創無新，即此一息已不生矣。[60]

Interpreting the *Changes*' construal of transformation through the lens of the Buddhist notion of instantaneous arising and ceasing, as Chan

Wing-tsit notes,[61] Xiong views life itself as a continuous process of creation and regeneration, whereby the new (*xin* 新) perpetually manifests itself by breaking free from all forms of attachment to the past.

That creativity involves breaking free from the hold of the past can be exemplified by the text's rather unusual reading of the relation between *yin* and *yang* as conveyed by the *Changes*, which Xiong views as the most important source of Confucian wisdom. While the two notions are usually interpreted as correlative polarities that complement each other and depend on each other for their existence, the text presents *yin* and *yang*, which are associated with the phenomenal realm of functions and Fundamental Reality, respectively, as "incompatible."[62] The ultimate goal is in fact for *yang* "to battle and defeat the darkness of *yin*" until the latter is "destroyed."[63] Once this goal is achieved, the wise, who embody "the virtue of *yang*," are no longer afflicted by the antithetical virtues of *yin*: softness and darkness.[64] Returning to the topic of self-cultivation, the text contends that "even when impeded by the physical body [and mired in] the layered darkness of reduplicated *yin*," "it is possible to rely on a solitary *yang*" to "develop and create unremittingly and to generate anew endlessly," and thus "head toward the new after getting rid of the old."[65]

The goal of self-cultivation is therefore to ensure that the mind remains in sync with the creative flow of the universe, which it does by freeing itself from the dual empires of the body and the past. The image of consciousness that emerges from such views is one in which reigns the unyielding dominion of the present—a present construed as a caesura with the past that perpetually renews itself at every instant. "Mind-consciousness," the text declares, "is able to flow uninterrupted only through constant renewal and a complete absence of abiding with the old [*wei you xinxin, dou wu gugu* 唯有新新，都無故故]."[66] As such, "transformation is ever renewing, sloughing off the past so that it does not linger."[67] Ontologically speaking, or in other words from the perspective of the mind that has recovered its original nature, there is no longer any room for any form of influence of the past on the present.[68] This entails that, like causation and continuity, tradition is but a misconstrued belief that prevents one's access to Fundamental Reality. Ontologically speaking, nothing of the past ever remains present.

The delusion of tradition

If consciousness and the universe repeatedly arise anew at every instant, without the existence of any form of causality linking the present to the past, how does the text account for its depiction of habituated tendencies as the residual power of past actions manifested in the present as mental associates?[69] And how is self-cultivation possible within this framework? Does the *New Treatise*'s ontology of continuous renewal not contradict its construal of self-cultivation as a gradual process of accumulation, *through time*, of wholesome mental associates? On the grounds that consciousness and the universe are continuously arising and ceasing, the text in fact rejects the possibility of evolution, since the latter relies on the assumption that "accumulation and retention" exist, a position that results from being "attached to things."[70]

Since there is no evolution, there is also no telos toward which the transformation of the universe evolves:

> Transformation has never been a thing; it has no outlines ["outline" here refers to a direction]. However, because arising and ceasing seem to follow one another in succession, there is the illusory appearance of an outline's being there. The foolish predetermine [that outline] and become attached to it in the mistaken belief that there is a thing there. **Hence they trace it back to a thing in the past [*ceng* 曾] [. . .] just as if it had been mechanically reduplicated. In the opposite direction, they conjecture about it as a future [*lai* 來] thing. [. . .] It is just as if the target had been determined beforehand.**[71] In terms of the principle of the transformation of the cosmos, there has certainly never been any target. Naturally, effortlessly, it is without purposiveness.

> 變本無物，即無輪廓。然以生滅相似隨轉，故幻似輪廓焉。愚者邀而執之以為有物也。故回溯曾物，……宛如機械重叠；逆臆來物，……儼若鵠的預訂。自宇宙化理言之，固無所謂鵠的，法爾任運，無作意故。[72]

Differentiating it from *Eastern and Western Cultures*, the *New Treatise*'s rejection of teleology provides an interesting critique of the notion of progress that had rapidly spread among the Chinese intellectual elite since the beginning of the twentieth century. But its denial of any form of evolution and teleology makes it difficult to account for its portrayal of self-cultivation as a gradual process of accumulation of wholesome mental associates.

Following the previous excerpt, however, the text goes on to argue that "for humans or other living things, as they struggle to move forward along the long road of imponderables, they secretly wish to seek the path to perfection—this can be said to be a target. This is because the target is the source of their [desire] to struggle to move forward."[73] Although this passage could be understood as meaning that the human desire to seek the path to perfection is itself mistaken—that the desire for enlightenment itself should be discarded for there to be enlightenment is a recurrent Buddhist theme, after all—in fact the text admits to certain targets being legitimate (those providing a "path to perfection"). This ability to fix a target explains why humans are described, later in the text, as "the most *evolved*" "among living things."[74] This suggests that evolution applies to humans. Humans, after all, can reach a union with the oneness of Reality that is inaccessible to other living things. As such, it is clear that humans have the capacity to evolve toward emancipation.[75] In fact, humans "lacking purpose"—in the sense of failing to pursue awakening—are described by the text as "comparable to animals and plants."[76]

Although the text never explicitly resolves the tension between its refutation of evolution and its portrayal of self-cultivation as an evolutive process, the distinction between Fundamental Reality and the phenomenal realm of functions, as well as that between inherent and habituated minds, can certainly account for it. From the perspective of Fundamental Reality and the inherent mind, there simply does not exist any form of retention from past to present: the mind simply continuously arises anew at each moment in a manner that provides it with the means to become one with the ceaseless flux of the universe. But from the perspective of the phenomenal realm of functions and the habituated mind that corresponds to it, the present does *appear* to result from the activation of habituated tendencies inherited from the past, and one does *appear* to work toward achieving awakening.[77] As soon as one enters the gates of wisdom, however, one realizes that one had been enlightened all along. The goal, according to the text, is to achieve a realization that "there has never been anything separating us from [our inherent nature]."[78] Once one has achieved this realization, one understands that the notion of habituated tendency and the seeking of perfection were but nominal constructs or skillful means one needed to break free from the confines of the habituated mind. Following the construal of "antitraditions" presented in the introduction, we could perhaps call them "antidelusions": delusions enabling one's final transcendence from all delusions.

This reading is supported by the text's endorsement of the Buddhist notion that truths come in either absolute or conventional forms. Once absolute truth is achieved, however, conventional truth is discovered to be ultimately false. On this basis, the existence of accumulation and retention, in the case of habituated tendencies and in the evolution of the mind toward awakening, should be understood as conventional truths to be dispelled once awakening is achieved.[79] This is further supported by the fact that the text regularly claims that its discussion of consciousness should be regarded as nominal only, and that the whole *New Treatise* merely uses language and nominal distinctions as expedient means aimed at facilitating the reader's progression toward awakening.[80]

Given these considerations, it appears that, ultimately, the text construes the very notion of continuity from past to present as a mistaken belief held by those who have not yet achieved enlightenment. Such enlightenment, however, cannot take place unless one first undergoes a process of cultivation of wholesome mental associates through which everything that was accumulated after birth and that is dissonant with the origin of the mind is annihilated. This entails that except when they accord with the inherent mind, traditions, even when regarded as existing conventionally, cannot but obfuscate the mind's ultimate goal of becoming one with the universe by continuously re-creating the origin in the present. Yet ultimately, even traditions of the self that accord with the origin—the pure habituated tendencies—are proven to be mistaken beliefs once awakening takes place.

(Un)learning

Although the *New Treatise* borrows the notion of inherent mind from the *Mencius*, its construal of the notion differs in important ways from it. In the *New Treatise*, self-cultivation is not conceived as a lengthy process during which one cultivates the seeds of goodness present in one's inherent mind to make them flourish—to give birth to something new on the basis of a mere potentiality (the seeds or sprouts). The text makes it clear that the inherent mind standing at the origin is already complete. Since "it is not the case that one can enhance what is innately possessed," self-cultivation, the text contends, can be simply regarded as "returning to the beginning."[81]

This reinterpretation of the Mencian inherent mind is significant, as it impacts in important ways the text's construal of what the mind inherits from the past; of the traditions of the self. If the *Mencius* builds its vision of the ethical life around agricultural metaphors of cultivation, the *New Treatise* reshapes "self-cultivation" into a process of unlearning everything one has acquired after birth. Such a process can best be described as one of "de-cultivation," of returning to the seeds of goodness themselves instead of cultivating them so that they can rise out of the soil of human nature in which they are sowed, to borrow from the agricultural cluster of metaphors of the *Mencius*.

The text upholds rather idiosyncratic views on learning (*xue* 學), conceiving it as a process whereby one "creates unceasingly" (*chuangxin buyi* 創新不已) to "generate pure habituated tendencies." "The functioning of this self-recognition and self-creativity," Xiong continues, "is collectively referred to as 'awakening' [*jue* 覺]—and it is this alone that constitutes true learning."[82] Learning therefore involves neither the incremental accumulation of knowledge nor the activation of a potential that must be built upon. Rather, it takes the form of the incessant flow of transformation of the universe, whereby the origin is constantly re-created anew (*chuangxin buyi*) in the present.

It is true that in doing so, one must rely on what the text calls the "sprouts" (*mengnie* 萌蘖) of pure dharmas or wholesome mental associates.[83] The Mencian sprouts, however, are but *potentialities* one must cultivate to achieve full-blown virtues. The *New Treatise*'s sprouts, on the other hand, are the few wholesome mental associates that enable the mind to gradually annihilate defiled mental associates. Undeniably, one *cultivates* wholesome mental associates, relying on the sprouts still accessible to the mind despite its having become habituated. Yet wholesome mental associates are but those mental associates that remain in complete accord with the inherent mind of the origin. Instead of being developed out of a mere potential, they allow for the mind's return to its original state. This explains why the text refers to the cultivation of sprouts as a process of creativity (*chuang* 創) and renewal (*xin* 新): they allow one to repeatedly re-create and renew the origin in the present.

Since the inherent mind is always already present in us, waiting to be rediscovered, Xiong holds that to achieve wisdom, one must seek within, and not without. The text in fact opens with this claim:

> **[Fundamental Reality] is not a perceptual field [*jingjie* 境界] detached from one's own mind, nor is it a cognitive object of knowledge. This is because it is only by seeking within that there is correspondence with true realization [*shizheng* 實證].** True realization is the self's recognizing the self, with absolutely nothing concealed. **Correspondence with true realization is called wisdom [*zhi* 智], because it differs from the mundane world, which is established on the basis of discernment [*hui*

慧]。[. . .] **The meaning of wisdom is that self-nature [*zixing* 自性] is awareness, and because it is inherently without a basis [*ben wuyi* 本無倚]。**

實體非是離自心外在境界，及非知識所行境界，唯是反求實證相應故。實證即是自己認識自己，絕無一毫蒙蔽。是實證相應者，名之為智，不同世間依慧立故。……智義云者，自性覺故，本無倚故。⁸⁴

That wisdom is achieved through a realization of the self by the self entails not only that one must seek within, and not without, but also that one must do so in a state of absolute autonomy from all that the habituated mind regards as external to itself. The text clarifies that "inherently without a basis," in the quote above, means that "awareness does not rely on sensory experience, nor does it rely on logical inference."⁸⁵ Sensory experience is unreliable because it is polluted by defiled mental associates, while logical inference fragments the oneness of the universe to make sense of it. Neither can be depended upon when seeking true realization.

Furthermore, awakening or awareness (*jue*), which as we saw is the ultimate meaning of learning, is related in the excerpt above to the concept of "self-nature." Something has self-nature, the text later explains, when it does not rely on anything external to it for its existence (*wudai* 無待).⁸⁶ Consciousness, for example, is deprived of self-nature, since its existence is established in opposition to cognitive objects. Without positing an external world of objects, we could simply not conceive of consciousness. This is not the case, however, with our awakening to the inherent mind, which takes place by reconnecting to the indivisible oneness of Fundamental Reality. Awakening thus denotes a state in which the mind no longer relies on an exterior, as one comes to see that nothing escapes the dominion of the mind. "Because the [inherent] mind is not transformed by material qualities," Xiong explains, "it is an aware, illuminating, pure, and clear Reality that stands by itself, relying on nothing [*duli wuyi* 獨立無倚]."⁸⁷

That learning-as-awakening should be undertaken in a state of isolation from the outside world also entails that others are of no help in one's pursuit of awakening:

> In learning, the thorough realization of principle [*qiongli* 窮理] is fundamental, and fully revealing the nature [*jinxing* 盡性] is its final goal. [. . .] The nature is not different from inherent pure mind, and principle is not different from the principle by

which *the mind is self-sufficient. They are not fused from outside, nor are they to be sought from others*. It is up to you students to experience them personally and to discern them clearly.

學以窮理為本，盡性為歸。……性即本來清淨之心，理即自心具足之理，不由外鑠，不假他求。此在學者深體明辨。[88]

It is little surprise that others are of no help in the process of learning, given how the text conceives the very concept of otherness as breaking the original unity of subject and object. One should in fact rely on "vigilance in solitude" (*shendu* 慎獨) to get a full grasp of the interconnectedness of the myriad things.[89] Even learning from the knowledge previous generations passed down in writing seems of no use to the solitary seeker of wisdom. "Skills acquired through scholarly learning," for example, are rejected by the text as a form of craving.[90]

By equating learning with a form of awakening that is achieved in complete autonomy from the outside and from others (contemporary or not), the *New Treatise* overturns the received meaning of learning, which is conventionally associated with the transmission of knowledge from one generation to the next, or with the accumulation of knowledge based on our experience of the external world. Such redefinition of learning appears to make no room for a positive assessment of tradition within the context of seeking wisdom.

There exists one exception to this rule, however. The teachings established in the past by Confucian sages and Buddhist masters are worth preserving and consulting, since they can help one find the right path leading to awakening. "Because the ignorant are stuck on a lost path," the text explains, "those who had first awakened bequeathed their teachings and thoughts. The import of these teachings and thoughts can also be depended upon."[91] Of the many traditions inherited from the past, in sum, only those passed down in written form by enlightened forefathers are of any value in one's quest for wisdom. But they are so only to the extent that they show their readers the right path to follow; once on the path, the seeker of wisdom must forge ahead alone.

Conclusion

Paradoxically, it is by undergoing a process of atomization or autonomization whereby the inner core of the self—the inherent mind—is purified and purged from any involvement with what is mistakenly regarded as external to it (cognitive objects, sensory experiences, the body, emotions, others, traditions, habits, etc.) that the self can recover a state of oneness with what used to be regarded as external—the universe—but is now realized to have always been one with the mind. The process of atomization that is self-cultivation thus leads to its own antithesis: a state in which the mind assimilates all that is other in its core, so much so that "there is nothing in the whole world that it does not look upon as not being me."[92]

Awakening is often described by the *New Treatise* as involving both a radical form of autonomy and a process whereby the boundary between self and non-self vanishes. In one passage, the text refers to awakening with the expression "unconditional freedom" (*xuan jie* 懸解), which it borrows from the *Zhuangzi* (莊子) and describes as a "great liberation" (*da jietuo* 大解脫).[93] Both expressions, in Chinese, connote a state of dislocation/separation (*jie* 解, *tuo* 脫) or isolation/elevation (*xuan* 懸) from one's surrounding. Yet in the same passage, the text also describes awakening as the disappearance of things and self (in the sense that they merge into a single Reality); as the end of "discriminative construction based on mental words."[94] Awakening thus comprises a dual process whereby one breaks free from limitations imposed by the phenomenal realm of functions (this is what the text means by referring to dislocation and isolation) to merge with the oneness of Fundamental Reality (and hence realize that functions and Fundamental Reality are one and the same).

The mind retains an ambivalent status within this soteriological framework. It is both the inner core of the self that must be purified from all that is other *and* the site of the ultimate demise of the self established in contradistinction to the non-self. Insofar as it is situated in the self yet rooted in selfless Reality, the inherent mind can serve as a bridge linking the two. And in its being accessible in the present yet rooted in the origin, it also has the ability to re-create anew the pure origin in the present. In other words, the inherent mind can bridge both spatial and temporal gaps: first, it fuses the part (mind) with the whole (the universe) after purifying the former from its outside; and second, it assimilates the present with the origin by annihilating the influence of the innumerable instants that separate them through a process of continuously breaking free from the past.

In both cases, what the mind needs to be purified of are spatial and temporal markers of the phenomenal realm of functions: external objects established in opposition to consciousness, and past habits manifesting themselves as defiled mental associates in the present. As such, despite the text's claim that functions and Reality are ontologically one and the same, it establishes a soteriological discourse according to which one must purify oneself from the phenomenal in order to be granted access to Fundamental Reality.

Within this soteriological framework, traditions can be viewed in essentially two ways, depending on whether one approaches them from a phenomenal or ontological perspective. Ontologically speaking, traditions simply do not exist, given that the mind-universe ceaselessly arises anew at every instant without any form of causality linking one moment to the next. To the awakened mind, traditions appear as mistaken constructs posited by the deluded mind to make sense of perceived continuities through time. Phenomenally speaking, the text does nominally accept the existence of habituated tendencies, which presume some form of transmission of habits from past experiences to present ones. Most of them, however, are described by the text as contributing to the mind's inability to directly perceive the universe as it is: one with the mind. Only pure habituated tendencies play a positive role in the self-cultivation process, although they do so by allowing the mind to break free from the habits it inherited from the past. Of the many traditions of the self, only those that mirror the original purity of the mind are worth preserving and cultivating. Continuously renewing such traditions in the present ensures that one can reshape the present in the image of the origin and in the process annihilate all that one acquired through experience after the birth of the body. The goal is to mirror the endless self-renewal of the universe by unceasingly re-enacting the origin, sloughing off the past so that one remains within the perpetual realm of presentism. Once one has achieved this goal, however, one realizes that even pure habituated tendencies, the only traditions of the self worth preserving from a phenomenal perspective, are misguided constructs.

Despite their vastly different scopes, one being a philosophy of culture and the other an ontology of the mind-universe, *Eastern and Western Cultures* and the *New Treatise* both find value in what is transmitted from the past only to the extent that it accords with a pure origin (the inherent mind or the ancient sage). Their construal of the origin thus provides the texts with a standpoint from which they can judge which traditions are still of value and which of them only limit the human potential to achieve liberation. Pure habituated tendencies, the only form of transmission from past to present that is presented in a positive light by the *New Treatise*, play a role in the soteriology of the text that is analogous, *mutatis mutandis*, to that of tradition-as-value in the metanarrative of *Eastern and Western Cultures*. They are manifestations in the present of a pure origin whose emancipatory potential can only be fully realized if one rids oneself of everything else one has inherited from the past: that is, tradition-as-history in *Eastern and Western Cultures* and defiled habituated tendencies in the *New Treatise*. Whether tradition-as-value or pure habituated tendencies, in short, only antitraditions retain any value in the emancipatory metanarrative and soteriology of the texts.

What distinguishes the *New Treatise* from *Eastern and Western Cultures* is that the traditions it admits the existence of, at least phenomenally speaking, remain for the most part *those of the self*. Certainly, such traditions arise out of the mind's phenomenal experiences with what it mistakenly regards as external objects, but the text does not seem to conceive of the possibility that different minds could belong to a community of habits shaped by a shared language, for example. Only in one instance does the text ask whether karmic power or habituated tendencies could inhere "in a race of people or in a society."[95] The text's conclusion is that although this is a logical possibility, this is not "the original import of the Buddhists." Nowhere else in the text is there a suggestion that the habituated tendencies stored in one's consciousness extend beyond the self, in the sense that they would be the product of one's participation in a community sharing certain customs, traditions, and a particular language. The only past that seems to influence the present, in Xiong's treatment of the unawakened consciousness, is the past of the consciousness itself, which is described in strongly autonomous terms as an entity essentially isolated from shared life.

One could perhaps retort that the absence of shared traditions in the discourse of the text is simply due to the narrow scope of its inquiry. After all, the *New Treatise* does not claim to be anything other than an ontological account of the mind-universe. Yet if the text had recognized that individual consciousnesses are formed through their relation with an exterior—family, community, customs, and so forth—it would certainly have presented an account of how this exterior informs the interior. But as Sang Yu notes in her monograph on Xiong's understanding of Reality and functions, the *New Treatise* suggests that every sentient being shares one and the same Reality.[96] This explains why the text can associate the mind with the whole universe. But precisely because everyone shares the same inherent mind, there is no sense in talking about the influence of others on one's mind, except when it comes to the level of the habituated mind, whose delusion is precisely what one must be purified of to achieve enlightenment. Yet even at the phenomenal level, the text does not seem to take into account the fact that the traditions or habituated tendencies that inform one's present could be shared. The narrow focus of the text on individual consciousnesses must therefore be explained, I suggest, by Xiong's presumption, perhaps inherited from Yogācāra, that the mind, habituated or inherent, is ultimately autonomous from such "external" factors.

As briefly mentioned in the introduction, there is a performative aspect to the text's disregard for the role played by external factors in the formation of the mind. By focusing narrowly on the inner workings of the mind, the *New Treatise* symbolically enacts the process of atomization integral to its discourse of emancipation. Given that Fundamental Reality cannot be described through language, the next best thing the *New Treatise* can do is not only to describe but also to *enact* the process whereby the mind frees itself from its own exterior to achieve a state of communion with the universe. The textual atomization of the mind, viewed from this angle, finds legitimacy in the soteriology of the text.

In any case, what matters for our purpose is that the text not only portrays tradition as a form of delusion from which one ought to awaken, but also overlooks the very possibility that traditions could be shared among a group of people. The only instance in which the text hints at traditions that escape the narrow confines of the self is when it provides a positive assessment of the teachings of former sages and masters. Such teachings, insofar as they were put down in writing and transmitted from one generation to another, can be viewed as traditions shared by a literate community.

It must be remembered, however, that the writings of the sages and masters of old cannot induce awakening in the readers in and of themselves. They can simply help them find the right path that might eventually lead them to awakening. Once on the right path, one finds oneself entirely alone, seeking within oneself for the remnants of one's inherent mind, and doing so by unremittingly renewing the origin and breaking free of the hold of the past at every instant. The teachings of sages and masters thus form a tradition that can help one emancipate from the hold of the past once and for all. As such, they can be described, although only phenomenally so, as an antitradition. As the interlude that follows will show, they are an antitradition that is shaped as an alternative to the May Fourth model of human autonomy.

Interlude

Contextualizing Teleological History and Individual Autonomy

Before moving on to the question of textual authority, it is worth taking a moment to reflect on the iconoclastic tendencies denoted in the discourses of *Eastern and Western Cultures* and the *New Treatise* and contextualize them in the intellectual milieu in which the texts were written and originally read.

Chapters 1 and 2 have argued that the discourse of both texts leaves very little room for a positive assessment of tradition's role in the quest toward human emancipation, regardless of whether this quest is construed as a historical odyssey or as something one ought to undertake in complete isolation from others. What remains to be shown—although I have hinted at it here and there—is that the texts reshape Confucianism into an anti-tradition: a tradition that can bring about a complete emancipation of the contemporary from the hold of the past. This I leave to the following two chapters. In this interlude, I discuss the texts' similar ends but dissimilar means before relating them to the intellectual context.

Similar ends

In terms of their depiction of the role—or lack thereof—tradition plays in the journey to emancipation, there are some striking similarities between the texts, and this in spite of their obvious asymmetry in terms of the scope of their inquiries. There is little doubt that the texts tackle vastly different topics and do so by adopting singular approaches. *Eastern and Western Cultures* deals with the issue of the survival and worth of Eastern traditions in the context of a fast-paced process of westernization of world cultures. As to the *New Treatise*, it offers an ontology of the mind-universe, and it does so for soteriological purposes, presenting itself as a guide readers can consult in their pursuit of enlightenment. The *New Treatise* appears much less concerned with the historical context in which it was written (although ultimately this is only apparently so, for a variety of reasons I hope will become clear in what follows).

Despite these differences, both texts offer emancipatory discourses—whether individual or collective. And both present emancipation as a state in which individuals, or humanity as a whole, are no longer defined, shaped, or influenced by what came before (before their birth, certainly, but also before the present moment). Yet both also make special room, in their iconoclastic discourse, for the unique moment that is the origin—the origin of the mind or that of cultures. In the *New Treatise*, only those traditions of the self that can mirror the pure origin of the mind have value, while in *Eastern and Western Cultures*, only the ideals proposed by two ancient geniuses situated at the fountainhead of Indian and Chinese cultures are salvaged from the text's strongly iconoclastic stance toward the *historical* traditions of China and India. In both cases, it is by re-enacting and manifesting the origin in the present that the emancipatory potential of the origin can be released and that the individual or humanity as a whole can free itself from the hold of the past, fusing in the process with the endless transformations of the universe.

The origin provides both texts with the sole criterion on the basis of which the value of traditions can be assessed. Only traditions that manifest the origin in the present are of value, and in the case of the *New Treatise*, they are only nominally or phenomenally so. Ontologically speaking, they are simply illusory. Although in theory many traditions could be assessed positively by presenting them as embodying the authentic value of the origin, in practice both texts propose drastically iconoclastic readings of the past. *Eastern and Western Cultures* discards Chinese history as the history of a failure to put in practice the ideal of Confucius, while the *New Treatise* casts a disparaging light on the entire process whereby past habits inform present cognition. Both texts, in sum, avail themselves of the iconoclastic potential of the origin—of the origin's ability, once reactivated in the present, to negate the entire scope of time that formerly kept the beginning alienated from the now.[1]

Interestingly, both texts also regard past and matter (including the body) as closely related culprits responsible for the degeneration of the mind or spirit. In *Eastern and Western Cultures*, matter, construed as the manifestation of past selves in the present, forms an obstacle to the free flow of spirit. Teleological history is rethought as a process whereby spirit gradually frees itself from the limitation imposed by the past-as-matter. In the *New Treatise*, habituated tendencies, which represent a medium through which the past shapes the present, are intricately tied to the birth of the body. The phenomenal effect of the past on the present, at the level of the mind, is in fact directly related to the gradual pollution of the mind by the body and matter. In both cases, the process by which one frees oneself from tradition is made one with that by which the mind vanquishes the body. Idealism, in both texts, is the handmaiden of iconoclasm.[2]

Both texts propose to their readers the historical or soteriological means through which the spirit or mind can be finally and utterly liberated from matter, the body, and the past. Liberation, however, is not construed as a state of absolute autonomy. On the contrary, both texts inscribe their discussion of emancipation within a largely traditional framework, one that regards the dissolution of the boundary between self and non-self as the ultimate goal. It is because matter, the body, and the hold of the past on the present sever the self from the non-self—the universe in constant transformation—that they must be transcended.

Despite the texts' strongly iconoclastic stances, significant features of their discourse are recycled from the many historical traditions that shaped, consciously or not, their authors. That both texts find ultimate value in a pure origin and in an ideal of oneness between self and universe will not come as a complete surprise to anyone familiar with Chinese intellectual history. Of course, this does not entail that the authors' views are entirely defined by the weight of historical traditions[3] or that the authors could not escape the determinism of their historical context. If this was the case, no disagreement of depth could ever come between two individuals formed by the same historical traditions. There are, undoubtedly, myriad ways in which traditions can be shaped into more or less coherent wholes at the level of the self—although ultimately, we never manage to entirely harmonize the various traditions that make us who we are. Like Walt Whitman, we all contain multitudes.

Both texts can be regarded as new textiles woven with the threads of the many traditions that informed their authors. Although they work with threads recycled from the past, the texts manage to weave relatively new patterns out of them, notably by making traditions previously at odds with one another intertwine in unexpected ways. This is the case with the texts' remarkable ability to knit together discourses in which threads usually associated with the Buddhist and Confucian traditions intersect in intricate and complicated ways with strands borrowed from their discursive rivals: the May Fourth group. That this is the case can be shown by taking a closer look at the dissimilar means through which a traditional fusion between self and non-self can be achieved according to the texts.

Dissimilar means

While the texts share striking similarities at the level of their aims, the means through which they argue such aims can be reached differ significantly. In the *New Treatise*, one's fusion with the universe comes at the end of a process of atomization of the mind. It is by gradually removing, one after another, the sedimented layers of impurity that are attached to the inherent mind and that represent the direct effect of the external world on the mind that the latter can be freed. While the aim remains one of fusion with all that is other, the means advocated by the *New Treatise* asks that the mind purifies itself from any sign of otherness. As the mind finds itself on the verge of reaching a state of perfect autonomy, however, a reversal of fate occurs, as autonomy gives way to a state of symbiosis between the mind and the universe.

In *Eastern and Western Cultures*, a similar fusion between the self and its exterior can be achieved by progressing along the predetermined course of teleological history. While the *New Treatise* makes emancipation directly available to its readers, *Eastern and Western Cultures* makes of liberation a collective goal that requires a long-term investment on the part of humanity as a whole. Yet the readers can find solace in the *fact*—the text presents its conclusions as vetted by the scientific method—that since the European Renaissance, humanity has finally entered the proper course of a teleological history proceeding in three distinct stages. In this case, it is the scientifically established trajectory of unilinear history, understood as the necessary result of the collective agency of humanity, that provides the means through which humanity can emancipate itself from tradition and fuse with the constant flux of the universe.

Individual autonomy and teleological history, in short, are the proper channels through which individual or collective emancipation can take place. It is far from coincidental that these also happen to be two of the most important components of an emancipatory discourse the May Fourth members adopted and adapted, for their own purposes, from the mainstream discourse of modernity. Undoubtedly, Xiong's autonomy differs in important ways from the kind of individual autonomy we are accustomed to associate with the Enlightenment. For one thing, reason is not the gateway through which the autonomous individual can access universality in Xiong's discourse. As to Liang's teleological history, it is far from a typical nineteenth-century European metanarrative of unilinear progress, if only because Buddhist enlightenment is the ultimate goal. Both authors also significantly depart from the May Fourth reinterpretation of autonomy and teleological history. Xiong and Liang did not simply reproduce ready-made discursive molds; they consciously or unconsciously adapted the discursive frameworks of their May Fourth rivals to their own needs and ends. If human autonomy and teleological history could buttress the agenda of May Fourth iconoclasts, could they not also instill new life in the largely traditional project of merging the self with the constant flow of the universe?

Teleological history

Teleological history had long served the purpose of sanctioning sociopolitical or geopolitical agendas as dissimilar as communism and colonialism. If one were able to abstract a set of laws from history and extrapolate from them the general course history could not but take, one could imbue one's vision for the future with an aura of scientific objectivity. By presenting humanity as partaking in a unilinear historical course that leads it from a state of heteronomy to one of absolute autonomy, for example, one could legitimize colonial enterprises as "charitable" attempts at imparting liberty to the colonial other.

Well-known are the dangers inherent in unilinear metanarratives of history. Although far from being unknown, what is perhaps *less* known are the differing ways in which the discursive framework of teleological history was adopted by those subjected to European colonialism and imperialism. Across the world, teleological history was put to the use of bolstering a variety of agendas, including agendas aimed at defending newly or soon-to-be established nation-states against the colonial or imperial advances of Europe, the United States, and Japan.

During the second half of the 1910s, leading May Fourth figures such as Hu Shi and Chen Duxiu made use of unilinear metanarratives of history and social Darwinist theories to argue China had but two options: retain its old ways and fall prey to foreign powers or modernize along Western models and achieve national sovereignty. This does not mean they merely saw science and democracy as tools needed to build a sovereign, powerful, and wealthy nation-state. Both Chen and Hu were in fact quite committed to their own understanding of science and democracy during this period. Yet both saw in teleological history a powerful means to present their own vision of China's future as the only possible outcome of history that was not disastrous for China. Teleological history proved to be a powerful tool to hegemonize the discursive field, as any alternative vision of the future in which Chinese traditions played a role could be attacked on the basis that such vision was unfit for the modern age. Iconoclasm and teleological history were closely knit into the discursive fabric of May Fourth.

In opposition to this model, intellectuals who wished to argue that Chinese traditions still retained some value in the modern period had a number of options available to them. They could accept the May Fourth model of teleological history but make the point that at least some aspects of the Chinese past were in agreement with the telos. If sprouts of science and democracy could be found in the arsenal of the past, one could make the argument that Chinese traditions were not to be rejected wholesale. One could even go further in making the bold claim that it was *because* science and democracy had the blessing of tradition that they had to be adopted. The obvious disadvantage of this option, however, is that only those aspects of tradition that could be made to fit the modern values vetted by May Fourth could be reauthorized.[4] By adopting this stance, one could reauthorize some traditions, but at the cost of subjecting oneself, and perhaps even admitting defeat, to May Fourth actors who acted as arbiters of truth and value.

The May Fourth challenge, for anyone wishing to argue that tradition retained some value in the context of modernity, is that one could either reject the teleological metanarrative of history and risk being depicted as an irrelevant traditionalist, or attempt to revalue tradition within the teleological framework and in the process concede to May Fourth more than one was willing to. The solution to this challenge proposed by *Eastern and Western Cultures* is to adopt a teleological historical framework that would make its discourse relevant to the discursive milieu of the time, while filling this framework with new content that peripheralized the role of the West. To be sure, the text admits to May Fourth iconoclasts, Western culture was the unavoidable telos toward which history evolved regardless of one's geographical location, but this was only the telos of the first phase of a developmental model oriented toward the revival of Chinese and Indian "cultures."

Unlike the other approach presented above, which could find value only in traditions equated with modern Western culture, what could be revalued of Chinese culture by *Eastern and Western Cultures*' approach was negatively predetermined by Western culture. Only that which differed from modern Western culture and could therefore complement it could be reauthorized by this approach.[5] This explains why the text's portrayal of Western and Eastern cultures often reproduces a variety of Orientalist tropes: the distinction between West and East (here China) along the lines of rationality versus intuition, the perception of Eastern cultures as stagnant and Western cultures as progressive, the West as providing an impetus for the entry of the East into teleological history, the portrayal of Chinese culture in terms of a number of "lacks" (by comparison to the Western "norm"), and the fetishization of national cultures into coherent and contradiction-free wholes that could then be contrasted to one another. *Eastern and Western Cultures* often adopts the Orientalist framework that made its way into May Fourth discourse, but reverses it on its head by abstracting the Eastern pole of the Orientalist divide from the dustbin of history before projecting it onto the telos of history in order to reauthorize it.[6] What could thus be reauthorized, however, had to be a spirit unaffected by the vicissitudes of premodern history. "Tradition" could be revalued only at the cost of being de-complexified, homogenized, universalized, and abstracted from history in such a way as to make it unclear how it could still be depicted as fundamentally "Chinese."

Although this discursive position is not devoid of shortcomings, it also presents a number of advantages. For one thing, it allowed *Eastern and Western Cultures* to steal a page from the Euro-American and May Fourth playbooks and depict Chinese culture as a truly universal culture. Making this argument was not without its challenges, however. While contemporary Western culture could be presented as universal by depicting it as the inescapable future toward which the rest of the world evolved, Liang could not easily do the same for *contemporary* Chinese culture. For one thing, he saw nearly as many flaws in contemporary Chinese culture as the May Fourth iconoclasts did. But there were also reasons pertaining to the discursive milieu that made it extremely difficult to reauthorize Chinese culture as it then was. The idea that contemporary Chinese culture was temporally behind that of the West had already become widespread enough that opposing it would prove exceedingly arduous. What is more, the issues that plagued China at the time could hardly be denied. As such, what could be revalued of Chinese culture were not only elements that significantly differed from Western culture, but also elements that could be insulated from contemporary China and what it had inherited from corrupt historical institutions and practices. Only a spirit, and one that had not been spoiled by the atrocities of history, could be revived without immediately falling prey to May Fourth attacks. This was precisely the role destined for tradition-as-value in the historical model of *Eastern and Western Cultures*.

This reading does not imply that Liang *consciously* went through all the possible options available to him before choosing the one that was better adapted to the discursive milieu of the time. The success of *Eastern and Western Cultures* certainly shows that Liang possessed a certain flair for the times he lived in, but it does not necessarily entail he consciously devised a plan to use the tools of his adversaries against them. Yet this is precisely what his text does: it employs the framework of May Fourth teleological history to reauthorize the unspoiled spirit of "Chinese culture" (read "Confucius") by making of it the inescapable future toward which humanity evolves. This shows the extent to which the teleological metanarrative of modernity had become a powerful tool to authorize discourses at the beginning of the Republican period, so much so that even revivalist projects sought legitimacy in it.

Human Autonomy

Intricately related to the teleological metanarrative of modernity is the notion of human autonomy. While this is not the place to revisit conventional narratives of the Enlightenment, suffice it to say, for our purpose, that modernity's purported break from the past was often construed as a passage from heteronomy to autonomy. Teleological metanarratives often drew a sharp contrast between pre-moderns, who found themselves subservient to external authorities such as the church, the monarch, the patriarch, and tradition; and moderns, who learned to rely on the authority of reason with which everyone is endowed at birth. The ideal of human autonomy thus reinforced the strict divide between the modern and the premodern, in such a way as to allow modern subjects to reject views that do not accord with their own by presenting them as the mere product of premodern heteronomy. The voice of reason could only be spoken by those graced with the gift of modern autonomy—a gift it was the white man's burden to pass on to others, through colonial means if necessary.

As a discursive tool, the notion of human autonomy could thus be put to the task of silencing alternative voices regarded as unreasonable or irrational. The rapid growth in value of individualism in the economy of May Fourth discourse can serve as an example. As Lydia Liu argues in *Translingual Practice*,[7] the notion of individualism allowed May Fourth actors to provide a multifaceted attack on the Confucian family model and the social hierarchies built around it. The individual had to be freed from the tyranny of the traditional family to become a citizen who could directly participate in politics. What individualism served to oppose, in May Fourth discourse, was not the infringement of the state in the private matters of its citizens, as one formed in classical liberalism would assume, but a patriarchal, family-centered model of sociopolitical organization depicted as feudal and unsuited to modern times.

Individualism therefore functioned as a means, in May Fourth discourse, to break free from the bonds of the feudal past. But it also served the discursive purpose of establishing a strict dichotomy between the autonomous voices of reason and heteronomous individuals who simply rehashed the old language of the feudal past. Defending tradition within this context made one prone to attacks on the grounds that one acted as the spokesperson of the feudal order. To answer this challenge, it certainly helped to concede defeat to May Fourth on the battlefield of history before attempting to win the war on the battlefield of value, as *Eastern and Western Culture* did. But the *New Treatise* adopted a different approach.

Although the *New Treatise*'s ultimate goal is not individual autonomy, the means through which the text attempts to achieve its goal borrows important resources from the discursive framework associated with the notion of individual autonomy. There is in fact something oddly cartesian about the *New Treatise*'s depiction of the body, matter, tradition, emotions, and the other as impediments limiting the proper functioning of the true core of the self: the mind. In *Meditations on First Philosophy* (1641), the mind could gradually free itself from its exterior by systematically casting doubt on everything it had learned from others and from its experience of the external realm. Once doubt had been applied to all previously held beliefs, one would be left with an atomized core, a faculty of thinking providing one with clear and distinct perceptions; the sole trustable source of universally valid truths.

The goal of the *New Treatise* is certainly not that of achieving truths about an external world of objects. In fact, its goal is to challenge the very existence of the latter. Yet the text parallels the *Meditations* in offering its reader the means to gradually purify the mind from its exterior.[8] Like the *Meditations*, the *New Treatise* gives pride of place to doubt in the process of purifying the mind. Doubt can help achieve awakening, the text explains, by allowing one to challenge the beliefs previously acquired by the habituated mind. Once doubt is given free reign, there is "a fundamental wavering [of trust] in those legends previously believed in, just as there is now a sudden awakening that the narrow views previously upheld were pure ignorance." Granting doubt the permission to challenge previous beliefs and "legends," the text concludes, "can lead to awakening [*qiwu* 啟悟]."[9]

It is significant that the *New Treatise* would link the soteriological process of atomization of the mind with a positive assessment of doubt as an antidote against received beliefs. In doing so, the text follows in the footsteps of May Fourth protagonists in promoting individualism and opposing superstitions (*mixin* 迷信). Although in the above quote the term used by the text is "legend" (*chuanshuo* 傳說) and not "superstition," both notions rely on a strict distinction between the reliable knowledge established by autonomous individuals and the unreliable knowledge one inherits from received opinion. According to the May Fourth actors, the scientific method provides the criteria on the basis of which knowledge and superstitions can be discerned. The *New Treatise* constitutes a significant departure from this position, insofar as it makes of awakening the sole criterion thanks to which one can distinguish true knowledge from legends. This represents an attempt to usurp from May Fourth the unique ability to access symbolic goods of universal value. Yet in both cases, legends and superstitions provide the intellectual elite with "others" against which its legitimacy can be firmly established in the figure of the autonomous individual.

Upon closer inspection, the *New Treatise*'s autonomy is neither that of Descartes nor of May Fourth. What is revealed through the process of atomization of the mind is not a faculty—reason—providing the individual access to irrefutable truths. Rather, it is an inherent mind posited as a reversed image of reason. While reason dissects the world into the subject and objects of cognition, the inherent mind shatters the subject-object divide and reconnects with the oneness of Reality. In a manner that resembles closely how *Eastern and Western Cultures* adopts the framework of teleological history but reverses the value judgment associated with the Orientalist tropes it served to sanction—premodern, intuitional East versus modern, rational West—the *New Treatise* employs the discursive framework of individual autonomy but puts it to the task of rejecting the very object it traditionally served to authorize: reason. In short, both texts oppose the discursive content of May Fourth by strategically deploying discursive frameworks borrowed from their adversary.

As in the case of Liang Shuming, I do not mean to suggest that Xiong Shili consciously drew on the language of his adversaries in opposing them. I find it highly unlikely that Xiong purposefully deployed the discursive framework of his opponents to gain purchase on an intellectual milieu defined by May Fourth rules of discursivity. It seems more likely that Xiong was simply a man of his time who shared with the May Fourth group a common attitude and a number of foundational assumptions regarding the human condition. But precisely because what the text *does* in the discursive milieu is not necessarily coextensive with what the author intended, an approach that draws from the literature on the death of the author can be an important ally in situating the text in a discursive milieu that both restricted and enabled what could be successfully argued.

While the adoption of teleological history shapes in important ways what could be logically and successfully presented as valuable of the past in *Eastern and Western Cultures*, the *New Treatise*'s embrace of the trope of individual autonomy also impacts in significant ways the resources from which it could borrow. Suffice it to say that its emphasis on introspection and inherent mind naturally brought the text closer to Wang Yangming and away from Zhu Xi, as one might expect. As in the case of *Eastern and Western Cultures*, the text's choices were to some extent negatively limited by what was valued in the mainstream discourse of modernity—in this case reason. Only that which could be presented as diametrically opposed to reason, as indisputably superior to it, and as capable of curing the very illness brought forth by it could be reauthorized within the discursive framework of the *New Treatise*. An inherent mind unplagued by the tendency to discriminate between subject and object fit the bill seamlessly.

Monopolizing tradition

On the surface, there appears to be an irreconcilable contradiction between the means and ends of *Eastern and Western Cultures* and the *New Treatise*: between their traditional goal of merging self with non-self and the means, borrowed from the antitradition of modernity, through which they attempt to achieve their goal. This apparent contradiction can certainly be explained, as I have done above, by appealing to the texts' need to adapt to the discursive milieu of the time. Yet we should be careful not to think of the texts' adoption of means borrowed from the resources of the antitradition of modernity as the result of the *passive* response of traditionalists to the changing historical context. There is something much more complex at work here.

Discursively speaking, both teleological history and human autonomy have historically served the purpose of providing their advocates with the tools to reject alternative visions of the future and the good, by reshaping their own views as the only viable option. Of course, this is not the only role played by both in history. There is little doubt that that the notion of human autonomy can be and has been put to the task of concretely contributing to freeing certain individuals or groups from oppression. Yet the modern notion of autonomy functions in such a way as to require, as Michel Foucault has shown, the continuous rejection and marginalization of its others: heteronomous, irrational, premodern, and unfree others. It is in this functioning that a potential of violence resides.

While this potential most forcefully manifested itself in the discourse meant to legitimize Euro-American and Japanese colonialism and imperialism, it also bore its mark on the development of a new discursive framework through which the modern Chinese intellectual elite rethought its place in society. After the collapse of traditional means of cultural and social distinction, May Fourth intellectuals found in the mainstream discourse of modernity new means to justify the claim that they, and only they, held the keys to the kingdom of value and truth.

As mentioned in the introduction, while in the 1920s May Fourth members splintered into different factions promoting competing agendas, the new factions continued to present themselves as the only legitimate representatives of the most advanced form of modernity, epitomized by Western Europe, North America, or the Soviet Union. The mainstream discourse of modernity, with its teleological view of history and its alleged monopoly over human autonomy, thus continued to serve as an important source of legitimacy for a variety of competing projects. Placing the rise of Confucian iconoclasm in this context allows us to see it not as a traditionalist project that merely recycles the discursive tools of teleological history and human autonomy to cater to the discursive milieu, but as one of the many projects aimed at hegemonizing the discursive field with the powerful tools of antitradition.

In doing so, Confucian iconoclasm essentially reproduced the exclusionary tendencies inherent in antitraditions. The discursive power of antitraditions resides in their ability to help their representatives monopolize the symbolic capital of truth and the good by rejecting all traditions but their own. May Fourth iconoclasts sought to harness this discursive power by presenting themselves as the only group possessing an unequivocal monopoly over the means of access to human emancipation and, by extension, over the means of ownership and distribution of cultural and symbolic capital. What the *New Treatise* and *Eastern and Western Cultures* seek to do, in opposition to May Fourth hegemony, is to reroute the discursive power of the antitradition of modernity in their favor and for their benefit.

Both texts do so, I argue in the following chapters, by presenting their own vision of Confucianism as the only antitradition capable of fulfilling the emancipatory promise of modernity. By weaving Confucianism into the modern fabric of antitraditionalism, the texts aspire to make of their Confucianism the only legitimate orthodoxy, against competing readings of Confucianism that emerged during and after the May Fourth period. And by presenting themselves as the authoritative interpreters of one of the only traditions worth reviving and transmitting—if not the only one—the texts exhibit a desire to monopolize the means of access to emancipation—and along with it cultural and symbolic capital—that is characteristic of hegemonic antitraditions such as those promoted by May Fourth iconoclasts.

This goes to show how issues of authority, orthodoxy formation, and the hegemonic monopolization of symbolic capital are central concerns of the texts. Such concerns inform the complex ways in which the texts intertwine the threads of historical traditions with strands borrowed from the antitradition of modernity, in such a way as to reshape Confucianism into an alternative modern antitradition. From this perspective, the texts' antitraditional means are far from contradicting their traditional goal. Such means provides them with counter-hegemonic resources to open up an intellectual space for their project in a discursive battleground shaped by the May Fourth group. And it makes it possible for them to do so while avoiding to appear as if they fought windmills on the battlefield of premodern Confucianism—a battlefield from which the intellectual elite had already slowly but steadily withdrawn.

3

Performing Sagely Authority

In chapter 1, we saw that *Eastern and Western Cultures'* metanarrative of history leaves little room for traditions in humanity's quest to transcend matter and the past. What remains to be seen is how the text attempts to reinstate the authority of Confucius, how it seeks to legitimize its discourse with this authority, and how redefining Confucianism as an antitradition helps it monopolize the authority of tradition in a way that is better adapted to the discursive milieu of the time.

Before entering the complex terrain of our main argument, however, it is worth pondering for a moment what "the authority of tradition" entails and how it can flow from the Confucian classics to their interpreters and the texts they produce. With the canonization of the classics from the Han dynasty onward, inserting oneself in the tradition by learning the language of the classics formed one of the most important means of acquiring symbolic, cultural, and political capital. In Neo-Confucian discourse, the canonized corpus often served as a site of sagely authority that could be reactualized in the present through a number of discursive means. One of the most important of such means was that of the commentary. By commenting on a text, one reaffirmed its authority as a classic and a repository of truths, and by performing one's mastery of the classic in a commentarial form, one could ascribe to oneself the authority of the ancient text.

Another means through which texts could reactualize the authority of tradition was the "genealogies of the way" (*daotong* 道統). Although the origin of such genealogies is often traced back to Han Yu (韓愈; 768–824) or even Mencius (孟子; 372–289 BCE),[1] Zhu Xi is often credited with popularizing one of the most enduring of such genealogies.[2] Simply put,

Zhu created an exclusive lineage of sages who embodied the *dao*. The latter was said to have passed from Confucius to Mencius, and, after more than a thousand years of decline, to Zhou Dunyi, the Cheng brothers (Cheng Hao 程顥 [1032–1085] and Cheng Yi 程頤 [1033–1107]), and finally, by implication, to Zhu himself.[3] Such genealogies, which soon became a mainstay of Neo-Confucian discourses, enabled texts and authors to produce symbolic conduits through which the authority of tradition could be conveyed and monopolized by drawing a sharp distinction between those in the lineage and those excluded by it.

The commentary and the genealogy of the way thus offered means to reactualize—and often monopolize—the authority of tradition. I return to these issues throughout the chapter, as they are closely related to the project of reclaiming the authority of Confucius I see at work in *Eastern and Western Cultures*. For now, I would like to address a possible objection to the project at hand. One might think it misguided to discuss the authority of tradition in Republican China, especially if one takes it, as I do, that the discursive milieu of the time was significantly shaped by May Fourth iconoclasm. Was there any authority left of tradition at the time, and if so, of which tradition exactly? Can we presume that the classics[4] retained some authority in Republican China? Have I not presented the metanarrative of history of *Eastern and Western Cultures* as having for its goal the *revaluation* of Confucianism, which takes for granted that the latter's value, and with it its authority, had all but vanished at the time?

My answer to this challenge is two-pronged. First, even if tradition had indeed lost its authority in the discursive milieu of Republican China, it would nevertheless still be possible to describe *Eastern and Western Cultures* as attempting to revive this authority before putting it to the task of legitimating its discourse. Although this is part of my answer, the success of the text, immediately following its publication, suggests that Confucianism most likely retained some of its authority in the eyes of many readers. Rather than appealing to the text's ability to successfully and single-handedly revive the authority of tradition in a discursive milieu entirely opposed to it, the success of the text can be explained with more ease by assuming that its readers were most likely already inclined to accept that Confucianism had not entirely lost its authority under the attacks of the May Fourth group. *Eastern and Western Cultures*, on such a reading, can be viewed as providing a metanarrative that tapped into the readers' desire to find some form of interpretative framework that could make sense of why Confucianism needed not lose its authority—at least not entirely—in the modern period.

It is after all extremely doubtful—and this is my second point—that the authority of Confucianism vanished overnight because of the May Fourth attacks. However poignant and discursively successful such attacks were, they could not in and of themselves do away with the remarkable power of symbolic commodities that had had such high value, historically, as the classics. Even the most iconoclastic of May Fourth thinkers found it necessary to display their command of the classical canon when attacking it.[5] This enabled them to perform their cultural capital and secure their membership in the intellectual elite. After all, the older May Fourth members were trained in classical scholarship. Although the authority of tradition, and especially of the classics, was not left unscathed by the May Fourth attacks, neither was it entirely obliterated by them.[6]

Of course, the kind of authority May Fourth members derived from the classics by showing their mastery of them differs in important ways from the kind of authority Confucian iconoclasm seeks in the classics. The former kind derives from a show of erudition, while the latter kind rests on the implication that the contemporary interpreter is of one mind with the sages of old. While the two should by no means be conflated, the fact that one could still find authority, as a member of the intellectual elite, by performing one's command of the classics, even if the latter were regarded as historical artifacts rather than repositories of truth, explains in part the success of a text like *Eastern and Western Cultures*.

In what follows, I identify the discursive means through which a text published in an intellectual milieu significantly shaped by May Fourth iconoclasm could reinstate the authority of tradition, and especially that of the Confucian sage, before attempting to subsume it. To achieve this goal, *Eastern and Western Cultures* implicitly presents its author as a modern sage who has reached spiritual simultaneity with Confucius. That "Liang"—by which I refer, in the context of this chapter, to the *image* of the author implicit in the discourse of the text[7]—mirrors the sage is then "demonstrated" by his ability (1) to intuitively grasp the ultimate meaning of the classics, as the text's commentaries on the classical corpus are meant to show, and (2) to use this intuitive grasp to judge which historical figure understood the true essence of Confucius's message—even if only partially so. I conclude by arguing that although the text seeks to discursively purify itself from history to recast itself as the product of a sage unbound by time and place, it can nevertheless be regarded, provided one does not make the kind of leap of faith the text asks of the reader, as taking part in *historical antitraditions*—that is, historical Confucian traditions (in contrast to the

Confucian traditions established *within the discourse of the text*) that seek to establish their transhistorical authority in at least *partial* opposition to tradition-as-history.

Naturalizing Confucius

Re-establishing the authority of tradition within the discursive context of the early 1920s was not without its challenges. Of course, texts could simply act as if May Fourth had not happened, but adopting this strategy would only invite the ire of the opposing camp, or perhaps even worse, their indifference. The superior strategy, within such a discursive milieu, consisted in arguing that a particular tradition retained its authority *not because of its status as tradition*, and even less because it was a *Chinese* tradition, but for the simple reason that it conveyed transhistorical truths still valuable to us moderns. Traditions could be more easily reauthorized by draping them in the garb of universality than by tying them down to a mundane history and a particular location.

In *Eastern and Western Cultures*, this strategy takes the form of a rhetoric of naturalization of the sage.[8] What this entails will become clearer by taking a closer look at the text's discourse on the most important notion it associates with the figure of Confucius: that of "intuition" (*zhijue* 直覺). In the sections that introduce the philosophy of life of Confucius, the text builds on the Mencian assumption that human nature is good. It describes intuition as a natural way of living that can be adopted by anyone who reacts to things by following their feelings (*suigan er ying* 隨感而應):

> Human beings naturally follow the right path, without the need to analyze and think things over [*caoxin daliang* 操心打量]. When encountering some difficulty, they immediately react by following their feelings. This reaction is always right. If they want to look for what is right externally, they will not find it. Human life follows the natural flow of things; it naturally takes the most righteous, the most appropriate, and the most suitable of paths. [. . .] So, in Confucianism it is said: "That which Heaven ordains is called nature, and to follow one's nature [*shuai xing* 率性] is called the way [*dao*]." In short, one simply needs to follow one's nature.

人自然會走對的路，原不須你操心打量的。遇事他便當下隨感
而應，這隨感而應，通是對的，要於外求對，是沒有的。我們
人的生活便是流行之體，他自然走他那最對，最妥帖最適當的
路。……所以儒家說：「天命之謂性，率性之謂道」。只要你率
性就好了。⁹

Whenever we act by following our feelings instead of reasoning, we take a natural path that is "always right." A metaphysical foundation to this natural path is then provided by the short quotation from the *Doctrine of the Mean* (*Zhongyong* 中庸), insofar as it is said to be what heaven ordains. To follow one's intuitions entails that one remains open to changes, which allows one to adapt and fuse with the constant transformations of the universe. This explains why the text later adds that living intuitively "means 'being in accord with the principle of Heaven' [*he tianli* 合天理]."¹⁰

The above passage contrasts intuition with a tendency to "analyze and think things over." This is an implicit reference to what the text terms *lizhi* (理智), which is somewhat akin to instrumental rationality in Max Weber. Although the text highlights a number of benefits that derive from the use of *lizhi*, notably in the realm of the sciences, it nevertheless retains a highly critical stance toward this form of reasoning it associates with the Western will to dominate the external world. A number of reasons explain why *lizhi* impedes the natural propensity of human beings to follow the right course. For one thing, *lizhi* tends to seek an understanding of the world as a *static* object of knowledge. In doing so, it makes it increasingly difficult for the subject to naturally react to the changing circumstances and thus mirror the endless transformations of the universe. Moreover, *lizhi* cannot but break the original unity of subject and object that characterizes intuition, as it must treat the world as an object distinct from the cognizing subject. With devastating effects, Westerners have applied this tendency to approach the external realm as a static object to other human beings, to the extent that the natural bond between human beings has collapsed in modern Western societies.¹¹

Eastern and Western Cultures also contrasts intuition with habits accumulated through experience. In passages that bear a sticking similarity to the *New Treatise*'s discourse of return to the origin, the text blames the deviation from the *dao* that characterizes the life of most of us common mortals on "defiled habits" (*zaran xiguan* 雜染習慣).¹² Habits limit our capacity to spontaneously follow our intuitions, in the sense that they originally arose in reaction to a particular situation, but then continue to arise regardless of the situation faced, so that they quickly become unsuited to deal with new challenges.[13] One must therefore work toward the "restoration" of the "original acuteness" of one's intuition.[14] Not unlike the *New Treatise*, the text makes it clear that it is because they are acquired, and not inscribed in human nature, that habits should be discarded. Regardless of whether they are good or bad, habits compel us to stray (*pian* 偏) from the right path (*zheng* 正).[15] *Lizhi*, we can deduct, is precisely one of the main habits that led the modern West to stray from an intuitive way of life.

The divide between acquired habits and innate intuitions is closely tied to an ethicized dichotomization of nature and culture. In a passage aimed at demonstrating how Confucius had no certainties, the text claims that

> Confucius invariably gave free reign to his intuition; he did not debate with himself, unlike most people who incessantly reason [with themselves]. [. . .] Therefore, most people are persistently holding on to a variety of principles, points of view, and opinions. Confucius had no fixed or preconceived ideas; he was devoid of the slightest opinion. This is why it is said that he had "no fixed teacher" [*wu chang shi* 無常師[16]]; that he "transmitted without innovating" [*shu er bu zuo* 述而不作].

> 孔子總任他的直覺，沒有自己打架，而一般人念念講理。……所以一般人心裡總是有許多道理、見解、主張的，而孔子則無成心，他是空洞無絲毫主張的。他因此就無常師，就述而不作。[17]

The assertion that Confucius "transmitted without innovating" is one of the most discussed passages of the *Analects* (7:1). While it has been traditionally interpreted to mean that Confucius saw himself as the transmitter (*shu* 述) of established traditions, we must remember that in *Eastern and Western Cultures*, Confucius is portrayed as a genius who single-handedly produced the cultural ideal of China. On this basis, we can assume that what Confucius transmitted were not first and foremost traditions he inherited from his forebearers, but transhistorical truths he achieved intuitively.

To be sure, the text does mention that "Chinese culture before Confucius was gathered more or less in its entirety in Confucius's hands." This suggests he might have indeed played the role of a transmitter of at least those aspects of the past that retained transhistorical value. Yet the text immediately adds that "Chinese culture after Confucius originated more or less in its entirety from Confucius."[18] This entails that Confucius transmitted to posterity ideals that originated in him. Yet if this is the case, what does it mean to say that Confucius did not innovate? On the basis of the longer quote above, we can assume this means that Confucius did not create anything *artificial*, a reading that is incidentally in accord with the ancient meaning of *zuo* (作).[19] This explains why the text claims Confucius had neither fixed or preconceived ideas nor opinions. By relying on his intuitions, Confucius could avoid straying (*pian*) from the middle path (by not adopting opinions on either side of a spectrum). Of course, that Confucius had neither opinions nor ideas does not entail that for him, anything goes. Given that he produced a cultural ideal still worth pursuing more than two thousand years later, he must have held certain views as to how things ought to be. But Confucius's views, unlike those of "most people," were expressed by giving voice to a natural way of life he *discovered* rather than invented.

In short, what Confucius transmitted to posterity are natural dispositions inscribed in us all. True, some of these natural dispositions might have been discovered by the ancient sage-kings who preceded him—this would explain the reference to Confucius gathering past culture "more or less in its entirety." But the reason why Confucius gathered past culture is *not* because of its status as tradition, but because it accorded with his intuitive discovery of transhistorical truths. The ultimate source of authority, in this discourse, is not the distant, mythologized past, but a realm of nature that escapes contestation. Confucius here serves as a mirror image of Liang: both are portrayed by the text as reactualizing past ideals, and in both cases these ideals are reactivated because they are recognized as transhistorically valuable and natural, and not because they are traditional or because they were produced by authoritative figures of the distant past.

At work in these claims is a distinction between natural and artificial ways of life, discourses, and cultures. Confucius's culture, insofar as it follows the *dao*, is what could paradoxically be called a culture-as-nature, while other cultures—and particularly Western culture, given how it is taken by the habit of *lizhi*—should be properly understood, within the context of this discourse, as cultures-as-artifice. As a natural way of life, intuition possesses a remarkable potential of iconoclasm, insofar as it entails that what one acquires after birth, that the culture one inherits from one's environment are but polluting practices that lead one astray from a natural way of life. As to Confucius's culture-as-nature, it is not properly speaking a tradition inherited from the past, insofar as it is a natural disposition inscribed in us at birth that must simply be activated and put in practice.[20] The spirit of Confucius is therefore one of transcendence from tradition.

The entire semantic field of the notions the above quotes posit as the true core of Confucianism betrays a strongly if latent iconoclastic force: nature (*ziran* 自然), intuition (*zhijue* 直覺), human nature (*xing* 性), the right path (*zheng* 正 or *dao* 道), and finally heaven (*tian* 天). The first three allow the text to redefine Confucianism into an antitradition-as-value, insofar as they represent transhistorical values that enable one to break free from all traditions regarded as artificial, except the one tradition that is truly natural: Confucius's (and by association Liang's). As to the last three notions (*zheng*, *dao*, *tian*), they are employed to create an orthodoxy (zheng*tong* 正統) celebrated as natural and decry opposing views as artificial heterodoxies straying (*pian* 偏) from the right path (*zheng*/*dao*) ordered by heaven (*tian*).

By reformulating Confucianism into an antitradition, the text not only seeks to escape May Fourth criticism; it aims to present its discourse as the only natural way to live against the artifice of its alternatives. By relocating the spirit of the sage in a natural realm informed by heaven, the text makes it immune from cultural and political fields that remain subject to contestation and disagreement. Confucius, after all, avoids positioning himself on either side of any debate; he has no opinion, no preconceived views. It is precisely because his ideal is content-free, because it is presented as the spirit of one who simply follows one's intuitions—and not intuitions reorganized into a dogmatic system passed down in history—that Confucius can be made to appear immune from contestation.[21] And it is by reshaping Liang into the contemporary representative of the sage, as we will see, that Confucius can serve as a conduit through which the text and its author can be transformed into privileged sites of transhistoricity.

Mirroring the sage

Once reinstated, the authority of the figure of the sage encoded in the classics can be reclaimed by the text. This is notably done by equating the program of the text with the ideal of Confucius. The text systematically presents the most important notions that characterize its vision of the future as reactivating the original message of the historical Confucius. For example, the text's rejection of "cost-benefit analysis" (*jijiao lihai* 計較利害), a notion associated with the modern West, finds legitimacy in the assertion that such rejection is "the attitude of Confucianism that most pointedly distinguishes it from that of other people" (despite the fact that the expression *jijiao lihai* is nowhere to be found in the classics).²² Unsurprisingly, the text also explicitly ties its metaphysics of constant transformation to the *Changes*. Perhaps more surprisingly, it also asserts that "not one sentence of Confucius does not discuss" this metaphysics, which is interpreted as "the single thread that binds" (*yi yi guan zhi* 一以貫之) the way of Confucius together mentioned in *Analects* 4:15.²³ Elsewhere, the text also maintains that "life" (*sheng* 生), an important piece of the puzzle of its metaphysics and its construal of culture, "is the most important concept [of Confucius]."²⁴

The core notion that sums up the ideal of Confucius, however, is that of "intuition." Unlike the notion of "resoluteness" (*gang* 剛) discussed in the first chapter, "*zhijue*" was a neologism at the time.²⁵ It therefore could not be linked to the classics by looking for passages in which the notion appears. To present intuition as the very core of Confucius's teaching, the text opts to equate *zhijue* with the cardinal notion of *ren* (humaneness), going so far as to claim that *zhijue* "is what Confucius meant by *ren*."²⁶ The text justifies this rather idiosyncratic interpretation by appealing to a passage from the *Analects* (17:21) to which we shall come back in a moment. For now, suffice it to say that *Eastern and Western Cultures* systematically presents Liang's program for China and the world as a reactivation of the ideal of the sage.

What the text endeavors to bring back to life is much more than the *ideal* of Confucius, however. After all, the text makes it clear that Confucius has no fixed doctrine or ideas to impart to his disciples. What Confucius teaches is a particular attitude centered on intuition that manifests itself in the *spirit* of what he says, rather than in a set of rules to follow. As such, his message cannot be passed down as a letter delivered by a courier unaware of what is being conveyed would. In the case of Confucius, the messenger *is* the message. Passing down the message involves much more than a process of decoding and explaining the meaning of the classics. One must become the messenger, by achieving spiritual simultaneity with him, to succeed in conveying his message. As we will see, it is this spirit of the sage that is meant to be embodied by Liang and conveyed to his students through recorded speech.²⁷

Eastern and Western Cultures provides a number of clues suggesting that the value of the classics resides in their ability to preserve the spirit of Confucius for future generations. Although the text does not discuss at any length hermeneutical issues—such as the question of how the original spirit of Confucius can be abstracted from the classics—we can nevertheless get a sense of the text's hermeneutics by taking a look at its critique—reminiscent of Zhu Xi's—of the exegetes of the Han dynasty:

> The Six Classics are not the product of Confucius; they are all the transmitted vestiges of the ancient past. If one makes use of the spirit of Confucius to comprehend them then they come to life; otherwise, they are all but dead things. At that time [i.e., the Han] the transmitters of the classics did not grasp the spirit of Confucius. Those who studied the classics during the Han did so as if studying ancient artifacts, without paying attention to the [spirit of] life of Confucius. These were but superficial studies and not in-depth [*neixin* 內心] ones.
>
> 六經並非孔子創作，皆古代傳留下來之陳跡，若用孔子之精神貫注起來便通是活的，否則都是死物；而當時傳經者實不得孔子精神。他們漢人治經只算研究古物，於孔子的人生生活並不著意，只有外面的研究而沒有內心的研究。²⁸

Reading the classics as the Han exegetes did is to treat them as dead artifacts of the past and to blind oneself to the living spirit of Confucius that inheres in them. This suggests that for the text, authority resides in the spirit of Confucius conveyed in the classics, and not in the classics themselves. To excavate Confucius's spirit from the classics, the text makes it clear that one must read them by adopting the spirit of Confucius. That is, one must read them *intuitively*. This explains why, as we will see, Liang is presented as having a full grasp of the ultimate meaning of the classics unmediatedly, without having to first situate them in their historical context and without the help of the commentarial or exegetical tradition.

The text remains unclear as to how the activation of one's sagely and intuitive mind takes place. How can intuition be the necessary condition of understanding the classics if it is our understanding of the spirit within the classics that helps us develop our intuitions in the first place? Presumably, although the text is not clear on this, through the process of reading one gradually learns to trust one's intuitions (which after all are part of human nature) at one and the same time as one increasingly understands that intuition is the core message *and* the spirit of Confucius. Alternatively, it is also possible that one develops one's intuition independently of the classics, but then discover, in the process of reading them, that one's acute intuitions are one and the same as those of the sage. This is made possible by the fact that in theory, we all possess one and the same intuitive mind rooted in heaven. The spirit of Confucius is already in all of us, awaiting to be activated.

Although in the above passage *Eastern and Western Cultures* retains a rather disparaging attitude toward the classics—they are but the "vestiges of the ancient past"—in other instances it treats the classics as a whole as the sum of Confucius's wisdom, even though "the Six Classics are not the product of Confucius," as the text readily admits. In one instance, quotes from the *Record of Rites* (*Liji* 禮記) and the *Doctrine of the Mean* are presented as the words of Confucius,[29] despite the fact that historically, the former was deemed to have been edited and not authored by Confucius, and the latter was ascribed to the sage's grandson Zisi (子思; c. 481–402 BCE). In another instance, a quote from the *Mencius* is introduced as being from Confucius, although the *Mencius* clearly identifies the passage as the words of Mencius himself (*Mengzi yue* 孟子曰).[30] Elsewhere, the text alleges that the expression *tianli liuxing* 天理流行 (the flowing principle of heaven) originates from Confucius, while in fact it does not appear in the classics at all.[31] Such mistakes might be attributed to the fact that the text originated in an oral lecture, a format that lends itself to improvisation and therefore mistakes (although Liang is said to have revised his students' notes of the lectures before publishing the book). They might also simply show the limits of Liang's knowledge of the canon—after all, he claims to have read the classics in their entirety for the first time only four years before presenting his lectures on Eastern and Western Cultures at Peking University.[32] Yet the above examples also epitomize the text's tendency to treat Confucius as a metonym for the entire corpus of the classics and the entire tradition-as-value.

This explains why *Eastern and Western Cultures* often reads one classic in light of another, as when it claims, as we saw above, that the *Changes'* metaphysics represents "the single thread that binds" Confucius's message according to the *Analects*, and this despite the reluctance of the *Analects'* Confucius to speak of things that are beyond one's reach. Given the ultimate purpose of the classics—conveying the spirit of the sage—it is little surprising that the text looks for "single threads" binding them together. A number of notions are in fact treated by the text as keys that unlock the entire meaning of the classics. By grasping the meaning of Confucius's notion of life (*sheng*), for example, it is said that "one can at once understand all the words of the Confucians."[33] Elsewhere, the notions of resoluteness, *ren/*

intuition, and *wu suowei er wei* (無所為而為; acting without finality), along with the rejection of cost-benefit analysis and habits, are made to represent the entire message of the sage.³⁴

Such statements are not only aimed at subsuming the polysemy of the classical canon under the unifying figure of the sage, who acts as a symbolic thread that weaves (*zhi* 織) into one textile everything that is of value in the classics (following the metaphor the *Shuowen jiezi* 說文解字 deploys in its definition of *jing* 經). Although Confucius is certainly the master weaver, with the passage of time his threads have become imperceptible to all but those who read the classics in the way they were meant to be read: with the spirit of the sage. That Liang is able to find the threads that bind the classical corpus together implies that he has reached an intuitive grasp of its message, and thus that he is of one mind with the sage.

Only in one instance does *Eastern and Western Cultures* give a clue as to how Liang achieved an intuitive grasp of the meaning of the classics. "In the summer of the fifth year of the Republic of China [1916]," Liang recalls, "I read through all the Confucian classics [*kongjia jingji* 孔家經籍] at once, and I self-consciously grasped their meaning, on the basis that nothing in the books seemed out of place."³⁵ It remains unclear whether Liang's intuitions evolved through the process of reading the classics or whether they were already significantly developed before the summer of 1916. Although given that this was the first time Liang read through the classics "seriously," as Guy S. Alitto notes,³⁶ we can assume Liang's intuitions were already developed enough that he could grasp the essence of Confucius's message at once, during the short period of a summer.

Regardless of whether Liang is meant to have developed his intuitive abilities independently of the classics or through them, by suggesting that Liang possesses an intuitive grasp of the meaning of the classics, the text implies that he has reached spiritual simultaneity with the sage. This further suggests that the text is meant to be read as the product of a modern sage who, like Confucius, is no longer bound by the sociohistorical limitations of human existence. The figure of the sage thus serves as a conduit through which the text is able to purify itself from the markers of its sociohistorical situatedness.

To secure its attempt at subsuming the authority of the sage, the text must "demonstrate" Liang's spiritual simultaneity with Confucius by enacting the intuitive spirit of the sage. To achieve this goal, the text deploys two closely interrelated discursive techniques. First, by *commenting* on the classics, the text "shows" that Liang has reached a complete understanding of the original message of Confucius hidden in them (the antitradition-as-value). And second, by providing a *genealogy of the way* (*daotong*), the text positions Liang as the ultimate judge of Confucian tradition-as-history.

Performing sagehood

Before addressing the first discursive technique, it is worth noting that most sections of *Eastern and Western Cultures* hardly quote or mention the Confucian classics. Outside the sections on Confucianism, most of the references of the text are to contemporary scholars: Liang's colleagues at Peking University (Li Dazhao, Hu Shi, Chen Duxiu), but also Japanese and Euro-American scholars. The text in fact often defers to a number of "modern authorities" by associating its discourse with them. The text explicitly relates its notion of "will," for example, to Arthur Schopenhauer (1788–1860), and it ties its concept of "intuition" to the philosophy of Henri Bergson. It is significant that in defining the concepts of "will" and "intuition," the text easily could have drawn from discursive resources of the Chinese past. The Buddhist notion of desire, for example, is relatively close to the text's portrayal of will, while Wang Yangming's construal of "innate moral knowledge" (*liangzhi* 良知) shares striking similarities with "intuition" as construed by the text.

The text's explicit appeal to Bergson and Schopenhauer can be regarded as an attempt to link the discourse of the text to European philosophers whose discourse was more likely to be regarded as objective and scientific by readers inscribed in the new episteme of 1920s China.[37] As Guy S. Alitto notes, "the tremendous prestige of Western ideas in post-May Fourth China led traditionalist thinkers of all shades into some strange contortions. Despite their antipathy toward things Western, they seemed to go to great lengths to try to tack the name of a Western thinker or theory onto the ideas of China's past they wished to exonerate. Liang [Shuming] was no exception: he sought to substantiate his theories with "evidence" he found in recent Western intellectual trends."[38] *Eastern and Western Cultures* in fact abounds with references to Euro-American scholarship; references that authorize the text insofar as they are deployed within a historical context that saw the rapid growth of scientism on the one hand, and a rather hasty association of Western discourses with science on the other.[39]

The text's tendency to appeal to modern and "scientific" authorities is however reversed in the sections that deal with Confucianism.[40] In these sections, a significant tonal shift occurs, as references to contemporary scholarship, with the notable exception of Hu Shi (for reasons I hope will become clear in a moment), are for the most part replaced with an important number of quotes from the classics and from figures associated with the long history of Confucianism. Moreover, while it is true that despite its acute attacks on *lizhi*, the text does rely heavily on argumentation and a method that bears the mark of the new scientific interest intellectuals of the early 1920s shared,[41] in the sections devoted to Confucianism, argumentation, while not entirely absent, tends to be supplemented or replaced by a reliance on the authority of the classics, and an approach to these classics that relies heavily on the authority of Liang himself. This is the result, I suggest, of the text's attempt at performing the kind of intuition said to be the core spirit of Confucius.

This can be exemplified by a passage in which the text comments on quotations from the classics. After mentioning that loving those near us to a greater extent than strangers, as Confucius encourages us to do, is an outcome that naturally flows from our intuitions, the text makes the following comments:

> However, the average person seeks an established doctrine, on the basis of which the import of what Confucianism says [regarding the fact that] one "can use a fishing line but not a fishing net; can use a corded arrow but not to shoot at roosting birds" or that "a noble person [*junzi*] stays far away from the kitchen," become invariably obscure.[42] If one uses a fishing line, why not also use a net? And if one should not use a net, then why not also forbid the use of a line? [Similarly], if one uses a corded arrow, why not shoot at roosting birds? And if one should not shoot at roosting birds, why not also forbid the use of a corded arrow? [. . .] The average person wants to reason (*jiangli* 講理); but Confucius does not reason. The average person seeks to make sense of these [statements] (*qiu qi tong* 求其通), while Confucius simply does not! Yet the result is that the average person's sense ultimately does not make sense, while Confucius's lack of sense is extremely sensical. Confucius invariably gave free reign to his intuition; he did not debate with himself, unlike most people who incessantly reason [with themselves].

> 然而一般人總要推尋定理，若照他那意思看，孔家所謂「釣而不綱，弋不射宿」，「君子遠庖廚」未免不通：既要釣何如綱，

既不綱也就莫釣；既要弋就射宿，既不射宿也就莫弋……。一般人是要講理的，孔子是不講理的［；］一般人是求其通的［，］孔子則簡直不通！然而結果一般人之通卻成不通，而孔子之不通則通之至。蓋孔子總任他的直覺，沒有自己打架，而一般人念念講理……。⁴³

This is an important passage, as it establishes that intuitions—which everyone in theory possesses, although in practice they are acute only in the case of sages like Confucius—literally make sense without making sense. This implies that however arbitrary they may sound, the above statements regarding fishing, hunting game, and staying away from the kitchen should be trusted on the authority of the speaker. This explains why the *Analects* and the *Record of Rites* do not provide reasons as to why one should not use fishing nets or enter the kitchen.

In other instances, the text makes it clear that the sage cannot always explain why he does what he does, as intuitions are properly speaking *without reasons* (the heaven inscribed in our nature cannot be pinned down by language, after all). Filial piety, for example, is simply "an intuitive reaction from the son or daughter toward the father and the mother."⁴⁴ Insofar as it is rooted in intuition, filial piety cannot be argued for and defended on the plane of *lizhi*. This goes to show the extent to which the notion of intuition is intricately related to the authority of the sage, which cannot be debated on the basis of reasoned arguments.

Of further interest for our purpose is the fact that in the above passage, the text does not elucidate why the use of fishing nets or corded arrows when aimed at roosting birds is forbidden by the *Analects*. The text's comments are targeted not at the explicit message conveyed by the quotes, but at the intuitive spirit that is assumed to justify their presence in the classics despite their apparent arbitrariness. By refraining from providing reasons as to why Confucius does what he does, *Eastern and Western Cultures* directly parallels the message of the classics and presents Liang as the mirror image of the sage. Liang performs the intuitive authority of the sage as much as he comments on it.

Commentaries on the classics often assume the role of metacommentaries on the text and its author. They allow the text to depict Liang as someone who possesses an unmediated access to the ultimate meaning of the classics, without the need to appeal to exegesis or historical commentaries. Examples of this hermeneutics of immediacy can be found throughout the sections devoted to Confucius's philosophy of life. In a passage meant to provide textual support for the contentious claim that Confucius meant "intuition" by "*ren*," for example, the text quotes the following section from *Analects* 17:21, in which Confucius converses with Zai Wo (宰我), also known as Zai Yu (宰予; 522–458 BCE), a disciple who questioned the necessity of mourning one's parents for a period of three years:

> The Master said, "Would you, then, feel at ease [*an* 安] eating your rice and wearing your finery [during the three years of mourning]?" "Yes. I would." "If you are able to feel at ease doing so, then by all means you should do it. The gentleman in mourning finds no relish in good food, no pleasure in music, and no comforts in his own home. That is why he does not eat his rice and wear his finery. But if you would feel at ease doing so, then by all means you should." After Zai Wo had left, the Master said, "How lacking in *ren* [仁] he is!"
>
> 子曰:「食夫稻,衣夫錦,於女安乎?」曰:「安。」「女安則為之!夫君子之居喪,食旨不甘,聞樂不樂,居處不安,故不為也。今女安,則為之!」宰我出。子曰:「予之不仁也!」[45]

Although the *Analects* 17:21 concludes with a quote in which Confucius gives two reasons that explain why Zai Wo is lacking in *ren*, as we will see in a moment, the text omits it. Instead, it proposes its own interpretation of Confucius's ultimate rationale in passing such a judgment on Zai Wo. In such a manner, Liang—that is, not the historical Liang but the "Liang" that emerges from the commentaries themselves—effectively substitutes the role of interpreter or judge assigned to Confucius in the *Analects*.

The text comments:

> The meaning of "*ren*" [in this passage] must be entirely sought in [the notion of] "feeling of ease" [*an*]. In this circumstance, Zai Wo feels at ease, yet Confucius says that he lacks in *ren*; so it follows from this that feeling ill at ease is *ren*. Is it not the case that [in Zai Wo,] "feeling at ease" refers to the poverty of [his] feelings and the interruption of [his use of] intuition, while "feeling ill at ease" denotes but an abundance of feelings and an acute intuition? For instance, it is abundantly clear that the heart of compassion [*ceyin zhi xin* 惻隱之心] and the heart of shame [*xiuwu zhi xin* 羞惡之心] are intuitive. Why is it [then]

that in a particular circumstance, some people feel compassion and shame while others do not? In every case, the difference is only that one feels at ease and is oblivious, while the other feels ill at ease. Being at ease or not; does it not depend once again on the acuity of one's intuitions?

這個「仁」就完全要在那「安」字上求之。宰我他於這樁事心安，孔子就說他不仁，那麼，不安就是仁嘍。所謂安，不是情感薄直覺頓嗎？而所謂不安，不是情感厚直覺敏銳是什麼？像所謂惻隱、羞惡之心，其為直覺是很明的；為什麼對於一樁事情，有人就惻隱，有人就不惻隱，有人就羞惡，有人就不羞惡？不過都是一個安然不覺，一個就覺得不安的分別罷了。這個安不安，不又是直覺敏銳的分別嗎？[46]

This passage concludes by asserting that "since Confucianism fully wants to give free reign to intuition, the only things that matter are the acuity and limpidity of intuition."[47]

The above commentary proceeds first by linking the notion of "*ren*" with that of "feeling ill at ease" before equating the latter with intuition. However, the notion of intuition is not introduced by finding textual evidence that "feeling ill at ease" means intuition, either from this passage or other passages of the *Analects*. Instead, the text appeals to "the heart of compassion" and "the heart of shame," notions it borrows from *Mencius* 2A.6 and interprets without looking at the textual context from which they are abstracted. Liang does not look for a textual proof that "feeling ill at ease" means "acute intuition" in the *Analects*; he provides us with a final judgment on the meaning of the passage. This effectively establishes a parallel between Liang and Confucius, in the sense that Liang's ability to judge the intentions of Confucius mirrors Confucius's own ability to judge the character of Zai Wo in the *Analects*. Both judgments rely heavily on the assumed authority of the speaker.

As noted above, the text's quote from *Analects* 17:21 leaves out Confucius's concluding remarks, in which he proposes two reasons as to why Zai Wo is lacking in *ren*: first, he is deficient in filial piety, and second, he fails to adhere to a custom "observed throughout the Empire."[48] This omission, which is at odds with the text's implicit goal of excavating the original meaning of Confucius, might be due to the fact that the reasons provided by the *Analects* cannot be easily tied to the notion of intuition (especially the second one). This gives a sense of how freely Liang interprets the text based on his own intuition, and how comfortable he is with replacing Confucius's judgments with his own.

Something similar is at work in the text's attempt at finding textual support for its notion of resoluteness (*gang*), which it does by commenting on *Analects* 5:11.[49] Regardless of whether its reading of this passage is accurate or not, it is worth noting that of the four passages in which the character *gang* 剛 appears in the *Analects* only, the text limits its comments to only one of them. Yet in another passage, *Analects* 17:8, the sage observes that unless it is matched with a love of learning, to be fond of *gang* "is liable to lead to indiscipline."[50] That the text omits such passages suggests it is more interested in finding legitimacy for its reading of *gang* by linking it to Confucius than it is in excavating the original meaning of the term. This does not imply the *historical* Liang was attempting to trick his readers or impose notions onto the classics that are at odds with them. Whether Liang truly believed this was the original import of *gang* in the *Analects* is something we can never ascertain, although I find no particular reason to doubt that he did. What we can extrapolate from Liang's approach to the classics, as constructed in the discourse of the text, is that it betrays a greater interest in having the classics comment on him (*liujing zhu wo* 六經註我) than in his commenting on the classics (*wo zhu liujing* 我註六經).

To support its understanding of *gang* and *ren*, the text does not provide linguistic (what was the meaning of *gang* and *ren* in the pre-Qin period?), intra-textual (how are *gang* and *ren* used in other passages of the *Analects*?), or inter-textual (how do other texts of the same period use *gang* and *ren*?) evidence. This is partly explained by the fact that *Eastern and Western Cultures* is not a work of textual exegesis, and Liang was not trained in the Qing philological tradition (*kaojuxue* 考據學), as he himself makes clear.[51] Despite this fact, the text could have nevertheless defended its readings of the classics by appealing to previous commentaries and the work done by Qing philologists.[52] Given that the text portrays the entire Confucian tradition-as-history as deviating from the original message of the sage, however, it is far from surprising that it does not. Moreover, insofar as Liang is meant to perform the spirit-ideal[53] of Confucius in reading the classics, which suggests he is of one mind with the sage, it is little surprising that the text presents him as having access to the ultimate message of the classics in an unmediated fashion, without the need of exegesis and commentaries.[54]

Such hermeneutics of immediacy allows for authority to flow back and forth between the contemporary text and the classics. The contemporary text first projects an absolute form of authority onto the classical canon before subsuming that authority by proposing final readings of the canon and by reshaping itself in the image of the classics. Finally, by presenting its author as having reached intuitions that escape the grasp of reason and that are meant to be the natural expression of heaven in us, the contemporary text can immunize itself from competing hermeneutics or interpretations of the classics. After all, even if we find, in the commentarial and philological traditions, interpretations of classical passages that are diametrically opposed to those of *Eastern and Western Cultures*, this should not, in theory, invalidate the text's reading of the classics, insofar as the object of its reading (the mind of Confucius) differs from that of the commentarial and philological traditions (the classics).

Instituting a genealogy of the way

Being of one mind with the sage, Liang can peruse through the classics, understand what binds them together, and identify apocryphal passages that are out of place within the general architecture of the canon. The text judges, for example, that the passage on the Great Harmony (*datong* 大同) in the "Liyun" (禮運) chapter of the *Record of Rites* is incongruous with the rest of the classics. Without addressing questions of authorship and composition from an exegetical perspective, Liang is presented as being in a position to judge the inauthenticity of a passage on the basis of his intuitive grasp of the "single thread that binds" the entire corpus together. The text readily admits, however, that Liang's lack of training in Qing philological research makes it difficult for him to *prove* this point (he can only *intuit* it). But the text does find support for his conclusion in a letter addressed to Chen Duxiu by Wu Yu (吳虞; 1872–1949), a fervent opponent of Confucianism and frequent collaborator of *New Youth*. In this letter, Wu provides three proofs that the notion of "Great Harmony" and the discourse surrounding it have their origin in Laozi (老子; n.d.).[55] This is a rare passage in which the text provides exegetical proofs that Liang's intuitive interpretation of the classics is indeed reliable.

By discarding the section on the Great Harmony, Wu Yu had sought to delegitimize Kang Youwei, who had made the notion of "Great Harmony" a cornerstone of his reinterpretation of Confucianism. *Eastern and Western Cultures* shares this goal, as, following the quote of Wu's letter, the text condemns Kang's utopian vision as a "vulgar" (*bi* 鄙) misinterpretation of Confucius rooted in subjective perspectives (*siqing* 私情). To avoid being subjected to similar criticisms as those advanced toward Kang by May Fourth thinkers, the text is extremely careful to distinguish its project from that of Kang, which centers on the establishment of a Confucian religion built in the image of the Christian church. The text provides a virulent critique of the financial interests at work in the church of Chen Huanzhang (陳煥章; 1880–1933), a "disciple" of Kang's. By reshaping Confucianism in the image of Christianity, the text decries, Kang and his clique adopted a vision of Confucianism as superficial as those of Mozi (墨子; c. 470—c. 391 BCE) and Westerners.[56]

Interestingly, the text also associates Mozi with Hu Shi, whose praise for Mozi's utilitarianism is explained by the fact that Hu was a pragmatist.[57] As mentioned above, the whole section on Confucianism in *Eastern and Western Cultures* makes few references to contemporary scholars, with the significant exception of Hu Shi, whose perspective on Confucianism is repeatedly criticized as failing to understand its true essence.[58] This is due to the fact that Hu, like Mozi, makes use of a calculating reason that explains things based on their uses. While Hu and Mozi incessantly ask the "why" (*weishenme* 為什麼) of things, Confucians act without having any reason, aim, or finality (*wu suowei er wei* 無所為而為).[59] To seek for reasons in the classics is therefore to significantly distort their meaning. The significance of Confucius's words, after all, can only be grasped intuitively.

In these passages, Hu Shi provides the text with a foil against which its own position can be firmly established as a genuinely Chinese and Confucian one. Mozi, in this discourse, is explicitly associated with, and often serves as a stand-in for, the Western will characterized by an excessive use of instrumental rationality.[60] The figure of Mozi, who has historically played the role, along with Yang Zhu (楊朱), of the archenemy of Confucian orthodoxy,[61] allows the text to oppose both the Confucian religionists, represented by Kang Youwei, and their May Fourth rivals, represented by Hu Shi, by depicting them as westernized thinkers who misunderstood the original meaning of Confucius. Furthermore, by associating Kang and Hu with Mozi, the text can present its disagreement with them as a re-enactment of the pre-Qin rivalry between the "schools" of Mohism and Confucianism, and in the process imply that Liang is the sole spokesperson of *genuine* Confucianism in modern China.

Liang's ability to pass final judgments regarding who has understood the core message of Confucius and who has failed to do so is not only deployed at the expense of contemporaries of Liang; it is also directed toward Confucian tradition-as-history. As we saw in the first chapter, the text upholds a rather idiosyncratic view of the history of Confucianism, going so far as to reject the entirety of its evolution as a failure to live up to the founder's spirit-ideal. This construal of the history of Confucianism implies that Liang is the sole direct inheritor of the way proposed by Confucius, the transmission of which had remained essentially broken the entire time, from the death of Confucius until Liang's reappropriation of the *dao*. Undoubtedly, Liang esteems some Neo-Confucian thinkers for their ability to partially intuit the *dao*, although they were ultimately unable to appreciate the full extent of Confucius's message. Liang, by contrast, was able not only to grasp the true message of the sage, but also to situate it in the proper framework of teleological history. Liang thus can be portrayed as the first sage who understood the proper means to bridge the gap between ideality (tradition-as-value) and reality (history) in such a way as to allow Confucianism to be historically realized.[62]

This implicit portrayal of Liang finds legitimacy in various judgments the text passes on Confucian tradition-as-history—judgments that ultimately amount to a genealogy of the way (*daotong*).[63] The text's narrative of Confucian tradition-as-history goes back to the transition from the Warring States period to the Qin empire and ends with the late Qing—just before Liang's revival of the way. As we saw above, the text upholds a strongly critical attitude toward Han exegesis, insofar as it treats the classics as dead artifacts of the past. Finding support in Wang Zhong's (汪中; 1745–1794) scholarship, the text suggests this development is in large part due to Xunzi (荀子; c. 310–c. after 238 BCE) (the text actually uses Xunzi's honorific title, Xun Qing 荀卿, which downplays his importance as an ancient master or *zi* 子). Xunzi misunderstood the true spirit of Confucius and only conveyed the rites. Although the rites are a manifestation of Confucius's spirit, they are merely an external and formal one. Because of Xunzi's influence, the overemphasis on the formal and superficial at the expense of the innermost message of the sage became a mainstay of Han scholarship.[64]

During the Three Kingdoms and Wei-Jin periods, the Confucian way rescinded further, being overshadowed by the "indulgent thought" exhibited in the "Yang Zhu" (楊朱) chapter of the *Liezi* (列子), for example.[65] In the Tang dynasty, the spread of Buddhism encountered no opposition from the Confucians, with the exception of Han Yu, who ultimately failed to bring the *dao* back to life because of his inability to comprehend Confucius. Then came the Song revival, toward which the text remains ambiguous. On the one hand, the text recognizes and commends the effort of Song Neo-Confucians to return to the original conception of life of Confucianism. Although they could only grasp a fraction of it, they nevertheless put Confucian studies back on the right path.[66] In one instance, the text even admits that Zhu Xi's commentaries, although not particularly imaginative, "remain faithful to the original meaning of Confucius."[67] Yet on the other hand, the text maintains that Song Neo-Confucianism ultimately deviated from Confucius's teaching, since it overemphasized the internal realm of the individual at the expense of the external world, and it based its understanding of the internal sphere on an external search for principles (*qiongli yu wai* 窮理於外).[68]

The Ming Neo-Confucians did better on this front. Wang Yangming dispelled the Song tendency to stress the external search for principle, replacing it instead with an intuitive approach. (The text here seems to equate its notion of intuition with Wang's concept of "innate moral knowledge" or *liangzhi*.) Yet despite Wang's attempt at correcting Zhu Xi's shortcomings, he was not entirely successful, as he also tended to neglect the external at the expense of the internal. His followers of the Taizhou school—Liang is particularly enthusiastic toward Wang Gen—came closer to a true understanding of Confucius. The text goes so far as to say that "the attitude toward life of Confucius is considerably revealed" by them, notably because, unlike their predecessors, they did emphasize putting the way of life of Confucius in practice in the external realm.[69]

The text's narration of Confucian tradition-as-history concludes by decrying Qing philological research, which is construed as a return to the exaggerated stress on form that rendered the classics lifeless during the Han. Moreover, under the Qing, Chinese society became overburdened by constraining rules having their origin in an overemphasis on intellect and doctrines that started in the Song. Only Dai Zhen managed to sow the seeds of a Confucian renaissance, although, because of the limited scope of his influence, his renaissance died in its infancy. Finally, Kang Youwei and Liang Qichao did attempt to reconcile their consideration for the classics (the New Texts) with a growing attention to the way of life of Confucius, although their understanding of the latter was ultimately in complete disaccord with the original attitude of the sage.[70]

Of Confucian tradition-as-history, only the Taizhou school—by which the text essentially refers to Wang Gen—and perhaps also to some extent Dai Zhen—although the text has little to say about him—have somewhat understood the way of life of Confucius. Yet at times, the text attacks Song-Ming Neo-Confucians as a whole, mainly because they failed to comprehend that Confucius did not have a fixed doctrine or dogma, but simply encouraged his students to follow their innermost intuitions. Although the text admits the Ming Neo-Confucians did better than their Song counterparts on this front, they nevertheless also tended to take particular principles (*daoli* 道理) as immutable and unalterable (*tianjing diyi* 天經地義).⁷¹ In doing so, they seriously misconstrued the spirit of Confucius, for whom, according to the text, "to establish that this is good and that is bad, that this is true and that false is in fact a huge mistake!"⁷²

By portraying Confucius's message as empty of content, as a spirit that must simply be embodied and performed, the text can depict the entire Confucian tradition-as-history as deviating from the original source, precisely because it is said to possess a content; a fixed doctrine. Of course, insofar as *Eastern and Western Cultures*' Confucianism is not entirely devoid of content itself, not much prevents it from being subjected to a similar criticism. By presenting the message passed down from Confucius to Liang as a natural way of life, however, the text can answer such criticism by arguing that its Confucianism is not the product of arrested views but of the implementation of the natural spirit of intuition. Such rhetoric of naturalization plays a central role in the text's attempt at rejecting tradition-as-history while making of its own tradition-as-value the only orthodox position.

Despite its radical critique of Confucian tradition-as-history, however, the text often supports Liang's performed understanding of Confucianism by appealing to quotes from, and references to, the very Confucian figures that are said to have deviated from Confucius's way of life. For example, the assertion that Confucius's *ren* ultimately refers to the kind of intuition the text promotes is first and foremost supported by an extensive commentary of *Analects* 17:21, as noted above. Yet the section on *ren* also quotes from the *Mencius* three times and the writings of Neo-Confucian scholars Wang Gen, Chen Baisha (陳白沙; 1428–1500), and Nie Shuangjiang (聶雙江; 1487–1563) once each.⁷³ This might be explained by the fact that the text finds better support for its reinterpretation of *ren* as intuition in the concepts of "inherent mind" (*benxin* 本心) and "innate moral knowledge" (*liangzhi* 良知), which are central to these texts, as opposed to comments on *ren* made in the *Analects*, which might not support such an interpretation as straightforwardly. But what matters for our purpose is that although the text theoretically rejects post-Confucius Confucianism as a degeneration from the pure origin, it does authorize its discourse with quotes from, and references to, texts written by the very historical figures it describes as having fallen short of a true understanding of the sage.

The method by which *Eastern and Western Cultures* appeals to the authority of Confucian tradition-as-history to legitimize its discourse thus appears to be at odds with the iconoclastic rejection of tradition-as-history in the very discourse it is said to authorize. This tension is revealing of the difficult task at hand for the text: to dissociate its Confucianism from that of May Fourth, it discursively rejects Confucian tradition-as-history, but in a bid to situate itself squarely within the Confucian camp, claiming that Liang is of one mind with the sage certainly helps, but it might not be sufficient to establish without doubt that Liang is indeed a legitimate Confucian. Authoritatively quoting from, and referring to, the entire corpus of tradition-as-history to show that Liang's views are not fully at odds with it can complement the authority the text seeks in the figure of Confucius. This does not negate the fact that *Eastern and Western Cultures* remains highly iconoclastic when it comes to tradition-as-history, but it does qualify the text's iconoclasm as one that seeks legitimacy by paradoxically situating itself in the very tradition-as-history it rejects. At work in these claims is an attempt to draw legitimacy from tradition-as-history while hiding this indebtedness by claiming to have entirely transcended the limitations of history.

Textual authority

The ambiguous rapport the text entertains with Confucian tradition-as-history is revealing of the complex gymnastics it must perform to reinstate the authority of tradition and ascribe it to the modern sage Liang, while avoiding relying too heavily on the authority of tradition-as-history in doing so, which would subject the text to the attacks of the progressive intellectuals of the time. This ambiguous rapport is also evocative of a tension between transhistoricity and historicity that is inherent in any antitradition. This can be clarified by taking a closer look at the inner workings of textual authority.

As noted in the introduction, textual authority is something quite precarious, insofar as it rests on a social dialectic of recognition over which texts can never exert full control. "An essentially *social* (rather than individual) phenomenon," as Alexandre Kojève notes, authority is "necessarily a *recognized* Authority; not to recognize an Authority is to negate it, and thereby destroy it."[74] Authority is not the property of texts themselves; it is imparted to them by the reading community. Of course, readers do not impart authority in a state of absolute freedom. Textual authorization is highly codified and depends on a variety of factors, including the social status and reputation of the author, the standing of the publishing house, the reception of the text by established authorities in the field, the ability of the text to deploy discursive tropes recognizable as legitimate by the readers, and so forth. This entails that the success of *Eastern and Western Cultures*' attempt at ascribing to itself the authority of tradition-as-value largely depends on factors over which the text and its author ultimately do not have full control.

Yet this is not to say that texts have no control over their own reception. There are a number of discursive techniques that can help texts present themselves to readers as already "possessing" authority. Texts have a vested interest in deploying such discursive techniques, as positing their authority as a fait accompli allows them to hide from the readers' view the fact that it is ultimately they, as a collective, who decide whether the text's claim to authority should be accepted as legitimate or not.[75] By inscribing within the text a source of authority (Confucius, the Buddha, etc.) that is expected to be recognized by the target readership and by having it recognize the legitimacy of the text's claim to authority, a text can internalize the dialectic of recognition *within its discourse* and thus hide the social dialectic of recognition between reader and text that is in effect responsible for instituting the authority of the text. It is of course imperative that the source of authority established in the text be regarded by readers as possessing an insight into truth and the good that far surpasses their own. This way, readers will be more inclined to accept that their role in recognizing the authority of the text is insignificant compared with that of the source of authority internalized within the text.

Inscribing sources of authority within one's text thus allows one to deflect the object toward which the readers' recognition is directed. The authority the reader is asked to recognize is no longer that of the text of a contemporary author whose reputation is precariously subject to social factors. Instead, it is that of a historical or legendary figure—oftentimes securely located in an ancient past of which little is known—whose authority has been accepted and recognized for centuries. Of course, readers must also recognize that the text's claim to already "possess" the recognition of the historical or legendary figure is legitimate. But if the text is successful in deploying discursive techniques that "demonstrate" the legitimacy of its authority, and if such discursive techniques have a long history and because of that long history tend to be viewed by readers as valid and unproblematic, then the likelihood that the text's claim to already possess the recognition of authoritative figures of the past will be accepted by readers significantly increases.

Coming back to *Eastern and Western Cultures*, there is little doubt that Confucius serves as a source of authority through which the text's program and its relation to the past—and therefore also its iconoclasm—can be sanctioned. By equating its program built around the notion of intuition with the message of Confucius, and by portraying Liang as embodying the intuitive spirit of the sage, the text effectively attempts to fuse the authority of Liang with that of the sage. Commenting authoritatively on the classics and the history of Confucianism serves as a performative proof of Liang's spiritual simultaneity with Confucius. This is done positively when it comes to the classics—Liang accesses the true meaning of the classics because he is of one mind with the sage—and negatively when it comes to history—Liang must have understood the core meaning of Confucianism if he can recognize how later Confucians deviated from it. Tradition-as-history here serves as a foil in contrast to which Liang can be relocated in a sagely realm of transhistoricity.

Readers who recognize the authority of Confucius as legitimate—and we can assume many still did in early Republican China—would thus be inclined to also recognize that of Liang, provided they accept the text's claim that Liang has indeed achieved spiritual simultaneity with the sage. The recognition the text asks of the reader is a *leap of faith*—faith in the veracity of the homology between Liang and Confucius, and faith in the text's claim to belong to a transhistorical realm of natural sagehood instead of that of history. Given that sagehood expresses itself through intuitions that are without reasons, the text cannot persuade readers through reasoned arguments as to why they should trust that Liang's intuitions are indeed what the text claims they are: the "proof" that Liang is of one mind with Confucius. The readers' willingness to perform the leap of faith asked of them depends heavily on the text's ability to reclaim, in the eyes of the readers, the authority of the spirit of Confucius that speaks through the classics.

In its bid to secure the readers' leap of faith, it is imperative that the text does not appear in any way concerned with its own reception, as exhibiting such explicit concerns would relocate the text in the mundane realm of social recognition and break the spell of its transhistoricity. Sages, after all, do not bother with concerns as mundane as the reception of their writings. The text must therefore seek the recognition of the readers, but do so in a disinterested manner that is worthy of a sage. Only by hiding its mundane entanglements in the May Fourth discursive field can the text secure the readers' leap of faith.

To do so, *Eastern and Western Cultures* essentially relies on the rhetoric of naturalization discussed above. By couching the spirit-ideal transferred from Confucius to Liang (and the authority that comes with it) in terms of an intuition that is entirely *natural*, the text seeks to relocate its discourse in a zone that is immune to contestation. The figure of Confucius serves as a conduit through which ideas enter as the product of an author situated in a discursive arena of competing claims and exit as naturalized inclinations rooted in heaven. Not unlike how naturalizing gender has historically served the purpose, and continues to serve the purpose, of hiding the social construction of gender, naturalizing one's discourse can help in hiding the important role social acts of recognition play in the process of providing such discourse with legitimacy. By appealing to a rhetoric of naturalization, texts can secure the recognition of readers without making it apparent that they want to do so and without revealing to readers the significant role they play in the process of authorization.

The rhetoric of naturalization, closely tied to the text's idealism,[76] is instrumental in hiding the text's indebtedness to history. And yet, to ensure that readers recognize the discursive techniques it employs as legitimate, the text must use historically established discursive techniques to which readers are accustomed, as readers tend to be more distrustful of new discursive techniques that appear contrived and interested. Discursive techniques that have a long history, by contrast, tend to be taken for granted by readers and authors, to such an extent that they are no longer regarded as discursive *techniques*, but simply appear to be what a *normal* (Confucian) text ought to look like. On the surface, *Eastern and Western Cultures* looks nothing like a "normal" Confucian text. But when it describes the essence of Confucianism, it reverts to a number of discursive techniques that do have a long history in Neo-Confucianism.

Neo-Confucian methods of reading

Much of the text's hermeneutics, of its assumptions regarding the classics and how they should be read, are inherited (consciously or not) from Neo-Confucian sources. Although it is outside the scope of the present research to trace the multiple resources from which *Eastern and Western Cultures* draws, a short discussion of Zhu Xi's hermeneutics will suffice to show the extent to which the text partakes in historically established discursive traditions—traditions that help the text secure the leap of faith of the readers, but that also threaten to relocate it in mundane tradition-as-history.

Not unlike Liang, Zhu Xi held a negative view of Han exegesis. In the preface to his commentary on the *Doctrine of the Mean*, Zhu explicitly states that the goal in reading the classics is not to "arrange and annotate" them, as the Han exegetes had done, but "to recover the ideas of the sages."[77] Zhu saw the classics as a medium through which the way was made accessible, but only to those who were able to pass "through words to the ultimate reality of the Way to which those words refer."[78] To do so, Daniel K. Gardner notes, Zhu "placed a great deal of value on the autonomy of the individual in the reading process."[79] This does not mean that readers should not consult the commentaries. But they should first try making sense of the classics by themselves, and only refer to commentaries, toward which a critical attitude should be adopted, when the meaning of certain passages remains obscure after several readings.[80]

Elucidated in his method of reading (*dushufa* 讀書法), Zhu's hermeneutics makes it clear that the ancients and the contemporaries share the same potential, stored in human nature, to develop a sagely mind. Reading the classics therefore is not intended as a means to fill an inherent lack in the human condition. On the contrary, by reading the way that speaks through the classics, what one does is to activate a potential inborn in all of us. By familiarizing oneself with the classics, the goal is for the mind to become a mirror of the way of the sages that speaks through the classics.[81]

While Liang is described as having found in the metaphysics of constant change and in the intuitive approach to it the "single thread that binds together" the message of the sage, Zhu Xi narrowed the "reality of the Way" down to a short sixteen-character passage from the "Counsels of Yu the Great" (*Dayu mo* 大禹謨) section of the *Documents* (*Shujing* 書經).[82] The passage reads: "The Human mind is precarious; the mind of *dao* is barely perceptible. Be discerning and single-minded. Hold fast to the mean" (人心惟危, 道心惟微, 惟精惟一, 允執厥中).[83] This message had been passed down, Zhu thought, from Yao (堯) to Shun (舜) and Yu (禹), and later Confucius, Yan Hui (顏回; c. 521–481 BCE), Zeng Shen (曾參; 505–435 BCE), Zisi—whom Zhu thought had written the *Doctrine of the Mean* to preserve the transmission—and finally Mencius. The way was then lost for more than a thousand years before being revived by Zhou Dunyi and the Cheng brothers.

The general structure of Zhu's hermeneutics bears striking similarities to *Eastern and Western Cultures'*. First, Zhu claims to have grasped the essential core of Confucianism, which he sums up in a sixteen-character passage. Then, based on this understanding, he performs his grasp of the essence of tradition by providing final judgments, in the form of commentaries, on the meaning of the classics. Zhu even goes so far as to produce his own version of the canon, the Four Books, which he claims are better suited, if read with the help of his own commentaries, to convey the core message of Confucianism.[84] Having performed his access to the truth of Confucianism,[85] Zhu then sets out to judge the entire history of Confucianism, identifying those who are securely located in the transmission of the *dao* (Zisi, Mencius, etc.) and, by implication, those who are not (Xunzi, Dong Zhongshu, etc.). Finally, as Hoyt Cleveland Tillman puts it, "Zhu uniquely and boldly construed the tradition to culminate with himself."[86] While this remains implicit in his preface to the *Doctrine of the Mean*, it is asserted more explicitly in other contexts, such as a list of orthodox Confucians Zhu drew in 1194, in which "he announced that he had come into contact with 'the conveyance of the [*dao*].'"[87]

By excluding Han figures such as Dong Zhongshu (董仲舒; 179–104 BCE) from the genealogy, Zhu, not unlike Liang, sought to immunize his Confucianism from that of the Han, which had become too closely intertwined with the affairs of the court. Ironically, Zhu's own commentaries on the Four Books would soon become the new orthodoxy in which young men were formed to pass the imperial examination and climb up the social ladder at the top of which stood the court. In this context, some Ming Neo-Confucians borrowed the discursive technique of the genealogy of the way Zhu had used to exclude the Han exegetes and applied it to Zhu himself. Wang Yangming, for example, accepted Zhu's contention that the way had been revived in the Song by Zhou Dunyi and the Cheng brothers, but also included Lu Xiangshan (陸象山; 1139–1193) in his genealogy. As Thomas A. Wilson notes, Wang thought this new inclusion "legitimated his own teachings," which were soon integrated into the genealogy by Wang's followers.[88]

Zhu's genealogy of the way incorporates both Confucians who received the transmission from their teachers (e.g., Yan Hui, Zeng Shen, Zisi, Mencius, and Zhu Xi himself[89]) and Confucians who accessed the *dao* without the help of a teacher (e.g., Confucius, Zhou Dunyi). It is in this latter group of Confucians that an iconoclastic potential resides—a potential further radicalized in Wang Yangming. Apart from serving the purpose of creating a new orthodoxy,[90] Zhu's genealogy of the way also functions as an antitradition: as the only tradition allowing human beings to transcend the limitations of time and place.

By discursively rejecting Confucian tradition-as-history, *Eastern and Western Cultures* establishes a radicalized genealogy that entirely does away with the need to posit intermediaries between the ancient sages and the contemporary. While in Zhu Xi the way of the ancient sages had at least been partially transmitted through the conduit of history, in *Eastern and Western Cultures* tradition-as-value finds itself entirely purified from any connection with history. The text is therefore far from the first to define Confucianism as an antitradition, although it is perhaps one of the most radical in fully activating the potential of this antitradition.

Although brief and necessarily incomplete, the above discussion of Zhu Xi's hermeneutics and genealogy of the way goes to show how *Eastern and Western Cultures* recycles a number of discursive tropes already present in Neo-Confucianism. This does not mean that Zhu and Liang's hermeneutics and genealogies of the way do not differ in important ways. Zhu certainly places a greater emphasis on the commentarial tradition, and he does not take Confucius to be the only true sage of the ancient period. Moreover, it should be noted that the similarities in their hermeneutics and genealogies do not necessarily entail that Zhu *directly* influenced Liang. By highlighting some of the similarities between them, my aim is to show that *Eastern and Western Cultures* does *partake in* a number of established discursive traditions, some of which were already in place during the Song.

It might be of importance, at this juncture, to reiterate that the above description of the text's attempt at re-establishing the authority of tradition, at subsuming it, and at securing the readers' recognition of its own authority is not meant to describe the *intentions* of the author. Whether Liang intended to deploy the discursive techniques I highlight or not and whether he deployed them for the purposes I suggest can never be ascertained. I find it highly unlikely, however, that what this chapter describes reflects the intentions of Liang in preparing his lectures. Instead of describing the discursive processes I explain in this chapter as the product of an author who intentionally borrows from various traditional resources to establish his authority, I find it more likely that established discursive practices *imposed themselves on Liang* because of his main goal (re-establishing the value of Confucianism within the May Fourth discursive milieu). What this chapter describes are the inner workings of such discursive practices; *not a process whereby Liang would have intentionally manipulated his readers into recognizing his authority as a modern sage.* If manipulation there is, it is in the historical discursive traditions in which the text *inserts itself*.[91]

Although in the discursive content of the text Confucian tradition-as-history is rejected, the form through which this rejection is performed partakes in *historical* antitraditions (by which I refer to discursive antitraditions that have taken place in history, in contrast to antitraditions-as-history, which refer to antitraditions established in the discourse of the text). The tension between the text's rejection of tradition-as-history and its use of historical antitraditions to legitimize its discourse is revealing of the need, inherent in antitraditions, of finding legitimacy for one's claim to transhistoricity in discursive means that are historically established and that can therefore be more readily recognized by readers as valid.

The text's claim to transhistoricity must find legitimacy in *historical* discursive techniques that cannot but challenge this legitimacy by laying bare the very historicity of transhistorical discourses. The condition of possibility of transhistorical textuality, in other words, is also its condition of impossibility. In light of this challenge, the value of the iconoclastic discursive techniques the text recycles from historical antitraditions is also that they can help the text hide the historical indebtedness of its discourse by performing an iconoclastic rejection of the very tradition from which it borrows (i.e., tradition-as-history).

Conclusion

Eastern and Western Cultures' rapport with the authority of tradition is shaped by a tension between transhistoricity and historicity, between transcending tradition and partaking of it. On the one hand, the text seeks to situate itself in the sagely realm of transhistorical naturalness, but on the other, it cannot do so successfully unless it also positions itself in the discursive milieu and unless it draws from traditional discursive techniques that buttress its claim to transhistoricity. Traces of the text's historicity thus continuously undermine its attempt at transposing itself in the realm of transhistoricity. It is only by hiding such traces that the text can secure the leap of faith of the readers that is responsible for providing the text's claim to transhistorical authority with recognition. Moreover, the very fact that the text's claim to sageliness must be recognized by readers to be successful must also be hidden from the readers' view, because the readers' acknowledgment of the significance of the social act of recognition would threaten to relocate the text in the mundane realm of the social. In sum, both the text's historicity and its reliance on social acts of recognition must be hidden from the view of readers if its attempt at relocating itself in the realm of transhistoricity is to be successful.

Discursive antitraditions are remarkably powerful tools that can reconcile the tension within such a difficult task by (1) claiming that one's tradition is the only one that transcends history and tradition, (2) by strengthening such claim by appealing to the authority of established traditions, and finally (3) by hiding one's indebtedness to such established traditions by discursively rejecting them as deviating from the true transhistorical core of the only tradition that remains of any value. What antitraditions allow for is a fusion of the authority of eternity (represented by heaven in *Eastern and Western Cultures*) with that of tradition, but one that makes it possible to conceal the mundane fact that one upholds a tradition because it is one's own. This is achieved by dressing this tradition up in the garments of eternity, undoubtedly, but also by deploying an iconoclastic discourse that pre-emptively disarms any attempt at tying one's tradition down to contingent historical factors.

The text systematically negates and hides the historicity of its Confucianism by deploying iconoclastic discursive techniques. Three examples will suffice to make this point. First, the historicity of the classics threatens to undermine the text's claim that they convey a spirit unbound by time and place. This explains why the text draws a sharp distinction between the historicity of the classics—as mere artifacts of the past—and the spirit of the sage the text excavates from them. It is not surprising that the text rejects exegetical approaches to the classics that tend to historicize them.[92] Second, it is imperative that the text draws a sharp distinction between the spirit of Confucius and Confucian tradition-as-history, as any association between the two would relegate spirit to the mundane realm of history—and not of any history, but the very history May Fourth iconoclasts mostly succeeded in presenting as cannibalistic (to use Lu Xun's metaphor). And finally, it is also of importance that the indebtedness of the text's discursive techniques to historical traditions remains hidden from the view of readers, as the text must imperatively be read as the product of a sage who simply gave free reign to his intuitive judgments, and not a skillful author who recycled established discursive techniques from history.

In all three cases, the text's rhetoric of naturalization plays a central role in relocating the text in the realm of the transhistorical while hiding the very historicity of its discourse. A transhistorical and natural authority is first projected by the text onto the figure of Confucius before it is reclaimed by the text through a hermeneutics that reshapes Liang Shuming in the mirror image of the sage. This allows for the text to hide its own historicity—Liang is simply meant to let the mind of heaven of the sage speaks through him—but also to hide the social dimension of the text. It is significant that the text should present Confucius as acting without finality, as it is precisely this lack of finality that readers must recognize in *Eastern and Western Cultures* for the text to appear truly unconcerned by its own reception and hide from the readers' view the central role they play in recognizing the authority of the text. Also of significance is the fact that the text portrays Confucius as having naturally intuited the transhistorical value of certain aspects of past culture, which offers a direct parallel with the text's implicit description of Liang's reactivation of the message of Confucius, which is meant to be the result of Liang's recognition of the message's transhistorical tenor, and not of Liang's nationalist predispositions.

Ultimately, the text's success depends on its ability to simultaneously situate itself in two discursive spaces: the historical space of Confucianism and the contemporary space of the post–May Fourth intellectual field. The text manages to do so by fusing the authority of tradition with that of eternity, the end result being an antitradition that can be more readily recognized as legitimate by readers situated in a discursive milieu in which emancipation is invariably associated with the necessity to break free from the shackles of the past. By reshaping Confucianism into an antitradition, the text can be both historically relevant and transhistorically valuable—that is, it can become historically relevant precisely by turning Confucianism into a transhistorical spirit capable of completing the May Fourth project of freeing the Chinese subject from tradition.

Successfully reclaiming the authority of the sage thus implies the need of first catering to the discursive antitradition of May Fourth, and second of hiding the extent to which the text's indebtedness to May Fourth is constitutive of its Confucian discourse. Iconoclasm also allows the text to purify the spirit of Confucius from historical Confucianism in order to exonerate it from the guilty verdict historical Confucianism received at the hands of the May Fourth group. It also makes it possible for the text to distance itself from Kang Youwei, his followers, and other intellectuals the May Fourth group succeeded in presenting as irrelevant traditionalists.

Yet the text also explicitly acknowledges its situatedness in the May Fourth discursive milieu. After all, it repeatedly refers to and quotes from the main figures associated with the May Fourth "canon": Hu Shi, Chen Duxiu, Li Dazhao, and Wu Yu. This is done most explicitly in the introduction, but also in the sections of the text not devoted to Confucianism. In the Confucian sections of the text, however, the May Fourth protagonists are mostly absent except for the specter of Hu Shi. Made a representative of a Western will rooted in an instrumental form of reason (*lizhi*), Hu Shi serves as a foil against which Liang can be presented as a Confucian sage whose authority, although clearly linked to Confucius, is ultimately rooted in a transcendent source (that of heaven). The text admits its presence in the May Fourth discursive field only to then relegate the main figures of May Fourth to a lower echelon of knowledge—that of science as opposed to the intuitive knowledge of heaven of the sage. The insertion of the Confucian sections in the general architecture of the text, which otherwise is mostly indebted to May Fourth, mirrors the text's attempt at re-establishing the authority of the sage in a discursive milieu hegemonized by May Fourth.

At work in these claims is an attempt at monopolizing transhistoricity; at recasting the modernity advocated by the May Fourth iconoclasts into a culture the value of which is restricted to a *particular* historical period: that of the first phase of teleological history. Although Confucianism is also situated in historical teleology, its value differs from that of Western culture insofar as the historical realization of Confucianism will see the incarnation, in the mundane realm, of a transhistorical spirit of heaven that speaks through us humans. Although the universality of Western culture is also recognized by the text, its goal is much more mundane: the satisfaction of basic human needs, which functions as a historical precondition for the incarnation of the transhistorical spirit of Confucius (and later of the Buddha) in history.[93]

Herein lies the iconoclastic potential of antitraditions. In the case of *Eastern and Western Cultures*, this potential is realized to its fullest by negating the transhistorical value of all traditions—including that of May Fourth and that of Confucian tradition-as-history—except that of a single sage. By reifying it into the figure of Confucius, the entire transhistorical value of tradition can then be subsumed by the text with more ease, by reshaping Confucius into a mirror image of Liang. The iconoclasm of the text thus serves the purpose of rejecting any alternative position, be they internal or external to the Confucian camp. Confucian iconoclasm, in other words, is both orthodox vis-à-vis competing Confucianisms (such as that of Kang Youwei) and hegemonic, if not in actuality at least in its intention of portraying competing perceptions of truth and the good (such as that of May Fourth) as inherently inferior.

In the final instance, an inherent weakness lies at the very heart of antitraditions such as that of *Eastern and Western Cultures*. Such antitraditions can never entirely sweep under the rug the traces of their own traditionality and historicity (and, in the case of *Eastern and Western Cultures*, of the nationalist scope of its discourse, rooted in its attempt at presenting at least one *Chinese* tradition as superior to that of the West[94]). Insofar as traces of historical traditions remain visible in the text's discourse on Confucianism, we can still call its Confucianism an anti*tradition*, although doing so inevitably involves challenging the text's claim to transhistorical authority by refraining from providing it with the recognition it needs.

4

Subsuming the Truth of Former Masters and Sages

In the previous chapter, we saw that *Eastern and Western Cultures* draws from both transhistorical and traditional sources of authority: on the one hand it claims that its author has intuited the transhistorical truths lodged in the message of Confucius, while on the other it seeks to bolster this claim by commenting authoritatively on the Confucian tradition. Transhistorical truths are not properly speaking transmitted through the medium of tradition in this model of textual authorization, as they are directly accessed by the author and only then confirmed by the author's ability to excavate the original meaning of the classics without the support of the commentarial or philological tradition.

This model effectively echoes Yü Ying-shih's description of what he calls the "anti-intellectualist" branch of Confucianism, which adopts "an attitude that tends to see *Dao* as lying in a higher realm than, and therefore beyond the reach of, intellectual knowledge." "A Confucian subscribing to this view believes that he can meet the minds of the sages without necessarily going through the medium of the sages' words," Yü continues. "And when he finally gets around to the sages' words—and this is often unavoidable as long as he professes to be a Confucian—he relies primarily on his own intuition and refuses to be bound by either the literal significance of a text or an earlier exegesis no matter how authoritative it may be, or both."[1] While this for the most part adequately describes Liang Shuming's relation to tradition as depicted in *Eastern and Western Cultures*, the text remains unclear as to whether Liang achieved a clear understanding of the *dao* without "going through the medium of the sages' words," or whether his intuitions were gradually sharpened through the process of reading the classics.

By comparison, the *New Treatise* offers a more paradigmatic example of the anti-intellectualist position. Its model of self-cultivation, as we saw in chapter 2, centers on a process of atomization of the inherent mind. Awakening must be reached by turning inward, in such a manner as to divorce oneself from one's surroundings. Once on the right path to awakening, book learning must also be put aside so that one can turn inward and reconnect with the inherent mind one shares with the sages and masters of the past. This self-cultivation model is meant as a guide for readers to follow. But it also represents a metacommentary that explains the process through which Xiong reached the *dao* autonomously before being able to discern the true meaning of the classics and Neo-Confucian texts in an unmediated fashion.

The *New Treatise*'s iconoclastic stance toward book learning falls short of being absolute, however (otherwise how would the text justify its own existence?). The *New Treatise* does find some value in certain types of texts: those that record the words of sages and masters who intuited the *dao*. Their words, as we saw in chapter 2, can help one find the right path toward awakening. Once awakened, one can also return to the words of former sages and masters, intuit their hidden meaning, and confirm that this meaning conforms with one's intuitions of the *dao* reached in complete isolation from the canon. The textual transmission of the words of former sages and masters therefore has value only to the extent that the words can show the proper way *before* one awakens and confirm one's insights *once* awakened. In and of themselves, they are powerless in eliciting the intuitions into the *dao* readers seek.

By comparison with *Eastern and Western Cultures*, in which the tension between historicity and transhistoricity relates to the text's attempt at inserting itself in the discursive traditions of Confucianism *and* May Fourth, the *New Treatise* appears significantly more disinterested. The text reads as a philosophical treatise that borrows from Yogācāra and Confucian resources without explicitly addressing May Fourth or Western sources of knowledge. Yet the lack of situatedness of the text is a mark of its situatedness—of its attempt at purifying Confucianism from its historical manifestation so that it can conform to the expectations of the discursive milieu of the time.

In what follows, I read the *New Treatise* as a complex performance of sagehood that builds on traditionally established rules that codify what a legitimate display of sagehood in writing ought to look like. The text's reliance on such traditional rules and discursive techniques continuously undermines the performance itself, which is meant to immunize the text from history by relocating it in the sovereign dominion of the inherent mind or Fundamental Reality. Fundamental Reality emerges from this reading as a discursive tool that allows the text to wash away the markers of its sociohistorical situatedness.

This chapter discusses the complex discursive means through which the *New Treatise* seeks to establish its authority by gaining the recognition of its readership. Like *Eastern and Western Cultures*, the *New Treatise* deploys a number of metacommentaries to present its author as someone who has achieved spiritual simultaneity with the sages of the past. Unlike *Eastern and Western Cultures*, however, the *New Treatise*'s claim to sagely authority relies first and foremost on epistemological distinctions grounded in the Buddhist theory of the two truths, which is also put to the task of immunizing the text from criticism. The chapter also addresses how the Yogācāra and Confucian traditions serve as historical "proofs" that the truth expounded by the *New Treatise* is indeed transhistorical, before concluding that the text seeks to entirely subsume and monopolize what is left of value in tradition.

A modern classic

As we saw in chapter 2, the *New Treatise* is shaped around a soteriological discourse according to which the self must first entirely free itself from markers of mundane existence—the body, emotions, desires, reliance of tradition, and so forth—before it can achieve a state of Oneness with the flux of the universe. Given the text's intricate knowledge of the process whereby one can reunite with the Oneness one had lost at birth, we can assume that implied in this discourse is the claim that Xiong Shili has already undergone the process of self-cultivation and has reached its ultimate objective. The very existence of the text further suggests that following the model of the Bodhisattva, Xiong is meant to have returned to the mundane realm after his awakening to guide others on their path to Oneness, by putting in writing the process whereby others can follow him "along the long road of imponderables."[2] Although it never makes this assertion explicitly (perhaps because claiming to be a sage is unsagely?), the text often implies, through a number of metacommentaries, that it originated from the pen of an awakened author. It is in the introduction that this claim is made most openly, when it is suggested that in discussing principle (*li* 理), Xiong cannot "put pen to paper" unless he is "in an expansive frame of mind in which [he] achieve[s] gnosis."³

The idea that the text is the product of an awakened author is reinforced by a number of statements that more or less implicitly frame the text as a guide readers can use to get a firmer grasp on Fundamental Reality. This is notably done by setting the parameters of the relationship between the text and its readers. Repeatedly, the text addresses readers as "students" (*xuezhe* 學者) who can learn about Fundamental Reality by reading various passages of the *New Treatise* "with an open mind" (*xuxin* 虛心)—or an "empty mind," if we translate the Chinese expression literally.⁴ Although in English "student" might give the impression that, by contrast, Xiong should be understood as a "teacher" or "master," the Chinese term employed by the text, *xuezhe*, also denotes a "learned person" or "scholar." In the many instances in which the *New Treatise* uses the term (I counted thirty-four), *xuezhe* can often be interpreted as "students *of the way*," and not "students *of Xiong*." That the text refers to Mencius as a "*xuezhe*" lends further support to this reading.⁵

In some instances, the text explicitly presents itself as a source of sagely truths from which readers, as students of the way, can learn. If readers approach the text with an empty mind free of preconceptions, the text implies, they can make use of the *New Treatise* as a self-cultivation guide. To understand the meaning of "transformation" (*zhuanbian* 轉變), which stands at the core of the text's metaphysics, for example, "students must not be attached to former accounts," as Xiong's perspective is not grounded "on the views of former masters."⁶ In some instances, the text directly instructs readers on how to proceed with their self-cultivation, as when it says that "students should first overcome pride" to become virtuous.⁷ Elsewhere, the text entrusts readers to properly reflect on the fact that the *New Treatise* "placed vigilance at the end of the various wholesome mental associates," as "the significance of this is profound."⁸ Such comments establish a certain rapport between text and reader, one that is shaped around the idea that the text offers valuable insights to readers interested in cultivating themselves.

Moreover, through four distinct discursive techniques, the *New Treatise* portrays itself as a modern sutra and Confucian classic, and thus by implication as the product of a Buddhist master or Confucian sage. In some instances, the text dictates how it should be read. One passage should be read "in one fell swoop,"⁹ for example, thus implying that as a modern classic or sutra, the *New Treatise* should be recited or read in a particular way to correctly apprehend its truth. Furthermore, the *New Treatise*, along with other texts written by Xiong, were originally signed with the character *zao* (造) following Xiong's name, a practice strictly reserved, in the Buddhist tradition, for scriptures having been authored by Bodhisattvas.[10]

A third means through which the *New Treatise* suggests it is the product of a Bodhisattva and sage—as we will see, the text equates the messages of Confucianism and Buddhism—is by inserting interlinear autocommentaries in the text. Traditionally, commentaries were employed to explicate the meaning of texts integrated in a canon believed to be a repository of transhistorical truths. The writing of interlinear commentaries was justified by the fact that the temporal distance between the classics and the contemporaries had rendered the meaning and language of the classics abstruse. Commentaries that made use of a more accessible language thus could be of great help in filling in the gap between the time of the classics and the time of the interpreter.[11]

In the case of the *New Treatise*, however, no temporal gap stands between the main text and the commentary. It is important to keep in mind that the text was not published without commentaries first, before being followed by a second edition with interlinear autocommentaries that explained some of the most abstruse passages of the first edition. The main text and the commentary were published at once in the first edition of the work in 1932 and were in all likelihood composed during the same period of time. This distinguishes the *New Treatise*'s use of interlinear commentaries from more conventional ones justified by the temporal gap that stands between text and commentary.

To be sure, the introduction provides an explanation—although not a very good one—as to why interlinear autocommentaries intersperse the main body of the *New Treatise*. It claims that they were "employed to resolve difficulties in the text."[12] On the one hand, this is evidently true, as throughout the text autocommentaries are put to the task of explaining the use of particular terms the meaning of which might not be obvious to readers. On the other hand, however, it remains unclear why interlinear autocommentaries are better equipped to provide such explanations. Could explanations not have been provided in the main body of the text directly? One example will suffice to make this point. In one passage, the main text reads: "Real dharmas [*youtifa* 有體法], in relation to the cognizing consciousness [*nengyuanshi* 能緣識], are that which are depended upon, enabling it to arise." This is followed by an interlinear autocommentary: " 'It' refers to the cognizing consciousness."[13] In this case, the text could have simply been edited in such a way as to replace "it" (*bi* 彼) in the main text with "cognizing consciousness." No autocommentary would have been needed, and "difficulties in the text" would have been straightforwardly resolved. The same could have been done, I suggest, for *all* autocommentaries inserted in the text without exception.

The above example shows that the use of interlinear autocommentaries gives the sense that the main text was fixed and could not have been altered. We can assume that this is because it was written, as claimed in the introduction, while Xiong was in a state of gnosis. The only temporal gap justifying the use of such autocommentaries is therefore the one that separates writing in "an expansive state of mind" from the mundane work of editing during which Xiong presumably was no longer in such a state of mind. This implies that the main body of the text should be viewed as a classic- or sutra-like repository of truths, so much so that even Xiong himself could not alter it once it had been composed. It should be further noted that whether this is how the historical Xiong Shili understood his use of autocommentaries is beside the point. What matters, for the present purpose, is that this interpretation follows from the metacommentaries on the text and its authorship inserted in the *New Treatise*.

Finally, it is also of significance that the text was written in classical Chinese, despite the fact that by 1932, when the work was published, vernacular Chinese had already become the norm. By then, it had already been twelve years since the Ministry of Education had issued a decree calling for the gradual transition from classical to vernacular Chinese in primary schools.[14] Publishing in classical Chinese in 1932 was a statement in itself—a sign that the author was supporting the preservation of at least some aspects of classical culture. It did not necessarily entail that the text was meant to be read as a classic or sutra, of course, but in the case of the *New Treatise*, classical Chinese is used in conjunction with discursive techniques clearly aimed at giving the text the aura of a classic or sutra. Through the use of classical Chinese, the text can present itself as temporally closer to the classics—although it should be kept in mind that the Chinese used by the *New Treatise* is that of late imperial China and not that of the pre-Qin classics. The text's relative proximity to the classics also distinguishes it from modern Chinese texts that fall short of the lofty goal of expounding "fundamental wisdom" (*xuanxue* 玄學)[15] set by the *New Treatise*—notably because of their reliance on a scientific language ill-equipped to grasp the Oneness of Fundamental Reality, as we will see.[16]

The dual positioning of the text

As the above shows, the authority of the *New Treatise* depends heavily on the readers' willingness to (1) accept the role of unawakened students of the way assigned to them by the text and (2) recognize that the text has indeed been authored by a master-sage. Once performed, such recognition is meant to be followed by a gradual bridging of the soteriological gap between author and reader, as the reader gradually advances toward the end goal of the self-cultivation process. Even before reaching this goal, however, a social distinction can already be established between readers who are on the path of self-cultivation and recognize the meaning of the text as "sublime," as it purports to be,[17] and the majority of human beings who are yet to embark on the road leading to enlightenment.

In various instances, the text makes disparaging comments on what it calls "ordinary people" (*yibanren* 一般人 or *fanren* 凡人)—that is, people who are entirely consumed by the mundane and fail to understand that striving to attain the supramundane is the very point of existence. "Ordinary people," the text explicates, "are not capable of possessing clear understanding." Although they are "innately endowed with this great treasure-store," the text continues in a Buddhist vein, "they do not take it upon themselves to develop it."[18] "Except for a very few exceptional individuals," the text states elsewhere, "the vast majority of people constantly let go of their minds so that they easily descend into the material."[19] Such passages not only imply that Xiong is indeed a member of this elite group of "exceptional individuals"—how else would he know what he knows?—but also that readers can join Xiong if not as part of the elite group itself, at least as part of a larger group of "students of the way" who are further advanced than "ordinary people" in their quest toward Fundamental Reality.

In terms of textual authority, the discursive trope of "ordinary people" follows a pattern similar to the social uses of irony. Irony can help establish a bond, a common identity between those who are "in on the joke" and who define themselves by their shared opposition to those who fail to grasp the ironic tenor of a comment. Of course, the social capital acquired by the person who performs the ironic statement is greater than the capital derived from simply recognizing the presence of irony. But through the act of recognition, one can nevertheless distinguish oneself from those objected to ironic remarks and those failing to identify the very presence of irony. Recognizing that the vast majority of human beings are "ordinary people" serves a similar function. It helps create a social bond between the readers and the author by showing that although they are soteriologically worlds apart, readers and author nevertheless share a common identity as students of the way when compared with such "ordinary people."

Central to the mode of textual authorization put forth by the *New Treatise*, the ordinary/exceptional gap finds legitimacy in the Buddhist theory of the two truths, the validity of which might have been accepted with relative ease by readers given how well inscribed in the Chinese intellectual milieu this theory had become through time.[20] On the distinction between absolute and conventional truths, the *New Treatise* has the following to say:

> Analyzing principles [to determine] if they are true or false [first requires] examining into the matter of the two truths [*erdi* 二諦]: absolute and conventional. [. . .] It is due to following conventional truth that the mundane world is accepted as proven. Earth is nothing but earth, water is nothing but water, right through to the myriad existents—all are differentiated and understood on the basis of specific and general attributes and do not run counter to the mundane world's [conventional truth]. Because absolute truth is experienced, however, there is a categorical refutation of conventional knowing. Hence, earth is not thought of as earth, because earth's nature is empty. [. . .] Water is not thought of as water because water's nature is empty. What is manifest before one is True Reality, perfectly clear. [. . .] As such, a single principle equalizes, cognition vanishes, and words disappear. This is because of what is realized by nothing other than self-nature's wisdom.
>
> 夫析理誠妄，咨於二諦: 曰真、曰俗。……順俗諦故，世間極成。地唯是地，水唯是水，乃至群有悉如其自相共相而甄明之，不違世間，入真諦故，決定遮撥世間知見。故於地不作地想，地性空故……。於水不作水想，水性空故，現前即是真體澄然……。此則一理齊平，慮亡詞喪，唯是自性智所證得故。[21]

"Ordinary people" refers to those individuals who only have access to conventional truth, while "exceptional individuals" are those who can grasp absolute truth and reach "True Reality."

Of central importance to our discussion of textual authority is the fact that in the realm of absolute truth, "cognition vanishes" and "words disappear." This is due to the fact that absolute truth is One—something alluded to by the text's reference to a "single principle" (*yi li* 一理) that "equalizes" all things, presumably by merging them into a single body. As we saw in chapter 2, the text conceptualizes awakening as a transition from fragmentation to a state of Oneness with the universe. It is precisely because Oneness should remain undivided that, once in this state, "cognition vanishes" and "words disappear," as both cognition and words cannot but bring about a fragmentation of the world. Absolute truth thus stands as the radical other of language and cognition.

This discourse, which the *New Treatise* recycles from Buddhist sources, stands at the core of the text's attempt at re-establishing the authority of the master-sage. Given that argumentation remains valid only for the realm of conventional truth, the text cannot persuade readers through argumentation that its depiction of absolute truth and Fundamental Reality is accurate. The absolute otherness of the Buddhist master and the Confucian sage entails that readers, unless masters or sages themselves, simply cannot judge whether the text's claim that Xiong has achieved "gnosis" is valid or not. The unawakened reader must perform a leap of faith that is responsible for providing the text with the recognition it seeks (regarding its claim to belong to a heightened state of consciousness). "Ordinary people," from this perspective, are simply those who have not yet performed the leap of faith asked of the readers.[22]

Neither in the excerpt above nor anywhere else does the text advance any argument to support its assertion that truths come in two forms: conventional and absolute. The text tends to use argumentation only when engaged in a direct dialogue with the Yogācāra tradition. This is especially the case of the second chapter called "Uniqueness of Consciousness" (*weishi* 唯識), in which the text sets out to refute the Yogācāra conception of consciousness. As the text moves on to discuss its own metaphysical position, however, the tone shifts and arguments are no longer proposed to sustain the text's key metaphysical claims.[23] While scholars have lamented this aspect of the *New Treatise*,[24] the absence of argumentation is consistent with its two truths epistemology and with the text's self-portrayal, through the metacommentaries discussed above, as the testament of an enlightened author.[25]

In various instances, the *New Treatise* reminds the reader that absolute truth simply cannot be subjected to language. Because "the principle [*li* 理] elucidated by the learning concerned with fundamental wisdom" is "recondite," the text advances in one such instance, "it becomes a hindrance [*kun* 困] to express it in words."[26] This explains why the text cannot directly express the absolute truth and must rely on what is known, in Buddhist terminology, as the apophatic mode of explanation (*zhequan* 遮詮), which expresses meaning indirectly. This can be achieved by making use of language as "an expedient means [*fangbian* 方便] for dispelling attachment."[27] The text goes on to explain that

> the functioning of discourse [*mingyan* 名言] relies on its capacity to express things. [. . .] Now, to seek to express the principle that extends beyond things using words that [can only] express things [. . .] will often [result in] speaking of them as if they are the same thing. Out of fear that those who are mired in the false discrimination of things will develop all sorts of mistaken interpretations when they hear [that words are being used to express the principle that extends beyond things], the words of those who specialize in learning concerned with fundamental wisdom, relying in particular on expedient means, frequently draw upon the apophatic mode of explanation. The abstruse contortions involved in this are certainly not something that ordinary people could understand.
>
> 名言緣表物而興，……今以表物之言而求表超物之理，……往往說似一物，兼懼聞者以滯物之情，滋生謬解，故玄學家言，特資方便，常有假於遮詮。此中奧隱曲折，誠有非一般人所可喻者。[28]

Because Fundamental Reality stands above the subject-object divide, it cannot be objectified by language. To discuss it, the text must engage in "abstruse contortions" that escape the grasp of ordinary people.

The language of the texts and its use of distinctions are meant to serve as means to transcend distinctions and language once and for all. The text makes it clear that the distinctions it establishes in writing are merely nominal in nature. They are aimed at helping readers find the path to awakening: "All the words and phrases of my thesis are but expedient/skillful means used to reveal [. . .] Fundamental Reality."[29] This explains why, although the text is against all distinctions, it can establish an impressive number of dualities itself, and although Fundamental Reality is supposed to be ineffable, it can describe it in a number of ways. From a nominal perspective, the text occasionally depicts Fundamental Reality as constantly changing, as "Supreme Change [*taiyi* 太易] before it is manifest as vital stuff [*qi* 氣]" in the phenomenal realm.³⁰ In other instances, the text describes Fundamental Reality as unchanging, insofar as it remains constant in manifesting itself in the myriad changes the phenomenal realm goes through.³¹ From an ontological perspective, however, the text cannot say anything at all, except that Fundamental Reality cannot be captured by language and as such should be regarded as neither changing nor unchanging; in fact, it should not be named at all.³²

The above suggests that "Fundamental Reality" is employed by the text as a signifier with two distinct signifieds: (1) a realm of constant change nominally established in contradistinction to the phenomenal realm of functions and used as a skillful means to help readers reach the shore of awakening, and (2) a realm of Oneness above language that is ontologically established in contradistinction to the nominal realm in which the distinction between Fundamental Reality in the former sense and the phenomenal realm of functions is used as a skillful means. Once one achieves the realm of Oneness above language, one realizes that Fundamental Reality (in the former sense) and the phenomenal realm of functions are one. Although this realm of Oneness is said to be unnameable, the text nevertheless employs "Fundamental Reality" as a shorthand for it. (In the following pages, all mentions of "Fundamental Reality" are to the second signified, unless it is explicitly contrasted with the phenomenal realm of functions.)

Although the nonduality of Fundamental Reality and the phenomenal realm of functions is generally regarded as the central tenet of the *New Treatise*, this tenet does not preclude the text from nominally using *ti* and *yong* as a foundation on which an entire edifice of dualisms is established: between mind and matter, between defiled and pure habituated tendencies, between exceptional individuals and ordinary people, and, as we will see, between Eastern wisdom and Western philosophy. While the text does portray the *tiyong* relation as nondual, in other words, this is only so *from the perspective of* ti. From the perspective of the text's *discursive use (yong)* of *ti* and *yong* as skillful means, the pair remains highly dichotomized, and it must remain so to preserve the integrity of the text's soteriological discourse. If all distinctions vanish, after all, there is no longer any need to undergo a transformation from ordinary person to sage.³³

The two signifieds of "Fundamental Reality" are revealing of the dual positioning of the text; of its being simultaneously situated in the realm of nominal distinctions, cognition, and language on the one hand and in the dominion of Oneness above language on the other. This dual positioning, I argue in what follows, plays a role similar to that of the rhetoric of

144 | Confucian Iconoclasm

naturalization in *Eastern and Western Cultures*: it enables the text to perform its iconoclastic function by rejecting, from the perspective of Fundamental Reality, alternative forms of discursivity as mired in the mundane realm of the many, while at the same immunizing its own discourse from similar criticism—despite its being steeped in similar distinctions and dualities—by appealing to the Oneness in the stead of which it presumably stands. This will become clearer by taking a closer look at the text's acute criticism of Dharmapāla (Hufa 護法; n.d.) and (Western) philosophy.

Iconoclasm and immunity from criticism

To advance its iconoclastic agenda, the text finds ample resources in the theory of the two truths, which enables it to discard alternative views by relegating them to the realm of conventional truth. This is reminiscent of a similar discursive technique used in *Eastern and Western Cultures*, whereby rationality is acknowledged as a valid means to achieve conventional truths about the world, although ultimately such truths are relegated to an inferior position vis-à-vis the intuitive grasp of the universe in flux said to be the core message of Confucius. Yet outside of the sections on Confucianism, *Eastern and Western Cultures* retains a rather positive attitude toward science and reasoning. By comparison, the *New Treatise* is far more critical of conventional truth. This can be exemplified by taking a closer look at the text's distinction between discernment (*hui* 慧) and wisdom (*zhi* 智), which closely parallels the divide between rationality (*lizhi* 理智) and intuition (*zhijue* 直覺) in *Eastern and Western Cultures*.[34]

Discernment, the *New Treatise* argues, produces knowledge by relying on a method of analysis that breaks things down (*fenxi* 分析). Although this method is of great use in establishing conventional truths pertaining to the phenomenal realm of functions, it takes for granted the ontological existence of its object of study, which is established in contradistinction to the cognizing subject. Discernment therefore cements our attachment to the subject-object dichotomy that breaks the original unity of Fundamental Reality. Scientists and philosophers—by which the text implies those engaged in *Western*-style philosophy—tend to fall in this trap, insofar as they pursue truths externally and discuss metaphysics and ontology through conceptual means.[35]

Discernment is opposed to wisdom, which provides access to absolute truth by returning to the inherent mind. Wisdom refers to a method of "understanding through personal experience" (*tiren* 體認) thanks to which "one is able mysteriously to intuit [*mingqi* 冥契] interconnection as a single whole."[36] Philosophers fail to grasp Fundamental Reality either because they remain ignorant of this method or because they assume that Fundamental Reality lies beyond our reach (in a Kantian fashion). This is what distinguishes philosophy from what the text calls "fundamental wisdom," a field of study that "strives to apprehend That Which Holds All [*zongchi* 總持]."[37] In short, while science and philosophy cannot pierce through nominal constructs to reach the Oneness behind them, fundamental wisdom allows one to do so by turning one's gaze inward to recover the inherent mind hidden away by the birth of the body.

As the above shows, the text draws from the Buddhist theory of the two truths to relegate Western knowledge to conventional truth while elevating the "fundamental wisdom" of Eastern forms of knowledge (Buddhism and Confucianism) to the status of absolute truth. Although in theory the *New Treatise* could follow *Eastern and Western Cultures* in acknowledging the relative value of conventional truth, in effect it presents conventional truth as standing in the way of enlightenment and argues that once awakening is achieved, all conventional "truths" are discovered to be ultimately false.[38]

On the basis of this epistemological position, the text can reject alternative positions held in the intellectual milieu of the time—the representatives of science and Western philosophy in Republican China—*without calling them out by their names*. This is fundamental, as addressing its adversaries directly would have made the *New Treatise* appear highly invested in the mundane realm of the politics of knowledge production of Republican China. By formulating its critique of Western knowledge and of its representatives in China in the seemingly disinterested language of epistemology, in other words, the text can position itself in the intellectual field without losing the aura of a text solely concerned with the supramundane realm of Fundamental Reality. Furthermore, the epistemological plane of the text's discussion entails that the value it ascribes to Eastern—and particularly Chinese[39]—wisdom is not the product of a nationalist stance.

The *New Treatise*'s distinction between the two levels of truth has a triple function with regard to textual authority. First, it serves an iconoclastic function vis-à-vis Western knowledges (and, as we will see, the Yogācāra school). Second, it is also employed to immunize the text from criticism by projecting it in a realm of Oneness that stands outside discourse, philosophy, and language. The figure of "ordinary people" plays an important role at this level. The text maintains that "ordinary people are incapable of putting aside craving for their own views or antipathy toward the views [of other sentient beings], and so they rely on their own views [*jijian* 己見] as the benchmark for what is true and false."[40] By contrast, extraordinary individuals transcend the narrow confines of subjective and selfish views: "When the nature is truly seen, there are no 'self views' [*jijian*] that can be attached to. [. . .] To follow the [principle of] things and not contravene, [that principle] is called wisdom. It does not involve using personal perspectives [*si* 私]."[41] Like the Confucius of *Eastern and Western Cultures*, the wise person, in the *New Treatise*, stands above all views and opinions. Wisdom is the expression of Reality as it is, without the distorting effects of subjectivity. This goes to show how the two truths epistemology of the text serves a purpose similar to the rhetoric of naturalization of *Eastern and Western Cultures*: it allows the text to relocate itself outside the contentious realm of disputation and discursivity.

Finally, as briefly mentioned above, epistemology also plays a pivotal role in establishing the authority of the text by securing the recognition of the readers. The distinction between conventional and absolute truths, which is presented by the text as a difference in kind rather than degree, provides an epistemological and soteriological source of legitimacy for the social distinction between author and readers. (Even if readers differ from "ordinary people" insofar as they are at least on the right path, they are ultimately standing with "ordinary people" on the side of conventional truth, at least for the moment being.) Because the difference between the wisdom of Xiong and the knowledge of readers is in kind, readers find themselves in no position to assess the validity of the text's claim to stand on the side of enlightenment. They are asked to perform a leap of faith, in exchange for which they are offered the title of "students of the way"—a significant advancement from the lowly social station occupied by "ordinary people." Readers who regard themselves as students of Confucian wisdom would thus be inclined to recognize the legitimacy of the text's claim to awakening and sagehood, without necessarily being aware that it is this act of recognition that is responsible for instituting the authority of the text.

Dharmapāla

To sum up, the notion of the two truths plays a central role in (1) the text's iconoclastic rejection of alternative views, (2) its immunization from similar iconoclastic moves, and (3) its attempt at securing the recognition of readers. Mutually reinforcing, the three discursive functions of the text's two truths epistemology will become clearer by taking a closer look at how they are implemented in the text's complex stance on the Yogācāra tradition.

The iconoclastic potential of the notion of conventional truth is nowhere more manifest than in the text's severe criticism of Dharmapāla. Dharmapāla is known for his commentary on the *Triṃśikā*—know in China as *Thirty Verses on Consciousness-only* (*Weishi sanshi lun song* 唯識三十論頌)—a central text of the Yogācāra tradition written by Vasubandhu (Shiqin 世親; fourth–fifth centuries), usually considered one of the two founders of the Yogācāra school, along with Asaṅga (Wuzhuo 無著; fourth century), who was possibly his half-brother. It is this commentary of the *Triṃśikā* that formed the basis of Xuanzang's (玄奘; 602–664) influential work of translation titled *Demonstration of Consciousness-only* (*Cheng weishi lun* 成唯識論), which became a central text of the East Asian school of Yogācāra. As John Makeham points out, "'Dharmapāla' effectively functions," in East Asian literature, "as a metonym for views expressed in *Cheng Weishi Lun* which is typically labeled as Dharmapāla's commentary."[42] As such, Xiong's attacks on Dharmapāla should be understood as criticisms of the *Demonstration of Consciousness-only*.

Dharmapāla is criticized for a number of reasons by the text, the main one being that he "had simply never seen Reality, and so the argument he upheld was riddled with confusion and mistakes."[43] Since he had not attained awakening, Dharmapāla relied on the method of analysis (*fenxi*) specific to discernment as opposed to fundamental wisdom. "So long as he employed methods of breaking down," the *New Treatise* explains, "he could not avoid succumbing to so-called preconceived, piecemeal characterizations." "An example of his breaking-down," the text adds in an interlinear autocommentary that follows, "is categories such as the eight consciousnesses, the fifty-one mental associates, and the three parts [*sanfen* 三分], each of which he broke down into separate discrete constitutive entities."[44] In short, Dharmapāla was guilty of fragmenting the original unity of the mind-universe.

Given that the *New Treatise* itself also distinguishes between the eight consciousnesses and given that it provides a detailed explanation of thirty-eight—rather than fifty-one[45]—mental associates, however, one would be tempted to ask whether it does not also depend on "methods of breaking down." But as we saw above, such distinctions are presented by the text as nominal constructs employed as skillful means to help readers along the path toward enlightenment. Moreover, the text makes it clear that once awakening is experienced, one can then use the method of breaking down *as a skillful means*. Presumably this is where Dharmapāla erred: he made use of the method of breaking down without having experienced awakening first.

Apart from his inability to achieve awakening, the main issue the *New Treatise* has with Dharmapāla is that instead of following Madhyamaka in adopting an apophatic mode of explanation, he, and all subsequent Yogācārins after him, made use of a kataphatic mode of explanation (*biaoquan* 表詮) that presumes the ontological existence of what is discussed.[46] Following Dharmapāla, Yogācārins mistakenly regarded the seeds stored in the eighth consciousness as the ontological cause and consciousness as their effect. As a result, seeds originally intended as skillful means came to be hypostatized, with the effect that consciousness was split into a subject and an object. This amounted to ontological dualism, the *New Treatise* concludes. Moreover, by individuating seeds according to the type of effect they produce (i.e., the fifty-one mental associates), and by postulating eight consciousnesses in relation to the type of object toward which they are directed, Yogācāra had broken the unity of consciousness into distinct units, thus treating it as if it were a material object that could be broken up into parts. Since the seeds were treated, in this account, as the ontological cause of consciousness, the *New Treatise* argues, it resulted in a form of ontological pluralism falling far short of the Oneness of Fundamental Reality.[47]

It is the distinction between nominal and ontological discourses—itself relying on the theory of the two truths—that justifies the text's rejection of Dharmapāla's conceptualization of consciousness (despite how closely it resembles the *New Treatise*'s).[48] It is important to note that there is nothing intrinsic in a discourse that makes it ontological or nominal by nature. To be sure, the *New Treatise* portrays the use of the concept of causation in Dharmapāla's discussion of seeds as a sign of its ontological nature,[49] but it remains unclear why this would necessarily be so. There is nothing intrinsic to the concept of causation, or any other concept for that matter, that makes it unsuited to nominal discussions serving as skillful means. As noted in chapter 2, the *New Treatise* itself portrays habituated tendencies as the result of past actions the residual power of which is manifested in the present. This presumes the existence of some form of causation between habituated tendencies and the mental associates they produce. Moreover, given its depiction of awakening as the end product of a *gradual* process of self-cultivation, the text clearly assumes that the notion of causality can be used nominally.

If the *New Treatise* can nominally use the notions of causality and continuity, then there is nothing intrinsic in Dharmapāla's assessment of the causality between seeds and consciousness that would make his discourse inherently ontological. This goes to show the arbitrariness of the distinction between nominal and ontological discourses. Given that distinctions are an unavoidable component of language, whether a discourse is regarded as emanating from the radical otherness of Oneness achieved by sages and masters is something that cannot be determined based on the nature of the discourse itself. Only someone who already has access to Oneness can judge whether a discourse is nominal or ontological. This is precisely what the *New Treatise* does when claiming that Dharmapāla "had simply never seen Reality."[50]

The arbitrariness of the nominal/ontological divide is instrumental in reinstating the authority of the master-sage, as the reader is asked to perform a leap of faith by recognizing the validity of the text's rather arbitrary judgments on the Yogācāra tradition—a recognition ultimately responsible for instituting the authority of the text and its author. Moreover, the text can deploy the nominal/ontological divide to immunize itself from criticisms similar to those it advances toward Dharmapāla. This will become clearer by taking a closer look at one instance in which the dual positioning of the text (between ontological Oneness and nominal discursivity) serves the purpose of pre-emptively inoculating the text from potential attacks.

In its assessment of Yogācāra, the text insists that the school's portrayal of Fundamental Reality as manifested through function is mistaken, as it

> fail[s] to understand that since there is certainly nothing in Reality that can be established, then how can it be established in function? Suppose we presume that function can be established because it is a real dharma; then function already stands in contrast to Reality, so how can one talk about function's being able to manifest Fundamental Reality?

> 不知體上固無可建立，又安可於用上建立乎？設計用為實法而可建立者，則用已與體對，談用何足顯體？[51]

On the grounds that Fundamental Reality transcends language and cannot be contrasted to function as it is One, the text condemns Yogācāra for suggesting that Fundamental Reality manifests itself in function. Yet elsewhere, the text makes a similar claim when it argues, as we saw above, that Reality "refers to Supreme Change before it is manifest as vital stuff"—that is, before it manifests itself in the phenomenal realm of functions.[52] That Fundamental Reality manifests itself in functions is repeated throughout the text, often with the explicit caveat that this is an illusion or that this claim remains nominal in nature.⁵³ This goes to show how the text can criticize an assertion made in Yogācāra from the ontological positionality of Fundamental Reality, while immunizing its reproduction of the same claim by positioning itself on the nominal side of skillful means.

By appealing to the nominal/ontological divide, the text draws a sharp distinction between what it says (nominally) and what it means (ontologically), so that any criticism can be brushed aside by retorting that the person advancing such criticism failed to understand what the text truly means and remained superficially confined to the nominality of what it says. The nominal/ontological distinction and the notion of the two truths thus serve as powerful discursive techniques of denial, which have the dual benefit, as Pierre Bourdieu notes in a different context, of "adding to the advantage of speaking the profit of denying what is said, through the manner of saying it."⁵⁴ In this passage on the work of Martin Heidegger, Bourdieu speaks of the imposition of the philosophical form on a discourse that participates in the conservative revolution of Weimar Germany, yet can deny this participation precisely by appealing to the autonomous nature of the philosophical language it deploys. The *New Treatise* similarly relies on the imposition of the philosophical form to distance itself from the mundane realm of politics, history, and discursive relations of power, as we will see shortly. But it is also its use of the nominal/ontological distinction that allows the text to double its benefits by saying what it wants to say on the one hand, while reserving for itself the possibility of denying that what it says is what it means on the other.

By moving across the nominal/ontological divide at will, the text can insert itself in the discursive milieu of its time to attack alternative subject positions (Western-style philosophers, scientists, students of Yogācāra), while simultaneously denying its own participation in the mundane discursive field of Republican China. Relocating itself on the side of ontological monism also serves as an important means of securing the recognition of the readers while hiding the fact that it pursues such recognition. As the following sections argue, the text also seeks to secure the readers' leap of faith by inserting an act of recognition within its discourse on Yogācāra and Confucianism.

The Yogācāra tradition

The complex rapport the *New Treatise* builds with the Yogācāra and Confucian traditions is significantly shaped by concerns with authority. On the one hand, the text relies on authoritative figures of the Yogācāra and Confucian traditions to legitimize its claim to sagehood and masterhood, insofar as such figures can provide historical "proofs" of the transhistoricity of the text's message. Moreover, the figures of former masters and sages serve to internalize the dialectic of recognition within the text itself, with the hope that this will help guarantee the readers' recognition. On the other hand, however, it is imperative for the text to distance itself from the mundanity of traditions transmitted historically and constrained by the contingency of the sociohistorical milieu within which they emerged. The text negotiates between these seemingly contradictory aims through two different discursive techniques, which it deploys in its exposition of the Yogācāra and Confucian traditions.

As the radical other of language and discursivity, Fundamental Reality allows for an external gaze on the whole Yogācāra and Confucian traditions from which Xiong can pass final judgements as to which historical figures had access to absolute truth and which did not. Regarding Yogācāra, the *New Treatise* is highly critical of Dharmapāla and the entire Yogācāra tradition as it evolved after him, as we saw above. This criticism is often presented as an attempt to reinstate the original form of Yogācāra before its insights were lost. The text builds a narrative according to which Asaṅga, presented as the founder of Yogācāra, "made assertions with ingenuity, sweeping them away no sooner than he had made them, never establishing anything and thereby distancing himself from any misguided conceptual elaboration."[55] Although Asaṅga did distinguish between the eight consciousnesses, he regarded them as mere nominal constructs.[56] The act of creation performed by Asaṅga—which the text implies it re-enacts—is meant to defy reification by making sure that Asaṅga's assertions are "swept away" as soon as they are made.

Asaṅga could not ultimately prevent the reification of his message, however. The process of hypostatization of consciousness gradually began with Vasubandhu, who "started having consciousness subsume the various dharmas and so came to look upon the dharma of consciousness as something relatively real."[57] Vasubandhu, the text goes on, "divided [consciousness] into [eight separate] cluster-categories [. . .] just like a machine."[58] Finally, Dharmapāla not only reproduced Vasubandhu's mistake in distinguishing between eight consciousnesses regarded as real, but also "identified deluded consciousness with inherent mind." Given these confusions, the text concludes that Dharmapāla's "perversity" is "unfathomable."[59]

This passage on the Yogācāra tradition finishes with the following assertion: "For the past one thousand years and several centuries, no one has sought to dispute him [Dharmapāla]—is this not strange?"⁶⁰ Implied by this short quote is the idea that Xiong is the first person who understood the historical process whereby Asaṅga's message was reified and polluted, and therefore also the first who fully grasped the import of Asaṅga's message and achieved spiritual simultaneity with him. Highly reminiscent of the role played by Confucius in the discursive architecture of *Eastern and Western Cultures*, the figure of Asaṅga provides the *New Treatise* with the metacommentarial means to comment on its own authorship.

The text's rejection of the entire tradition of Yogācāra following Asaṅga also serves the implicit purpose of attacking contemporary Yogācāra advocates, including Xiong's former teacher and classmates at the China Institute of Inner Learning.⁶¹ Ouyang Jingwu, Xiong's former teacher, was at the time engaged in the project of retrieving what he and other members of his institute considered authentic Buddhism.⁶² According to them, the authentic form of the tradition had been conveyed in certain sutras and translations, including the *Demonstration of Consciousness-only* that the *New Treatise* implicitly attacks through the figure of Dharmapāla. Furthermore, Ouyang singled out *The Awakening of Mahāyāna Faith*, and its theory that the mind is originally awakened but hidden from us because of defilements, as bearing the responsibility for the deviation of Sinitic Buddhism from the authentic source of Indian Buddhism. As John Makeham and Sang Yu have argued, the *New Treatise* was significantly influenced by *The Awakening of Mahāyāna Faith*.⁶³ As such, the text significantly departed from the orthodox interpretation of Yogācāra promoted at the China Institute of Inner Learning. The above goes to show that the text's severe attacks on Dharmapāla were obliquely aimed at Ouyang Jingwu and his students. By directing its criticism toward Dharmapāla instead of Ouyang, the text can retain an appearance of disinterestedness and autonomy vis-à-vis its opponents and hide its active participation in the politics of authentic Buddhism of Republican China.

In a manner that echoes its description of self-cultivation as a reactivation of the origin in the present, the text presents itself as reactivating the originary message of Yogācāra before its corruption.⁶⁴ Indeed, the text explicitly states that "through accumulated transmission, true meaning is gradually lost sight of," and "Buddhism is not unique in this regard."⁶⁵ This explains why the text portrays itself, "compared with Buddhist [writings]," as "fundamentally innovative." "In all of the terms I use," the text affirms, "there are some where I continue to use the old term but change its meaning [. . .] and there are some where I adopt conventional language but change its meaning."⁶⁶ Even though the *New Treatise* borrows an impressive number of terms from Buddhist sources, its innovative use of language ensures that it is not ensnared in the mundanity of the traditional. Similar claims to novelty and innovation, contrasted to traditional accounts, are repeated in various instances.[67] The text goes so far as to redefine the meaning of "*weishi*" in "*weishilun*" (唯識論; Yogācāra), which in the *New Treatise* stands for the "unique" (*wei* 唯) ability of consciousness (*shi* 識) to discern cognitive objects.[68]

Although at times Asaṅga serves as a mirror image that supports the text's self-portrayal as a transhistorical act of creation, in other instances the text's attitude toward Asaṅga is far more ambiguous. In one case, the text judges that "since the beginning of the Existence school [Yogācāra] with Asaṅga, talk about function has especially involved breaking down [*fenxi*]."[69] Elsewhere, it is said that "Mahāyāna masters," as a whole, "became narrowly concerned with phenomenal characteristics and their names," and that "in doing so, they all used formal logic, and although reasoned arguments are repeatedly in evidence," their "treatises suffer from an excess of empty theorizing that borders on sophistry."[70] It is in this regard that Confucianism is superior to Buddhism. "The six perfections of which the Buddhists speak mostly elucidate phenomena. They do not measure up to the five virtues of which the Confucians speak in being as precise in pointing directly to Fundamental Reality."[71] This is because in China, "former wise men [. . .] were unwilling to develop [their] understanding in the form of doctrinal discussions."[72] In short, Confucians were better at using a language that could avoid the pitfalls of reification. It is therefore the very absence of "theorizing," "reasoned arguments," and doctrine that makes Confucianism particularly well suited to point readers in the direction of Fundamental Reality.

The overall superiority of Confucianism lies in its mode of discourse. In terms of its message, however, Confucianism shares a "common insight" with Mahayana masters, which is that "cognitive objects are not separate from consciousness."[73] "Although Cheng Hao, Lu Xiangshan, and Wang Yangming had read a few Chan recorded sayings," the text adds, "they had certainly never read any Yogācāra [*faxiang weishi* 法相唯識] texts, yet what they had realized is a precise match with Yogācāra."[74] The fact that *without knowing the existence of each other*, Mahayana masters and Neo-Confucians arrived at the very same insight reinforces the idea that this insight is not bound to a particular time or place.

The Confucian tradition

The *New Treatise* ambiguously attempts, at least in certain instances, to insert itself in the Yogācāra family, but it does so by claiming that what it recycles from the tradition is merely the untransmitted and transhistorical spirit of its founder. This effectively echoes the divide between tradition-as-value and tradition-as-history central to *Eastern and Western Cultures*.

When it comes to the Confucian tradition, however, the *New Treatise*'s attitude differs in significant ways from the discursive model in which iconoclasm is the by-product of a return to the origin.[75] Although the text conceives of Confucius as the source of the Confucian tradition,[76] it suggests that the original insight achieved by the founder was not entirely lost to his successors. After Confucius experienced the recondite truths, some of his followers, including Zhu Xi, "profoundly grasped Confucius's meaning."[77] The text in fact builds its own genealogy of the way (*daotong*), claiming that "from Confucius, Mencius, to the various masters of the Song and Ming periods—all of them applied themselves to this [acting without having tried to act; i.e.: an ethical praxis based on the inherent mind]. [. . .] They personally experienced recondite [truths] and pursued wondrous [insights] to their limits."[78]

Although the text's genealogy of the way seems to suggest that Confucian truths were transmitted through the conduit of tradition, this is only apparently so. First, it should be noted that the text's genealogy, not unlike Zhu Xi's, is not unbroken: the period from the Han to the Song dynasty and the whole Qing dynasty are conspicuously absent from the text's lineage. Two early figures of the Qing period, Huang Zongxi (黄宗羲; 1610–1695) and Wang Fuzhi (王夫之; 1619–1692), are portrayed in a positive light by the text, but apart from them, the Confucian way seems to have receded during the Qing period according to the *New Treatise*. Second, the text makes it clear that Confucius, Mencius, and the masters of the Song and Ming periods "personally experienced recondite [truths]" (*tixuan* 體玄). What the Neo-Confucians did is not merely to *transmit* the recondite truths of the ancients; they personally *embodied* (*ti*) them—as *tixuan* could alternatively be translated.

Given that the text repeatedly reminds the readers that recondite truths can only be achieved by turning inward, and not by learning from others and tradition, we can safely assume that Mencius and the Neo-Confucians reached one and the same insight independently of the Confucian tradition. Of course, the *New Treatise* acknowledges that the "teachings and thoughts" of former masters "can also be depended upon" to find the right path leading to awakening, but once on the path, one must make the journey alone.[79] It is therefore entirely possible that the Neo-Confucians personally experienced truth after the classics had shown them the way toward awakening. But their insight into the recondite truths could not but have taken place through a process whereby they reconnected with their inherent mind in a state of absolute isolation from all that is exterior to it—including the classics. What is historically transmitted by the Confucian tradition is therefore not the insight into the *dao* itself, but a mode of self-cultivation that can show the way to such insight.

The genealogy of the way of the *New Treatise* should not be confused with a "transmission of the way," as "*daotong*" (道統) is sometimes translated. After all, the *dao* was not transmitted but personally experienced by Confucius, Mencius, and the Neo-Confucian masters *independently of one another*. The genealogy is therefore the product of a retrospective judgment passed by a master-sage able to assess who of the past Confucians truly and independently accessed recondite truths. Authority, in such genealogy of the way, does not flow forward through time, but is rather projected onto the Confucian figures of the past by the genealogist before being subsumed by the latter through the very act of performing a final judgment on tradition.

As we saw in chapter 3, a text can be said to be authoritative only to the extent that it is recognized as such by a significant number of readers. As in the case of *Eastern and Western Cultures*, by claiming that Xiong is of one mind with the sages of the past, the *New Treatise* internalizes a symbolic act of recognition within its discourse. It is now the figures of the sages inscribed in the canon who are meant to perform the all-important role of recognizing the legitimacy of the claim to sagely authority made by the text. To be sure, the authority of the text still entirely relies on the recognition of the readers, but it is safe to assume that their recognition will be more easily secured if Confucius, Mencius, and Neo-Confucians have already performed this recognition within the text. Readers who do not feel particularly confident in their ability to decode the original meaning of the classics but who are inclined to believe that transhistorical truths are hidden within them will be predisposed to provide recognition to a text particularly skilled at presenting its reading of the classics as final judgments before equating its own message with that of past sages.

Attempts at equating the texts' central claims with the words of former sages are made throughout the *New Treatise*. After asserting that the goal of self-cultivation is for the mind to see itself (*xin zijian* 心自見), for example, the text maintains that "that which the *Doctrine of the Mean* calls 'genuineness completing itself' [*chengzhe zicheng* 誠者自成], or what the [*Changes*] calls 'the self-illuminating illustrious virtue' [*zizhao mingde* 自昭明德], or the *Analects* calls 'silently taking note' [*mou er shi zhi* 默而識之]

all mean that the mind sees itself."⁸⁰ In another instance, that "cognitive objects are not separate from consciousness" is confirmed by quotes from the *Mencius*, Cheng Hao, Lu Xiangshan, and Wang Yangming,⁸¹ while the text's reading of the relation between the moral nature (*yili zhi xing* 義理之性) and the psycho-physical nature (*qizhi zhi xing* 氣質之性) is supported by references made to the *Analects* as well as the thought of the Cheng brothers, Zhang Zai (張載; 1020–1077), and Zhu Xi.⁸² The text also justifies its interpretation of what being a Bodhisattva means by appealing to quotes taken from Confucian sources (the *Changes*, Zhou Dunyi, the *Analects*), thus reinforcing the notion that the Buddhists and Confucians share a similar insight into Reality.⁸³

The *New Treatise* shares with *Eastern and Western Cultures* an unmediated hermeneutics, made possible by the fact that according to the text, all human beings share one and the same inherent mind.⁸⁴ By retrieving his inherent mind—or more properly *the* inherent mind shared by all—Xiong naturally became of one mind with the previous sages and could thus directly access the original import of their teachings. This explains why the text's reading of the canon finds no justification in textual evidence or arguments. The *New Treatise* entirely disregards the commentarial tradition, the philological tradition of the Qing period, the sociohistorical context of the texts from which it quotes, and the textual context of the short quotes it abstracts from the canon.

Although they share an unmediated hermeneutics, the *New Treatise* and *Eastern and Western Cultures* differ on one point. While in *Eastern and Western Cultures* it is unclear whether Liang is meant to have intuited the truth of Confucianism independently of the classics or through them, the *New Treatise*'s repeated claim that awakening must be achieved on one's own suggests that Xiong reached his insight autonomously before being able to recognize the equivalence between his own insight and that of former sages and masters hidden away in the canon. This is in fact exactly how the vernacular edition of the *New Treatise*, published in 1944, describes Xiong's awakening and his original intent in writing the 1932 *New Treatise*:

> There was a period when I was inclined toward Indian Buddhist thought [. . .]. Later on, I gradually rejected the theories of various schools. Totally putting aside Buddhism and other systems (including even Confucianism), I searched within myself with singleness of purpose. I thought that truth is not remote from us. We can never lay hold of truth by turning around under the

spell of verbal and written words of others [. . .]. After a long time, I suddenly awoke to the realization that what I inwardly witnessed agreed entirely with the meaning of the *Changes* in the Confucian transmission. Thereupon I completely destroyed the draft of *A General Account of Consciousness-Only Learning* which I had written on the basis of Asaṅga and Vasubandhu and avowed to compose a *New Treatise on the Uniqueness of Consciousness* of my own in order to save myself from the defect of the old. *Hence what I gained from the learning of Confucius was not through books but rather through personal realization.* Only then did I feel that it was verified by what is in his writings. This kind of experience is extremely difficult to explain to ordinary people.

我從前有一個時［代］，是很傾向於印度佛家思想的。……其後，漸漸離開百家之說，佛家和其他連孔家也在內。一概不管，只一意反己自求。我以為，真理是不遠於吾人的，決定不是從他人的語言文字下轉來轉去，可以得到真理的。……久之我所證會者，忽然覺得與孔門傳授之《大易》的意思，若甚相密契。因此，才把舊日所依據無著和世親一派的主張而造作的《唯識學概論》，全毀其稿，又誓改造《新唯識論》，以救其失。我之有得於孔學，也不是由讀書而得的，卻是自家體認所至，始覺得和他的書上所說，堪為印證。這個甘苦，也無法向一般人說了。 [85]

Although this account of Xiong's awakening and of his motivations in writing the *New Treatise* should not be taken for granted, it does support my reading of the *New Treatise* as a text engaged in an attempt to present Xiong as a sage having reached the same insight as Confucius, yet independently of him and of the Confucian tradition that followed.

Subsuming tradition

The goal of the *New Treatise* is not merely that of *preserving* the insights of past sages and masters obscured by the passage of time, however. To be sure, the text proposes a syncretic philosophy meant to subsume the truth of both Yogācāra and Confucianism. But it also makes repeated claims to novelty, as we saw above. Perhaps the greatest novelty of the *New Treatise* resides in its attempt to elucidate its syncretic truth in the form of a *philosophical system*, with the hope of making it clearer and better adapted to the times. As John

Makeham argues, the text "provides us with the first substantive attempt to respond to the modernist challenge of providing Chinese philosophy with 'system,' and Xiong did this in the form of an ontology."[86] The text's emphasis on building an independent philosophical system that "synthesizes Buddhism and Confucianism," Makeham adds, should be understood as a direct response "to claims initially made by Japanese scholars that Chinese philosophy lacked systemization, that in method and organization it was simple and naive, and that it fell far short of the standards set by Western philosophy."[87] To reauthorize Confucianism, and to a lesser extent Yogācāra, the text reshapes them in the form of philosophical system—a form expected to be more easily recognized by readers as a legitimate means of conveying transhistorical truths in the 1930s.

This reading is further supported by the following passage abstracted from a letter to Tang Junyi (唐君毅; 1909–1978) published in 1947, in which Xiong describes the goal of the *New Treatise* as that of systematizing the wisdom of the Confucian and Buddhist traditions. Although we should not take the accuracy of Xiong's description of the text for granted, and although I have thus far avoided appealing to Xiong's oeuvre to understand his *New Treatise*, given that the following quote directly addresses the writing of the *New Treatise*, it can—as the quote at the end of the previous section—be treated as a secondary source, and one that accurately describes the text's ambition as revealed by a number of metacommentaries inserted in the text. The passage reads as follows:

> Works in China are always unsystematic and they do not excel in reasoning, so these works are largely incomprehensible to readers in later times, and those of shallow understanding tend to reject Chinese philosophy or metaphysics as un-philosophical. The publication of the *New Treatise* introduces a brand-new theory [*pikong jianli* 劈空建立], which makes use of a systematic and meticulous approach to reveal, in an oblique manner, the incomparable and ultimate truth. If learners study this book with prudence and modesty, they are bound to find herein the basic lessons about life and the universe as discussed not only by eminent Confucian scholars in this land from the late Zhou dynasty to the Song and Ming dynasties, but also by eminent Buddhist thinkers. Extensive and deep, the book leaves nothing out.

此土著述，向無系統，以不尚論辨故也。緣此而後之讀者求了解乃極難。亦緣此而淺見者流不承認此土之哲學或形而上學得成為一種學。《新論》劈空建立，卻以系統謹嚴之體製而曲顯其不可方物之至理。學者誠肯虛心、細心，熟習此論，必見夫此土晚周儒道以迄宋明，旁及印土大乘，其諸哲學家中，對於宇宙人生諸大問題無不網羅融合貫穿於《新論》之中。旁皇周浹，無所遺憾。[88]

By presenting the *New Treatise* as "a brand-new theory," what this passage suggests is not that the insights it conveys are entirely new. After all, the book encompasses the "basic lessons about life and the universe" taught by both Confucians and Buddhists. The *New Treatise* is therefore "new" in terms not of its message, but of the medium through which this message is transmitted to readers. This medium is precisely what Makeham calls the "systematic and meticulous approach" that "respond[s] to the modernist challenge of providing Chinese philosophy with 'system.'"

Despite its vehement attack on (Western) philosophy and the method of analysis, the *New Treatise* seeks to reauthorize Eastern traditions of "wisdom" by translating them in the form of philosophical system. The goal of the system is to leave "nothing out," so that the entirety of what is transhistorically valuable of the past finds itself subsumed within it. This explains why Xiong presented the *New Treatise* as "the crystallization of Oriental philosophy."[89] Yet by deploying a philosophical system, the aim is also to convey the entirety of "Oriental philosophy" in a medium that improves on what has been written about the *dao* in the past.[90] After all, the *New Treatise* is "systematic" and "meticulous" whereas in the past, Chinese works have remained "unsystematic," so much so that they have become "largely incomprehensible to readers in later times." By imposing the form of philosophical system onto the message of Confucianism and Buddhism, in sum, the text seeks to render this message clearer and more readily available to readers. The text thus betrays a desire not only to *subsume* the entirety of what it regards as valuable of Eastern traditions, but also to *substitute* itself for it.

Conclusion

As in the case of *Eastern and Western Cultures*, the establishment of the *New Treatise*'s authority is shaped by a tension between historicity and transhistoricity. On the one hand, it is clear that the main source of authority from which the *New Treatise* draws is that of a transhistorical realm of ontological Oneness to which the author is said to have access—an access readers can hope to achieve one day, provided they read the text in the way it wants to be read. By performing the leap of faith the text requires of them, readers can be introduced into the small family of students of the way. Although not yet awakened, their status as students distinguishes them from the mundanity of so-called "ordinary people." Moreover, insofar as it is meant to have been authored in a transhistorical realm untainted by the mundane world of politics, the text provides readers with a symbolic purification from the sociopolitical issues of the Nanjing decade.

By equating its message with the insight of former masters and sages, the text attempts to buttress its claim to transhistoricity by appealing to the authority of tradition. To ensure that the values the text subsumes from the Confucian and Yogācāra traditions do not sully its claim to transhistoricity, it is imperative that the text pre-emptively refutes the traditionality and historicity of these values. To do so, the *New Treatise* on the one hand negates the value of the entirety of the Yogācāra tradition—although the text at times exonerates its founder—and on the other hand portrays former sages and masters as having achieved the same insight independently of one another and of any form of cultural transmission. If Xiong's insight into Fundamental Reality was also reached by former Confucians independently of one another, and if the very same insight was also achieved by Buddhist masters who lived in an entirely different historical and cultural context, the universal and transhistorical nature of this insight can be presented as *historically proven.*

The text's rapport with the authority of tradition is therefore highly ambiguous. It needs tradition to authorize its discourse, by making of former sages and masters mirror images of the author, but it also needs it not to take on the appearance of tradition. What it needs, in short, is an antitradition. Confucianism serves precisely this purpose, insofar as it is reshaped by the text into an ouroboric antitradition that births itself by killing itself. The truth lodged in the heart of the Confucian tradition is first reauthorized only so that it can, in a second step, be subsumed by the text in a manner that ultimately de-authorizes the tradition again.

To reauthorize the Confucian tradition in the discursive context of Republican China, the text employs modern means, such as that of the philosophical system. Moreover, by drawing a sharp distinction between discernment and wisdom, it clearly seeks to re-establish the authority of

Confucian wisdom in opposition to Western philosophy, insofar as the former can grasp absolute truth while the latter can merely access conventional "truths" revealed to be false once awakening takes place. The text's claim to have subsumed the truth of tradition in a discursive format that is both clearer and more systematic than previous accounts cannot but lead to a devaluation of previous Confucian works, however. We can presume that readers who accept the validity of the *New Treatise*'s self-portrayal would in theory find no interest in decoding the message hidden away in the complex language of the Confucian classics and the Buddhist sutras, as the very same message is made accessible by the *New Treatise* in a manner that is much less demanding of the readers. Of course, we can expect that in practice, readers would still feel the need to read the classics, especially since their use in producing social distinction cannot be matched by the *New Treatise*, unless the latter is recognized by a significant number of individuals as a modern classic. Yet this does not alter the fact that the text does attempt to substitute itself for the entirety of tradition—or, to be more precise, for the entire transhistorical value said to reside in its midst.

Ouroboric traditions, such as that of the *New Treatise*'s Confucianism, are shaped around a constituting fissure that runs through their very core: between (1) the imperative that the text's traditionality be recognized by readers, so that the validity of its claim to belong to the elite group of Buddhist masters and Confucian sages can be accepted by them, and (2) the need for the text to continuously negate its own traditionality and safeguard the purity of its claim to originate in the transhistorical realm. Any reader familiar with the Buddhist and Confucian traditions will readily recognize how open the *New Treatise* is in borrowing vocabularies and discursive tropes from traditional sources. On the one hand, the text draws from Buddhist distinctions between absolute and conventional truths, apophatic and kataphatic modes of explanation, nominal and ontological discourses, and awakened individuals and ordinary people, not to mention its indebtedness to the duality of the mind expressed in *The Awakening of Mahāyāna Faith*, as well as to Yogācāra terminologies such as "habituated mind," "habituated tendency," "mental associates," and so forth. From Confucianism, on the other hand, the text borrows the notion of inherent mind (*benxin*), an ontology of constant transformation, and a self-cultivation model heavily indebted to Wang Yangming. Much more could be said of the traditional inheritances of the *New Treatise*. Suffice it to say, for our purpose, that the text openly acknowledges that it adopts the language of tradition, but only to then argue it uses this language in a thoroughly novel manner that ensures its claim to transhistoricity is not undermined by the traditional language through which it is conveyed.

To cumulate the symbolic benefits of situating itself both within and above tradition, the text deploys a number of discursive strategies of denial. Iconoclasm is one such strategy that adds to the benefit of drawing from the authority of tradition that of denying that it does so in order to ascribe to itself the authority of the transhistorical. Another discursive strategy of denial deployed by the text is its clever use of the distinction between nominal and ontological discourses. By presenting what it says as entirely nominal and what it means as pointing toward the ontological Oneness of Fundamental Reality, the text can relegate any sign of traditionality to what it says, while securing what it means from any association with non-canonical tradition. The dual positioning of the text thus allows it to double its benefits by legitimizing its pretention to transhistoricity with the authority of the Confucian and Buddhist traditions, while simultaneously denying its reliance on tradition by presenting itself as standing in the transhistorical realm of Fundamental Reality.

Along with the dual positioning of the text, the imposition of the philosophical form, in Bourdieu's sense, also serves as an important means through which the text can position itself in the discursive milieu and deny that it does so at one and the same time. What the language of philosophy allows is for the text to frame its implicit attack on "westernized" intellectuals as entirely disinterested—that is, as the mere product of the author's investment in the search for truth in the field of epistemology. The same holds true of its attacks on Yogācāra, the philosophical tenor of which makes it possible for the text to hide the fact that these attacks are aimed at intellectuals who occupy a competing position in the discursive field. By purging itself from any mention of the sociopolitical issues of the day, the text performs philosophical autonomy discursively instead of making its claim to autonomy explicit—which would have made it appear as if the text's disinterestedness were ultimately very interested. Of course, my point is precisely that *it is interested*, but it must hide this interest by continuously performing disinterested autonomy through the imposition of the philosophical form.

We saw in the previous chapter that *Eastern and Western Cultures* builds a complex narrative aimed at absolving Confucian tradition-as-value from tradition-as-history. To achieve a similar goal, the *New Treatise* adopts a different approach: that of simply discursively performing the cleansing of Confucianism from history by philosophizing it in such a way that history is simply left undiscussed by the text. Indeed, nowhere does the text address the issue of Confucianism's relation to imperial polity or its important role, as a state-sponsored ideology, in sanctioning social and gendered hierarchies. The sociopolitical dimensions of Confucianism are also entirely evacuated from the text, which is silent on the notions of ritual and music (*liyue* 禮樂) or the three bonds and five relationships (*sangang wuchang* 三綱五常). While the text's silence on these issues might be accounted for by the fact that the *New Treatise* presents itself as an ontology of the mind-universe, in relation to which sociopolitical concerns are entirely irrelevant, I suggest the reverse is in fact more accurate: intentionally or not, the text reshapes Confucianism into an ontology of the mind-universe to ensure it would be in no way liable to the criticism that Confucianism was but the ideology of a bygone era.

There is a subtle irony in the imposition of the philosophical form of system onto Confucianism by the text, given how the *New Treatise* values Confucianism over Yogācāra for its refusal to build systematic "treatises and discourses." This irony is revealing of the double bind of Chinese or Asian philosophies. As Amy Olberding notes, "this double bind consists in the need to demonstrate that Asian philosophies offer novel elements not found elsewhere in the Western canon and in the need to make Asian philosophies conform to dominant existing interests, methods, and paradigms: Asian philosophy needs to be different, but never *too* different."[91] This double bind manifests itself, in the *New Treatise*, in the difficult task of writing a philosophical defense of Chinese or Asian philosophical traditions in opposition to Western philosophy—hence the text's contrast between "wisdom" and "philosophy"—but within a historical context in which Western philosophical standards had become widely adopted. To answer this challenge, the text opposes Western philosophy with tools borrowed from it, with the ultimate consequence that the form of the text undermines its content.

Traces of the situatedness, mundanity, historicity, and traditionality of the text continuously threaten to undercut the text's claim to emanate from a position of ontological Oneness that transcends the mundane, the historical, and the traditional. Its imposition of philosophical system, for example, threatens to reveal the text's concern with its own reception in the discursive milieu of its time on the one hand, and to undermine the text's rejection of (Western) philosophy and systems because of their blindness toward the Oneness of Fundamental Reality on the other. This explains why the text presents its use of philosophical system, language, and distinctions as a skillful means pointing the way toward an escape from the grasp of philosophy, system, language, and distinctions. This entails that language, system, and philosophy are valuable only insofar as they point the way toward a realm within which all three vanish to give way to a totalizing Oneness. This effectively echoes how tradition is rendered valueless by the text unless it has the ability to lead one on the path at the end of which awaits a complete transcendence from the realm of the traditional.

The text's iconoclasm is nearly absolute, insofar as it is directed toward all competing positions in the discursive milieu, but also extends, in an ouroboric fashion, to the very traditions the text seeks to subsume. Finally, iconoclasm is also directed at the text itself—not the ultimate meaning the text purports to obliquely reveal, of course, but the markers of mundanity and historicity that are intrinsic to textuality, such as the use of language (which is inherently both social and historical) as well as the imposition of a philosophical form that betrays the historical conditions within which the text was written.

Whether directed at philosophy, language, system, or Confucianism, iconoclasm plays a similar role: that of a hegemonic discursive device whereby all forms of tradition, language, and philosophy are rejected except for those subsumed and deployed by the text itself. The rhetoric of Oneness further strengthens the hegemonic contentions of the text, as it enables it to reject pluralism and present itself as the only means to reach absolute truth. As we saw above, the implicit targets of the text's hegemonic rejection of otherness are not only students of Yogācāra, but also Chinese philosophers—and intellectuals more generally—who adopt "Western" approaches. As such, the *New Treatise* can be read as a counter-hegemonic project aimed at decentering the intellectual inheritors of May Fourth in the discursive milieu of the time, as the conclusion will make clear.

Conclusion

Hegemony and the Politics of Antitradition

Located in between a closed past and an open future, in between a finite here and a timeless there, human beings have been inclined to project zones of authority onto the ends of time: in the ancients of the beginning, in the utopias of history's end, or in dominions that escape the supremacy of time. Such projected zones of authority were then put to the task of justifying the present state of affairs or condemning it, depending on whether the present was demonstrated to be in continuity with the authoritative origin or not, whether it was oriented toward the liberating telos of history or not, or whether it was justified in the timeless eyes of the transhistorical or not. In final analysis, however, it is first and foremost timelessness that has served as an ultimate marker of authority. When the end of history is deemed salvatory, it is as the manifestation of a transhistorical mode of existence forever awaited. And when the origin of a tradition is regarded as authoritative, it is usually as a manifestation of a timeless truth that ought to remain unchanged throughout the ages. The authority of tradition is therefore often closely allied to that of the transhistorical.[1]

Traditions can serve, among other purposes, as remarkably powerful vessels of the transhistorical, as their point of origin often remains shrouded in mystery and can thus more readily serve as relatively blank screens on which finite beings can project reversed images of themselves: images of individuals unbound and unfettered by their sociohistorical location. By restraining individuals embodying the transhistorical in the straightjacket of tradition, the transhistorical can be monopolized by groups seeking to control the transmission of the only tradition in the midst of which the transhistorical stands. Traditions often are, after all, the product of a discursive process whereby the chaotic occurrences of the past are translated into a relatively homogeneous and reasoned unity. We can always emphasize the many tensions that inhere in them, but the very act of reifying and abstracting a tradition out of the past is already to find some form of unity or pattern in it, even if this pattern is one of tensions. As the end product of a process of reification, traditions lend themselves to attempts at monopolizing the transhistorical source said to be located in the distant past.

Traditions said to convey transhistorical value have often served as precious commodities that could justify social distinctions and mark off the identity of an elite group. Monopolizing such traditions is not an easy task, however, as competing groups can always condemn the tradition benefiting the hegemonic group as a perverted simulacrum having lost all ties with the transhistorical origin it claims to embody. New traditions that profess to be more faithful to the originary moment of inception can then be initiated, or through a more radical gesture, the bold claim can be made that the transhistorical can be accessed without the need to first embody the tradition of the hegemon—a claim that can, if successful, be subsequently treated as the beginning of a new tradition. Traditions thus undergo various moments at which they are re-reified, re-packaged, and re-homogenized into new unities. While the past is a dominion whose scope expands incessantly, absorbing in its midst the heterogeneity of human life, human beings strive, equally incessantly, to abstract from this dominion homogeneous traditions that can be more readily handled and possessed.

By virtue of their ability to abstract homogenized cores from the chaotic scope of the past, and do so in such a way that the transhistorical value said to reside in "our" beginnings can be monopolized by a group or individual, antitraditions are remarkably valuable commodities. They allow one to reject all traditions but one, monopolize the only tradition whose transhistoricity enables our emancipation from the sociohistorical confines of the human condition, condemn competing groups as mired in the domain of the traditional, and immunize one's position by presenting it as non-traditional—as a natural disposition emerging from the ashes of the past or as an innate potential, residing in the depths of our mind, that can transform us in our own reversed image. Antitraditions, in short, are perfectly suited to serve hegemonic purposes. The rise of Confucian iconoclasm in Republican China can be seen as one of many attempts to harness the power of antitraditions to serve such purposes.

Level playing field

The discursive analysis of *Eastern and Western Cultures* and the *New Treatise* conducted in the previous chapters has brought to the fore the remarkably iconoclastic tenor of both texts, which reject the value of tradition except when it comes to emancipatory antitraditions (Confucianism, and to some extent Buddhism) said to be entirely subsumed by the texts. Owing to the fact that both texts reshape Confucianism into an antitradition capable of freeing humanity from all traditions, I have described them as partaking in an alternative to the iconoclasm of May Fourth I call "Confucian iconoclasm."

As noted in the introduction, although "Confucian iconoclasm" refers to a common discursive project shared by both texts, this project should not be thought of as the product of a coalition between Liang Shuming and Xiong Shili, who would have joined forces against the opponents they had in common. Although the objects of my study are not the historical figures of Liang Shuming or Xiong Shili, and although the previous analysis remains for the most part agnostic as to the authorial intentions behind the writing of the texts, important dimensions of the two historical figures have nevertheless obliquely come to the fore through the analysis of their texts, such as their remarkable sense of mission and hubris. We can extrapolate from the fact that both texts present their author as the *sole* incarnation of the transhistorical core of the Confucian tradition that Xiong and Liang might have been reluctant to form close alliances with other intellectuals claiming to represent Confucianism. And indeed, we know from historical accounts that Liang and Xiong had a fraught relationship.[2]

That *Eastern and Western Cultures* and the *New Treatise* share a common discursive strategy and project should rather be accounted for by the fact that both texts were equally shaped by their discursive milieu. To better understand Confucian iconoclasm as a project, it is of great importance that we situate it in its sociohistorical and discursive contexts and pay close attention to the competing projects against which it emerged. As Joseph R. Levenson argued more than fifty years ago,[3] holding the value of some aspects of Chinese traditions in the early nineteenth century and doing so one hundred years later meant something entirely different, as the issues one dealt with in the early twentieth century were no longer those of the early nineteenth. Partly, this is due to the fact that, as Levenson notes, there was a viable alternative to tradition in the early twentieth century. However, we must be careful not to assume, as Levenson did, that this alternative (Western knowledges) became dominant in Republican China because of its inherent universality, which was simply recognized by those Chinese intellectuals who could keep in check their emotional attachment to the Chinese past.

Of central importance is that we situate both May Fourth and Confucian iconoclasm on a level playing field, so that claims to the universality of Western knowledges *and* Confucianism can be equally read as hegemonic operations invested in attempts to occupy central subject positions in the intellectual field. The danger in not doing so is that we reproduce the assumption that underscores Levenson's analysis regarding the universality of Western knowledges and the particularism of Chinese traditions, and that on this ground, we only perceive defenses of the latter as the result of particular interests, while failing to see appeals to the universality of Western knowledges as similarly shaped by the particular interests of their advocates.

While one solution to this problem would be to portray both groups as disinterested seekers of universal truths, I suggest it is historically more accurate to describe both camps as interested parties engaged in hegemonic practices aimed at presenting their views as the only truly universal ones. By doing so, we can challenge the predominant narrative according to which modern Confucianism emerged as an attempt to preserve the value of Chinese or Eastern traditions, and did so in answer to the problem of the gradual erosion of such traditions from the May Fourth period onward. By conceptualizing the main challenge faced by Confucian iconoclasm—understood as the most successful form of modern Confucian textuality—as the *hegemonic dimension* of May Fourth,[4] Confucian iconoclasm can be reinterpreted as a counter-hegemonic project.

The amputated authority of tradition

The difficult task faced by Confucian iconoclasm was that of establishing textual authority in opposition to the May Fourth hegemonic group, yet in a manner that fulfilled discursive criteria set by this group, so as to avoid being viewed as the handmaiden of the feudal traditions decried by it. To achieve a better sense of how Confucian iconoclasm responded to this difficult challenge, it is useful to appeal to Alexandre Kojève's subtle analysis of the concept of authority.

Regarding the authority of tradition, Kojève notes that "the Past which exerts an *Authority* over me is a *historic* Past; it is *my* Past, that is to say the Past that is the 'cause' of my Present and the 'basis' of my Future; it is the Past that is held to determine the Present with the Future in mind. In other words, the Past does not acquire an Authority except in so far as it presents itself in the guise of a *tradition*."[5] There can be no authority of tradition without historical causality, in short. With the advent of modernity, the authority of tradition was, in Kojève's words, "amputated."[6] Although he does not explicitly describe the historical process that led to this amputation, it is relatively easy to see how the historical caesura modernity is purported to have performed would weaken the authority of tradition, insofar as the present is no longer regarded as significantly caused by the past.[7]

In the Chinese setting, the symbolic amputation of the authority of tradition, although far from complete, was discursively performed with remarkable force by the May Fourth group. This did not entail the end of authority, however. May Fourth members successfully managed to present themselves as the sole representatives of two other kinds of authority discussed by Kojève. First is the authority of the future, represented in Kojève's typology by political leaders who guide the people toward a future they claim to foresee more clearly than anyone else. The intellectuals who emerged out of the May Fourth Movement were remarkably successful in monopolizing the authority of the future by claiming to represent the modern West or communism, which they regarded as the universal future of humanity.

Second is the authority of eternity, epitomized in Kojève by the judge whose rulings are meant to incarnate the atemporal laws of the state.[8] In May Fourth discourse, this authority was monopolized by claiming that a universal and infallible faculty of judgment was accessible to those who could free themselves from the shackles of feudal traditions and achieve modern autonomy. The authorities of the future and eternity were ultimately fused in May Fourth discourse, insofar as what awaited humanity in the future was a thorough emancipation from particularism that went hand in hand with access to the universalism of eternity. Teleological history and individual autonomy thus provided important discursive means through which the May Fourth group could monopolize the authorities of the future and eternity and reshape the rules that codified social distinction in the intellectual field.

Confucian iconoclasm emerged as an answer to the conundrum of how to reinstate and monopolize the authority of some form of tradition in a discursive milieu in which this authority had been amputated, and do so in a way that could compete with the May Fourth hegemon in a discursive battle the rules of which had been set by the hegemon. Confucian iconoclasm met this challenge by taking part in the hegemonic politics of antitradition of its opponents. The first step in Confucian iconoclasm's politics of antitradition was to ensure that the value of tradition was not established on the grounds that it was a tradition—on the grounds that it was the cause of China's present. It was of central importance that any attempt at infusing value back into Chinese traditions did not appear motivated by one's "emotional tie" to tradition *on the basis that it is one's own*.[9] Universal value could perhaps be found in tradition, but only insofar as this value was recognized by a modern subject entirely autonomous from the empire of the traditional.

Instead of rejecting the legitimacy of the symbolic amputation of tradition performed by May Fourth, Confucian iconoclasm acknowledges its value in freeing humanity from the shackles of the past. *Eastern and Western Cultures* does this by recasting the entire history of Confucianism as a failure to live up to its potential—a potential that found itself embodied in the person of Confucius. To be sure, despite the historical failure of Confucianism, Confucius could still be looked upon as the cause of China's present, as he had set in place the particular will that determined the entire course of Chinese history. But this is not the explicit reason why the text regards Confucius as authoritative. The sage represents, after all, a cause whose effects have been entirely distorted by history. Insofar as it rejects the effects, the text cannot acclaim the cause, at least not on the basis of what it has caused.

Instead, the authority of Confucius, in *Eastern and Western Cultures*, finds its source in eternity: in a natural way of life that transcends the limitations of time and place. Everyone possesses the intuitive faculty of the sage that allows them to escape the determinism of culture and history, although only Confucius was able to activate the full potential of this faculty. Confucius's authority is shaped by the text in the image of the impartial judge, to borrow from Kojève. The final judgments Confucius passes on Zai Wo, hunting, fishing, and cooking, to name but a few examples, find their legitimacy not in argumentation, but in the authority of the judge who embodies a natural way of life and gives free reign to an intuitive faculty that is not bound by time and place.

The *New Treatise* also performs the amputation of the authority of tradition by presenting any form of inheritance from the past as a limitation imposed on the innate state of awakening of the mind. Various Confucians throughout history have retrieved their awakened inherent mind, but they have done so in a state of complete isolation from one another. It is entirely possible that they did so by following the path charted out by the Confucian classics, but once on the path, they could only achieve awakening on their own, in total isolation from tradition and others. Confucianism is not authoritative, in this discursive model, on the basis that it is the cause of the present—in fact, it is not even the proper cause of the state of awakening enjoyed by previous sages. Confucianism's authority is first and foremost rooted in eternity: in an inherent mind with which everyone is endowed at birth and through which humanity can directly access the transhistorical. Although this eternal authority is not utterable, it is nevertheless obliquely hinted at in the classics. The eternal truth residing in the classics can thus be unlocked by anyone who has retrieved their inherent mind, in such a way as to allow them to pass final judgments on tradition from the transhistorical plane of eternity.

Both texts therefore make it clear that they value Confucianism not because of its traditionality, and even less because it is a *Chinese* tradition, but because one or several former sages have embodied the same transhistorical insight as that reached by their authors, through intuitions that are theoretically accessible to everyone. Once the authority of Confucianism is transplanted in eternity instead of tradition, the texts offer complex narratives through which they present themselves as the only conduits through which the insight of Confucianism can be *transmitted*, in such a way as to enable the texts to symbolically reshape themselves into the authoritative cause of the future.

In *Eastern and Western Cultures*, this is achieved through a complex metanarrative enabling the fusion of temporal and eternal forms of authority. Although the main source of authority he embodies is that of eternity, Confucius also personifies the authority of the leader who foresees the future and sets out to guide humanity toward it. In the second stage of teleological history, the intuitive spirit of Confucius is expected to be revived and transform the way human beings relate to one another as well as to nature and the cosmos. Confucius had foreseen this future. Only he had done so too precociously. In the past, China had fallen victim to the fact that the future Confucius had foreseen was too far ahead to implement. But this fate was about to change. Humanity was about to realize the value of Confucius as his ideal took shape in history.

That Confucius embodies an authority that transcends his situatedness in time and space was meant to be historically demonstrated, in the near future, by the fact that his ideal would be universally realized throughout the world. The modern authority of the future central to teleological history is therefore put to the task, in *Eastern and Western Cultures*, of supplementing and supporting the eternal authority of Confucius. The authority of the future is auxiliary to that of eternity insofar as it is because of its eternal value that Confucius's ideal will reappear in the future—and it is not because it will reappear that it has eternal value.

The text's Confucius thus fuses the authorities of eternity and the future, but ultimately also that of tradition. In the past, the eternal message of Confucius had not been transmitted historically, and as such it was not properly speaking a "tradition," except to the extent it had been passed down in a hidden form in the classical canon (although this message had been so well hidden that nobody had grasped it before Liang).[10] As humanity reaches the second phase of teleological history, however, it would finally recognize Confucius as *the* cause of the present, and therefore as a tradition. Although this cause was not properly speaking *historical*, given that Confucius's message was not historically transmitted, Confucius could nevertheless be viewed as the *spiritual* cause of the second phase of teleological history. This goes to show that the future would bring about the reinstatement of the authority of the Confucian tradition, although not of *any* Confucian tradition, of course. What was inexorably set to be reauthorized by the determinism of history was a Confucian antitradition that could release humanity from its enslavement to tradition by recasting it in a realm of naturalness.

Within this discourse, Liang serves as a conduit through which the eternal authority of Confucius, alienated from the historical process in the past, can finally be made manifest in history.[11] Insofar as he is portrayed by the text as the living embodiment of the spirit of the ancient sage,[12] Liang is meant to share with Confucius the authority of eternity, although unlike Confucius, Liang was able to foresee the *historical means* through which the eternal and natural way of life of the sage could be made accessible to all.[13] It is therefore through Liang that the authority of eternity can be fused with that of the future, which has for consequence the re-establishment of the authority of the Confucian (anti)tradition (as cause of the future).

In sum, the text first rejects the authority of tradition before reintroducing it through the back door by deploying a complex historical metanarrative in which eternal and temporal authorities can be fused. The tradition thus reauthorized, however, is not that of the historical Confucianism at which May Fourth attacks were targeted. It is a new form of tradition, spiritual in character, that would be established in the near future. While in the context of the historical tradition Liang would be but one link in a long chain of Confucian figures, in the soon-to-be-established tradition his role

Conclusion | 173

is not only that of the sole contemporary incarnation of the sage, but also that of the only conduit through which the eternal ideal of Confucius can be made real in the realm of temporality. Liang serves, in other words, as the bridge connecting the shores of heaven and earth, thanks to which the latter can be reshaped in the image of the former. Of central importance to *Eastern and Western Cultures*' complex metanarrative is not only that the authority of tradition can be reinstated, but that it can be reinstated *around the figure of Liang Shuming*.

As to the *New Treatise*, it reinstates the authority of tradition through a triple gesture. First, it sharply distinguishes between the authority of tradition (the canon) and the authority of eternity (awakening) before claiming that the latter cannot be fully conveyed in the language of the former. At best, texts can pass on their authors' experience of the path that led them to awakening, but they cannot describe the state of awakening itself, except through indirect means. Second, the *New Treatise* performs iconoclasm by suggesting that Buddhist sutras are ill-equipped to convey truth through such indirect means. Although Confucian texts have done a better job at pointing toward the truth without naming it, they have done so in such an unsystematic manner that their message barely can be grasped by readers.

Once it has challenged previous textual claims to embody and convey the transhistorical truth of the sages and masters of the past, the *New Treatise* sets out—in a third step—to portray itself as uniquely equipped to transmit this truth to readers. It can do so by deploying skillful means and by synthesizing the entire transhistorical message of tradition in a textual form that is both clearer and more systematic than any Confucian text of the past. The *New Treatise*, in short, presents itself as the only viable means through which the truth can be *indirectly* transmitted. The text's rejection of the authority of tradition is thus followed by a gesture that reinstates it in such a way as to situate the *New Treatise* as its only medium—as the subsumption of the entire scope of tradition that can then be transmitted to readers.

The texts thus reshape Confucianism into an ouroboric antitradition: a tradition that births itself by rejecting the value of all traditions, including that of Confucianism itself. By deploying such radical iconoclastic discursive techniques, the texts can reinstate the authority of Confucianism on eternal and universal grounds no longer sullied by the vagaries of history before subsuming it in its entirety. The symbolic killing of tradition performed by the texts' ouroboric act of creation is thus meant to reposition the texts themselves as the new point of origin of tradition, in the sense that the transhistorical truth of Confucianism is properly *transmitted* for the first time in the act of reading performed by the readers.

In such a way, the texts can speak to two audiences at once: on the one hand, their ouroboric discourse is meant to pre-emptively inoculate the texts against the rebuke of iconoclasts who see in the Confucian tradition but the remnants of feudal heteronomy, and on the other, by positioning themselves as the new fountainhead of tradition, the texts can instill a renewed sense of national pride in readers uninclined to reject the value of Confucianism. Insofar as they put forth a discourse that partakes in the politics of antitradition of the time, however, the texts do much more than provide the discursive means to reauthorize Confucianism. By suturing the universality of Confucianism with their own message, they also undertake to establish an alternative epistemic hegemony to that of May Fourth.

Counter-hegemonic operations

As Ernesto Laclau and Chantal Mouffe point out, hegemonic operations are never entirely finalized, as within them resides a "tension between universality and particularity."[14] Counter-hegemonic groups can always reveal the suture between the universal and the particular that sustains the hegemon as historically contingent and fabricated. They can then engage in counter-hegemonic operations at one of two levels. At one level, they can use the established rules of discursivity to displace the hegemonic group by filling in the universal that legitimizes it with content that is beneficial to the counter-hegemonic group. At another level, they can attempt to change the rules of discursivity—through what Slavoj Žižek calls "the authentic act"[15]—by challenging the universals co-opted by the hegemon and by producing new ones. As a shorthand, I call these two levels "intrinsic" and "extrinsic counter-hegemonic operations," respectively.

To explain a similar distinction, Judith Butler uses the example of the potential approaches toward marriage lesbian and gay rights activists can opt for. Either the universality of the institution of marriage can be accepted by the activists who can then ask for same-sex marriage to be accommodated within that institution, or they can challenge the conception of marriage as a universal institution.[16] Although the first option—the intrinsic counter-hegemonic operation—reiterates and even reinforces the rules established by the hegemon, it might be a strategy better suited to those situated in a marginal position from which challenging the rules of discursivity is exceedingly difficult, if not simply unfeasible.

Coming back to Confucian iconoclasm, it would appear, at least at first sight, that it deploys counter-hegemonic operations of the intrinsic type by using the rules of the hegemon in opposition to it. The texts do so through the discursive media of historical teleology and human autonomy. Before going into the details of how each text does so, however, it is worth reiterating that the processes discussed in what follows are not meant to describe *intentional choices* made by Liang Shuming and Xiong Shili. My point is not that Liang and Xiong purposefully borrowed hegemonic operations from their May Fourth opponents to oppose them. Although we cannot rule out that they did so intentionally, it is overall more likely that both authors simply had a refined sense of the intellectual field, of the limits of what could be successfully argued, and of the discursive rules one had to abide by to be accepted in the field. What I describe below therefore can be regarded as the effects the hegemonic rules of discursivity that became widespread at the turn of the 1920s had on the texts.

Eastern and Western Cultures is the most explicit of the two texts in turning discursive means borrowed from May Fourth against May Fourth. It adopts a modernization discourse of its own, but one that remains extremely close to that of May Fourth in that it rests on a unilinear and teleological model of history understood as a gradual process of emancipation from the limitations of the past.[17] The text acknowledges that the future and not the past is the temporal marker of human liberty, and it further accepts the May Fourth claim that the "modern West" represents the universal future toward which humanity evolves. Where the text departs from May Fourth is of course in the fact that it supplements the historical teleology of May Fourth with two horizons: that of Confucianism and that of Buddhism.

Although the universal future the text seeks to fill in with particular content differs from that of May Fourth, the discursive means through which it attempts to do so—by projecting its agenda onto the future of unilinear history—reproduces the May Fourth use of modernization discourse. As in the case of May Fourth,[18] *Eastern and Western Cultures*' hegemonic operations follow a two-step process. In a first step, the text sutures Confucianism with the universal future of teleological history. To make this act of suture appear irrefutable and hide its fabricated nature, the text deploys three distinct discursive techniques.

First, it presents its reading of the future as scientific, so that the equation of Confucianism with the universal future can be interpreted as the inevitable outcome of unalterable historical trends. Second, *Eastern and Western Cultures* steals a page from the May Fourth playbook by presenting the Confucian future as having already happened, or at least as having already begun to happen in the West. It does so by reviewing new intellectual and societal trends, which it interprets as objective proofs of the confucianization and sinicization of the West. Just as in May Fourth discourse, that the future has already happened in the West is meant to make the suture between the particular agenda of the text and the universal future of humanity appear as an irrefutable historical *fact*.[19] And finally, the text employs a rhetoric of naturalization to present the Confucian sage as what naturally emerges once humanity manages to satisfy its primordial needs. This rhetoric effectively echoes the portrayal of human autonomy as the natural outcome of humanity's breaking free from the shackles of tradition at work in May Fourth hegemonic operations.

In the second step of its hegemonic operations, the text deploys a number of discursive devices meant to suture the universalism of the Confucian sage with Liang Shuming. It does so by equating the message of Liang with that of Confucius and by portraying Liang as uniquely capable of passing intuitive and final judgments on the meaning of the classics and on the history of Confucianism. By performing the naturalness of the sage, the text can describe its authorship as thoroughly disinterested and dissimulate the hegemonic project behind the equation between Confucius, Liang, and the universal future. Moreover, by presenting itself as the mere translation into language of the natural way of life of the sage, the text can more easily secure the readers' leap of faith, which is responsible for instituting the authority of the text through an act of recognition that confirms the validity of the suture between the sage and Liang Shuming.

Insofar as the text recycles the hegemonic operations of May Fourth to oppose May Fourth, it can be regarded as deploying counter-hegemonic operations of the intrinsic type. This type of operation allows the text to present its own brand of Confucianism as *supplementing*, rather than *supplanting*, the "modern West" as a universal future filled in with May Fourth content. This makes it possible for the text to accept the discursive rules set by the hegemon, but put them to the task of marginalizing the hegemon by relocating it to the first and lower stage of teleological history. This type of operation was better suited to the discursive milieu of the time, as attempting to challenge the hegemonic group by rejecting the universality of the "modern West" in all likelihood would have been met with severe criticism and might have made the text appear obsolete to a significant portion of the readership.

The counter-hegemonic operations of the *New Treatise* are also—at least partially, as we will see—of the intrinsic type, insofar as the text uses the discursive tools of the hegemon against it. In the case of the *New Treatise*, however, it is the figure of the autonomous individual, and not teleological history, that is put to the task of hegemonizing the text's agenda by universalizing it. In May Fourth, human autonomy had been portrayed as the natural and universal outcome of the process whereby the Chinese would gradually but surely free themselves from servile traditions of heteronomy—Confucianism being the prime example of such heteronomy. What the *New Treatise* does is to recycle the image of the autonomous individual no longer defined by its exteriority in order to reauthorize the Confucian sage. It does so by claiming that the natural outcome of the process whereby the self gradually frees itself from its exteriority is not the rational subject of the modern West but the Confucian sage whose mind "embodies" the entire universe. This suture between the universal figure of the autonomous individual and Confucian sagehood represents the first step of its counter-hegemonic operations.

In a second step, the text establishes an equivalence between Xiong on the one hand and Confucian sagehood and human autonomy on the other. To do so, the text provides a number of metacommentaries aimed at making sure that the text will be read as the product of a modern sage. The insertion of interlinear autocommentaries, for example, gives readers the sense that the text is a sutra or classic that cannot be altered, as it was written while Xiong was in a state of gnosis. That the text purports to reveal to readers the path that will take them to the shore of enlightenment, and that it continuously claims to obliquely hint at Fundamental Reality, further strengthen the impression that Xiong must have already achieved awakening. This impression finds additional support in the fact that Xiong can pass final judgments on the meaning of the classics without appealing to the commentarial or philological tradition.

The text performs the suture between Xiong and human autonomy by adopting the language and the textual form most closely associated with such autonomy: those of philosophy. The philosophy of the *New Treatise*, however, is not the product of a philosopher accessing universal truths through the medium of reason; it is the creation of an autonomous sage intuiting Fundamental Reality. The text also performs autonomy by eliminating any reference to the sociohistorical context in which it was written. The ritual of purification the text exhorts its readers to perform to free their mind from external influences is thus matched by a symbolic act purifying Confucianism and the text's philosophical system from any sign of involvement in politics, academic debates, and history.

The text's performance of disinterestedness and absolute autonomy plays a central role in dissimulating its (definitely interested) participation in counter-hegemonic operations from the view of readers. To dissimulate its involvement in the hegemonic politics of antitradition, the *New Treatise* also relies on the discursive technique of denial. Closely related to the dual positioning of the text, this technique allows the text to immunize itself from criticism by sharply distinguishing what it says (in language) from what it means (which transcends linguistic expression). If any objection should be raised that the *New Treatise* is in fact deeply concerned with its reception and is engaged in hegemonic operations, the text can dispel such objection by retrieving into the Oneness of sagehood from which it claims to have been written.

The *New Treatise* thus borrows from its opponents the discursive trope of the autonomous individual, and the discursive form of the philosophical system closely associated with it, to reject the claim that the European rational subject, and the May Fourth group acting as its stand-in in Republican China, are the sole legitimate representatives of individual autonomy. It does not entirely reject the rational subject, however. Through the use of the Buddhist theory of the two truths, the text can accept the validity of the suture between human autonomy and May Fourth rationality, but relegate it to a lower epistemic status: that of conventional truths. By comparison, the kind of autonomy achieved through Eastern wisdom, which leads to a reconnection with the flux of the universe, pertains to a higher epistemic realm. Once the absolute truth of Eastern wisdom is fully grasped, however, the conventional "truths" established by "Western" science and philosophy are revealed to be ultimately false.

Sagehood and hegemony

Confucian iconoclasm seeks to reauthorize and monopolize the figure of the sage through hegemonic discursive techniques it borrows from its adversaries. In doing so, its goal is dual. First, it seeks to peripheralize the hegemon by relegating Western knowledge—and its May Fourth representatives—to a lower echelon of a hierarchy of intellectual goods rooted in historical teleology or two truths epistemology. Moreover, it does so in such a way that the rules of discursivity set by the hegemon can be preserved (at least momentarily) and put to the counter-hegemonic tasks of the texts. Second, by adopting the hegemonic discursive tools of its opponents, Confucian iconoclasm also aspires to establish new rules of intellectual/social distinction. By presenting the sage as the figure of universality par excellence, the texts strive to institute new discursive rules that codify how universality can be accessed, embodied, and monopolized. This suggests that Confucian iconoclasm employs *intrinsic* counter-hegemonic operations, whereby it seeks to displace the hegemon by using the discursive tools of the hegemon, to support its *extrinsic* counter-hegemonic operations, whereby it attempts to change the rules that codify discursivity by appealing to a new form of universality personified by the Confucian sage.

The figure of the sage is particularly well suited to the needs of hegemonic operations, insofar as sagehood is both universal *and* particular: it is universally shared by all of us as a potential, yet this potential is fully activated only in extremely rare cases. As such, sagehood represents an archetypical example of a discursive device through which individuals can claim to incarnate the universal. Moreover, insofar as sagehood defies any attempt to pin it down in language, its meaning is never fully fixed. As a tendentially empty signifier of universality,[20] sagehood is prone to serve as a battleground over which various factions and individuals wage a struggle to monopolize universality.

The figure of the sage thus echoes that of the modern autonomous individual incarnated by the European rational subject in being both universal in potential yet particular in terms of who has managed to activate this potential. Both figures point to an originary source, in the sense that they represent a potential endowed to us at birth. Both can also be projected onto the horizon of the future, insofar as they present an image of what naturally springs forth once individuals free themselves from the hindrances of the past. As such, both figures are prone to co-option by individuals or groups who wish to portray themselves as the only means through which the emancipatory horizon of the future can be reached.

Compared with the modern rational subject, however, the figure of the sage seems relatively more predisposed to serving exclusionary purposes. After all, only a handful of sages are said to have existed throughout history. Moreover, while groups have often sought to monopolize the figure of the modern rational subject, sagehood appears to be a prerogative of individuals, not groups. Yet although in *Eastern and Western Cultures*, Liang Shuming is presented as the sole individual incarnating sagehood after Confucius, the natural lifestyle of the sage is expected to be within the reach of humanity as a whole in the near future. As to the *New Treatise*, although its soteriology appears first and foremost invested in saving individuals rather than groups, ultimately the text can be read as an appeal to the ethical revolution of the Chinese people. Therefore, although the figure of the sage seems particularly exclusionary, in effect both texts present themselves as the only conduit through which its universality, a prerogative of the happy few in the past, can be democratized and incarnated by the multitudes in the future. This echoes how the May Fourth group sought to make of itself the only representative of the modern autonomous individual before promoting and disseminating its vision of autonomy throughout the Republic.

The figure of the sage enables the texts to perform two closely intertwined hegemonic operations: one that makes the universal the prerogative of the texts and their authors, and another that sutures the universal with China. While through the first hegemonic operation, the texts seek to position themselves at the center of the discursive field, through the second one, they set out to oppose Eurocentric discourses making of the modern European subject the very incarnation of human autonomy. To propose an alternative form of universality rooted in the Chinese soil, the texts avoid the narrowly nationalistic assertion that only Chinese can become sages. Instead, by opposing Western rationality to Chinese wisdom or intuition, they make the more subtle claim that the Chinese possess a privileged access to the *cultural toolkit* thanks to which we can learn to become sages.

Given that the meaning of sagehood is tendentially empty, it would be tempting to argue that in theory, anyone can claim to be a sage. If sagehood escapes the dominion of language, after all, linguistic proofs of its presence should theoretically be unnecessary, if not counterproductive. In effect, however, there are a number of rules, inscribed in the tradition, that codify access to sagehood. Successfully claiming to be a sage can only be done by individuals who are educated and well versed in the traditional language associated with Confucianism. As such, it is the exclusivity of the *language* of sagehood that limits who can claim to be a sage—a claim the success of which depends on a variety of other factors, such as charisma, social status, institutional affiliation, and so forth.

Confucian iconoclasm ultimately seeks to recenter the intellectual field around new rules of access to universality—rules that require a high level of education and familiarity with the traditional discursive techniques through which one can successfully present oneself as a sage. The discursive means through which the texts seek to obtain the leap of faith of readers, which I describe in chapters 3 and 4, are precisely the new rules of discursivity around which Confucian iconoclasm seeks to reshape the field. Such rules are only available to the Chinese (thus excluding Westerners), to the intellectual elite (thus excluding those with less education), and to those members of the intellectual elite who are well versed in the language of sagehood in particular (thus excluding the members and heirs of the May Fourth group). The figure of the sage, and the rules of discursivity associated with it, are thus put to a counter-hegemonic task by the texts.

The fact that Confucian iconoclasm seeks to recenter the authority of the sage through discursive means borrowed from the May Fourth group makes it all too clear that May Fourth members had been successful in fixing the discursive rules of intellectual/social distinction in Republican China. Traces of the May Fourth hegemon are in fact scattered throughout both texts: in the use of teleological history, in the distinction between Western rationality and Eastern wisdom, in the fetish of human autonomy, in the ideal of the philosophical system, in claims to scientific objectivity, and so forth. Such traces continuously undermine the texts' claim to represent a mode of existence, that of Confucian sagehood, far superior to the autonomous and rational subject of Western modernity. *Eastern and Western Cultures*' appeal to the scientific objectivity of its reading of history, for example, calls into question the idea that the text is the product of an author relying on a Confucian mode of intuition contrasted to the overemphasis on rationality in "Western" science. Similarly, the adoption of the form of philosophical system by the *New Treatise* imperils the text's self-portrayal as standing on the side of Eastern wisdom, and *not* Western philosophy.

The texts are shaped by a tension between (1) their use of extrinsic counter-hegemonic operations to establish sagehood as the only gateway to universality and (2) their need to legitimize sagehood through intrinsic counter-hegemonic operations—operations that ultimately reinforce the hegemon's claim to possess the only means of access to true universality and thus challenge the texts' original goal of monopolizing universality. Nowhere is this tension more visible than in the texts' radical iconoclasm. Reshaping Confucianism into an antitradition certainly contributed to the success of the texts, insofar as it made them better adapted to the discursive milieu. But it also entailed that Confucianism could be successfully reauthorized only through discursive means that continuously negated the traditionality of Confucianism. The texts' overt rejection of historical Confucianisms continuously undermines their attempt at reinstating the language of tradition as the main conduit through which universality could be embodied.

That the texts are riddled with tensions and filled with traces of the hegemon that undermine their claim to sagely universality might partially account for the fact that their counter-hegemonic project was ultimately little successful (even though Confucian iconoclasm remains the most successful modern Confucian textual response to May Fourth in the Republican period). Of course, factors external to the texts most likely played a prominent role in the relative failure of their project. For one thing, the historical context was in all likelihood not yet fully ripe for texts aimed at reauthorizing the figure of the sage. Yet the failure of the texts' counter-hegemonic project might also be explained by the remarkable exclusivity they ascribe to the figure of the sage. Both texts put forth exclusionary claims to orthodoxy, insofar as they present their authors as the sole representatives of Confucian sagehood in modern China. As such, they are exceptionally ill-equipped to establish close ties or chains of equivalence with other intellectuals similarly opposed to the May Fourth hegemonic group. This made it impossible for them to find allies, not only among Buddhists but also among other Confucians.

Despite their inability to forge ties with potential intellectual allies, the texts could nonetheless secure the leap of faith of a number of those readers eager to find a Chinese or Eastern alternative to the contention that universality entirely stood on the side of Western knowledges. However, the success of the texts, among the readership, depended heavily on the readers' willingness to recognize the legitimacy of the texts' claim to emanate from the transhistorical plane of sagehood and perform a leap of faith that rendered the traces of hegemonic struggle scattered throughout them unrecognizable. Such readers might have been inclined to read the texts as attempts to "preserve" tradition in a historical period that saw its authority amputated by members of the May Fourth Movement. By refusing to perform such a leap of faith, however, we can more readily see the texts as engaged in a politics of antitradition aimed at the monopolization of intellectual commodities associated with universality, autonomy, and liberty. And by situating the texts in the context of an intellectual field the rules of which had been set by the May Fourth hegemonic group, we can see more readily how Confucian iconoclasm represents a counter-hegemonic project.

Notes

Introduction

1. I refer to *Analects* 3:14 and 7:1 respectively. For an English translation, see D. C. Lau, trans., *The Analects* (London: Penguin, 1979), 69, 86.

2. See, for example, Roger T. Ames and David L. Hall, *Thinking Through Confucius* (Albany: State University of New York Press, 1987), 24; Tan Sor-hoon, "Balancing Conservatism and Innovation: The Pragmatic *Analects*," in *Dao Companion to the* Analects, ed. Amy Olberding (Dordrecht: Springer, 2014), 335–54; Tan Sor-hoon, "Three Corners for One: Tradition and Creativity in the *Analects*," in *Confucius Now: Contemporary Encounters with the* Analects, ed. David Jones (Chicago: Open Court, 2008), 59–79; Alan Chan, "Philosophical Hermeneutics and the *Analects*: The Paradigm of 'Tradition,'" *Philosophy East & West* 34, no. 4 (October 1984): 421–36. On this topic, see also Michael Puett, *The Ambivalence of Creation: Debates Concerning Innovation and Artifice in Early China* (Stanford: Stanford University Press, 2001).

3. See, for example, Chang Hao, "New Confucianism and the Intellectual Crisis of Contemporary China," in *The Limits of Change: Essays on Conservative Alternatives in Republican China*, ed. Charlotte Furth (Cambridge: Harvard University Press, 1976), 276–302. John Makeham argues there was no self-aware and integrated New Confucian philosophical movement until the 1970s in "The Retrospective Creation of New Confucianism," in *New Confucianism: A Critical Examination*, ed. John Makeham (New York: Palgrave, 2003), 25–54.

4. I use "May Fourth" in its broadest sense, including the New Culture Movement as an integral part of it. Lin Yü-sheng argues that "May Fourth iconoclasm was a result of the interplay of the intellectual change of the content of thought and a traditional Confucian mode of thinking" regarding ideas as the main impetus of historical change. Lin Yü-sheng, "Radical Iconoclasm in the May Fourth Period and the Future of Chinese Liberalism," in *Reflections on the May Fourth Movement: A Symposium*, ed. Benjamin I. Schwartz (Cambridge: Harvard University Press,

1973), 42. On May Fourth iconoclasm, see also Lin Yü-sheng, *The Crisis of Chinese Consciousness: Radical Antitraditionalism in the May Fourth Era* (Madison: University of Wisconsin Press, 1979).

5. See for example Hon Tze-ki's rereading of the place of the supposedly conservative *Journal of National Essence* (*Guocui xuebao* 國粹學報) in China's path to modernity in *Revolution as Restoration*: Guocui xuebao *and China's Path to Modernity, 1905–1911* (Leiden: Brill, 2013). Another example is Lin Shaoyang, who challenges the dichotomy between reformists and revolutionaries that has shaped late Qing intellectual history by showing how intellectuals associated with both camps took part in a single intellectual and cultural movement (*sixiang wenhua yundong* 思想文化運動). Lin Shaoyang 林少阳, *Dingge yi wen: Qingji geming yu Zhang Taiyan "fugu" de xin wenhua yundong* 鼎革以文：清季革命与章太炎「复古」的新文化运动 [*Revolution by Words: Late Qing Revolution and Zhang Taiyan's "Antiquarian" New Culture Movement*] (Shanghai: Shanghai renmin, 2018). Yü Ying-shih has also argued that, strictly speaking, there are no real conservative intellectuals in Republican China, as no one wished to conserve or preserve the status quo. Yü Ying-shih 余英時, "Zhongguo jindai sixiangshi shang de jijin yu baoshou" 中國近代思想史上的激進與保守 [Radicalism and Conservatism in Modern Chinese Intellectual History], in *You ji feng chui shuishang lin: Qian Mu yu xiandai Zhongguo xueshu* 猶記風吹水上鱗－錢穆與現代中國學術 [*Like Recording the Wind Blowing over Shimmering Water: Qian Mu and Modern Chinese Scholarship*] (Taipei: Sanmin shuju, 1991), 199–242. On this topic, see also Yü Ying-shih, "The Radicalization of China in the Twentieth Century," *Daedalus* 122, no. 2 (1993): 125–50.

6. As Eske J. Møllgaard puts it: "the confrontation between Confucius and Mr. Science in the late nineteenth and early twentieth century was also a fight over who should occupy the space of a 'subject supposed to know.'" Eske J. Møllgaard, *The Confucian Political Imagination* (Cham: Palgrave Macmillan, 2018), 30.

7. Edward Shils, *Tradition* (Chicago: University of Chicago Press, 1981), 12. This definition includes both what I call continuous and discontinuous traditions.

8. Liang Shuming 梁漱溟, *Dongxi wenhua ji qi zhexue* 东西文化及其哲学 [Eastern and Western Cultures and Their Philosophies], in *Liang Shuming quanji* 梁漱溟全集 [The Complete Works of Liang Shuming], ed. Committee of the Academy of Chinese Culture (Jinan: Shandong Remin, 1989), vol. 1, 319–547. There is no English translation of this work. I refer to the following French translation for readers who do not know Chinese: Liang Shuming, *Les cultures d'Orient et d'Occident et leurs philosophies*, trans. Luo Shenyi (Paris: You Feng, 2011).

9. Xiong Shili 熊十力, *Xin weishi lun (wenyanwen ben)* 新唯识论（文言文本）[New Treatise on the Uniqueness of Consciousness: Classical Chinese Edition], in *Xiong Shili quanji* 熊十力全集 [The Complete Works of Xiong Shili], ed. Xiao Shafu 萧萐父 (Wuhan: Hebei Jiaoyu chubanshe, 2001), vol. 2, 1–149; Xiong Shili, *New Treatise on the Uniqueness of Consciousness*, trans. John Makeham (New Haven:

Yale University Press, 2015). Unless specified otherwise, all references to the *Xin weishi lun* are to the classical Chinese edition.

10. Shils discusses three significant modern antitraditions: those of originality (the idea of the genius qua creator ex nihilo; elsewhere Shils calls this antitradition "emancipationism"), scientism, and progressivism. All three are closely related to what I call, in what follows, the antitraditional discourse of modernity. Shils, *Tradition*, 235–39.

11. Simon Leys regards the "Chinese attitude toward the past" as one greatly informed by iconoclasm, so much so that he views the Cultural Revolution as "the latest expression of a very ancient phenomenon of massive iconoclasm, which was recurrent all through the ages." Although I do not fully share Leys's views on this point, his reminder that iconoclasm was far from foreign to the Chinese *attitudes*—I would emphasize the importance of the plural form here—toward the past before the modern period suggests that the traditional sources of Confucian iconoclasm could very well be multiple and dispersed. Simon Leys is quoted in Møllgaard, *Confucian Political Imagination*, 34.

12. On modernization as detraditionalization, see Paul Heelas, Scott Lash, and Paul Morris, eds., *Detraditionalization: Critical Reflections on Authority and Identity* (Cambridge: Blackwell, 1996). For reasons that will become clear in what follows, I disagree with scholars, including Anthony Giddens and Peter Taylor, who hold the view that modern societies are "post-traditional": Peter Taylor, *Modernities* (Minneapolis: University of Minnesota Press, 1999) and Anthony Giddens, *The Consequences of Modernity* (Cambridge: Polity Press, 1990), 107. On Giddens, see also John Walliss, "The Problem of Tradition in the Work of Anthony Giddens," *Culture and Religion* 2, no. 1 (2001): 81–98.

13. Jürgen Habermas, *The Philosophical Discourse of Modernity: Twelve Lectures*, trans. Frederick Lawrence (Cambridge: Polity Press, 1987), 6–7.

14. I borrow the metaphor of textiles from the Latin etymology of "text" (*textus* means "woven"), but also from the meaning of *jing* (經; classics), which the *Shuowen jiezi* 說文解字 defines as "weaving" (*zhi* 織). On this, see Michael Nylan, *The Five "Confucian" Classics* (New Haven: Yale University Press, 2001), 11–12.

15. Monotheistic religions might have played an important role in this process, to the extent that the claim to possess a monopoly on truth, in the antitraditional discourse of modernity, can be viewed as a secularization of the rejection of other traditions in monotheistic discourses. As the case of Confucian iconoclasm suggests, however, non-monotheistic traditions also seem to have provided sufficient iconoclastic resources from which the moderns could draw to monopolize truth. This view challenges the myth of European exceptionalism in the work of Marcel Gauchet on the relation between secularization and modernity. Although we can perhaps view modernity as a "European phenomenon," as Enrique Dussel suggests, it is "one constituted in a dialectical relation with a non-European alterity that is

its ultimate content. Modernity appears when Europe affirms itself as the 'center' of a *World* History that it inaugurates; the 'periphery' that surrounds this center is consequently part of its self-definition." It is this relation to its other that I find lacking in Gauchet's, as well as Taylor's, metanarratives of secularization. Marcel Gauchet, *The Disenchantment of the World: A Political History of Religion*, trans. Oscar Burge (Princeton: Princeton University Press, 1997); Charles Taylor, *A Secular Age* (Cambridge: Belknap Press, 2007); Enrique Dussel, "Eurocentrism and Modernity (Introduction to the Frankfurt Lectures)," *Boundary 2* 20, no. 3 (Fall 1993): 65.

16. François Hartog calls this process *restitutio*, i.e., an "operation allowing one to legitimize a new present through an appeal to the authority of the past." François Hartog, "Ouverture: Autorités et temps," in *Les Autorités: Dynamiques et mutations d'une figure de référence à l'Antiquité*, ed. Didier Foucault and Pascal Payen (Grenoble: Éditions Jérôme Million, 2007), 32. Elsewhere, Hartog goes so far as to suggest that "authority is another name for tradition." François Hartog, "Temps du monde, histoire, écriture de l'histoire," *L'inactuel* 12 (2004): 102.

17. John B. Henderson notes that "the most universal and widely expressed commentarial assumption regarding the character of almost any canon is that it is comprehensive and all-encompassing, that it contains all significant learning and truth." John B. Henderson, *Scripture, Canon, and Commentary: A Comparison of Confucian and Western Exegesis* (Princeton: Princeton University Press, 1991), 89.

18. *Auctoritas* "derives from the verb *augere*," as Hannah Arendt reminds us, which means "to augment." "What authority or those in authority constantly augment is the foundation." Hannah Arendt, "What Is Authority?," in *Between Past and Future: Six Exercises in Political Thought* (New York: The Viking Press, 1961), 121–22.

19. Pascal Payen, "Introduction: Les Anciens en figures d'autorité," in *Les Autorités*, 19. The internal quote is from Paul Ricoeur: tradition "signifies that the temporal distance separating us from the past is not a dead interval but a transmission that is generative of meaning. Before being an inert deposit, tradition is an operation that can only make sense dialectically through the exchange between the interpreted past and the interpreting present." Paul Ricoeur, *Time and Narrative, Volume 3*, trans. Kathleen Blamey and David Pellauer (Chicago: University of Chicago Press, 1988), 221.

20. On the social dialectic of recognition at the basis of authority, see Bruce Lincoln's insightful analysis in *Authority: Construction and Corrosion* (Chicago: University of Chicago Press, 1994). The recognition of the ruled can simply take the form of the passive acceptance of the authority of the ruler, and even, as Bruce Lincoln notes (p. 8), of the act of *pretending* to accept that authority.

21. On rites of institution, see Pierre Bourdieu, "Rites of Institution," in *Language and Symbolic Power*, ed. John B. Thompson, trans. Gino Raymond and Matthew Adamson (Cambridge: Polity, 1991), 117–26.

22. Arendt traces back the central idea of authoritarian governments—"that the source of their authority, which legitimates the exercise of power, must be beyond

the sphere of power and, like the law of nature or the commands of God, must not be man-made"—to Plato's political philosophy, while she ascribes to the Romans the idea that political authority has its origin in "the sacredness of foundation," that is, in the point of origin of tradition. See Arendt, "What Is Authority?," 111, 120. The notion of "mandate of heaven" (*tianming* 天命) and rulership succession were also central to political authority in China: a mandate was bestowed from heaven onto the first ruler of a dynasty, before such mandate was passed down to subsequent rulers of the dynasty through the conduit of lineage. Wang Aihe sees a contradiction at work here, "between receiving the mandate of the dynasty on the basis of moral qualifications and inheriting the mandate through lineage." Wang Aihe, *Cosmology and Political Culture in Early China* (Cambridge: Cambridge University Press, 2000), 207.

23. Arendt, "What Is Authority?," 92.

24. On Gadamer's positive reassessment of the notion of "prejudice," see Hans-Georg Gadamer, *Truth and Method*, trans. Joel Weinsheimer and Donald G. Marshall (New York: Continuum, 2003), 268–306.

25. John Marincola defines literary authority, in the context of ancient historiography, as "the rhetorical means by which the ancient historian claims the competence to narrate and explain the past, and simultaneously constructs a persona that the audience will find persuasive and believable." The following chapters pay close attention to the construction of the figures of "Liang Shuming" and "Xiong Shili" by the texts, a central component of what I call "textual authority." See John Marincola, *Authority and Tradition in Ancient Historiography* (Cambridge: Cambridge University Press, 2004), 1. On textual authority, see also Amit Assis, "Author-ity," *Mafte'akh* 2 (2011): 1–28; and Larry Scanlon, *Narrative, Authority and Power: The Medieval Exemplum and the Chaucerian Tradition* (Cambridge: Cambridge University Press, 1994). On the question of the relation between authorship and authority, see Seán Burke's discussion of the French debate regarding the death of the author in *The Death and Return of the Author: Criticism and Subjectivity in Barthes, Foucault and Derrida* (Edinburgh: Edinburgh University Press, 1998). For a treatment of authorship and authority in the East Asian context, see Christian Schwermann and Raji C. Steineck, eds., *That Wonderful Composite Called Author: Authorship in East Asian Literatures from the Beginnings to the Seventeenth Century* (Leiden: Brill, 2014).

26. This Promethean task is related to the atomistic subject of the Enlightenment that has been under attack for quite some time, notably by a group of Anglophone scholars more or less closely associated with the communitarian movement. See Alasdair MacIntyre, *After Virtue* (Notre Dame: University of Notre Dame Press, 1981) and Charles Taylor, *Sources of the Self: The Making of Modern Identity* (Cambridge: Harvard University Press, 1989).

27. Alexandre Kojève argues that the authority of tradition (or of the Father, in his terminology) was "amputated" in the modern period. See Alexandre Kojève, *The Notion of Authority (A Brief Presentation)*, trans. Hager Weslati (London: Verso,

2014), 64. I come back to Kojève's work on authority in the conclusion. For an application of Kojève's insightful analysis of the notion of authority to comparative philosophy, see Ralph Weber, "Authority: Of German Rhinos and Chinese Tigers," in *Comparative Philosophy Without Borders*, ed. Arindam Chakrabarti and Ralph Weber (New York: Bloomsbury Academic, 2016), 143–74.

28. As Gérard Leclerc notes, "there exists a mythological history according to which Western culture passed, following the initial rupture of the Renaissance, from a reign of authority, which would be archaic, arbitrary, and illegitimate by nature [. . .], to a reign of pure reason." According to this logic, Leclerc sums up, modernization was conceptualized as "'a scientific and cultural progress' that would amount to a gradual transition, slow and arduous yet palpable and irreversible, from the principle of authority to the principle of rationality." This is also attested by Revault D'Allones, who sees modernity as answering "to an aspiration for rational self-foundation and political self-institution at once; both are inseparable and share precisely a common claim to a mode of legitimacy that detaches itself, not without violence, from tradition and the past." Habermas also makes a similar claim: "Modernity can and will no longer borrow the criteria by which it takes its orientation from the models supplied by another epoch; *it has to create its normativity out of itself*. Modernity sees itself cast back upon itself without any possibility of escape." Gérard Leclerc, *Histoire de l'autorité. L'assignation des énoncés culturels et la généalogie de la croyance* (Paris: Presses Universitaires de France, 1996), 9; Myriam Revault d'Allonnes, *Le pouvoir des commencements: Essai sur l'autorité* (Paris: Seuil, 2006), 3; Habermas, *Philosophical Discourse of Modernity*, 7.

29. Wang Hui, *The Politics of Imagining Asia*, ed. Theodore Huters (Cambridge: Harvard University Press, 2011), 266.

30. As Shih Shu-mei notes in *The Lure of the Modern*, "the ideology of linear temporality produced, so to speak, 'tradition' in order to repudiate it as old and outdated, and celebrated 'modernity' as discontinuity from the past, in order to create a new subjectivity that prioritized the present and the future." Shih Shu-mei, *The Lure of the Modern: Writing Modernism in Semicolonial China, 1917–1937* (Berkeley: University of California Press, 2001), 50. James C. Scott also notes how what he calls "high modernism" has needed the "other" of tradition, "this dark twin, in order to rhetorically present itself as the antidote to backwardness." James C. Scott, *Seeing Like a State: How Certain Schemes to Improve the Human Condition Have Failed* (New Haven: Yale University Press, 1998), 331.

31. Habermas, *Philosophical Discourse of Modernity*, 6–7. On the idea of modernity as caesura with the past, see also Michel Foucault, "What Is Enlightenment?," in *The Foucault Reader*, ed. Paul Rabinow (New York: Pantheon Books, 1984), 39–42; Fredric Jameson, *A Singular Modernity: Essay on the Ontology of the Present* (London: Verso, 2002), 17–22; David Harvey, *The Condition of Postmodernity: An Enquiry into the Origins of Cultural Change* (Oxford: B. Blackwell, 1989), 12; Hannah Arendt, "Tradition and the Modern Age," in *Between Past and Future*,

17–40; and Michel de Certeau, *Histoire et psychanalyse, entre science et fiction* (Paris, Gallimard, 2002), 85–88.

32. In *Futures Past,* Reinhart Koselleck argues "that during *Neuzeit* the difference between experience and expectation has increasingly expanded; more precisely, that *Neuzeit* is first understood as a *neue Zeit* from the time that expectations have distanced themselves evermore from all previous experience." François Hartog summarizes that "for Koselleck, the temporal structure of the modern period is characterized by an asymmetry between experience and expectation that is produced by the idea of progress and the opening of time onto a future. This asymmetry grew ever more extreme from the end of the eighteenth century, as time speeded up." François Hartog, *Regimes of Historicity: Presentism and Experiences of Time*, trans. Saskia Brown (New York: Columbia University Press, 2015), 17. Reinhart Koselleck, *Futures Past: On the Semantics of Historical Time*, trans. Keith Tribe (New York: Columbia University Press, 2004), 263.

33. Although the question of the "spatialization of time" has been tied to the work of Fredric Jameson, among others, I borrow it from Johannes Fabian, who discusses, in *Time and the Other*, the denial of coevalness at work in anthropology—that is, the denial that the anthropologist and the people he or she studies belong to the same historical era—as a form of spatialization of time. See Johannes Fabian, *Time and the Other: How Anthropology Makes Its Object* (New York: Columbia University Press, 1983).

34. See Charles Taylor, "Two Theories of Modernity," in *Alternative Modernities*, ed. Dilip Parameshwar Gaonkar (Durham: Duke University Press, 2001), 172–96.

35. On the new unilinear consciousness of time characteristic of Chinese thought during the Republican period, and on its origin in late Qing thought, see Leo Ou-fan Lee, "In Search of Modernity: Some Reflections on a New Mode of Consciousness in Twentieth-Century Chinese History and Literature," in *Ideas Across Cultures: Essays in Honor of Benjamin Schwartz*, ed. Merle Goldman and Paul A. Cohen (Cambridge: Harvard University Press, 1990), 109–35. On the notion of progress in late Qing and Republican China, see Thomas Fröhlich and Axel Schneider, eds., *Chinese Visions of Progress, 1895 to 1949* (Leiden: Brill, 2020).

36. In *Chinese Intellectuals in Crisis*, Chang Hao argues that the crisis faced by Chinese intellectuals at the turn of the twentieth century was not only political in nature, but should rather be characterized as a "crisis of orientational order" or a "crisis of meaning." Because this crisis was quite broad in scope, in that it spread to the political, social, moral, and existential realms, modern Chinese intellectuals tended to look for all-encompassing solutions. Scientism provided such a solution for a majority of May Fourth thinkers. Modern Confucians, Chang argues elsewhere, separated the spiritual and material aspects of the crisis. This allowed them to suggest that science could only resolve issues related to the latter, while Confucianism could be of help with the spiritual crisis Chinese were facing at the time. See Chang Hao, *Chinese Intellectuals in Crisis: Search for Order and Meaning (1890–1911)* (Berkeley:

University of California Press, 1987) and "New Confucianism and the Intellectual Crisis of Contemporary China," 276–302.

37. Lin Yü-sheng explains the extremely broad scope of the crisis experienced by modern Chinese intellectuals—a "crisis of Chinese consciousness"—by the fact that traditionally, the cultural, political, and social orders were regarded as integrated in, and subsumed under, "universal kingship" in China. Lin, *Crisis of Chinese Consciousness*, 10–55.

38. That May Fourth discourse achieved a hegemonic status around the years 1919 and 1920 is attested by the fact that, as Elisabeth Forster has argued, the "New Culture Movement" became "a buzzword used by a variety of people to market an even larger variety of competing agendas." Unlike Forster, who emphasizes that Hu Shi and Chen Duxiu came to be regarded as the main protagonists of the movement thanks to "lesser-known people" who sought to propagate their agenda by equating it with Hu and Chen's "new culture," however, I suggest the protagonists played a central role in producing a hegemonic discourse that reshaped the rules of discursivity. See Elisabeth Forster, *1919—The Year That Changed China* (Berlin: De Gruyter Oldenbourg, 2018), 3, 8.

39. My understanding of hegemony is indebted to the collaborative work of Ernesto Laclau and Chantal Mouffe, *Hegemony and Socialist Strategy: Towards a Radical Democratic Politics* (London: Verso, 2014), as well as Laclau's *Emancipation(s)* (London: Verso, 1996) and his contributions to the following edited volume: Judith Butler, Ernesto Laclau, and Slavoj Žižek, *Contingency, Hegemony, Universality: Contemporary Dialogues on the Left* (London: Verso, 2000). On "organic crises," see Laclau and Mouffe, *Hegemony and Socialist Strategy*, 122.

40. As Laclau and Mouffe note, hegemony is never truly finalized and can always be contested. Laclau and Mouffe, *Hegemony and Socialist Strategy*, xiii. I come back to this issue in the conclusion.

41. On the porousness of the philosophical field in Republican China, for example, see Matthew Chew, "Academic Boundary Work in Non-Western Academies: A Comparative Analysis of the Philosophy Discipline in Modern China and Japan," *International Sociology* 20, no. 4 (December 2005): 530–59.

42. Chen Duxiu can exemplify this point. He studied the classics and passed both the county-level and provincial-level examinations at the very end of the nineteenth century. His experience of the examination system left a deep mark on the young Chen, who abhorred the experience, but it also played an important role in Chen's ability to gain access to a prestigious position at Peking University. On this experience, see Lee Feigon, *Chen Duxiu: Founder of the Chinese Communist Party* (Princeton: Princeton University Press, 1983), 28–32.

43. As Ernesto Laclau argues, hegemonic operations succeed to the extent that they manage to suture—although always precariously and temporarily so—the particular interests of the group deploying them with the universal, so that the very meaning of the universal will be thought of in terms that benefit the hegemonic

group. The goal is to produce, in Perry Anderson's words, the "passive resignation to the way of the world and diffidence in any possibility of changing it." Perry Anderson, "The Antinomies of Antonio Gramsci," *New Left Review* 100 (1976), 30. Laclau, *Emancipation(s)* (especially pp. 20–46).

44. Leigh K. Jenco notes that a characteristic distinction between late Qing and May Fourth discourses is the passage from a spatialized to a historicized understanding of East-West differences. Leigh K. Jenco, *Changing Referents: Learning Across Space and Time in China and the West* (Oxford: Oxford University Press, 2015), 171. On this topic in relation to Chen Duxiu's thought, see also Wang Hui 汪晖, *Xiandai Zhongguo sixiang de xingqi* 现代中国思想的兴起 [The Rise of Modern Chinese Thought] (Beijing: Sanlian, 2008), vol. 2:2, 1295–96 and Yang Zhende 楊貞德, *Zhuanxiang ziwo: jindai Zhongguo zhengzhi sixiang shang de geren* 轉向自我: 近代中國政治思想上的個人 [Turning Toward the Self: The Individual in Modern Chinese Political Thought] (Taipei: Zhongyang yanjiuyuan Zhongguo wenzhe yanjiusuo, 2009), 277.

45. Chen Duxiu 陈独秀, "Jinggao qingnian" 敬告青年 [Call to Youth], in *Chen Duxiu zhuzuo xuanbian* 陈独秀著作选编 [Selected Works of Chen Duxiu], ed. Ren Jianshu 任建树 (Shanghai: Shanghai Renmin, 2009), vol. 1, 160.

46. See for example Chen, "Jinggao qingnian," 160. A similar conception of evolution, rooted in a *voluntarist* social Darwinism, even though the role of historical actors remained limited to bringing about history's inevitable end, was already present in Yan Fu (嚴復; 1854–1921). In "On the Speed of World Change" (*Lun shibian zhi ji* 論世變之亟; 1895), Yan had argued that the sages cannot change the course of history but can foresee its future and contribute to realizing it. On this point, see Ady Van den Stock, *The Horizon of Modernity: Subjectivity and Social Structure in New Confucian Philosophy* (Leiden: Brill, 2016), 158–59. On the uses of the logic of social Darwinism at the time, see James Reeve Pusey, *China and Charles Darwin* (Cambridge: Harvard University Press, 1983).

47. "One is the bright path of republicanism, science, and atheism, while the other is the dark path of autocracy, superstition, and divine right." Chen Duxiu 陈独秀, "Kelinde bei" 克林德碑 [The Von Ketteler Monument], in *Chen Duxiu zhuzuo xuanbian*, vol. 1, 447.

48. Consciously or not, May Fourth members redefined the meaning of science and democracy. For example, Wang Hui argues Chen Duxiu emphasized science's role in the ethical development of the individual and believed that social progress relied on this project of scientific self-cultivation. Wang points out that this understanding of science essentially amounts to a re-actualization of the Neo-Confucian ideal of *gewu zhizhi* 格物致知 (investigating things and extending knowledge). Wang, *Xiandai Zhongguo sixiang de xingqi*, vol. 2:2, 1218–19. On this topic, see also Wang Hui, "The Fate of 'Mr. Science' in China: The Concept of Science and Its Application in Modern Chinese Thought," *Positions* 3, no. 1 (Spring 1995): 1–68. Chen treats "science" as a means to achieve a utopian fusion of the individual with the world

in Chen Duxiu 陈独秀, "Zai lun kongjiao wenti" 再论孔教问题 [On the Issue of Confucianism Again], in *Chen Duxiu zhuzuo xuanbian*, vol. 1, 278.

49. Chen Duxiu 陈独秀, "Bo Kang Youwei *Gonghe pingyi*" 驳康有为《共和评议》 [Refuting Kang Youwei's *Impartial Words on Republicanism*], in *Chen Duxiu zhuzuo xuanbian*, vol. 1, 388–404.

50. Chen Duxiu 陈独秀, "Zai zhiwen *Dongfang zazhi* jizhe" 再质问东方杂志记者 [Further Questions for the Correspondents of *The Eastern Miscellany*], in *Chen Duxiu zhuzuo xuanbian*, vol. 2, 39–48. Leo Ou-fan Lee argues that while in theory Chen upheld the values of intellectual freedom and pluralism, in practice he made use of his iconoclastic rhetoric to attack any alternative voice. Leo Ou-fan Lee, "Incomplete Modernity: Rethinking the May Fourth Intellectual Project," in *The Appropriation of Cultural Capital: China's May Fourth Project*, ed. Milena Doleželová-Velingerová and Oldřich Král (Cambridge: Harvard University Press, 2001), 39–45.

51. The three bonds refer to the hierarchical bonds between ruler and minister, father and son, and husband and wife.

52. The idea that May Fourth was not as antitraditional as it was made out to be in twentieth-century historiography can be found in the literature aimed at decentering May Fourth in modern Chinese history. See, for example, Doleželová-Velingerová and Král, *Appropriation of Cultural Capital*, and Chow Kai-Wing, Hon Tze-ki, Ip Hung-yok, and Don C. Price, eds., *Beyond the May Fourth Paradigm: In Search of Chinese Modernity* (Lanham: Lexington, 2008). On Chen Duxiu, see Joseph Ciaudo, "Replacer Chen Duxiu dans son vocabulaire: *La nouvelle jeunesse* et le problème de la culture chinoise," *Oriens Extremus* 54 (2015): 23–57. Lin Yü-sheng also argues that May Fourth iconoclasts were *in fine* quite traditional. Yü Ying-shih also suggests that various aspects of May Fourth find their root in Chinese traditions in "Wusi yundong yu Zhongguo chuantong" 五四運動與中國傳統 [The May Fourth Movement and Chinese Traditions], in *Shixue yu chuantong* 史學與傳統 [*Historiography and Tradition*] (Taipei: Shibao wenhua, 1982), 93–107.

53. On the incompatibility of Chinese and modern Western cultures, see Chen Duxiu 陈独秀, "Dongxi minzu genben sixiang zhi chayi" 东西民族根本思想之差异 [The Differences in the Fundamental Thinking of Eastern and Western Peoples], in *Chen Duxiu zhuzuo xuanbian*, vol. 1, 193; "Xianfa yu kongjiao" 宪法与孔教 [Constitution and Confucianism], in *Chen Duxiu zhuzuo xuanbian*, vol. 1, 252; "Da peijian qingnian (kongjiao)" 答佩剑青年 (孔教) [Answering the Sword-Bearing Youth (Confucianism)], in *Chen Duxiu zhuzuo xuanbian*, vol. 1, 311; "Kelinde bei," 447; and "Tiaohelun yu jiu daode" 调和论与旧道德 [The Reconciliation Theory and the Old Morality], in *Chen Duxiu zhuzuo xuanbian*, vol. 2, 133–36.

54. On the importance of the growth of scientism in the first half of the twentieth century in China, see D. W. Y. Kwok, *Scientism in Chinese Thought, 1900–1950* (New Haven: Yale University Press, 1965).

55. Chen Duxiu 陈独秀, "Yijiuyiliu nian" 一九一六年 [1916], in *Chen Duxiu zhuzuo xuanbian*, vol. 1, 198. On the idea that modernity produced a complete break from the past in the context of Europe, see also Chen Duxiu 陈独秀, "Falanxiren yu jinshi wenming," 法兰西人与近世文明 [The French and Modern Civilization], in *Chen Duxiu zhuzuo xuanbian*, vol. 1, 165. Yü Ying-shih notes that "the idea of total demolition of tradition as a precondition for the building of a new society was wholly inconceivable to the traditional Chinese imagination, but it was one of the absolute presuppositions of the May Fourth iconoclastic antitraditionalism." Yü, "Radicalization of China," 133.

56. On chains of equivalence, see Laclau and Mouffe, *Hegemony and Socialist Strategy*, 113–20 and Laclau, *Emancipation(s)*, 38–42, 54–58.

57. Chang Hao notes that the number of newspapers and journals published in China passed from 64 during the late nineteenth century to 487 in 1913. See Chang Hao 張灝, "Zhongguo jindai sixiangshi de zhuanxing shidai" 中國近代思想史的轉型時代 [The Transitional Period of Modern Chinese Intellectual History], *Ershiyi shiji* 二十一世紀 52 (April 1999): 29.

58. Milena Doleželová-Velingerová and David Der-wei Wang, "Introduction," in *Appropriation of Cultural Capital*, 23.

59. Given this reading of May Fourth, I agree with Yü Ying-shih in rejecting the use of "Enlightenment" to qualify the movement. See Yü Ying-shih, "Neither Renaissance nor Enlightenment: A Historian's Reflections on the May Fourth Movement," in *Appropriation of Cultural Capital*, 299–324. The classic work referring to the May Fourth Movement as a "Chinese Enlightenment" is Vera Schwarcz, *The Chinese Enlightenment: Intellectuals and the Legacy of the May Fourth Movement of 1919* (Berkeley: University of California Press, 1986). See also Zhang Wei, *What Is Enlightenment: Can China Answer Kant's Question?* (Albany: State University of New York Press, 2010).

60. See, for example, Mark Edward Lewis, *Writing and Authority in Early China* (Albany: State University of New York Press, 1999); Thomas A. Wilson, *Genealogy of the Way: The Construction and Uses of the Confucian Tradition in Late Imperial China* (Stanford: Stanford University Press, 1995); Henderson, *Scripture, Canon, and Commentary*; Julia Ching, "Truth and Ideology: The Confucian Way (*Tao*) and Its Transmission (*Tao-T'ung*)," *Journal of History of Ideas* 35, no. 3 (1974): 371–88.

61. See N. Serina Chan, *The Thought of Mou Zongsan* (Leiden: Brill, 2011), 219–54. John Makeham provides historical accounts of the modern formation of the discourse of the genealogy of the way in "The New *Daotong*," in *New Confucianism*, 55–78 and *Lost Soul: "Confucianism" in Contemporary Chinese Academic Discourse* (Cambridge: Harvard University Asia Center, 2008), 149–67.

62. Yü Ying-shih 余英時, "Qian Mu yu xin rujia" 錢穆與新儒家 [Qian Mu and New Confucianism], in *You ji feng chui shuishang lin*, 31–98. See also the following responses to Yü's article: Lee Ming-huei 李明輝, "Dangdai xin rujia de

daotonglun" 當代新儒家的道統論 [The Discourse of the Genealogy of the Way in New Confucianism], in *Dangdai ruxue zhi ziwo zhuanhua* 當代儒學之自我轉化 [*The Self-Transformation of Contemporary Confucianism*] (Taipei: Zhongyang yanjiuyuan Zhongguo wenzhe yanjiusuo, 1994), 149–73; and Zheng Jiadong 鄭家棟, "Dangdai xin rujia de daotonglun" 當代新儒家的道統論 [The Discourse of the Genealogy of the Way in New Confucianism], in *Dangdai xin ruxue lunheng* 當代新儒學論衡 [A Critical Evaluation of New Confucianism] (Taipei: Guiguan, 1995), 1–37. For an analysis of Yü's article and Li's and Zheng's answers to it, see Makeham, *Lost Soul*, 149–67.

63. Zheng Jiadong, for example, argues that Liang Shuming does not discuss the issue of *daotong*, although he does not consider that a genealogical logic does in fact appear in Liang's construal of the history of Confucianism. See Zheng, "Dangdai xin rujia de daotonglun," 1–37.

64. Although my distinction between history and value is indebted to Joseph R. Levenson, this does not entail that I approve of Levenson's tendency to associate value with Western culture and history to Chinese culture. I discuss this issue at greater length in the conclusion. On Levenson's distinction between history and value, see his "'History' and 'Value': The Tensions of Intellectual Choice in Modern China," in *Studies in Chinese Thought*, ed. Arthur F. Wright (Chicago: University of Chicago Press, 1953), 146–94. My use of "tradition-as-value" is also perhaps reminiscent of Feng Youlan's (馮友蘭; 1895–1990) notion of abstract inheritance. On abstract inheritance, see Xiaoqing Diana Lin, *Feng Youlan and Twentieth Century China: An Intellectual Biography* (Leiden: Brill, 2016), 114–21.

65. The introduction of philosophy as an academic discipline at the beginning of the twentieth century in China played a significant role in the reformulation of Confucianism into an iconoclastic tradition. On the birth of philosophy as an academic discipline in China, see John Makeham, ed., *Learning to Emulate the Wise: The Genesis of Chinese Philosophy as an Academic Discipline in Twentieth-Century China* (Hong Kong: The Chinese University of Hong Kong Press, 2012). On the philosophization of Confucianism and the question of historical (dis)continuity, see Van den Stock, *Horizon of Modernity*, 104–96 and Joël Thoraval, "Sur la transformation de la pensée néo-confucéenne en discours philosophique moderne. Réflexions sur quelques apories du néo-confucianisme contemporain," *Extrême-Orient, Extrême-Occident* 27 (2005): 91–119.

66. Xiong Shili 熊十力, *Shili yuyao* 十力語要 [Important Remarks of Shili], in *Xiong Shili quanji*, vol. 4, 425; referenced in Chak Chi-shing, "The Contemporary Neo-Confucian Rehabilitation: Xiong Shili and His Moral Metaphysics" (PhD diss., University of California, 1990), 217.

67. In this, the texts echo May Fourth iconoclasm, which remained rather textual, especially compared to the iconoclasm that took place during the Cultural Revolution.

68. In practice, antitraditions such as that of Confucian iconoclasm can still have for effect the re-establishment of the authority of tradition and of the classics in the eyes of the readers. After all, readers can accept the texts' assertions regarding the authority of the Confucian tradition-as-value while remaining ambivalent as to the texts' claim that they have entirely subsumed this authority and clarified the message of the ancients. I come back to these issues in the conclusion.

69. Carl Jung notes that the ouroboros is "a symbol of immortality, since it is said of the [ouroboros] that he slays himself and brings himself to life, fertilizes himself and gives birth to himself." It is this process of rebirthing oneself by killing oneself that I refer to here by my admittedly playful use of the term "ouroboric." Carl Gustav Jung, *Mysterium Coniunctionis: An Inquiry into the Separation and Synthesis of Psychic Opposites in Alchemy*, trans. R. F. C. Hull, in *The Collected Works of C. G. Jung*, 2nd ed., ed. Sir Herbert Read, Michael Fordham, Gerhard Adler, and William McGuire (Princeton: Princeton University Press, 1970), vol. 14, paragraph 513.

70. Alan Cole, *Fetishizing Tradition: Desire and Reinvention in Buddhist and Christian Narratives* (Albany: State University of New York Press, 2015), 28.

71. Eske J. Møllgaard makes a similar claim, but for the entire Confucian tradition. I doubt whether this re-enactment of the sagely caesura of the origin can be applied to every Confucian, as Møllgaard suggests, but it certainly describes what is at work in Confucian iconoclasm. See Møllgaard, *Confucian Political Imagination*, 11–12, 20.

72. Whereas continuous traditionalists can be to some extent conflated with conservatives who wish to preserve the sociopolitical and cultural orders as they are, discontinuous traditionalists seek to revive traditions in opposition to the current order of things. In an article on Shils' conception of tradition, Struan Jacobs discusses discontinuous traditions and whether they should be conceptualized as pseudo-traditions or traditions in their own right. He also uses the distinction between "tradition" and "traditional" to denote what I call here "continuous" and "discontinuous" traditions, respectively. I consider discontinuous traditions to be traditions in their own right, although traditions in which the weight of the contemporary is much more important. See Struan Jacobs, "Edward Shils' Theory of Tradition," *Philosophy of the Social Sciences* 37, no. 2 (June 2007): 156–58. It should further be noted that traditionalists can be categorized as "cultural conservatives" under Benjamin I. Schwartz's scheme. See his "Notes on Conservatism in General and in China in Particular," in *Limits of Change*, 3–21.

73. To give but one example, the attempt to return to the "original" Confucius made by Kang Youwei paradoxically paved the way to May Fourth iconoclasm, insofar as it entailed a thoroughly critical attitude toward Confucianism as it then existed, while also shedding doubt on the authenticity of a number of classics. On this topic, see Wang Fansen 王汎森, "Cong chuantong dao fan chuantong: liangge sixiang mailuo de fenxi" 從傳統到反傳統——兩個思想脈絡的分析 [From Tradition-

alism to Anti-Traditionalism: An Analysis of Two Intellectual Trends], in *Cong wusi dao xin wusi* 從五四到新五四 [From May Fourth to New May Fourth], ed. Yü Ying-shih 余英時 and Bao Zunxin 包遵信 (Taipei: Shibao wenhua, 1989), 242–67.

74. Yü Ying-shih, "Some Preliminary Observations on the Rise of Qing Confucian Intellectualism," in *Chinese History and Culture, Volume 2, Seventeenth Century Through Twentieth Century*, ed. Josephine Chiu-Duke and Michael S. Duke (New York: Columbia University Press, 2016), 20.

75. Lydia H. Liu, *Translingual Practice: Literature, National Culture, and Translated Modernity—China, 1900–1937* (Stanford: Stanford University Press, 1995).

76. Various scholars have argued for the inclusion of conservative intellectuals in what we understand as the May Fourth Movement. See for example Peng Hsiao-yen 彭小妍, *Weiqing yu lixing de bianzheng: Wusi de fanqimeng* 唯情與理性的辯證：五四的反啟蒙 [Dialectics Between Affect and Reason: The May Fourth Counter-Enlightenment] (Taipei: Lianjing chuban, 2019) and Edmund S. K. Fung, *The Intellectual Foundations of Chinese Modernity: Cultural and Political Thought in the Republican Era* (Cambridge: Cambridge University Press, 2010). For an earlier example, see Charlotte Furth, "May Fourth in History," in *Reflections on the May Fourth Movement*, 59–68.

77. Scientific truths are relegated to a lower echelon of truth, in the texts studied, by an epistemic division—inherited from Buddhism—between two levels of truth or through a historical metanarrative oriented toward the disclosure of increasingly higher forms of truth.

78. Republished five times and selling perhaps more than 100,000 copies within the space of a year, *Eastern and Western Cultures* was highly popular at the time of its publication. On the popularity of the work, Feng Youlan had the following to say: "His talks on 'Eastern and Western Cultures and Their Philosophies' provoked such widespread interest at the time since regardless of whether his conclusions were accurate or not, the issues he discussed were on many people's minds; it could even be said that they were issues on everyone's mind at the time." Moreover, *Eastern and Western Cultures* was highly influential in the formation of the debate on science and metaphysics (*kexue yu xuanxue lunzhan* 科學與玄學論戰) that emerged in 1923. Zhang Junmai's (張君勱; 1887–1969) position in this debate was greatly indebted to this work. By presenting the future of humanity as Confucian, Liang opened the door for a revaluation of Confucianism within the context of modernity, and for a critique of the hegemony of scientific discourse during the Republican period.

On the number of copies of *Eastern and Western Cultures* sold, see Zheng Dahua 鄭大華, *Liang Shuming yu xiandai xin ruxue* 梁漱溟與現代新儒學 [Liang Shuming and New Confucianism] (Taipei: Wenjin, 1993), 27–28 (Feng's quote is taken from pp. 28–29 of this work). It should be noted, however, that Zheng believes the number of copies sold might have been exaggerated. For works highlighting the influence of Liang's text on the science and metaphysics debate, see S. J. O. Brière, *Fifty Years of Chinese Philosophy, 1898–1950*, trans. Laurence G. Thompson

(Westport: Greenwood Press, 1979), 29; Charlotte Furth, *Ting Wen-chiang: Science and China's New Culture* (Cambridge: Harvard University Press, 1970), 99; and Zheng, *Liang Shuming yu xiandai xin ruxue*, 30–31.

79. John Makeham notes that "with the publication of the 1932 [classical edition of the *New Treatise*], Xiong was catapulted to national prominence (and controversy)." Guo Qiyong regards it as Xiong's most important work, while in Chen Yongjie's opinion, the philosophical system of the *New Treatise* "established Xiong's position in the history of modern Chinese philosophy, and his being regarded by all as a representative of the orthodoxy of modern New Confucianism." See John Makeham, "Translator's Introduction," in *New Treatise*, xiv–xv; Guo Qiyong 郭齊勇, *Tiandi jian yige dushuren: Xiong Shili zhuan* 天地間一個讀書人: 熊十力傳 [A Scholar Between Heaven and Earth: A Biography of Xiong Shili] (Taipei: Yeqiang chubanshe, 1994), 50–54, 61 (Makeham mentions this in his "Translator's Introduction," xiv); and Chen Yongjie 陈永杰, *Xiandai xin rujia zhijueguan kaocha: yi Liang Shuming, Feng Youlan, Xiong Shili, He Lin wei zhongxin* 现代新儒家直觉观考察: 以梁漱溟、冯友兰、熊十力、贺麟为中心 [An Inquiry into the Concept of Intuition in New Confucianism: The Cases of Liang Shuming, Feng Youlan, Xiong Shili, and He Lin] (Shanghai: Dongfang chuban zhongxin, 2015), 128.

80. Chapters 1 and 2 point out two further assumptions the texts share with the May Fourth group: first, that it is the intellectuals' important role and mission to save China, if not from its imminent doom at least from a number of ills that were regarded as plaguing it; and second, that the solution to China's crisis is to be found in the cultural realm, notably through a thorough ethical transformation of the citizenry. The former is a rather pervasive assumption that predates the May Fourth Movement and that survives to this day in at least an important segment of the Chinese intelligentsia, as Gloria Davies argues in *Worrying about China: The Language of Chinese Critical Inquiry* (Cambridge: Harvard University Press, 2007). The latter relates to what Lin Yü-sheng calls the "cultural-intellectualistic approach" to resolving problems, which he sees as widely shared by May Fourth intellectuals (Lin, *Crisis of Chinese Consciousness*, 26–55). Such a "cultural-intellectualistic approach" is far from a prerogative of the May Fourth group, however. Maurice Meisner, for example, draws a parallel between Chen Duxiu's writings of the second half of the 1910s and the Cultural Revolution, as "both were undertaken with a basic assumption that the immediate and essential problems afflicting Chinese society were in fact, broadly speaking, 'cultural.'" See Maurice Meisner, "Cultural Iconoclasm, Nationalism, and Internationalism in the May Fourth Movement," in *Reflections on the May Fourth Movement*, 15.

81. *Eastern and Western Cultures* is presented as a foundational text of New Confucianism in Umberto Bresciani, *Reinventing Confucianism: The New Confucian Movement* (Taipei: Taipei Ricci Institute for Chinese Studies, 2001), 59 and Liu Shu-hsien, *Essentials of Contemporary Neo-Confucian Philosophy* (Westport: Praeger, 2003), 16. Liang is also often presented as the founding father of modern Confucianism,

or of the modernization of Confucian thought. See Guo Qiyong 郭齐勇 and Gong Jianping 龚建平, *Liang Shuming zhexue sixiang* 梁漱溟哲学思想 [The Philosophical Thought of Liang Shuming] (Beijing: Peking University Press, 2011), 311; Zheng, *Liang Shuming yu xiandai xin ruxue*, 18; Zheng, "Dangdai xin rujia de daotonglun," 5; Cao Yueming 曹躍明, *Liang Shuming sixiang yanjiu* 梁漱溟思想研究 [Research in the Thought of Liang Shuming] (Tianjin: Tianjin remin chubanshe, 1995), 402; and He Xinquan 何信全, *Ruxue yu xiandai minzhu: dangdai xin rujia zhengzhi zhexue yanjiu* 儒學與現代民主——當代新儒家政治哲學研究 [Confucianism and Modern Democracy: Studies in the Political Philosophy of New Confucianism] (Taipei: Zhongyang yanjiuyuan Zhongguo wenzhe yanjiusuo, 2009), 1.

For positive appraisals of the book by Tang Junyi (唐君毅; 1909–1978), Mou Zongsan, and others, see Ma Yong 马勇, ed., *Modai shuoru: mingren bixia de Liang Shuming, Liang Shuming bixia de mingren* 末代碩儒——名人笔下的梁漱溟 梁漱溟笔下的名人 [The Last Generation of Great Confucians: Liang Shuming in the Writings of Famous Intellectuals and Famous Intellectuals in the Writings of Liang Shuming] (Shanghai: Dongfang chuban zhongxin, 1998), 25–29. In 1963, Xiong Shili himself praised Liang's book in the following manner: "During the period of the May Fourth Movement, in the extremely difficult atmosphere of opposition to Confucianism [*kongxue* 孔學] and ancient Chinese culture, Mr. Liang showed courage and insight by arguing that the future world culture would be a revival of Chinese culture." Quoted in Li Yuanting 李淵庭 and Yan Binghua 闫秉华, *Liang Shuming nianpu* 梁漱溟年谱 [A Chronicle of Liang Shuming's Life] (Beijing: Shangwu yinshuguan, 2018), 50.

82. Mou Zongsan played a central role in establishing Xiong Shili as the founder of a modern form of Confucianism. On this topic, see Makeham, "New *Daotong*," 55–78. The *New Treatise* itself is interpreted as laying the metaphysical foundation for the New Confucian movement in Guo Qiyong 郭齊勇, *Ruxue yu ruxueshi xinlun* 儒學與儒學史新論 [New Articles on Confucianism and Its History] (Taipei: Xuesheng shuju, 2002), 341. Cheng Zhongying 成中英 makes a similar claim in "Zonglun xiandai Zhongguo xin rujia zhexue de jieding yu pingjia wenti" 综论现代中国新儒家哲学的界定与评价问题 [A Comprehensive Discussion of the Issues of the Definition and Evaluation of Modern Chinese New Confucian Philosophy], in *Xuanpu lunxueji: Xiong Shili shengping yu xueshu* 玄圃论学集: 熊十力生平与学术 [Collected Essays from Xuanpu: Xiong Shili's Life and Work], ed. Cao Yuetang 曹月堂 (Beijing: Sanlian, 1990). Zheng Jiadong also presents Xiong as the "founder of New Confucian ontology," in Zheng Jiadong 郑家栋, *Xiandai xin ruxue gailun* 现代新儒学概论 [A General Account of New Confucianism] (Nanning: Guangxi renmin chubanshe, 1990), 139 (referenced in Makeham, "New *Daotong*," 74n22). Makeham also notes that Liu Shu-hsien "is following Du Weiming in identifying Xiong as the founding figure of Third Epoch Confucianism or New Confucianism, and in regarding Xiong to be the first *daotong* inheritor after the Ming" (Makeham, "New *Daotong*," 75n44). For praises of Xiong's work by later modern Confucian

thinkers associated with the second generation of the movement, see Guo Qiyong 郭齊勇, *Xiong Shili yu Zhongguo chuantong wenhua* 熊十力與中國傳統文化 [Xiong Shili and Traditional Chinese Culture] (Hong Kong: Tiandi, 1988), 221–26.

83. Michel Foucault, "What Is an Author?," in *Textual Strategies: Perspectives in Post-Structuralist Criticism*, ed. Josué V. Harari (London: Methuen, 1979), 151.

84. In the following chapters, most references to "Liang Shuming" and "Xiong Shili" should be read as metonymic, in the sense that they refer to *Eastern and Western Cultures* and the *New Treatise* respectively, and not to the historical authors (unless specified otherwise). When "Liang" and "Xiong" are used to refer to the historical actors, however, they are treated as actors shaped by the discursive traditions that speak through them, and not as ex nihilo producers of meaning.

85. This is what I take the notion of the "death of the author" to mean in Barthes: what is dead is a particular notion of authorship that casts the author as a deified figure. It is not a coincidence that the expression Barthes uses mirrors the Nietzschean death of God.

86. Roland Barthes, "The Death of the Author," in *Authorship: From Plato to Postmodernism: A Reader*, ed. Seán Burke (Edinburgh: Edinburgh University Press, 1995), 128.

87. I share with Lionel M. Jensen a critical attitude toward essentialized readings of "Confucianism." My understanding of the agent-tradition relation differs somewhat from his, however, insofar as it emphasizes how agents are shaped by traditions in ways that are not always conscious. Although he at times describes tradition as "a frame within which invention is contained," overall Jensen tends to lay greater emphasis on human agency in the process of manufacturing. Lionel M. Jensen, *Manufacturing Confucianism: Chinese Traditions and Universal Civilization* (Durham: Duke University Press, 1997), 277.

88. I discuss other texts written by Liang and Xiong only insofar as they explicitly mention and clarify some aspect of the texts under study here. In such cases, I treat these texts as secondary sources supplementing my analysis of the *New Treatise* or *Eastern and Western Cultures*.

89. A growing trend in Anglophone scholarship has been to highlight the Buddhist aspects of *Eastern and Western Cultures* and the *New Treatise*. Thierry Meynard and John J. Hanafin have argued that Liang Shuming should be mainly regarded as a Buddhist thinker (although a highly syncretic one), while John Makeham has emphasized the influence of Buddhism on the *New Treatise*. Although I stress, in the context of this book, that both texts *portray themselves* as reactivating the Confucian *dao*, this does not entail that the texts might not also present themselves as conveying the message of Buddhism. On Buddhism, *Eastern and Western Cultures* remains ambivalent: on the one hand it portrays the ultimate salvation of humankind as Buddhist in nature, yet it also maintains that this salvation remains inaccessible to us moderns living in the early stages of teleological history. This explains why the text spends much more time discussing Confucius and Confucianism and has

comparatively little to say about the Buddha and Buddhism. To this extent, therefore, and even if we agree with Meynard and Hanafin that Liang was ultimately a Buddhist, *Eastern and Western Cultures* mainly presents itself as conveying the Confucian *dao*, leaving the spread of Buddhism to a further stage of history. As to the *New Treatise*, although its language is highly indebted to Yogācāra, the text remains overall extremely critical of Yogācāra, except at times when it comes to Asaṅga. The text in fact presents both the Yogācāra and Confucian traditions as sharing the same insight into wisdom, although ultimately it does portray the Confucian tradition as superior to that of Yogācāra, as chapter 4 makes clear. Of course, that the texts *present themselves* as Confucian does not preclude the fact that scholars can disagree with this self-portrayal and classify the texts and/or their authors as solely or mostly Buddhist. But this should not change our understanding of how the texts portray themselves, which is what interests me in the context of this study.

For the relevant literature on the Buddhist dimensions of the works of Liang and Xiong, see John J. Hanafin, "The 'Last Buddhist': The Philosophy of Liang Shuming," in *New Confucianism*, 187–218; Thierry Meynard, "Is Liang Shuming Ultimately a Confucian or Buddhist?," *Dao* 6 (2007): 131–47; Thierry Meynard, *The Religious Philosophy of Liang Shuming: The Hidden Buddhist* (Leiden: Brill, 2011); John Makeham, "Xiong Shili's Critique of Yogācāra Thought in the Context of His Constructive Philosophy," in *Transforming Consciousness: Yogācāra Thought in Modern China*, ed. John Makeham (Oxford: Oxford University Press, 2014), 242–82. On this issue, see also Zhang Wenru, "Liang Shuming and Buddhist Studies," trans. Jaroslaw Duraj, *Contemporary Chinese Thought* 40, no. 3 (2009): 67–90. On Liang's claim, made in the 1980s, that he had always remained a Buddhist, see Liang Shuming 梁漱溟, "Meiguo xuezhe Ai Kai xiansheng fangtan jilu zhaiyao" 美国学者艾恺先生访谈记录摘要 [Summary of the Record of the Interview with American Scholar Guy S. Alitto], in *Liang Shuming quanji*, vol. 8, 1178; Wang Zongyu 王宗昱, "Shi rujia, haishi fojia: fang Liang Shuming xianshen" 是儒家，還是佛家：訪梁漱溟先生 [Confucian or Buddhist? A Discussion with Mr. Liang Shuming], *Wenxing* 文星 115 (1988): 67–69.

90. I prefer the less connoted term "modern Confucianism" to "New Confucianism," as the latter refers to a narrower group of philosophers genealogically and generationally taxonomized. Since one of my goals, in focusing on Confucianism as a contested site of power relations, is to challenge the idea that modern Confucians simply *inherited* and *preserved* the tradition, I wish to avoid reiterating genealogical models of understanding that are implied in the title "New Confucianism." "Modern Confucianism," by contrast, is used to refer to any text *claiming* to represent Confucianism within the modern context.

91. Of course, this would in turn imply that I—and not Xiong and Liang—know what authentic Confucianism is.

92. I avoid terminologies, such as "ruist" or "ruism," that reinforce the idea that it is possible, and desirable, to return to the authentic origin of the tradition,

before it was corrupted by the introduction of a foreign vocabulary ("Confucius," "Confucianism," etc.). Although useful to challenge certain assumptions about Confucianism upheld in the Euro-American region, Lionel M. Jensen's distinctions between Kongzi and Confucius on the one hand and *ru* and Confucianism on the other cannot avoid the implication that Kongzi and *ru* are somewhat more authentic than the latter. The contrast between Kongzi and Confucius, moreover, might occult the fact that both equally served as authority figures onto which differing views were projected. Jensen is aware of this issue, as he insists that "the history of Kongzi, like that of Confucius, is one of differential invention and local manufacture." But when stating that "what we know of Confucius is not what the ancient Chinese knew as Kongzi," Jensen seems to presuppose that the ancient Chinese knew of only one authentic Kongzi, while in effect the figure of Kongzi was contested and polysemous from the very beginning, as was the notion of *ru*, as Mark Csikszentmihalyi shows in *Material Virtue*.

Despite his acknowledgement that the meanings of "*ru*" and "Kongzi" were always contested, Csikszentmihalyi prefers the use of "*ru*" to "Confucianism," notably because the latter "mistakenly suggests a tradition that grew out of the foundational teachings of one person." This might indeed be a legitimate reason to reject the use of "Confucianism" for a specialist of the pre-Qin period, but not for studies of modern texts, such as *Eastern and Western Cultures* and the *New Treatise*, which portray Confucius as *the* source of Confucianism. I should note, however, that my preference for "Confucianism" over "*ru*" is first and foremost rooted in my rejection of the language of authenticity. This preference, however, does not imply that I follow Jensen's account, which tends to overemphasize (1) the role of the Jesuits in "manufacturing" Confucianism (at the expense of the role played by Chinese actors) and (2) the influence such manufacture had on the reinterpretation of Confucianism by modern East Asian scholars, whose work, according to Jensen, "reproduces in another form the interpretive predilections of the Jesuits." Jensen, *Manufacturing Confucianism*, 5, 14, 22. Mark Csikszentmihalyi, *Material Virtue: Ethics and the Body in Early China* (Leiden: Brill, 2004), 15 (on "*ru*," see chapter 1).

93. As Edmund S. K. Fung notes, Chinese cultural conservatism was less antimodern than it was suggesting alternative forms of modernity that would not relegate Chinese traditions to the dustbin of history. Fung sees cultural conservatives as "raising the idea of what contemporary scholars call 'alternative modernities'" (although they do so from a conservative perspective, and not a progressive, anti-colonial one). Edmund S. K. Fung, "Nationalism and Modernity: The Politics of Cultural Conservatism in Republican China," *Modern Asian Studies* 43, no. 3 (2009): 782. Hon Tze-ki also describes how cultural conservative critics of May Fourth "supported what we call 'alternative modernity' by charting a unique path for China's modernization based on its historical and cultural background." Hon Tze-ki, *The Allure of the Nation: The Cultural and Historical Debates in Late Qing and Republican China* (Leiden: Brill, 2015), 75.

Chapter 1

1. Liang and his work have been labeled "romantic" by Wang Hui, "conservative" by Jing Haifeng, "cultural conservative" by Zheng Dahua and Guo Qiyong, "politico-cultural conservative" by Edmund S. K. Fung, and "new conservative" by Wang Zongyu. Lyman P. Van Slyke portrays Liang as a traditionalist, while Guy S. Alitto associates Liang with "a world-wide conservative response" to modernity that regards "a traditional form of society as the touchstone for social excellence." Yang Zhende and Lin Yü-sheng see Liang as a conservative whose thought nevertheless incorporates antitraditional elements (Lin even labels Liang an "antitraditional conservative"). Wang, *Xiandai Zhongguo sixiang de xingqi*, vol. 2, no. 2, 1316–17; Jing Haifeng 景海峰, *Xin ruxue yu ershi shiji Zhongguo sixiang* 新儒学与二十世纪中国思想 [New Confucianism and Twentieth-Century Chinese Thought] (Zhengzhou: Zhongzhou guji chubanshe, 2005), 53; Zheng, *Liang Shuming yu xiandai xin ruxue*, 169; Guo Qiyong 郭齐勇, "Wusi de lingyige bei ren hulüe de chuantong: wenhua baochengzhuyi de xingcheng, fazhan ji qi yiyi" 五四的另一个被人忽略的传统：文化保成主义的形成、发展及其意义 [Another Forgotten Tradition of May Fourth: The Formation, Development, and Meaning of Cultural Conservatism], accessed April 16, 2022, https://www.aisixiang.com/data/30184.html; Fung, "Nationalism and Modernity," 777–813; Wang Zongyu 王宗昱, *Liang Shuming* 梁漱溟 [Liang Shuming] (Taipei: Dongda, 1992), 298; Lyman P. Van Slyke, "Liang Sou-ming and the Rural Reconstruction Movement," *The Journal of Asian Studies* 18, no. 4 (1959): 458; Guy S. Alitto, *The Last Confucian: Liang Shu-ming and the Chinese Dilemma of Modernity* (Berkeley: University of California Press, 1986), 9–10; Yang, *Zhuanxiang ziwo*, 333, 382; Lin Yü-sheng 林毓生, "Hu Shi yu Liang Shuming guanyu *Dongxi wenhua ji qi zhexue* de lunbian ji qi lishi hanyi" 胡適與梁漱溟關於《東西文化及其哲學》的論辯及歷史涵義 [Hu Shi and Liang Shuming's Debate on *Eastern and Western Cultures and Their Philosophies* and Its Historical Significance], in *Zhengzhi zhixu yu duoyuan shehui* 政治秩序與多元社會 [Political Order and Pluralistic Society] (Taipei: Lianjing chuban, 1989), 303–24.

2. Catherine Lynch depicts Liang as "a modern, cosmopolitan thinker," while Wang Yuanyi emphasizes Liang's progressivism and his close ties to Marxism, rejecting the idea that he could be labeled a conservative. Catherine Lynch, *Liang Shuming and the Populist Alternative in China* (Leiden: Brill, 2018), 39; Wang Yuanyi 王遠義, "Ruxue yu makesizhuyi: xilun Liang Shuming de lishiguan" 儒學與馬克思主義：析論梁漱溟的歷史觀 [Confucianism and Marxism: An Analysis of Liang Shuming's View of History], *Taida wenshizhe xuebao* 臺大文史哲學報 56 (2002): 145–95.

3. Chen Lai and Thierry Meynard argue that Liang opposed the portrayal of modernity and tradition as antithetical, insofar as he promoted a synchronic cultural pluralism rather than a diachronic opposition between the modern and the premodern. Chen Lai 陈来, "Liang Shuming de *Dongxi wenhua ji qi zhexue* yu qi wenhua duoyuanzhuyi" 梁漱溟的《东西文化及其哲学》与其文化多元主义 [Liang

Shuming's *Eastern and Western Cultures and Their Philosophies* and Its Cultural Pluralism], in *Xiandai Zhongguo zhexue de zhuixun: xin lixue yu xin xinxue* 现代中国哲学的追寻——新理学与新心学 [*The Search for Modern Chinese Philosophy: New Cheng-Zhu Studies and New Lu-Wang Studies*] (Beijing: Renmin, 2001), 3–40; Meynard, *Religious Philosophy of Liang Shuming*, 34.

4. I make this argument in Philippe Major, "Tradition and Modernity in Liang Shuming's *Eastern and Western Cultures and Their Philosophies*," *Philosophy East & West* 68, no. 2 (April 2018): 460–76.

5. On this debate, see Jenco, *Changing Referents*, 169–87. On the retrospective creation of the New Culture Movement, see Forster, *1919*.

6. For example, see Chen, "Dongxi minzu genben sixiang zhi chayi," 193–96.

7. Li Dazhao 李大钊, "Dongxi wenming genben zhi yidian" 东西文明根本之异点 [The Fundamental Differences Between Eastern and Western Civilizations], in *Li Dazhao quanji* 李大钊全集 [The Complete Works of Li Dazhao], ed. The Chinese Li Dazhao Research Association (Beijing: Renmin, 2006), vol. 2, 211–24. On the influence that these colleagues and their articles on the topic of the differences between Eastern and Western cultures had on Liang Shuming, and on the importance of Liang's close friendship with Li Dazhao, see Lynch, *Liang Shuming and the Populist Alternative*, 73–79.

8. On this topic, see Wang Fansen 王汎森, "Zhongguo jindai sixiang zhong de 'weilai'" 中国近代思想中的「未来」[The "Future" in Modern Chinese Thought], *Tansuo yu zhengming* 探索与争鸣 9 (2015): 64–71.

9. On the influence of Liang Qichao's publications on Liang Shuming, see Lynch, *Liang Shuming and the Populist Alternative*, 50–51.

10. Liang's interest in this topic began in 1917 or 1918, according to his own recollections. See Liang, *Dongxi wenhua*, 338; *Cultures d'Orient et d'Occident*, 3.

11. First published by the Beijing Ministry of Finance Press (*Beijing caizhengbu yinshuaju* 北京财政部印刷局) in October 1921, *Eastern and Western Cultures* was republished in January 1922 by the Shanghai Commercial Press (*Shanghai shangwu yinshuguan* 上海商務印書館). While composing the final text on the basis of Luo's notes taken during the Jinan lectures, Liang also referred to notes taken by another student of his, Chen Zheng (陳政; n.d.), during the Peking University lectures of 1920. The last chapter was directly written by Liang, however, without reference to written notes, as Luo Changpei was hired in Tianjin before he could attend the last lectures of Liang's in Jinan. On this, see Léon Vandermeersch, "Préface," in *Cultures d'Orient et d'Occident*, xix–xx. As Vandermeersch notes in his preface, the French translator of *Eastern and Western Cultures*, Luo Shenyi, is none other than the daughter of Luo Changpei, the redactor of the Jinan notes.

12. The preface is reproduced in Liang, *Dongxi wenhua*, 542–45. For an English translation of the section in which Liang announces his choice to "lead a Confucian life," see Alitto, *Last Confucian*, 125. It should be noted that an underlying assumption that informs my interpretation of *Eastern and Western Cultures* is that

despite the many tensions and contradictions of its discourse, and despite its being the product of lecture notes, the text nevertheless *seeks* to build a relatively systematic philosophy of culture. This assumption is grounded in a number of features of the text itself. First, although the book is based on lectures, these lectures were part of a series that was meant as Liang's answer to the debate of Eastern and Western cultures. The lectures were thus designed around a single and overarching theme. Second, the text discusses its own methodology, shaped around a dialectic between induction and deduction (although the text does not explicitly use these terms), which suggests that it wants to be read as scientific and systematic. Finally, the text proposes an all-encompassing metanarrative that subsumes its various discussions of epistemology, metaphysics, life, and culture. It is not a coincidence that the text distinguishes between three epistemologies, three problems that beset human life, three approaches to solving problems, etc. In doing so, the text can subsume its discussion of epistemology and life under its three-tiered historical metanarrative. On the text's methodology, see Liang, *Dongxi wenhua*, 352–53; *Cultures d'Orient et d'Occident*, 26–28.

13. Lynch, *Liang Shuming and the Populist Alternative*, 76. On Liang's critique of the conservatives of his time, see Alitto, *Last Confucian*, 118.

14. Given that he fiercely opposed what he saw as a group of insulated traditionalists, Lynch concludes that "Liang Shuming was very much a part of the May Fourth period in its broader sense." She also states that *Eastern and Western Cultures* "was the product of the years surrounding the May Fourth incident and bears their marks." Interestingly, in a review of the book published in 1921, Taixu (太虛; 1890–1947) called *Eastern and Western Cultures* "the best book of the recent New Culture Movement." Liang himself felt distressed at Hu Shi and Chen Duxiu's portrayal of his book as going against the New Culture Movement, as he regarded himself as part of it. On this, see Alitto, *Last Confucian*, 128–29. Lynch, *Liang Shuming and the Populist Alternative*, 79, 90. Taixu's statement is quoted in Meynard, *Religious Philosophy of Liang Shuming*, 134.

15. I mostly use "tradition" (as opposed to "historical tradition") when dealing with the discourse of the two texts studied, but I also use it to denote traditions established in other discourses, such as that of May Fourth.

16. Shils, *Tradition*, 12.

17. Liang, *Dongxi wenhua*, 338; *Cultures d'Orient et d'Occident*, 10. All translations are mine unless specified otherwise, and all are based on the original Chinese text.

18. Liang, *Dongxi wenhua*, 376; *Cultures d'Orient et d'Occident*, 52 (emphasis mine). On Liang's metaphysics of constant flux, see Wu Chan-liang 吳展良, "Liang Shuming de shengsheng sixiang ji qi dui Xifang lixingzhuyi de pipan (1915–1923)" 梁漱溟的生生思想及其對西方理性主義的批判 (1915–1923) [Liang Shuming's Generative Thought and Its Critique of Western Rationalism (1915–1923)], in *Zhongguo xiandai xueren de xueshu xingge yu siwei fangshi lunji* 中國現代學人的學術性格與思維

方式論集 [A Collection of Articles on the Academic Nature and Mode of Thinking of Modern Chinese Scholars] (Taipei: Wunan, 2000), 183–238.

19. Liang, *Dongxi wenhua*, 411; *Cultures d'Orient et d'Occident*, 91. The text also uses the Buddhist terms "seeing-part" (*jianfen* 見分) and "image-part" (*xiangfen* 相分), which refer to the subjective and objective realms, respectively, to discuss this demand-and-answer phenomenon.

20. On the Buddhist and Schopenhauerian sources of Liang's notion of "will," see Wu Chan-liang, "Western Rationalism and the Chinese Mind: Counter-Enlightenment and Philosophy of Life in China, 1915–1927" (PhD diss., Yale University, 1993), 131–32; and Meynard, *Religious Philosophy of Liang Shuming*, 31–32.

21. Liang, *Dongxi wenhua*, 352; *Cultures d'Orient et d'Occident*, 27.

22. The text gives as an example someone who would seek immortality or would want flowers not to wither away. The law of impermanence simply cannot be avoided. On these three types of demands, see Liang, *Dongxi wenhua*, 380; *Cultures d'Orient et d'Occident*, 56–57. The text also points out certain kinds of issues, such as artistic ones, which do not call for a resolution or satisfaction at all, and thus are excluded from this typology.

23. It is clear that what the text refers to here is the *modern* West. In fact, the text classifies the European Middle Ages in the third orientation explained below, since this historical period is associated with the ascetic attitude toward desire Liang sees as central in Christianity.

24. Liang, *Dongxi wenhua*, 382; *Cultures d'Orient et d'Occident*, 58.

25. Liang, *Dongxi wenhua*, 381; *Cultures d'Orient et d'Occident*, 58.

26. Liang, *Dongxi wenhua*, 381–82; *Cultures d'Orient et d'Occident*, 58.

27. Lin Anwu calls Liang's view of culture a form of "cultural anthropomorphism" (*wenhua nirenlun* 文化擬人論; translated as "cultural personification" by Meynard). See Lin Anwu 林安梧, "Liang Shuming ji qi wenhua sanqi chongxian shuo: Liang zhu *Dongxi wenhua ji qi zhexue* de xingcha yu shitan" 梁漱溟及其文化三期重現說——梁著《東西文化及其哲學》的省察與試探 [Liang Shuming and His Theory of the Reappearance of Three Cultural Periods: Analysis and Evaluation of Liang Shuming's *Eastern and Western Cultures and Their Philosophies*], in *Dangdai xin rujia zhexue shi lun* 當代新儒家哲學史論 [On the History of New Confucian Philosophy] (Taipei: Wenhai jijinhui, Mingwen, 1996), 99–125; translated as Lin Anwu, "Liang Shuming and His Theory of the Reappearance of Three Cultural Periods: Analysis and Evaluation of Liang Shuming's *Eastern and Western Cultures and Their Philosophies*," *Contemporary Chinese Thought* 40, no. 3 (2009): 16–38. On the question of the text's analogy between person and civilization, see also Wang, *Xiandai Zhongguo sixiang de xingqi*, vol. 2:2, 1316.

28. Liang writes: "I cannot but praise and admire the clarity of Mr. Chen's mind! Although it is easy for people to be confused about the differences in these two cultures, Mr. Chen is very able to recognize them clearly, and moreover, sees that Western culture is an integrated whole that cannot be looked at superficially

and piecemeal." Liang, *Dongxi wenhua*, 335 (on Chen, see also 531–32); *Cultures d'Orient et d'Occident*, 7 (241). The translation is from Alitto, *Last Confucian*, 88.

29. Liang, *Dongxi wenhua*, 375, 392 (on the three cultures being holistic wholes distinct from one another and embarked on different paths, see also 441); *Cultures d'Orient et d'Occident*, 51, 68 (128).

30. On Liang's cultural pluralism, see Chen, "Liang Shuming de *Dongxi wenhua ji qi zhexue*," 3–40.

31. On the three stages of modern history, see Liang, *Dongxi wenhua*, 493–94; *Cultures d'Orient et d'Occident*, 195–97.

32. Liang, *Dongxi wenhua*, 526; *Cultures d'Orient et d'Occident*, 234.

33. Liang, *Dongxi wenhua*, 485; *Cultures d'Orient et d'Occident*, 184.

34. Liang, *Dongxi wenhua*, 480; *Cultures d'Orient et d'Occident*, 178.

35. Liang, *Dongxi wenhua*, 528; *Cultures d'Orient et d'Occident*, 237.

36. On the "sinicization" of Western culture, see Liang, *Dongxi wenhua*, 503–12; *Cultures d'Orient et d'Occident*, 206–18.

37. I discuss the text's distinction between intuition and rationality in the third chapter. On intuition, see Liang, *Dongxi wenhua*, 452–57; Liang, *Cultures d'Orient et d'Occident*, 141–48. Regarding Bergson's influence on Liang's notion of intuition, see An Yanming, "Liang Shuming and Henri Bergson on Intuition: Cultural Context and the Evolution of Terms," *Philosophy East & West* 47, no. 3 (1997): 337–62. On harmonious interpersonal relations, see Liang, *Dongxi wenhua*, 478–80; Liang; *Cultures d'Orient et d'Occident*, 176–78. Regarding the relation between intuition and the unity of heaven and the human, see Wu, "Western Rationalism and the Chinese Mind," 111, 183–84; Wang, *Liang Shuming*, 121–24; and Guo and Gong, *Liang Shuming zhexue sixiang*, 93.

38. The distinction between tradition-as-value and tradition-as-history maps onto what Chen Lai calls "the two meanings of 'Chinese culture'" in Liang's work: one being "the whole culture produced by the Chinese people, with Confucian culture at its core," and the other being "a kind of spirit that is made manifest in Chinese history and culture." That the world would "sinicize" means it would adopt the *spirit* of Chinese culture, and not the actual shape it took in history. See Chen Lai 陈来, "Dui xin wenhua yundong de zai sikao: cong 'wusi' houqi de Liang Shuming shuoqi" 对新文化运动的再思考——从「五四」后期的梁漱溟说起 [Rethinking the New Culture Movement: On Liang Shuming in the Late Period of the May Fourth Movement], *Nanchang daxue xuebao (rensheban)* 南昌大学学报 (人社版) 1 (2000): 2.

39. Liang, *Dongxi wenhua*, 472–77; *Cultures d'Orient et d'Occident*, 168–75. Of course, implied in this view is the idea that Liang himself was the first Confucian to decipher the Confucian message thoroughly. Alitto points this out in *Last Confucian*, 104.

40. Liang, *Dongxi wenhua*, 481–82, 526; *Cultures d'Orient et d'Occident*, 180, 234.

41. Liang, *Dongxi wenhua*, 375, 472, 529; *Cultures d'Orient et d'Occident*, 51, 168, 238. On this topic, see Wang, "Ruxue yu makesizhuyi," 165.

42. Wang Zongyu uses the Chinese expression *shutu tonggui* (殊途同歸), somewhat equivalent to the expression "all roads lead to Rome," to qualify Liang's view of history. Wang, *Liang Shuming*, 247.

43. Liang, *Dongxi wenhua*, 338; *Cultures d'Orient et d'Occident*, 10–11.

44. I refer to history evolving along Liang's three stages as "teleological history," as opposed to history before the Renaissance in the West and before the impetus of the West in China and India, which were not teleologically oriented toward human emancipation, but remained stagnant in their own course. Catherine Lynch calls the former "natural history" and the latter "actual history" in *Liang Shuming and the Populist Alternative*, 105.

45. Liang, *Dongxi wenhua*, 388–89; *Cultures d'Orient et d'Occident*, 65.

46. Liang, *Dongxi wenhua*, 390; *Cultures d'Orient et d'Occident*, 66.

47. Liang, *Dongxi wenhua*, 362–65; *Cultures d'Orient et d'Occident*, 38–41.

48. Liang, *Dongxi wenhua*, 479; *Cultures d'Orient et d'Occident*, 177. The translation is adapted from Alitto, *Last Confucian*, 103.

49. Liang, *Dongxi wenhua*, 362–70; *Cultures d'Orient et d'Occident*, 37–45.

50. See for example Chen Duxiu 陳獨秀, "Kongzi zhi dao yu xiandai shenghuo" 孔子之道与现代生活 [The Way of Confucius and Modern Life], in *Chen Duxiu zhuzuo xuanbian*, vol. 1, 264–69. A partial English translation is available in Chen Duxiu, "The Way of Confucius and Modern Life," in *Sources of Chinese Tradition*, ed. Wm. Theodore de Bary and Richard Lufrano (New York: Columbia University Press, 2000), vol. 2, 353–56.

51. Liang, *Dongxi wenhua*, 360; *Cultures d'Orient et d'Occident*, 35. I consulted the following English translation: Liang Shuming, "The Cultures of the East and West and Their Philosophies," trans. Andrew Covlin and Jinmei Yuan, *Dao* 1, no. 1 (2001): 117.

52. Liang, *Dongxi wenhua*, 443–44; *Cultures d'Orient et d'Occident*, 130–31.

53. See for example Chen's distinction between Western science and Chinese "imagination" (*xiangxiang* 想像) in "Jinggao qingnian," 162–63. On the May Fourth criticism of superstitions and religion, see Prasenjit Duara, *Rescuing History from the Nation: Questioning Narratives of Modern China* (Chicago: University of Chicago Press, 1996), 85–113.

54. Liang, *Dongxi wenhua*, 479; *Cultures d'Orient et d'Occident*, 178.

55. Liang, *Dongxi wenhua*, 472; *Cultures d'Orient et d'Occident*, 168.

56. I discuss this issue in Philippe Major, "Rethinking the Temporalization of Space in Early Republican China: Liang Shuming's *Eastern and Western Cultures and Their Philosophies*," *International Communication of Chinese Culture* 4, no. 2 (May 2017): 171–85.

57. It should be noted that the text employs *Dongfanghua* (東方化), *Zhongguohua* (中國化), and *Xifanghua* (西方化) in an idiosyncratic manner to denote

"Eastern culture," "Chinese culture," and "Western culture" respectively, and not, as a contemporary reader of Chinese might expect, "easternization," "sinicization," and "westernization." Luo Shenyi's French translation reflects this, as does the English translation of sections of the second chapter of *Eastern and Western Cultures* published in Liang, "Cultures of the East and West," 107–27.

58. Liang, *Dongxi wenhua*, 340; *Cultures d'Orient et d'Occident*, 13. This quote is reminiscent of similar claims Liang makes in the first text he wrote on the topic of Eastern and Western cultures, written in the summer of 1919, a full year before he gave his lectures on the topic at Peking University. See Liang Shuming 梁漱溟, "*Dongxi wenhua ji qi zhexue* daoyan" 《东西文化及其哲学》导言 [Preface to *Eastern and Western Cultures and Their Philosophies*], in *Liang Shuming quanji*, vol. 1, 261; *Cultures d'Orient et d'Occident*, 264. This text is misleadingly called a "preface" (*daoyan*) to *Eastern and Western Cultures*, despite the fact that it was written two years before the publication of the book and did not appear in its original publication.

59. On this topic, Joël Thoraval comments that Chinese culture "is a kind of genius but premature child who has been waiting for his blossoming for centuries." Joël Thoraval, "Liang Shu ming : qu'était devenu le 'dernier confucéen' sous le régime communiste? (première partie)," *Bulletin de Sinologie* 52 (1989): 26.

60. Liang, *Dongxi wenhua*, 388; *Cultures d'Orient et d'Occident*, 65.

61. Liang, *Dongxi wenhua*, 366–68, 390; *Cultures d'Orient et d'Occident*, 41–44, 66.

62. Liang, *Dongxi wenhua*, 466; *Cultures d'Orient et d'Occident*, 159.

63. Liang, *Dongxi wenhua*, 360; *Cultures d'Orient et d'Occident*, 35. Although the text's mention of the need to rejoice in heaven's mandate is aimed at our rejoicing in the *natural* course of life, I suggest this also applies to teleological history as the natural and inevitable course history must take. Thierry Meynard argues that "Liang's evolutionary scheme should not be considered deterministic. It contains no law of necessity, since the encounter between the three types of culture was accidental. Without such an encounter, the three cultures would have followed their own specific paths indefinitely." This is mistaken, I believe. The historical model of development discussed by Liang follows what he took to be a natural process of evolution from material to interpersonal to existential issues. Even if the three cultures had never met, this evolutionary scheme would have remained inevitable. This is why China could never materialize the Confucian ideal historically, since it had failed to complete the first stage of history beforehand. But Meynard's point is also that the three cultures would have remained on their respective paths, and humanity would have never reached the second stage of evolution if the three cultures had never met. This is doubtful as well, however, since the West was moving toward the second stage of historical development on its own, and not because it had been in contact with China (on this, see Liang, *Dongxi wenhua*, 529; *Cultures d'Orient et d'Occident*, 238). See Meynard, *Religious Philosophy of Liang Shuming*,

37. On determinism and freedom in Liang's metanarrative, see also Alitto, *Last Confucian*, 117.

64. Liang, *Dongxi wenhua*, 372; *Cultures d'Orient et d'Occident*, 48.

65. Meynard notes that the difference between consciousness and spirit is that the former is "momentary and individual," while the latter is "permanent and collective." Meynard, *Religious Philosophy of Liang Shuming*, 36.

66. Liang, *Dongxi wenhua*, 372 (see also 481 regarding "Chinese culture" being the product of ancient geniuses); *Cultures d'Orient et d'Occident*, 48 (179).

67. A Buddhist term opposed to "the world of sentient beings" (*youqing shijian* 有情世間), *qi shijian* is usually translated to "receptacle world," "container world," or "insentient world" in Buddhist literature, since it refers to what sentient beings regard, in the outside world, as there for the satisfaction of their cravings and desires; as tools or utensils that can be grasped either physically or conceptually by sentient beings. But in the case of *Eastern and Western Cultures*, *qi shijian* is described as an obstacle to the present self (which is equated with spirit) and as "unwieldy things." It is clear that the text does not emphasize their being tools to be used by the present self. Moreover, *qi shijian* is here explicitly associated with the previous self, which is itself equated to the material world (*wuzhi* 物質) in the text (on this, see Liang, *Dongxi wenhua*, 377; *Cultures d'Orient et d'Occident*, 54). As such, I translate *qi shijian* into "material world," which seems more adequate within the particular textual context in which it is used here. Luo Shenyi also translates *qi shijian* as "monde matériel" within this context. On the notion of *qi shijian* in Buddhism, see Charles Muller, "Qi shijian" 器世間 [Receptacle World], *Digital Dictionary of Buddhism*, accessed April 16, 2022, http://www.buddhism-dict.net/cgi-bin/xpr-ddb.pl?q=器世間.

68. Liang, *Dongxi wenhua*, 378; *Cultures d'Orient et d'Occident*, 54.

69. Liang, *Dongxi wenhua*, 377; *Cultures d'Orient et d'Occident*, 54.

70. On the eight consciousnesses in Yogācāra, see Peter Harvey, *An Introduction to Buddhism: Teachings, History and Practices* (New York: Cambridge University Press, 2013), 130–33; Paul Williams, *Mahāyāna Buddhism: The Doctrinal Foundations* (London: Routledge, 2009), 97–100; and Dan Lusthaus, "Yogācāra School," in *Encyclopedia of Buddhism*, ed. Robert E. Buswell (New York: Macmillan Reference/Thomson/Gale, 2004), vol. 2, 918–19.

71. Liang, *Dongxi wenhua*, 426; *Cultures d'Orient et d'Occident*, 108.

72. Liang, *Dongxi wenhua*, 428–30; *Cultures d'Orient et d'Occident*, 111–13. The text also characterizes the end of history as a kind of "suicide" (*zisha* 自殺), which I interpret to entail the death of the body but not of the spirit. Liang, *Dongxi wenhua*, 429; *Cultures d'Orient et d'Occident*, 111. On Liang's explanation of the conceptualization of awakening in Yogācāra, see also Liang, *Dongxi wenhua*, 412–13; *Cultures d'Orient et d'Occident*, 93–94. Meynard points out that the Indian will allows the negation of the previous self "in a radical way." Meynard, *Religious Philosophy of Liang Shuming*, 34.

73. Meynard, *Religious Philosophy of Liang Shuming*, 68.

74. See Liang Shuming 梁漱溟, "Zishu" 自述 [Autobiography], in *Liang Shuming quanji*, vol. 2, 9; "Wo de zixue xiaoshi" 我的自学小史 [A Brief History of My Self-Study], in *Liang Shuming quanji*, vol. 2, 659–98; "Zishu zaonian sixiang zhi zaizhuan zaibian" 自述早年思想之再转再变 [An Account of the Many Changes in My Early Thought], in *Liang Shuming quanji*, vol. 7, 177; and "Wo dui renlei xinli renshi qianhou zhuanbian butong" 我对人类心理认识前后转变不同 [On the Differences Between My Early and Late Understandings of Human Psychology], in *Liang Shuming quanji*, vol. 7, 131.

75. Meynard provides a description of Liang's self-narratives of his "conversions" in *Religious Philosophy of Liang Shuming*, 167–74.

76. Interestingly, in *Fifty Years of Chinese Philosophy*, Brière misunderstands the text in precisely this manner, claiming that Liang found the superiority of Confucianism in its being a balance between the extremes of Western and Indian cultures. See Brière, *Fifty Years of Chinese Philosophy*, 28. Chan Wing-tsit provides a similar interpretation in *Religious Trends in Modern China* (New York: Columbia University Press, 1953), 23.

77. Eske J. Møllgaard sees Confucians in general as wanting "to repeat the creative act of *instituting* the social imaginary as opposed to simply being caretakers of the *instituted* social imaginary." I doubt whether this applies to all Confucians, but it does certainly apply to *Eastern and Western Cultures*' construal of Confucianism. Møllgaard, *Confucian Political Imagination*, 20.

78. Liang, *Dongxi wenhua*, 529; *Cultures d'Orient et d'Occident*, 238. Liang claims the West passed from the third will to the first in the transition from the Middle Ages to the Renaissance. This does not contradict his assessment of the stagnancy of Chinese culture and its inability to return to the will of a previous phase, however, since Liang explicitly appeals, to explain the transition from the "dark ages" to the Renaissance, to the dual origins of Western culture, in Hebraic culture and Greek culture, representing the third and first wills, respectively. Liang in fact suspects Hebraic culture has its origin in India. See Liang, *Dongxi wenhua*, 383–87; *Cultures d'Orient et d'Occident*, 59–63.

79. Liang, *Dongxi wenhua*, 532–33; *Cultures d'Orient et d'Occident*, 242.

80. The detrimental effects of excessive rationality could be perceived at three levels of modern Western culture. At the level of what the text calls "material life," rationality led to an alienation of human life from nature. Moreover, to study nature, Western rationality had to dissect it and shatter to pieces what was originally holistic. At the level of social life, rationality resulted in people who "drew a demarcation between themselves and others and held a utilitarian attitude toward others, so much so that their relations became mechanistic." This led in turn to a capitalism in which individuals regard one another as competition, a view that incapacitated human cooperation. At the level of spiritual life, rationality led not only to the demise of religion and metaphysics, but also to a form of Western philosophy that

focused on the natural world at the expense of human affairs. Liang, *Dongxi wenhua*, 485; *Cultures d'Orient et d'Occident*, 184.

81. Liang, *Dongxi wenhua*, 528; *Cultures d'Orient et d'Occident*, 237.

82. Zhang Dongsun (張東蓀; 1886–1973) pointed this issue out early on. On this, see Zheng, *Liang Shuming yu xiandai xin ruxue*, 87–88. On this contradiction in the text, see also Yang, *Zhuanxiang ziwo*, 358 and Alitto, *Last Confucian*, 121–22. Catherine Lynch attempts to demonstrate that Liang does not contradict himself by appealing to Liang's "apparent inconsistency in his use of the word, 'culture,' a use sometimes inclusive, for patterns of daily life, and sometimes exclusive, for the attitudes underlying such patterns." Lynch, *Liang Shuming and the Populist Alternative*, 106.

83. For example, He Lin argued that Liang's "advocating a resurrection of the Confucian attitude while at the same time advocating science and democracy still does not completely escape the snare of 'Chinese learning for the basis; Western learning for utility.'" He Lin 賀麟, *Dangdai Zhongguo zhexue* 當代中國哲學 [Contemporary Chinese Philosophy] (Taipei: Shidai shuju, 1974), 9. The translation is from Alitto, *Last Confucian*, 133. On this topic, see also Zheng, *Liang Shuming yu xiandai xin ruxue*, 86–87; Jing, *Xin ruxue yu ershi shiji Zhongguo sixiang*, 57; and Fang Keli 方克立 and Cao Yueming 曹躍明, "Liang Shuming de feilixingzhuyi zhexue sixiang shuping" 梁漱溟的非理性主義哲學思想述評 [A Critique of Liang Shuming's Non-Rational Philosophical Thought], in *Cong wusi dao xin wusi*, 370–71.

84. Liang, *Dongxi wenhua*, 537; *Cultures d'Orient et d'Occident*, 247–48.

85. *Analects* 5:11. The translation is from Lau, *Analects*, 77–78. I return to the text's discussion of *gang* in the *Analects* in the third chapter.

86. Liang, *Dongxi wenhua*, 537; *Cultures d'Orient et d'Occident*, 248.

87. Liang, *Dongxi wenhua*, 538; *Cultures d'Orient et d'Occident*, 249.

88. Liang, *Dongxi wenhua*, 538; *Cultures d'Orient et d'Occident*, 250.

89. The text claims that "Chinese culture before Confucius was gathered more or less in its entirety in Confucius's hands, while Chinese culture after Confucius originated more or less in its entirety from Confucius." It is clear that the text refers to tradition-as-value and not tradition-as-history here; otherwise Liang's statement that Chinese history represents a failure to put into practice Confucius's ideal would not make sense. Liang, *Dongxi wenhua*, 472; *Cultures d'Orient et d'Occident*, 168.

90. As John Henderson notes, depicting Confucius in one's own image was a common trope from the Han dynasty onward, as commentators of the classics built an image of the sage as the greatest commentator and expurgator of tradition, for example. Henderson calls this "commentatorization" of Confucius "commentarial transfiguration." Henderson, *Scripture, Canon, and Commentary*, 30–32.

91. Shils, *Tradition*, 12.

92. On the abstraction and simplification of the three cultures in Liang's thought, see Chen, "Liang Shuming de *Dongxi wenhua ji qi zhexue*," 23–24; Zheng, *Liang Shuming yu xiandai xin ruxue*, 69; Lin, "Liang Shuming and His Theory of

the Reappearance of Three Cultural Periods," 30; Meynard, *Religious Philosophy of Liang Shuming*, 29–39. On the tendency of modern Chinese intellectuals to portray the Chinese tradition as a homogeneous whole, see also John Makeham, "Disciplining Tradition in Modern China: Two Case Studies," *History and Theory* 51 (2012): 89–103.

93. In *Eastern and Western Cultures*, Liang does not use the term "philosophy of culture" (*wenhua zhexue* 文化哲學) to describe his approach, although years later he admitted his approach amounted to a philosophy of culture. On this, see Meynard, *Religious Philosophy of Liang Shuming*, 27–28.

94. Liang himself highlights that since he completely endorses science and democracy, his "advocacy of Eastern cultures has nothing to do with those conservatives [literally: "old brains" *jiu tounao* 舊頭腦] who reject Western culture." Liang, *Dongxi wenhua*, 338; *Cultures d'Orient et d'Occident*, 24. He also refused to be categorized as a conservative later on in his life: see Liang, *Liang Shuming quanji*, vol. 8, 1175 and Liang Shu Ming and Guy S. Alitto, *Has Man a Future? Dialogues with the Last Confucian* (Heidelberg: Springer, 2013), 201.

95. On this topic, see Nicholas Rescher, *Philosophical Textuality: Studies on Issues of Discourse in Philosophy* (Frankfurt: Ontos Verlag, 2010), 5.

96. Lu Xun 鲁迅, *Kuangren riji* 狂人日记 [Diary of a Madman], in *Lu Xun quanji* 鲁迅全集 [The Complete Works of Lu Xun] (Beijing: Renmin wenxue, 2005), vol. 1, 444–56. For an English translation, see Lu Xun, *Diary of a Madman, and Other Stories*, trans. William A. Lyell (Honolulu: University of Hawai'i Press, 1990).

97. I emphasize this point as even if what remains of value in Confucianism does not amount to a tradition *within the text's discourse*, it might still be possible to show that this discourse itself partakes in *historical* antitraditions that purport to enable a transcendence from tradition. This is precisely what I set out to do in the third chapter.

Chapter 2

1. Most scholars date this work to 1930, although Sang Yu has recently put in doubt the veracity of this dating. See Sang Yu, *Xiong Shili's Understanding of Reality and Function, 1920–1937* (Leiden: Brill, 2020), 169–71.

2. A significantly altered "vernacular edition" was later published in 1944 before an abridged version of the vernacular edition came out in 1953. The classical Chinese edition used here was originally published in October 1932 in the press of the Zhejiang Provincial Library (*Zhejiang shengli tushuguan* 浙江省立圖書館).

3. I discuss the text's critique of Yogācāra in chapter 4.

4. See Makeham, "Xiong Shili's Critique of Yogācāra Thought," 242–82.

5. Makeham, "Xiong Shili's Critique of Yogācāra Thought," 281. Thierry Meynard interprets the *New Treatise* as "a philosophical elaboration which used

elements of Buddhist epistemology and served the larger project of developing a Confucian ontology." Thierry Meynard, "Introducing Buddhism as Philosophy: The Cases of Liang Shuming, Xiong Shili, and Tang Yongtong," in *Learning to Emulate the Wise*, 199.

6. On Liang's epistemology, see Thierry Meynard, "Liang Shuming and His Confucianized Version of Yogācāra," in *Transforming Consciousness*, 201–41.

7. Thierry Meynard interprets Liang as a syncretist who makes of Confucianism a skillful means aimed at facilitating the coming of the Buddhist end of history. See Meynard, "Is Liang Shuming Ultimately a Confucian or Buddhist?," 146.

8. By then, it had already been twelve years since the Ministry of Education had issued a decree calling for the gradual transition from classical to vernacular Chinese in primary schools. On this, see Chow Tse-tsung, *The May Fourth Movement: Intellectual Revolution in Modern China* (Cambridge: Harvard University Press, 1960), 279. On the vernacular movement (*baihuawen yundong* 白話文運動), and particularly on Hu Shi's involvement in it, see Yü Ying-shih 余英時, *Zhongguo jindai sixiangshi shang de Hu Shi* 中國近代思想史上的胡適 [Hu Shi in Modern Chinese Intellectual History] (Taipei: Lianjing chuban, 1984), 29–35.

9. One notable exception is that of Ma Yifu (馬一浮; 1883–1967), who wrote a foreword to the *New Treatise*. The text mentions and quotes him on four separate occasions. On the influence of Ma on the *New Treatise*, see Li Qingliang 李清良, "Lun Ma Yifu dui Xiong Shili *Xin weishi lun* zhi yingxiang" 論馬一浮對熊十力《新唯識論》之影響 [On the Influence of Ma Yifu on Xiong Shili's *New Treatise on the Uniqueness of Consciousness*], *Taiwan Dongya wenming yanjiu xuekan* 臺灣東亞文明研究學刊 7, no. 1 (2010): 201–32.

10. Li and Yan, *Liang Shuming nianpu*, 40–41, 48.

11. For a biographical account of Xiong, see Guo, *Tiandi jian yige dushuren*. For an account of his years leading to the Xinhai revolution, see Chak, "Contemporary Neo-Confucian Rehabilitation," 153–282.

12. On this topic, see John Makeham, "Introduction" and "The Role of Masters Studies in the Early Formation of Chinese Philosophy as an Academic Discipline," *Learning to Emulate the Wise*, 1–25, 73–101.

13. Makeham, "Translator's Introduction," lxviii.

14. Ng Yu-kwan notes that Xiong chose the path of academic learning after he felt disillusioned with the soldiers of the Wuchang Uprising (*Wuchang qiyi* 武昌起義; 1911), whom he thought were more interested in personal gain than service to the nation. "He felt that if one were to start a revolution, it would be best to purify and cultivate the people's minds before revolting. Therefore, he gave up his career in the army and began an academic life." Ng Yu-kwan, "Xiong Shili's Metaphysical Theory about the Non-Separability of Substance and Function," in *New Confucianism*, 221.

15. On this tendency, see Davies, *Worrying about China*, 17. For instances in which the *New Treatise* resorts to metaphors of the body politics, see Xiong, *New Treatise*, 173, 175; *Xin weishi lun*, 77, 78.

16. On this topic, see Sung-chiao Shen and Sechin Y. S. Chien, "Turning Slaves into Citizens: Discourses of *Guomin* and the Construction of Chinese National Identity in the Late Qing Period," in *The Dignity of Nations: Equality, Competition, and Honor in East Asian Nationalism*, ed. Sechin Y. S. Chien and John Fitzgerald (Hong Kong: Hong Kong University Press, 2006), 49–69.

17. See for example Chen Duxiu 陳獨秀, "Wuren zuihou zhi juewu" 吾人最后之觉悟 [Our Final Awakening], in *Chen Duxiu zhuzuo xuanbian*, vol. 1, 201–04 and "Wo zhi aiguozhuyi" 我之爱国主义 [My Patriotism], in *Chen Duxiu zhuzuo xuanbian*, vol. 1, 231–36.

18. While I see Xiong's emphasis on saving China from the cultural and ethical grounds up as characteristic of the May Fourth approach, it should be kept in mind that in this work, Xiong rejects the idea that China's chaos is due to the tension between old and new intellectual trends; rather, its cause is to be found in the abandonment of humaneness and righteousness. I thank John Makeham for pointing this out to me. Xiong Shili 熊十力, *Xinshu* 心书 [Book of the Mind], in *Xiong Shili quanji*, vol. 1, 36. The translation is adapted from Yu Jiyuan, "Xiong Shili's Metaphysics of Virtue," in *Contemporary Chinese Philosophy*, ed. Chung-Ying Cheng and Nicholas Bunnin (Malden: Blackwell Publishers, 2002), 127.

19. Xiong Shili 熊十力, *Shili yuyao chuxu* 十力语要初续 [First Sequel to the Important Remarks of Shili], in *Xiong Shili quanji*, vol. 5, 8–9. The translation is from Yu, "Xiong Shili's Metaphysics of Virtue," 129. The letter was first published in the journal *Xueyuan* (學原; vol. 2, no. 1) in May 1948 before being republished in the *First Sequel to the Important Remarks of Shili* the following year. For a translation of another letter in which Xiong describes his decision to work on scholarship to enlighten the masses, see Sang, *Xiong Shili's Understanding of Reality and Function*, 17.

20. Ng Yu-kwan, Yu Jiyuan, Thierry Meynard, and Sang Yu make similar assertions regarding the relation between Xiong's ontology and his concern for China, and Jing Haifeng and Shimada Kenji regard Xiong as a May Fourth thinker in his own right. See Yu, "Xiong Shili's Metaphysics of Virtue," 128; Meynard, "Introducing Buddhism as Philosophy," 210; Sang, *Xiong Shili's Understanding of Reality and Function*, 22; Ng, "Xiong Shili's Metaphysical Theory," 221; Jing Haifeng 景海峰, *Xiong Shili* 熊十力 [Xiong Shili] (Taipei: Dongda, 1992), 1; Shimada Kenji 島田虔次, *Shin Jukka tetsugaku ni tsuite: Yū Jūriki no tetsugaku* 新儒家哲学について: 熊十力の哲学 [On New Confucian Philosophy: The Philosophy of Xiong Shili] (Kyoto: Tōhōsha, 1987), 6–8.

21. Xiong, *New Treatise*, 281; *Xin weishi lun*, 129.

22. My goal in using the metaphor of "the fall" is not to force a Christian reading on the discourse of the *New Treatise*. It is clear to me that this discourse does not borrow from the Judeo-Christian notion of fall. Rather, my use of this term is meant to emphasize the fact that the rhetoric whereby a fall is first narrated by a text before a remedy is offered to the reader is one of the most established narrative devices used in religious and philosophical texts both East and West. It should be

noted, however, that the text does not systematically use the term "fall" to denote the process whereby the mind becomes deluded. The verb *luo* (落), translated by "fall" in Makeham, is used once by the text to describe one's fall into the trap of the opposition between subject and object, while the verb *duo* (墮), also translated as "fall" in Makeham, is used to metaphorically denote one who has "fallen back into conventional views." As to the compound *chenzhui* (沉墜), again translated into "fall," it is used once to refer to contaminated habituated tendencies. The notion of fall is only used systematically in one passage that expounds on the danger of "fall[ing] [*duo*] into the error of the extreme view of eternalism" or "the extreme view of nihilism." See Xiong, *New Treatise*, 55, 71, 141, 268–70; *Xin weishi lun*, 24, 31, 61, 123–24.

23. Xiong, *New Treatise*, 186–87, 266; *Xin weishi lun*, 85, 122.

24. Xiong, *New Treatise*, 58, 285–88; *Xin weishi lun*, 25, 131–33.

25. "Human emotions [*renqing* 人情]," the text advances, "are one-sided in their attachments, being obsessed with divisions but blind to the whole." Later, the *New Treatise* maintains that "the obfuscation brought about by human sentiments [*renqing*] most certainly dulls the precious storehouse of numinous clarity [*shenming* 神明] [. . .] such that humans regard themselves as things." Xiong, *New Treatise*, 172, 183; *Xin weishi lun*, 77, 83.

26. Xiong, *New Treatise*, 186; *Xin weishi lun*, 85.

27. On this, see Makeham, "Translator's Introduction," liii.

28. Xiong, *New Treatise*, 289; *Xin weishi lun*, 133.

29. Xiong, *New Treatise*, 137; *Xin weishi lun*, 59. Another definition of "habituated tendencies" given by the text is that they are "the force constituted by habit." Xiong, *New Treatise*, 135; *Xin weishi lun*, 59.

30. Xiong, *New Treatise*, 132; *Xin weishi lun*, 57.

31. The eighth or storehouse consciousness (*alaiyeshi* 阿賴耶識) functions as the repository of one's previous experiences of craving, which are due to the *manas*' (the seventh consciousness) attachment to selfhood. Previous experiences of craving produce karmic "seeds" (*zhongzi* 種子), which are stored in the eighth consciousness and which serve as the cause (*yinyuan* 因緣) of present and future conscious experiences, which in turn produce more seeds. This process, caused by self-attachment, accounts for the karmic cycle of life and continued existence. On this topic, see Lusthaus, "Yogācāra School," 918–19 and Charles Muller, "Bashi" 八識 [Eight Consciousnesses], *Digital Dictionary of Buddhism*, accessed April 16, 2022, http://www.buddhism-dict.net/cgi-bin/xpr-ddb.pl?q=八識.

32. Xiong, *New Treatise*, 227; *Xin weishi lun*, 103–04.

33. On the one and the many, see for example Xiong, *New Treatise*, 199; *Xin weishi lun*, 91.

34. Xiong, *New Treatise*, 302; *Xin weishi lun*, 138.

35. "In relation to the nature, habituated tendencies can accord with it or be contrary to it. If they accord with the nature, then they are undefiled, and if

they are contrary to it, they are defiled. [. . .] It is by means of undefiled [or pure] habituated tendencies that the nature is realized." Xiong, *New Treatise*, 144; *Xin weishi lun*, 63.

36. The text here deviates from Yogācāra orthodoxy, in which there are fifty-one mental associates. On the latter, see Tagawa Shun'ei, *Living Yogācāra: An Introduction to Consciousness-Only Buddhism*, trans. Charles Muller (Boston: Wisdom Publications, 2009), 19–27.

37. There are seven wholesome mental associates: concentration (*ding* 定), conviction (*xin* 信), contra-craving (*wutan* 無貪), contra-malevolence (*wuchen* 無瞋), contra-ignorance (*wuyi* 無疑), sustained effort (*jingjin* 精進), and vigilance (*bu fangyi* 不放逸). See Xiong, *New Treatise*, 280–307; *Xin weishi lun*, 128–41.

38. On this topic, the text has the following to say: "Habituated tendencies are divided into two kinds: defiled and pure, which wax and wane in response to one another, unable to flourish together. Just like two puppets—as one enters the stage, the other departs. If defiled habituated tendencies are acute, they impede pure habituated tendencies, stopping them from arising and making it seem that they are severed. Also, if pure habituated tendencies are created and gradually dominate, then even if defiled habituated tendencies always occur together with them from the time of birth, because pure habituated tendencies now dominate, they are able to cause defiled habituated tendencies to be gradually subdued and eventually to be extinguished." Xiong, *New Treatise*, 152–53; *Xin weishi lun*, 67.

39. Xiong, *New Treatise*, 142; *Xin weishi lun*, 62.

40. "If one includes all things in the cosmos, and refers to their origin, it is called Reality. If one refers strictly to one's own origin, it is called self-nature. This is because although verbally they are different, what they refer to is the same." Xiong, *New Treatise*, 21; *Xin weishi lun*, 10.

41. Xiong's doctrine of nonduality of Reality and functions is made clear in his critique of Yogācāra's "mistake of severing Fundamental Reality and function in two." Against Yogācāra, the *New Treatise* holds that "as soon as 'Reality' is uttered, 'function' is included within it." On this, see Xiong, *New Treatise*, 91–92; *Xin weishi lun*, 39. Xiong claimed that the *New Treatise* was based on the notion of "the nonduality of Reality and functions" (*tiyong bu'er*) in his *First Sequel to the Important Remarks of Shili*, but to my knowledge, he did not use this expression in the *New Treatise* itself. See Xiong, *Shili yuyao chuxu*, 225. On the influence of the historical Neo-Confucian tradition on Xiong's adoption of this doctrine, see Tu Wei-ming, "Hsiung Shih-li's Quest for Authentic Existence," in *Limits of Change*, 269. On the evolution of Xiong's thought on the relation between *ti* and *yong*, see Sang, *Xiong Shili's Understanding of Reality and Function*.

42. As my use of the plural form of "function" suggests, the relation between Reality and functions is an iteration of the One-many polarity. The vernacular *New Treatise* uses the metaphor of an ocean and its waves to describe the relation between

Reality and functions (respectively), but this metaphor does not appear in the text under study here. On this metaphor, see Xiong Shili 熊十力, *Xin weishi lun (yutiwen ben)* 新唯识论 (语体文本) [New Treatise on the Uniqueness of Consciousness: Vernacular Edition], in *Xiong Shili quanji*, vol. 3, 446. My use of "function" in the plural is borrowed from Tan Sor-hoon, "Contemporary Neo-Confucian Philosophy," in *History of Chinese Philosophy*, ed. Bo Mou (Abingdon: Routledge, 2009), 540. Sang Yu argues that for the *New Treatise*, every phenomenon manifests the whole of reality, so that Reality is not the sum of the multitude of phenomena. Reality is however still one and phenomena many in this account. See Sang, *Xiong Shili's Understanding of Reality and Function*, 210.

43. Xiong, *New Treatise*, 50; *Xin weishi lun*, 22. That Fundamental Reality itself undergoes an endless process of transformation suggests that it should not be regarded as a unique substance. The text remains rather vague, however, as to the relation between Reality and functions. In any case, "Reality" is better suited than "substance" as a translation for *ti* within this context. I borrow this translation from Makeham. On "Reality" meaning "transformation," see also Xiong, *New Treatise*, 124; *Xin weishi lun*, 53.

44. These terms originate from the *Changes*, although Xiong might have been more directly influenced by Yan Fu's use of the terms in his translation of Thomas Huxley's *Evolution and Ethics*. On this, see Makeham, "Translator's Introduction," xxxiv n.76, and Cai Yuanpei's (蔡元培; 1868–1940) forward to the *New Treatise* in Xiong, *New Treatise*, 6; *Xin weishi lun*, 4. Wang Zhongjiang also argues that Xiong's use of these two terms is mainly influenced by Yan Fu and Bergson, rather than the *Changes*. See Wang Zhongjiang 王中江, "Xiong Shili de 'benxin' jinhua lun" 熊十力的「本心」进化论 [On the Evolution of the "Inherent Mind" in Xiong Shili], *Tianjin shehui kexue* 天津社会科学 2 (2011): 131–32. On Yan Fu's use of these terms, see Max Ko-wu Huang 黃克武, "Hewei tianyan? Yan Fu 'tianyan zhi xue' de neihan yu yiyi" 何謂天演？嚴復「天演之學」的內涵與意義 [What Is *Tianyan*? The Meaning and Significance of Yan Fu's *Theory of Natural Evolution*], *Zhongyang yanjiuyuan jindaishi yanjiusuo jikan* 中央研究院近代史研究所集刊 85 (September 2014): 129–87.

45. On contraction and expansion, see Xiong, *New Treatise*, 96–100; *Xin weishi lun*, 41–43. It should be noted that in the vernacular *New Treatise*, the tendencies of contraction and expansion are more explicitly said to be nondual, while this claim remains rather implicit in the classical Chinese text, given the monistic discourse of the *New Treatise*. On the vernacular discussion of the tendencies of contraction and expansion being nondual, see Xiong, *Xin weishi lun (yutiwen ben)*, 252.

46. Xiong, *New Treatise*, 110; *Xin weishi lun*, 48. It should be noted that the text mentions idealists and materialists "in the West." It seems that the text assumes that this distinction mainly applies to Western philosophers still not freed from attachments.

47. Xiong, *New Treatise*, 99; *Xin weishi lun*, 42.

48. On the idealist tendency revealed by the distinction between contraction and extension in the vernacular *New Treatise*, see Van den Stock, *Horizon of Modernity*, 240–45.

49. Xiong, *New Treatise*, 98–99, 182; *Xin weishi lun*, 42, 82.

50. Xiong, *New Treatise*, 289; *Xin weishi lun*, 133.

51. Xiong, *New Treatise*, 184; *Xin weishi lun*, 83.

52. Xiong, *New Treatise*, 292; *Xin weishi lun*, 134.

53. On the impossibility of naming Reality, see Xiong, *New Treatise*, 92, 158, 176; *Xin weishi lun*, 39, 70, 79.

54. The soteriological divide between enlightened and unenlightened minds is also epistemological, insofar as it depends on whether one has realized or not that the ontological Reality of the universe is one. Of course, given that mind and universe are ultimately one, it is not surprising that Fundamental Reality refers to both the ontological reality of the universe and the mind that has recovered its original purity in the *New Treatise*.

55. Xiong, *New Treatise*, 97; *Xin weishi lun*, 41.

56. On the notion of "self-animation," see Xiong, *New Treatise*, 66–69; *Xin weishi lun*, 28–30.

57. On the text's treatment of Yogācāra causation, see Xiong, *New Treatise*, 62–85; *Xin weishi lun*, 27–36. On this topic, see Liu Shu-hsien, "Hsiung Shih-li's Theory of Causation," *Philosophy East & West* 19, no. 4 (1969): 399–407.

58. Xiong, *New Treatise*, 111–12; *Xin weishi lun*, 48.

59. Xiong, *New Treatise*, 59; *Xin weishi lun*, 26.

60. Xiong, *New Treatise*, 192; *Xin weishi lun*, 87.

61. Chan Wing-tsit contends that Xiong "applies it [the Buddhist concept of instantaneous arising and ceasing] to the doctrine of production and reproduction in the *Book of Changes* and reinforces it." Chan Wing-tsit, *A Source Book in Chinese Philosophy* (Princeton: Princeton University Press, 1963), 764.

62. Xiong, *New Treatise*, 318; *Xin weishi lun*, 145.

63. Xiong, *New Treatise*, 188; *Xin weishi lun*, 86. Guo Qiyong argues that Xiong's ontology was inherited from that of the *Changes* and the *Laozi* (老子), which he characterizes as claiming that although *ti* is one, it is dichotomized at the level of *yong*, before one of the two poles of the dichotomy is emphasized at the expense of the other. Guo calls this form of ontology *yiti liangmian* (一體兩面; a single *ti* with two aspects). See Guo, *Xiong Shili yu Zhongguo chuantong wenhua*, 190–91. Guo Meihua 郭美华 also notes that Xiong clearly emphasizes Reality at the expense of functions in *Xiong Shili bentilun zhexue yanjiu* 熊十力本体论哲学研究 [Research on the Ontological Philosophy of Xiong Shili] (Chengdu: Bashu, 2004), 85–86.

64. Xiong, *New Treatise*, 318; *Xin weishi lun*, 145.

65. Xiong, *New Treatise*, 189; *Xin weishi lun*, 86. On the topic of Xiong's reading of the *Changes*, it is also worth noting that according to him, the hexagram

of *qian* (乾), which is pure *yang*, means Fundamental Reality, while that of *bo* (剝), which tends toward pure *yin*, is equated with the phenomenal realm of functions. Xiong seems to prefer *bo* to represent a state in which *yin* is prevailing to the extreme, as opposed to *kun* (坤), which depicts pure *yin*. While *kun* is composed of six *yin* lines (broken lines), *bo* is composed of five *yin* lines upon which stands a single *yang* line. The reason why Xiong prefers *bo* seems to be that it better represents the fact that Reality is never entirely absent, so that one "can always rely on a solitary *yang*" to "develop and create unremittingly and to generate anew endlessly," as quoted above. This interpretation of the text's use of *bo* instead of *kun* is also suggested by the following remark: "Even when *bo* is extreme, when has there ever been a break in the continuity of Reality's incessant generation and procreation?" See Xiong, *New Treatise*, 189; *Xin weishi lun*, 86.

66. Xiong, *New Treatise*, 70–71; *Xin weishi lun*, 31.

67. Xiong, *New Treatise*, 168; *Xin weishi lun*, 74. The text also proposes nine arguments aimed at demonstrating that no dharma abides even temporarily. See Xiong, *New Treatise*, 100–11; *Xin weishi lun*, 43–48.

68. Yu Jiyuan also points out that "since change is instantaneous, nothing in this world has a history, for nothing stays." Yu, "Xiong Shili's Metaphysics of Virtue," 137.

69. This tension is widely discussed in Buddhist literature. The Yogācāra notion of storehouse consciousness can in fact be regarded as one of many Buddhist attempts at reconciling the doctrines of karma and impermanence. On this theme, see Bryan J. Cuevas, "Rebirth," in *Encyclopedia of Buddhism*, vol. 2, 712–13. On the Yogācāra notion of storehouse consciousness as an answer to this problem, see William S. Waldron, *The Buddhist Unconscious: The Ālaya-vijñāna in the Context of Indian Buddhist Thought* (London: Routledge Curzon, 2003), 18–19; Jiang Tao, "*Ālayavijñāna* and the Problematic of Continuity in the *Cheng Weishi Lun*," *Journal of Indian Philosophy* 33 (2005): 243–84; and Lambert Schmithausen, *Ālayavijñāna: On the Origin and the Early Development of a Central Concept of Yogācāra Philosophy* (Tokyo: The International Institute of Buddhist Studies, 1987).

70. Xiong, *New Treatise*, 108; *Xin weishi lun*, 47.

71. In indented quotes, when the quoted text includes interlinear commentaries, I distinguish between the main text and Xiong's interlinear commentaries by highlighting the main text in bold. I discuss the text's use of interlinear commentaries in chapter 4.

72. Xiong, *New Treatise*, 119; *Xin weishi lun*, 51.

73. Xiong, *New Treatise*, 119; *Xin weishi lun*, 51.

74. Xiong, *New Treatise*, 181; *Xin weishi lun*, 82 (emphasis mine). On the distinction between humans, animals, and plants, see also Xiong, *New Treatise*, 185–86, 289–90; *Xin weishi lun*, 84, 133.

75. See Xiong, *New Treatise*, 181; *Xin weishi lun*, 82. Yet a few pages later, the text claims: "Being grounded in magnificent Reality, [the universe and humans] have

no alternative but to act [as they do], yet from the beginning it has never been the case that in doing so there was any purposefulness." Xiong, *New Treatise*, 184; *Xin weishi lun*, 84–85. Again, the dual positioning of the text might be held responsible for this apparent contradiction: from the perspective of Reality, everyone is already awakened and without purpose, yet from the perspective of the phenomenal realm of functions, it appears that one can aim for such an awakening, although one ultimately has always been awakened. I come back to this topic shortly.

76. Xiong, *New Treatise*, 279; *Xin weishi lun*, 128.

77. This reading finds support in the *New Treatise*'s discussion of the notion of instantaneous arising and ceasing, according to which knowledge of former things is possible "because the dharma that subsequently arises *resembles* the preceding dharma." Xiong, *New Treatise*, 104; *Xin weishi lun*, 45 (emphasis mine).

78. Xiong, *New Treatise*, 317; *Xin weishi lun*, 145. As Makeham points out, "the notion of the mind as inherently enlightened, but obscured by defilements," is "a view common to several Sinitic systems of Buddhist thought—Tiantai, Huayan, and Chan—influenced by the [*Awakening of Mahāyāna Faith*]. This was also a view that shaped Neo-Confucian philosophy." John Makeham, "Xiong Shili's Understanding of the Relationship Between the Ontological and the Phenomenal," in *Chinese Metaphysics and Its Problems*, ed. Li Chenyang and Franklin Perkins (Cambridge: Cambridge University Press, 2015), 208.

79. The text mentions that our consciousness of continuity is but a conventional truth proved to be ultimately false once awakened: "If there was someone who [. . .] presumed that [the movement of] mind-consciousness is from past to present and is then directed to the future, then this would be as if one had fallen back into conventional views and had not yet heard the Superior Truth [*shengyi* 勝義]." Xiong, *New Treatise*, 71; *Xin weishi lun*, 31.

80. Xiong, *New Treatise*, 127; *Xin weishi lun*, 55.

81. Xiong, *New Treatise*, 192; *Xin weishi lun*, 88.

82. Xiong, *New Treatise*, 309; *Xin weishi lun*, 141–42.

83. Xiong, *New Treatise*, 190–91; *Xin weishi lun*, 87. The text might have employed *mengnie* as an implicit reference to *Mencius* 6A:8, although this is not where the argument on the sprouts of goodness is made in the text (which is in *Mencius* 2A:6).

84. Xiong, *New Treatise*, 21; *Xin weishi lun* 10. Elsewhere, the text reads: "The mind is not different from the constant transformation that is Fundamental Reality. One's own root, one's own trunk—one cannot rely on something else in making an effort to seek it. To seek Fundamental Reality externally is to rely on something else." Xiong, *New Treatise*, 178; *Xin weishi lun*, 80. Given Xiong's doctrine of the nonduality of Reality and functions, it is not entirely clear why Reality cannot be achieved by a study of phenomena regarded as external, since this doctrine suggests that external phenomena and internal Reality are one and the same. Yu Jiyuan points

this issue out in "Xiong Shili's Metaphysics of Virtue," 141. It should be noted, however, that Reality and functions are said to be one only from the perspective of someone who has already entered the realm of Reality. For someone still seeking awakening, Reality and functions can still be nominally distinguished.

85. Xiong, *New Treatise*, 22; *Xin weishi lun* 10.

86. Xiong, *New Treatise*, 61; *Xin weishi lun*, 27. Although the text here discusses *ziti* (自體) and not *zixing* (自性), it is made clear on the same page that the two refer to the same signified.

87. Xiong, *New Treatise*, 24; *Xin weishi lun*, 11.

88. Xiong, *New Treatise*, 309; *Xin weishi lun*, 142 (emphasis mine).

89. Xiong, *New Treatise*, 212; *Xin weishi lun*, 97. On solitude as a gateway to inherent mind and Reality, see also Xiong, *New Treatise*, 57, 182; *Xin weishi lun*, 25, 82.

90. Xiong, *New Treatise*, 276; *Xin weishi lun*, 126. Xiong reiterates in various instances that learning should not be sought from others. For example: "Whether one succumbs to or retreats from [defilement] does not depend on other people; rather, victory relies on oneself." Xiong, *New Treatise*, 155; *Xin weishi lun*, 68. On learning or self-cultivation being something that only the self can achieve, independently of others, see also Xiong, *New Treatise*, 298, 317; *Xin weishi lun*, 136–37, 145.

91. Xiong, *New Treatise*, 145; *Xin weishi lun*, 63.

92. Xiong, *New Treatise*, 289; *Xin weishi lun*, 133.

93. Xiong, *New Treatise*, 206; *Xin weishi lun*, 94. The actual term used by the *Zhuangzi* is in fact *xian jie* (縣解) and not *xuan jie* (懸解), as it is written in the *New Treatise*.

94. Xiong, *New Treatise*, 206; *Xin weishi lun*, 94.

95. "Examining this account of karmic power or habituated tendencies, then, since it is acknowledged that it abides for a long time, could this possibly mean that collective karma perpetually exists in a race of people or in a society? Although this also makes sense, the original import of the Buddhists was quite different from this. They frankly stated that a person's total karmic power or habituated tendencies intermix to form a concentration of power that gets born over and over. And even though this person dies, this concentration of power never disappears or dissipates. Rather, it constitutes a continuous life for the person after he or she dies. In broad terms this is how it is. Again, logically, it is a possibility." The text considers this option, but it does not take a stand on the issue. This is rather odd, since nowhere else in the text is Xiong displaying any sense of uncertainty; after all, as we will see in the fourth chapter, the text portrays him as having access to absolute truth. It is clear that Xiong has not considered this option thoroughly, and merely mentions it in passing to remind the reader that karma is traditionally regarded as individual. Xiong, *New Treatise*, 132–33; *Xin weishi lun*, 57.

96. Sang, *Xiong Shili's Understanding of Reality and Function*, 174–81.

Interlude

1. Eske J. Møllgaard makes a similar point, although in his case he makes it about the entire Confucian tradition: "Confucians do not interpret the historical tradition but fix a correct line of transmission that serves to immediately connect the present moment with the moment of the inception of Confucianism in Confucius and Mencius, and in doing so they leap over the entire historical tradition that separates the two." He also characterizes Confucians as attempting to "jump out of history and return to the beginning when their culture was instituted and revive it in the splendor of its origin. They are militant revivalists rather than cultural conservatives." The origin, in such discourse, often plays the role of the great other against which the present state of affairs can be criticized and decried. Insofar as the origin is partially created by the contemporary, it would be tempting to interpret it as a form of transcendence that allows space for critique. This might in part challenge Max Weber's immanent reading of Confucianism as too much of this world to provide the impetus for radical changes along the lines of those enabled by protestant ethics. Møllgaard, *Confucian Political Imagination*, 12, 30.

2. The texts' idealist rejection of the body as a limitation imposed on our ability to reconnect with the constant flow of the universe goes against recent portrayals of Confucianism as inherently non-cartesian in the emphasis it lays on embodied experience. Tu Weiming has played an important role in bringing forth a non-cartesian reading of Confucianism. He has notably argued that "the Confucians do not take the body as, by nature, an impediment to full self-realization. To them, the body provides the context and the resources for ultimate self-transformation." While this description might accurately characterize some Confucian texts, it certainly does to apply to the *New Treatise* and *Eastern and Western Cultures*. Tu Wei-ming, *Confucian Thought: Selfhood as Creative Transformation* (Albany: State University of New York Press, 1985), 172.

3. I use "*historical* traditions" to refer to traditions that existed historically. By contrast, "traditions-as-history" refers to traditions established in writing within the texts.

4. For example, Xiaoqing Diana Lin comments that "in discussing what constituted Chinese philosophy" in his *History of Chinese Philosophy* published between 1931 and 1934, Feng Youlan "would define Chinese philosophy only as those parts of Chinese scholarship that could fit into the Western definition of philosophy . . ." Lin, *Feng Youlan and Twentieth Century China*, 164.

5. This also applies to "Indian culture" in *Eastern and Western Cultures*. Thierry Meynard notes that Buddhism is also valued by Liang "for its foreignness," for its ability to provide an alternative to both Western and Chinese cultures. See Meynard, "Liang Shuming and His Confucianized Version of Yogācāra," in *Transforming Consciousness*, 213. On this topic, see also Meynard, "Introducing Buddhism as Philosophy," 187–216.

6. Alitto describes Liang's dichotomization of Western and Chinese cultures in the following terms: "The West was the equivalent of mechanistic positivism, intellectualization, purposeful [*you suo wei* 有所為] action, selfishness, and ethical nihilism. [. . .] The alternative was China and Confucianism—the equivalent of emotion, intuition, noncalculation, ethics, unselfishness, and absolute value." Alitto, *Last Confucian*, 101.

7. Liu, *Translingual Practice*, 77–99.

8. I argue elsewhere that Xiong's construal of self-cultivation as a process of atomization in fact appears closer to the atomistic portrayal of the individual associated with the Enlightenment than the description, in the works of Roger T. Ames and Henry Rosemont Jr., of the Confucian person as the "irreducibly social" "sum of the roles we *live*—not *play*—in our relationships and transactions with others." Roger T. Ames, "Achieving Personal Identity in Confucian Role Ethics: Tang Junyi on Human Nature *as* Conduct," *Oriens Extremus* 49 (2010): 151. See Philippe Major, "The Confucian Atomistic Individual? Selfhood in Xiong Shili's New Treatise on the Uniqueness of Consciousness," *Philosophy East & West* 71, no. 4 (October 2021): 938–58.

9. Xiong, *New Treatise*, 248; *Xin weishi lun*, 113–14.

Chapter 3

1. See for example Joseph A. Adler, *Reconstructing the Confucian Dao: Zhu Xi's Appropriation of Zhou Dunyi* (Albany: State University of New York Press, 2014), 23–25.

2. Zhu Xi most probably drew inspiration from the Chan discourse of mind-to-mind transmission in developing his genealogy. Thomas A. Wilson argues that the "[*daotong*] project is more properly understood as part of a general discourse on lineages of truth beginning in the [Tang], which both Buddhist and Confucian genealogists shared." See Wilson, *Genealogy of the Way*, 114. On the genealogy of the way in Neo-Confucianism, see also Thomas A. Wilson, "Genealogy and History in Neo-Confucian Sectarian Uses of the Confucian Past," *Modern China* 20, no. 1 (1994): 3–33; Julia Ching, "Truth and Ideology," 371–88; Wm. Theodore de Bary, *Neo-Confucian Orthodoxy and the Learning of the Mind-and-Heart* (New York: Columbia University Press, 1981), especially 2–13; Hoyt Cleveland Tillman, *Confucian Discourse and Chu Hsi's Ascendancy* (Honolulu: University of Hawai'i Press, 1992). On Chan Buddhist lineage-making, see Alan Cole, *Fathering Your Father: The Zen of Fabrication in Tang Buddhism* (Berkeley: University of California Press, 2009).

3. On Zhu's discussion of the genealogy of the way in the preface to the *Doctrine of the Mean*, see Wilson, *Genealogy of the Way*, 85–89.

4. I use the term "classic" not in the specific sense of the Five Classics (*wujing* 五經) but in a general sense for any ancient work that came to be regarded

as encompassing some form of timeless truth at one point in history. This includes not only the Five Classics but also the Four Books (*sishu* 四書).

5. See for example Chen's extensive quoting from the classics in Chen, "Kongzi zhi dao yu xiandai shenghuo," 264–69. Hu Shi's authority also relied on his ability to comment authoritatively on ancient texts, although from a perspective indebted to Euro-American historiography. See for example Hu Shih, *The Development of the Logical Method in Ancient China* (Shanghai: The Oriental Book Company, 1922).

6. The resurgence of anti-Confucian campaigns and sentiments in twentieth-century China might in itself attest to the remarkable resilience of the authority of the Confucian tradition. Although the motivations behind such campaigns are usually political rather than intellectual, the very fact that Confucius and the Confucian tradition were the chosen object of criticism in political campaigns goes to show that their authority had not entirely vanished. The value of criticism is directly proportionate to the authority of what is being subjected to criticism. After all, few would bother criticizing someone who commands no authority whatsoever.

7. Apart from a few instances in which "Liang" obviously refers to the historical figure in this chapter, in all other cases I use it to refer to the implicit portrayal of the author that emerges from the discourse of the text.

8. On the rhetoric of naturalization of the text, see also Philippe Major, "Textual Authority and Its Naturalization in Liang Shuming's *Dong-Xi wenhua ji qi zhexue*," *Monumenta Serica* 65, no. 1 (June 2017): 123–45.

9. Liang, *Dongxi wenhua*, 452; *Cultures d'Orient et d'Occident*, 141–42. The internal quote is from the *Doctrine of the Mean*. For the text's equation of intuition with *suigan er ying*, see Liang, *Dongxi wenhua*, 452–57; *Cultures d'Orient et d'Occident*, 141–48.

10. Liang, *Dongxi wenhua*, 454; *Cultures d'Orient et d'Occident*, 145. On the topic of intuition allowing one to fuse with the constant changes of the universe, see also Liang, *Dongxi wenhua*, 456; *Cultures d'Orient et d'Occident*, 147.

11. On the distinction between *lizhi* and *zhijue/ren*, see Liang, *Dongxi wenhua*, 454–45, 460–62; *Cultures d'Orient et d'Occident*, 145, 152–54. This distinction is also rooted in a complex epistemology heavily indebted to Yogācāra. While this epistemology lies outside the scope of the topic covered here, readers can consult Thierry Meynard's detailed explanations in "Liang Shuming and His Confucianized Version of Yogācāra," 227–31.

12. Liang, *Dongxi wenhua*, 452; *Cultures d'Orient et d'Occident*, 142.

13. Liang, *Dongxi wenhua*, 458; *Cultures d'Orient et d'Occident*, 149–50.

14. Liang, *Dongxi wenhua*, 452; *Cultures d'Orient et d'Occident*, 142.

15. Liang, *Dongxi wenhua*, 458; *Cultures d'Orient et d'Occident*, 149.

16. "*Wu chang shi*" appears to be an implicit reference to Han Yu's "On Teachers" (*Shishuo* 師說). For the original passage in which Han explains that Confucius followed various teachers, see Han Yu 韓愈, "Shishuo" 師說 [On Teachers], in

Han Yu wenji huijiao jianzhu 韓愈文集彙校箋注 [Collected Writings of Han Yu: Compiled Recensions and Annotations], compiled and annotated by Liu Zhenlun 劉真倫 and Yue Zhen 岳珍 (Beijing: Zhonghua shuju, 2010), vol. 2, 140.

17. Liang, *Dongxi wenhua*, 451; *Cultures d'Orient et d'Occident*, 140–41.

18. Liang, *Dongxi wenhua*, 472; *Cultures d'Orient et d'Occident*, 168.

19. I thank Tan Sor-hoon for pointing this out to me. On the meaning of *zuo* as "manufacture," see Jensen, *Manufacturing Confucianism*, 23.

20. Catherine Lynch highlights Liang's indebtedness to Wang Gen in the association he makes between Confucianism and the realm of nature. See Lynch, *Liang Shuming and the Populist Alternative*, 83.

21. In *Un sage est sans idée*, François Jullien addresses the topic of the sage who is "without ideas." His analysis fails to highlight how authority is a central component of such claims, however. See François Jullien, *Un sage est sans idée: ou l'autre de la philosophie* (Paris: Seuil, 1998).

22. Liang, *Dongxi wenhua*, 458; *Cultures d'Orient et d'Occident*, 150.

23. This is more surprising as the *Analects*' Confucius has often been regarded as unconcerned with metaphysical issues. Liang, *Dongxi wenhua*, 447; *Cultures d'Orient et d'Occident*, 135.

24. Liang, *Dongxi wenhua*, 448; *Cultures d'Orient et d'Occident*, 136.

25. On *zhijue* as neologism, especially in relation to the reception of Bergson's thought in China, see Joseph Ciaudo, "Introduction à la métaphysique bergsonienne en Chine: échos philosophiques et moralisation de l'intuition," *Noesis* 21 (2013): 293–328; "Bergson's 'Intuition' in China and Its Confucian Fate (1915–1923): Some Remarks on *Zhijue* in Modern Chinese Philosophy," *Problemos* 35 (2016): 35–50.

26. See Liang, *Dongxi wenhua*, 453; *Cultures d'Orient et d'Occident*, 143.

27. Although coincidental, it is of interest that *Eastern and Western Cultures* represents the collation of a series of speeches given by Liang and recorded by his students. Liang's rapport to the text thus at least partially echoes that of Confucius in the *Analects* (although of course we cannot assume this was in any way intended by Liang Shuming himself). It should be noted, however, that *Eastern and Western Cultures* is presented to its readers as a relatively systematic work of philosophy, and not as the record of the conversations of the sage. In that it could be regarded as betraying the original spirit of the sage, which is devoid of any doctrinal core according to the text.

28. Liang, *Dongxi wenhua*, 473; *Cultures d'Orient et d'Occident*, 169. In the first edition of *The Complete Works of Liang Shuming*, the last *er* 而 in the passage is mistakenly rendered as *mian* 面. This was corrected in the second edition.

29. Liang, *Dongxi wenhua*, 448 (see also p. 451 for another quote from the *Record of Rites* the text ascribes to Confucius); *Cultures d'Orient et d'Occident*, 136 (140). In the same passage, the text also presents quotations from the *Xici* 繫辭 appendices to the *Changes*, traditionally ascribed to Confucius, as the words of the sage.

30. Liang, *Dongxi wenhua*, 450; *Cultures d'Orient et d'Occident*, 140. A. T. Roy points this out in an early article on Liang: "Liang Shu-ming and Hu Shih on the Intuitional Interpretation of Confucianism," *Chung Chi Journal* 1, no. 2 (July 1962): 145.

31. Liang, *Dongxi wenhua*, 456; *Cultures d'Orient et d'Occident*, 147. To my knowledge, this expression first appears in Zhu Xi's commentaries on the classics.

32. See Alitto, *Last Confucian*, 74.

33. Liang, *Dongxi wenhua*, 448; *Cultures d'Orient et d'Occident*, 136.

34. Liang, *Dongxi wenhua*, 457 (on *ren*), 458 (for the rejection of cost-benefit analysis and habits), 461 (on *wu suowei er wei*), 537 (on resoluteness); *Cultures d'Orient et d'Occident*, 148, 150, 153, 247.

35. Liang, *Dongxi wenhua*, 462; *Cultures d'Orient et d'Occident*, 154.

36. Alitto, *Last Confucian*, 74.

37. Modern Euro-American authorities are also put to the task of legitimizing Confucianism (by appealing to Bergson's intuition) and Yogācāra. Regarding the latter, the text explicitly makes use of Bergson, Russell, and Einstein's theory of relativity to bring legitimacy to Yogācāra's doctrine of impermanence. See Liang, *Dongxi wenhua*, 414; *Cultures d'Orient et d'Occident*, 94.

38. Alitto, *Last Confucian*, 96.

39. It is also worth noting that the text presents its philosophy of culture as the result of an inquiry that puts into practice both inductive and deductive methods (although the text itself does not use these terms). *Eastern and Western Cultures* falls short of calling this method "scientific," although there is no doubt that its methodological discussion relies on scientific resources. Moreover, the text employs a number of philosophical neologisms, such as *xingershangxue* 形而上學 (metaphysics) and *zhishilun* 知識論 (epistemology), that authorize the text's positioning in the field of philosophy. On Liang's method, see Liang, *Dongxi wenhua*, 352–53; *Cultures d'Orient et d'Occident*, 26–28.

40. For these sections on Confucianism, see Liang, *Dongxi wenhua*, 441–82, 537–40; *Cultures d'Orient et d'Occident*, 127–80, 247–52.

41. Liu Boming (劉伯明; 1887–1923) made this point in his review of the text. On this, see Alitto, *Last Confucian*, 130.

42. The first quote is from *Analects* 7:27 and the second appears in both the "Yu Zao" (玉藻) section of the *Record of Rites* and the *Mencius* 1A.7. My translation of *Analects* 7:27 borrows from Lau, *Analects*, 89.

43. Liang, *Dongxi wenhua*, 451; *Cultures d'Orient et d'Occident*, 140.

44. Liang, *Dongxi wenhua*, 461; *Cultures d'Orient et d'Occident*, 153.

45. The translation is based on D. C. Lau's, although it also borrows from Slingerland's. Lau, *Analects*, 147 (17:21); Edward Slingerland, trans., *Analects: With Selections from Traditional Commentaries* (Indianapolis: Hackett Publishing Company, 2003), 210. I quote the received Chinese edition here, with added punctuation.

Liang quotes it slightly differently, changing the character *nü* (女) into *ru* (汝), for example, although this change does not affect the meaning of the sentence.

46. Liang, *Dongxi wenhua*, 453–54; *Cultures d'Orient et d'Occident*, 144.
47. Liang, *Dongxi wenhua*, 454; *Cultures d'Orient et d'Occident*, 144.
48. The translation is based on Lau, *Analects*, 147 (17:21).
49. Liang, *Dongxi wenhua*, 537–38; *Cultures d'Orient et d'Occident*, 247–50. I discuss this passage of the text in chapter 1.
50. The translation is from Lau, *Analects*, 145.
51. Liang, *Dongxi wenhua*, 462; *Cultures d'Orient et d'Occident*, 155.
52. The text could have found support for its interpretation of the meaning of *gang* in the commentarial tradition on *Analects* 5:11. Slingerland notes that both Huang Kan (皇侃; 488–545) and Sun Qifeng (孫奇逢; 1585–1675) interpret the passage to mean that while desire is object- and external-driven, *gang* is a strength of will that can limit such desires. As to the text's reading of *ren*, it could have found support in historical commentaries, such as that of Kang Anguo (孔安國; 156–74 BCE), for whom "lacking in *ren*" involves an emotional failure related to a lack of compassion or empathy. As Edward Slingerland notes, however, other commentators, such as Miao Bo [繆播; ?–309], emphasize that "Zai Wo's failure is not one of feeling, but rather of ritual propriety." See Slingerland, *Analects*, 44, 210.
53. Having established that Confucius's cultural ideal (intuition) is one and the same as his spirit of transcendence from sociohistorical limitations, in what follows I use "spirit-ideal" as a shortcut.
54. It should be noted that on rare occasions, the text does mention the commentarial tradition in passing. For example, in its explanation of the *qian* (乾) hexagram from the *Changes*, the text does mention commentaries by Rao Lu (饒魯; 1193–1264) and Wang Yangming. See Liang, *Dongxi wenhua*, 462; *Cultures d'Orient et d'Occident*, 134–35.
55. See Liang, *Dongxi wenhua*, 462–63; *Cultures d'Orient et d'Occident*, 155–56. Interestingly, the three proofs offered by Wu are also not properly speaking exegetical (although the text presents them as such), but rely on the authority of the statements of Song historical figures Zhu Xi, Lü Zuqian (呂祖謙; 1137–1181), and Li Qingchen (李清臣; 1032–1102).
56. Liang, *Dongxi wenhua*, 463; *Cultures d'Orient et d'Occident*, 156.
57. Liang seems to conflate utilitarianism and pragmatism here. Liang, *Dongxi wenhua*, 460; *Cultures d'Orient et d'Occident*, 152.
58. Liang, *Dongxi wenhua*, 453, 455, 457–62, 465; *Cultures d'Orient et d'Occident*, 143, 145, 148–54, 158.
59. Liang, *Dongxi wenhua*, 461; *Cultures d'Orient et d'Occident*, 152–53.
60. Liang, *Dongxi wenhua*, 460; *Cultures d'Orient et d'Occident*, 152.
61. On this, see Carine Defoort, "Unfounded and Unfollowed: Mencius's Portrayal of Yang Zhu and Mo Di," in *Having a Word with Angus Graham: At*

Twenty-Five Years into His Immortality, ed. Carine Defoort and Roger T. Ames (Albany: State University of New York Press, 2018), 165–84; "Five Visions of Yang Zhu Before He Became a Philosopher," *Asian Studies* 8, no. 2 (2020): 235–56.

62. It is worth noting that twenty-one years after the publication of *Eastern and Western Cultures*, Liang described his own writings to his sons as the only chance for the Confucian way to be revived and for the world to evolve along the right path: "The learning of Confucius and Mencius has sunk into obscurity. Perhaps some can comprehend its meaning, but no one can see that it is rooted in an understanding of human life, and no one can establish its doctrine of the mind [*xinlixue* 心理學] in order to then expound its ethics. This only *I* can do. [. . .] Our forefathers used to say: 'carry on the extinct learning for the sages of old, and open up the age of Great Peace for those to come.' This has been the mission of my whole life. Only after completing the three books, including *Human Mind and Human Life*, can I die. I cannot die now. Also because I am equally indispensable to the coming fate of China and the work of nation-building, I cannot die. If I died, the color of heaven and earth would change and the course of history would be diverted. This can barely be imagined, let alone can we let it happen!" This quote gives a sense of the messianic task with which Liang had entrusted himself, while making clear that Liang regarded himself as a modern sage. Alitto notes that "Liang felt that in the present age he and he alone had fully comprehended the [*dao*], and so was under the awful imperative of transmitting it" (*Last Confucian*, 7). The quote is from Liang Shuming, "Xianggang tuoxian ji Kuan Shu liang er" 香港脫險寄寬恕兩兒 [Letter to My Two Sons [Pei]kuan and [Pei]shu upon My Escape from Hong Kong], in *Liang Shuming quanji*, vol. 6, 343. I consulted the following translations of sections of this quote: Wu Longcan, "Xiong Shili: A Founder of Contemporary New Confucianism," *Confucian Academy* 3, no. 1 (2016): 157; and Alitto, *Last Confucian*, 7–8, 59. The internal quote is from Zhang Zai, although instead of "open up the age of Great Peace *for all times*" (*wanshi* 萬世), Liang writes *for those to come* (*laishi* 來世), perhaps because of his teleological view of history in which the age of Great Peace is located in the future (not unlike in Kang Youwei). This quote is part of what Feng Youlan called "the four sentences of Hengqu" (*Hengqu siju* 橫渠四句). Zhang Zai was known as Mr. Hengqu, a reference to his hometown in Shaanxi.

63. Although, as Zheng Jiadong (鄭家棟) notes, *Eastern and Western Cultures* does not explicitly propose a genealogy of the way, such a genealogy does implicitly emerge from the sections of the book on Confucian tradition-as-history. Zheng highlights how in most modern Confucians, the genealogical logic often remains rather implicit and hidden away in their narrative of the evolution of Confucianism. This judgment certainly applies to *Eastern and Western Cultures*. Alitto also mentions that Liang "relates most specifically to this tradition of [*daotong*]," but in this case he is referring to the Old Text school wishing to preserve the "transmission of the transcendental [*dao*]" in opposition to New Text members like Kang Youwei who wished to institutionalize the *dao* in a state religion. Alitto does not imply that

Liang had his own views of the *daotong* in this case. See Alitto, *Last Confucian*, 7 and Zheng, "Dangdai xin rujia de daotonglun," 3–5.

64. Liang, *Dongxi wenhua*, 473; *Cultures d'Orient et d'Occident*, 169–70.
65. Liang, *Dongxi wenhua*, 474; *Cultures d'Orient et d'Occident*, 171.
66. Liang, *Dongxi wenhua*, 475; *Cultures d'Orient et d'Occident*, 172.
67. Liang, *Dongxi wenhua*, 453; *Cultures d'Orient et d'Occident*, 143.
68. Liang, *Dongxi wenhua*, 476; *Cultures d'Orient et d'Occident*, 174.
69. Liang, *Dongxi wenhua*, 476; *Cultures d'Orient et d'Occident*, 174.
70. Liang, *Dongxi wenhua*, 476–77; *Cultures d'Orient et d'Occident*, 174–75.
71. Liang, *Dongxi wenhua*, 450; *Cultures d'Orient et d'Occident*, 139.
72. Liang, *Dongxi wenhua*, 450; *Cultures d'Orient et d'Occident*, 139.
73. See Liang, *Dongxi wenhua*, 452–57; *Cultures d'Orient et d'Occident*, 142–48.
74. Kojève, *Notion of Authority*, 8, 10 (emphases in original).
75. On this point, I disagree with Kojève, for whom authority "presupposes both the *possibility* of opposing it and the *conscious* and *voluntary* renunciation of realising this possibility." My analysis suggests that the readers' recognition of the authority of a text does not need to be conscious. Texts can in fact hide the significance of the readers' recognition from their view, as will become clear, to secure their (unconscious) recognition more readily. Such analysis could perhaps also be extended to political authority, in the sense that the ruled may not be aware of their role in recognizing the authority of the ruler; they may simply take for granted the state of affairs as it is, particularly if they have been legitimized through a process of naturalization. Kojève, *Notion of Authority*, 8 (emphases in original).
76. The text's tendency to celebrate the transcend spirit of the sage at the expense of the historicity and embodied nature of human existence—in short, its idealism—is closely tied to the rhetoric of naturalization. That is, by ascribing the spirit of transcendence from history and matter of the sage to its author, the text can present itself as standing on the firm ground of heaven, and not on the contentious grounds of history, culture-as-artifice, and the discursive field of Republican China.
77. Quoted in Henderson, *Scripture, Canon, and Commentary*, 10.
78. Wilson, *Genealogy of the Way*, 84.
79. Chu Hsi, *Learning to Be a Sage: Selections from the* Conversations of Master Chu, Arranged Topically, trans. with commentary by Daniel K. Gardner (Berkeley: University of California Press, 1990), 55.
80. See for example Chu, *Learning to Be a Sage*, 47–48 (passages 5.48 and 5.58).
81. For Zhu Xi's comments on this in his "method of reading," see for example Chu, *Learning to Be a Sage*, 48 (passage 5.10), 128 (passages 4.2 and 4.3). In his "method of reading," Zhu also highlights (1) the possibility of "speaking with [the sages] face to face" (passage 4.6 on p. 129), which resembles what I call "spiritual simultaneity," (2) the idea that the coherence of the classics reveals itself to readers by looking for an opening in the texts (passage 4.11 on p. 130), which is close to Liang's assumption that one key can unlock the hidden message of Confucius

in the classics, and (3) the emphasis on letting calculation aside when reading the classics (passage 4.16 on p. 131).

82. This goes to show how Zhu's hermeneutics assumes that Confucius was not the only sage of the ancient period, while in Liang we see a rather radical refocus on the figure of Confucius himself; a refocus that bears some similarities to the work of Kang Youwei, despite Liang's own critique of the latter's "misunderstanding" of Confucianism.

83. I adapted the translation from Wilson, *Genealogy of the Way*, 86.

84. Although Zhu hoped to bypass the commentaries of Han exegetes to "return to the pristine core of the canonical texts, unencumbered by exegetical traditions," as Michael Nylan notes, he himself produced commentaries that replaced those of the Han and came to be treated as the orthodox interpretation. Nylan also notes how "five centuries later, when Zhu Xi's own commentaries had themselves become encumbrances to the desired direct insight, Zhang Dai [. . .] urged readers to put aside Zhu Xi's commentaries." Nylan, *Five "Confucian" Classics*, 55.

85. Daniel K. Gardner notes how Zhu saw in the classics transhistorical and universal truths about the entire cosmos. This distinguishes him from the pre-Song classicists, who Gardner suggests were more interested in what he calls "situational truths." See Daniel K. Gardner, *Chu Hsi and the* Ta-hsueh*: Neo-Confucian Reflection on the Confucian Canon* (Cambridge: Harvard University Press, 1986), 48–49.

86. Hoyt Cleveland Tillman, "Reflections on Classifying 'Confucian' Lineages: Reinventions of Tradition in Song China," in *Rethinking Confucianism: Past and Present in China, Japan, Korea, and Vietnam*, ed. Benjamin A. Elman, John B. Duncan, and Herman Ooms (Los Angeles: UCLA Asian Pacific Monograph Series, 2002), 36. Tillman also argues that Zhu "evoked, as his own fictive ancestor, the spirit of Confucius." On this, see his "Zhu Xi's Prayers to the Spirit of Confucius and Claim to the Transmission of the Way," *Philosophy East & West* 54, no. 4 (2004): 489–513.

87. Tillman, *Confucian Discourse*, 255 (on this, see also p. 138). Tillman also points out Zhu's eulogy to Lü Zuqian and his epitaph to Cao Jian (曹建; 1147–1183) as particularly explicit instances in which Zhu claimed to be a contemporary representative of the genealogy of the way (see pp. 254–55). Zhu's appointed successor, Huang Gan (黃榦; 1152–1221), was even more explicit in presenting Zhu Xi "as the culmination of the [*daoxue*] tradition." See Tillman, *Confucian Discourse*, 237.

88. On this, see Wilson, *Genealogy of the Way*, 94–97 (the quote is from p. 97). Wilson notes that Wang Yangming also singled out the Counsels of Yu the Great as the core of the tradition, although he presented his interpretation of it as significantly departing from that of Zhu Xi.

89. By including the Cheng brothers, Zhu's genealogy reverts to a master-disciple form of transmission, given that Zhu can trace a lineage between his teacher and the Cheng brothers. Indeed, Zhu's teacher, Li Tong (李侗; 1093–1163), had studied with Luo Congyan (羅從彥; 1072–1135), who was a student of Yang Shi (楊時; 1053–1135)—although Li Tong also studied directly under Yang Shi—who

was a disciple of the Cheng brothers. This suggests that apart from the gap that separates Mencius and Zhou Dunyi, Zhu does emphasize direct transmission.

90. As Thomas A. Wilson notes, such genealogies were "regularly invoked to enunciate an exclusionary conception of the Confucian past that served sectarian agendas." Wilson, *Genealogy of the Way*, 9.

91. This explains the importance of the notion of the death of the author for my project. Without it, my analysis would resort to the figure of the author-God who manages to manipulate his readers into recognizing his own sagely authority. The notion of the death of the author enables us to see how both Liang and Xiong are shaped by various discursive traditions (various strands of Confucianism, May Fourth, Buddhism, etc.) that speak through them. My point is that the reason why the texts insert themselves in historical traditions that have a strong potential for iconoclasm is related to the historical context within which the texts were written.

92. As John B. Henderson notes, "insofar as a canon is generally supposed to express truths and beauties that transcend particular times and places, it is usually convenient, if not absolutely necessary, to remove it from the limiting historical and cultural context that nurtured it." Henderson, *Scripture, Canon, and Commentary*, 37.

93. This explains why, as I mention in the first chapter, my reading departs from that of Thierry Meynard, who argues that Confucianism functions as a skillful means in Liang's historical metanarrative. As to Buddhism, it provides humanity with a transcendence from this world altogether, and not just from the limitations of one's situatedness in time and space.

94. I follow Zbigniew Wesołowski's analysis on this point. Wesołowski reads *Eastern and Western Cultures* as a "sinodicy," by which he means "a theory of the justification of Chinese culture." See Zbigniew Wesołowski, "Understanding the Foreign (the West) as a Remedy for Regaining One's Own Cultural Identity (China): Liang Shuming's (1893–1988) Cultural Thought," *Monumenta Serica* 53 (2005): 397.

Chapter 4

1. Yü, "Some Preliminary Observations," 26.
2. Xiong, *New Treatise*, 119; *Xin weishi lun*, 51.
3. Xiong, *New Treatise*, 17; *Xin weishi lun*, 9.
4. Xiong, *New Treatise*, 177; *Xin weishi lun*, 79.
5. Xiong, *New Treatise*, 181; *Xin weishi lun*, 81.
6. Xiong, *New Treatise*, 94; *Xin weishi lun*, 40.
7. Xiong, *New Treatise*, 265; *Xin weishi lun*, 121.
8. Xiong, *New Treatise*, 307; *Xin weishi lun*, 141.
9. "[The passage beginning with] 'Is it possible that [these people] understand' up to here should be read in one fell swoop." Xiong, *New Treatise*, 262; *Xin weishi lun*, 120.

10. In full, Xiong's signature reads as follows: *Huanggang Xiong Shili zao* (黃岡熊十力造). This signature does not appear in the *New Treatise* as reproduced in the *Complete Works of Xiong Shili*, but it does appear in the following edition of the same text: Xiong Shili 熊十力, *Xin weishi lun* 新唯識論 [New Treatise on the Uniqueness of Consciousness] (Taipei: Taiwan xuesheng shuju, 1985), 1. On this topic, see Guo, *Tiandi jian yige dushuren*, 53. I thank John Makeham for pointing this out to me.

11. Michael Nylan notes that "writing an authoritative commentary on a venerated text (a) closes the text, after which nothing, except more commentaries, may be added; (b) marks the canonical status of the text; and (c) adapts the message of the venerated text to present concerns." Nylan, *Five "Confucian" Classics*, 22.

12. Xiong, *New Treatise*, 16; *Xin weishi lun*, 8.

13. Xiong, *New Treatise*, 74; *Xin weishi lun*, 32.

14. Chow, *May Fourth Movement*, 279.

15. *Xuanxue* is usually translated as "metaphysics." As we will see shortly, however, the text uses it in contradistinction to "philosophy" (*zhexue* 哲學). The former denotes a field of knowledge that has for object the holism of Reality as opposed to the myriad phenomena studied by philosophy. The use of "metaphysics" to translate *xuanxue* would as such be misleading, as Xiong clearly does not refer to metaphysics as a branch of philosophy, but to something that stands altogether opposed to philosophy. I therefore follow Makeham in translating *xuanxue* as "fundamental wisdom."

16. That Xiong later published a vernacular edition of the *New Treatise* might be explained by the fact that he gradually acknowledged that by adapting it to a readership no longer accustomed to classical Chinese, his work might have a greater impact.

17. Xiong, *New Treatise*, 35; *Xin weishi lun*, 16.

18. Xiong, *New Treatise*, 298; *Xin weishi lun*, 136–37. On "ordinary people," see also, among other instances, Xiong, *New Treatise*, 89, 104, 260–61; *Xin weishi lun*, 38, 45, 119.

19. Xiong, *New Treatise*, 185–86; *Xin weishi lun*, 84.

20. On the theory of two truths in Buddhist discourse, and especially in Nagarjuna, see Jiang Tao, "Incommensurability of Two Conceptions of Reality: Dependent Origination and Emptiness in Nāgārjuna's *MMK*," *Philosophy East & West* 64, no. 1 (January 2014): 25–48 and Jay L. Garfield, *Empty Words: Buddhist Philosophy and Cross-Cultural Interpretation* (Oxford: Oxford University Press, 2002), 24–106.

21. Xiong, *New Treatise*, 159; *Xin weishi lun*, 70–71.

22. Jing Haifeng maintains that "life supported by faith is essential for Xiong in constructing his philosophical ontology." I agree with this statement, but only to the extent that one speaks of the faith the readers must have in recognizing that the text is a testimony from an awakened individual. Faith has no use to Xiong

because he has purportedly reached awakening. Jing, *Xiong Shili*, 25. The English translation is from Liu Junping and Qin Ping, "Contemporary Chinese Studies of Xiong Shili 熊十力," *Dao* 5, no. 1 (December 2015): 164.

23. On the absence of arguments in the text's discussion of the interaction between contraction and expansion, for example, see Xiong, *New Treatise*, 96–100; *Xin weishi lun*, 41–43.

24. See for example Yu, "Xiong Shili's Metaphysics of Virtue," 134.

25. Regarding the relation between the text's epistemology and its "lack" of argumentation, it is of interest to note Liu Shu-hsien's understanding of Xiong's epistemology, especially as expounded in his vernacular rendering of the *New Treatise*. Liu notes that Xiong's epistemology "was very much influenced by the school of Nyaya and consciousness-only Buddhism." "According to Nyaya," Liu continues, "there are four means of knowledge: perception, inference, analogy, and testimony. The Buddhist tradition never trusts perception and inference, which start from something phenomenal and can never get to the bottom of things; and analogy, though helpful, is never precise. Thus only testimony from an enlightened person can guide us to follow the right way. There is no doubt that Xiong was in this tradition, which presupposed a source of knowledge higher than the empirical knowledge built on sense perception and logical inference." In other words, only an inner enlightenment or a testimony offered by one who has achieved such an enlightenment should qualify as an adequate method to discern the nature of Reality. Xiong's *New Treatise* should be understood precisely as such a testimony. See Liu Shu-hsien, "Xiong Shili (Hsiung Shih-li)," in *Encyclopedia of Chinese Philosophy*, ed. Antonio S. Cua (New York: Routledge, 2003), 802.

26. Xiong, *New Treatise*, 88–89; *Xin weishi lun*, 38.

27. Xiong, *New Treatise*, 88; *Xin weishi lun*, 38.

28. Xiong, *New Treatise*, 89; *Xin weishi lun*, 38.

29. Xiong, *New Treatise*, 127; *Xin weishi lun*, 55. Elsewhere, the text asserts that "names have only ever been traps and snares [. . .]. If by inner reflection there is gnosis, then there will be no distorted interpretations to bind oneself—it is as if one's confusion had suddenly melted away!" Xiong, *New Treatise*, 159; *Xin weishi lun*, 70. The text moreover repeatedly reminds the reader that mental objects (Xiong, *New Treatise*, 127, 156; *Xin weishi lun*, 55, 69), the phenomenal realm of functions (Xiong, *New Treatise*, 30–49, 214; *Xin weishi lun*, 14–21, 98), and consciousness itself (Xiong, *New Treatise*, 61–62, 68, 86; *Xin weishi lun*, 27, 29, 37) are ultimately illusory; i.e., they are employed as skillful means.

30. Xiong, *New Treatise*, 50; *Xin weishi lun*, 22.

31. Xiong, *New Treatise*, 156–57, 177; *Xin weishi lun*, 69–70, 79. On this, see Tan, "Contemporary Neo-Confucian Philosophy," 542.

32. The text claims that "the Reality of mind and things when forcefully named is constant transformation. It is said to be forced because [the Reality of mind

and things] cannot be named yet is given a name." Xiong, *New Treatise*, 176; *Xin weishi lun*, 79. On the impossibility to name Reality, see also Xiong, *New Treatise*, 92, 158; *Xin weishi lun*, 39, 70.

33. My focus on the *use* of the *tiyong* pair in the discourse of the text distinguishes my approach from that of most philosophical readings of the text, which tend to emphasize the ontological nonduality of the pair. On this point, see Philippe Major, "Review of *Xiong Shili's Understanding of Reality and Function, 1920–1937*, by Sang Yu," *Dao* 20, no. 1 (2021): 165–69.

34. The *New Treatise* itself equates discernment with rationality (*lizhi*). See Xiong, *New Treatise*, 22; *Xin weishi lun*, 10. On Xiong's epistemology, see Jana Rošker, *Searching for the Way: Theory of Knowledge in Pre-Modern and Modern China* (Hong Kong: The Chinese University of Hong Kong Press, 2008), 215–25 and, especially for Xiong's later writings from the 1940s onward, Van den Stock, *Horizon of Modernity*, 221–34.

35. Xiong, *New Treatise*, 21–27, 299–301; *Xin weishi lun*, 10–13, 137–38. On Xiong's view of science and philosophy, see Chen, *Xiandai xin rujia zhijueguan kaocha*, 143–50. Xiong's distinction between discernment and wisdom maps onto the divide between science and views of life, which was heavily discussed in the 1923 debate. This debate was partly influenced by the distinction between science and intuition established in *Eastern and Western Cultures*. On the debate, see Huang Yushun 黃玉順, *Chaoyue zhishi yu jiazhi de jinzhang: "Kexue yu xuanxue lunzhan" de zhexue wenti* 超越知识与价值的紧张:「科学与玄学论战」的哲学问题 [Transcending the Tension Between Knowledge and Value: The Philosophical Issue in the "Debate on Science and Metaphysics"] (Chengdu: Sichuan renmin chubanshe, 2002) and Peng Hsiao-yen 彭小妍, 'Renshengguan' yu Ouya houqimeng lunshu「人生觀」與歐亞後啓蒙論述 ["Views of Life" and the Eurasian Post-Enlightenment Discourse], in *Wenhua fanyi yu wenben mailuo: wanming yijiang de Zhongguo, Riben yu Xifang* 文化翻譯與文本脈絡——晚明以降的中國、日本與西方 [Cultural Translation and Textual Contexts: China, Japan, and the West Since the Late Ming] (Taipei: Zhongyang yanjiuyuan Zhongguo wenzhe yanjiusuo, 2013), 221–67.

36. Xiong, *New Treatise*, 204; *Xin weishi lun*, 93.

37. Xiong, *New Treatise*, 201; *Xin weishi lun*, 92. Interestingly, fundamental wisdom is in at least one instance portrayed by the text as a form of sudden enlightenment equated with a return to the origin: "If one is skilled at 'returning' [*fan* 反], then immediately [fundamental wisdom] will be there. There is no need for endless searching." Xiong, *New Treatise*, 27; *Xin weishi lun*, 13.

38. Xiong, *New Treatise*, 159, 261–64; *Xin weishi lun*, 70, 119–20.

39. The nationalist intent behind the text is at times more explicit, as when the text claims that "by and large, Chinese students have all followed [the path of] pure authenticity in the context of ethical praxis, in which the ego-self's preoccupation with petty advantage is transcended, thereby [enabling them] to come to know the mind itself." Xiong, *New Treatise*, 181; *Xin weishi lun*, 81.

40. Xiong, *New Treatise*, 260; *Xin weishi lun*, 119. Makeham's commentary on this quote reads: "Ordinary people—as distinct from those who are awakened—find it difficult to treat all views equally; instead they are biased toward their own preferred views." Xiong, *New Treatise*, 261n47.

41. Interestingly, this excerpt is followed by a quote taken from the *Zhuangzi*: "The way has never had borders, and speech has never had that which makes it constant." Xiong comments on this quote in the following way: "When wisdom [*zhi* 知] is used for one's personal ends, [. . .] borders begin to be established and 'the paths of affirming and denying are inextricably confused.'" Xiong, *New Treatise*, 288; *Xin weishi lun*, 132–33.

42. John Makeham, "The Significance of Xiong Shili's Interpretation of Dignāga's *Ālambana-parīkṣā* (Investigation of the Object)," *Journal of Chinese Philosophy* 40, no. 5 (2013): 218. It should however be noted that commentaries from other sources were also included in the *Demonstration of Consciousness-only* (which Makeham refers to here as *Cheng Weishi Lun*), although the main source of the translation was Dharmapāla's commentary on the *Triṃśikā*. On this, see Charles Muller, "Cheng weishi lun" 成唯識論 [Demonstration of Consciousness-only], *Digital Dictionary of Buddhism*, accessed April 18, 2022, http://www.buddhism-dict.net/cgi-bin/xpr-ddb.pl?q=成唯識論.

43. Xiong, *New Treatise*, 127; *Xin weishi lun*, 55.

44. Xiong, *New Treatise*, 122–23; *Xin weishi lun*, 53.

45. On this point, the text departs from Yogācāra orthodoxy, in which there are fifty-one mental associates.

46. Xiong, *New Treatise*, 89–91; *Xin weishi lun*, 38–39. For Xiong Shili's earlier critique of Dharmapāla, as advanced in his 1926 work *A General Account of Consciousness-Only Learning*, see Sang, *Xiong Shili's Understanding of Reality and Function*, 127–36.

47. Xiong, *New Treatise*, 65, 200–1; *Xin weishi lun*, 28, 91–92. For a critique of Xiong's interpretation of Yogācāra, see Lin Chen-kuo, "Hsiung Shih-li's Hermeneutics of Self: Making a Confucian Identity in Buddhist Words," *NCCU Philosophical Journal* 8 (2002): 78–80. Soon after the publication of the *New Treatise*, a number of Buddhist thinkers, such as Yin Shun (印順; 1906–2005), Juzan (巨贊 1908–1984), and Liu Dingquan (劉定權; 1900–1987), had already taken offense at Xiong's claim that Yogācāra had hypostatized the seeds and had fallen in the trap of ontological dualism or pluralism. On this, see Guo, *Xiong Shili yu Zhongguo chuantong wenhua*, 209–10.

48. Although the *New Treatise* claims to present a monist ontology in contrast to the dualism or pluralism of Yogācāra ontology, Chang Hao has rightfully argued that Xiong's "intellectual outlook in fact contained a dichotomous view of the world which emphasizes the division between the phenomenal realm and the realm of metaphysical reality." Chang, "New Confucianism," 284.

49. See Xiong, *New Treatise*, 62–85; *Xin weishi lun*, 27–36.

50. See Xiong, *New Treatise*, 127; *Xin weishi lun*, 55.
51. Xiong, *New Treatise*, 90; *Xin weishi lun*, 39.
52. Xiong, *New Treatise*, 50; *Xin weishi lun*, 22.
53. Xiong, *New Treatise*, 156–57, 177; *Xin weishi lun*, 69–70, 79. On this, see Tan, "Contemporary Neo-Confucian Philosophy," 542.
54. Pierre Bourdieu, *The Political Ontology of Martin Heidegger*, trans. Peter Collier (Stanford: Stanford University Press, 1991), 78.
55. Xiong, *New Treatise*, 207; *Xin weishi lun*, 95.
56. Xiong, *New Treatise*, 207–08; *Xin weishi lun*, 95. Note that the text does not provide any textual support for its claim that Asaṅga, as opposed to Dharmapāla, described the eight consciousnesses in a nominal effort to help readers experience awakening.
57. Xiong, *New Treatise*, 208; *Xin weishi lun*, 95.
58. Xiong, *New Treatise*, 209; *Xin weishi lun*, 95.
59. Xiong, *New Treatise*, 210; *Xin weishi lun*, 96.
60. Xiong, *New Treatise*, 210; *Xin weishi lun*, 96.
61. Xiong spent two years at the China Institute of Inner Learning as a student under the guidance of Ouyang Jingwu from 1920 to 1922, before he began his appointment at Peking University. In 1932, the year of the publication of the *New Treatise*, Liu Dingquan, under the supervision of Ouyang Jingwu, published "A Rebuttal of the *New Treatise on the Uniqueness of Consciousness*" (*Po Xin weishi lun* 破新唯識論), in response to which Xiong wrote a "A Rebuttal of 'A Rebuttal of the *New Treatise on the Uniqueness of Consciousness*'" (*Po po Xin weishi lun* 破破新唯識論) the following year. Following the publication of Liu's text, a series of influential Buddhist thinkers, some of whom were Xiong's former classmates at the China Institute of Inner Learning, published essays criticizing Xiong's treatment of Yogācāra. This includes Taixu, Zhou Shujia (周叔迦; 1899–1970), Yin Shun, Lü Cheng (呂澂; 1896–1989), Wang Enyang (王恩洋; 1897–1964), Chen Mingshu (陳銘樞; 1889–1965), and Juzan. That so many intellectual figures associated with the China Institute of Inner Learning took offense at the publication of the *New Treatise*, and that a number of them took the time to write rebuttals to some of the claims made by the text regarding Yogācāra, further support my assessment that the text's stance on Yogācāra represents an oblique criticism of Xiong's former teacher and his institute. For a review of the Buddhist critiques of the *New Treatise*, see Guo Qiyong's detailed account in *Xiong Shili yu Zhongguo chuantong wenhua*, 207–19. For the original articles, see *Xiong Shili quanji*, annex 1, 1–590. For an English-language biographical account of this period of Xiong's life, see Chak, "Contemporary Neo-Confucian Rehabilitation," 304–11.
62. On this project, see Eyal Aviv, *Differentiating the Pearl from the Fish-Eye: Ouyang Jingwu and the Revival of Scholastic Buddhism* (Leiden: Brill, 2020) (see especially chapter 3 for Ouyang's strident critique of *The Awakening of Mahāyāna Faith*) and Sang, *Xiong Shili's Understanding of Reality and Function*, 61–69.

63. Makeham, "Xiong Shili's Critique of Yogācāra Thought" (especially 273–77), Makeham, "Translator's Introduction," xxv–xxvi, and Sang Yu, "The Role of the *Treatise on Awakening Mahāyāna Faith* in the Development of Xiong Shili's *Ti-yong* Metaphysics," in *The* Awakening of Faith *and New Confucian Philosophy*, ed. John Makeham (Leiden: Brill, 2021), 132–71. On the influence of *The Awakening of Mahāyāna Faith* on New Confucian philosophy in general, see Makeham, ed., *The* Awakening of Faith *and New Confucian Philosophy*.

64. Focusing on the problem of textual authority might explain, at least in part, why the text exonerates Asaṅga, reasons that, as Makeham notes, "are not immediately apparent." See Makeham, "Translator's Introduction," lii. The text's exoneration of Asaṅga might also account for the fact that Brière believed that in this work, Xiong "undertakes to reconstruct the system [of Yogācāra] with the aid of Wang Yangming and Bergson." See Brière, *Fifty Years of Chinese Philosophy*, 48.

65. Xiong, *New Treatise*, 207; *Xin weishi lun*, 95.

66. Xiong, *New Treatise*, 16; *Xin weishi lun*, 8.

67. For example: "in talking about the meaning of transformation, I definitely do not base myself on the views of former masters. To understand me, students must not be attached to former accounts." Or: "This is why [my view] is vastly different from all the conventional views. Students must engage the full import of what I am saying. Only by adopting a transcendent [*chaoran* 超然] and free-moving [*shen* 神] interpretation can one avoid being impeded by such views." Xiong, *New Treatise*, 94, 108; *Xin weishi lun*, 40, 47.

68. Traditionally, the character *wei*, in this particular compound, was understood to mean "only," and *weishi* signified that only consciousness truly existed. According to the *New Treatise*, *wei* rather denotes the uniqueness (*shute* 殊特) of consciousness. According to this redefinition of "*weishi*," cognitive objects do exist, but they should not be regarded as external objects separate from consciousness. Rather, the *New Treatise* argues that consciousness and cognitive objects "are the same whole and are not separated," although, as Sang Yu points out, both "exist only from the perspective of conventional truth." See Sang, *Xiong Shili's Understanding of Reality and Function*, 180n21. On the text's redefinition of *weishi*, see Xiong, *New Treatise*, 53–54; *Xin weishi lun*, 23–24.

69. Xiong, *New Treatise*, 90; *Xin weishi lun*, 39.

70. Xiong, *New Treatise*, 56; *Xin weishi lun*, 24.

71. Xiong, *New Treatise*, 316; *Xin weishi lun*, 144.

72. Xiong, *New Treatise*, 54; *Xin weishi lun*, 24. This claim is highly reminiscent of the portrayal of Confucius as devoid of doctrine in *Eastern and Western Cultures*.

73. Xiong, *New Treatise*, 54; *Xin weishi lun*, 24.

74. Xiong, *New Treatise*, 56; *Xin weishi lun*, 24.

75. In later writings, Xiong would apply this discursive model to Confucianism as well, thus echoing in significant ways the portrayal of Confucianism in *Eastern and Western Cultures*. In *The Origin of Confucianism* (*Yuanru* 原儒; 1956), Xiong

238 | Notes to Chapter 4

rejected the authority not only of the sages of antiquity who preceded Confucius but also of the Confucians of later generations. In his *Elucidating the Mind* (*Ming xin pian* 明心篇; 1959), he went on to claim that the teaching of Confucius was no longer transmitted after Mencius. In his *Exposition of the Qian and Kun Hexagrams* (*Qiankun yan* 乾坤衍; 1961), he built a distinction between the "Confucians of the Limited Unity" (*xiaokang zhi ru* 小康之儒) and the "Confucians of the Great Way" (*dadao zhi ru* 大道之儒) to immunize Confucianism from its historical manifestations, before concluding that even Mencius had failed to transmit Confucius's teaching. See Van den Stock, *Horizon of Modernity*, 222–25 and Liu Shu-hsien, "Xiong Shili," 805.

76. Although Xiong is known for making the bold claim that Confucius authored the six classics, the *New Treatise* is not explicit about this. It does however mention Confucius as the author of the *Record of Rites* (Xiong, *New Treatise*, 303; *Xin weishi lun*, 139). Xiong would later become more explicitly interested in the Confucian tradition in works like *The Origin of Confucianism*, in which he would claim that "the goals of the hundred schools and various sages of late Zhou, the various schools of Song-Ming [Neo-Confucianism], and of Buddhism can all be traced back to Confucius." See Wang Kun 王锟, *Kongzi yu ershi shiji Zhongguo sixiang* 孔子与二十世纪中国思想 [Confucius and Twentieth-Century Chinese Thought] (Jinan: Qilu Shushe, 2006), 224. On the six classics having been written by Confucius according to Xiong, see Liu, *Essentials of Contemporary Neo-Confucian Philosophy*, 67. Ng Yu-kwan points out that Xiong "often relied on subjective views to make his decision [regarding the Confucian classics], without paying much attention to objective textual proofs or to the rules of developments in the history of thought. For instance, he believed that the *The Book of Changes* had been written by Confucius. From a historical standpoint, a mature onto-cosmological system of thought such as that described in the *The Book of Changes* could not have been established in Confucius' time." Ng, "Xiong Shili's Metaphysical Theory," 243.

77. Xiong, *New Treatise*, 149; *Xin weishi lun*, 65.

78. Xiong, *New Treatise*, 181; *Xin weishi lun*, 81–82.

79. Xiong, *New Treatise*, 145; *Xin weishi lun*, 63.

80. Xiong, *New Treatise*, 24; *Xin weishi lun*, 11. The quote from the *Analects* is from 7:2. See D. C. Lau's translation in Lau, *Analects*, 86. For the passages from the *Doctrine of the Mean* and the *Changes*, and their translation by James Legge, see https://ctext.org/dictionary.pl?if=en&id=10286 and https://ctext.org/book-of-changes/jin2 (accessed April 18, 2022).

81. Xiong, *New Treatise*, 55–56; *Xin weishi lun*, 24.

82. Xiong, *New Treatise*, 147–49; *Xin weishi lun*, 64–65.

83. Xiong, *New Treatise*, 273–74; *Xin weishi lun*, 125. This syncretism appears in other instances as well. In one passage, the text argues that "the single *yang* [陽] line on the Peeling hexagram [*bogua* 剝卦] in the [*Changes*]" is "what the schools of [Sinitic] Buddhism call 'original face [*benlai mianmu* 本來面目],'" and what Wang Bi (王弼; 226–249) "referred to as 'the few are able to control the many [*gua neng*

zhi zhong zhe 寡能制眾者].'" Elsewhere, the text's discussion of the wholesome mental associate called "vigilance" (*bu fangyi* 不放逸) makes passing references to the *Demonstration of Consciousness-only*, the *Record of the Transmission of the Lamp Published in the Jingde Period* (*Jingde chuan denglu* 景德傳燈錄), the *Recorded Sayings of Chan Master Dahui Pujue* (*Dahui Pujue Chanshi yulu* 大慧普覺禪師語錄), the *Śūraṃgama-sūtra* (*Da foding shoulengyan jing* 大佛頂首楞嚴經), the *Record of Rites*, the *Odes* (*Shijing* 詩經), the *Changes* (which Xiong regards as a Confucian classic), Zhou Dunyi, the Cheng brothers, Zhu Xi, and the *Zhuangzi*. See Xiong, *New Treatise*, 304–7, 310–11; *Xin weishi lun*, 139–41, 142.

84. On this point, see Sang, *Xiong Shili's Understanding of Reality and Function*, 182–83.

85. Xiong, *Xin weishi lun (yutiwen ben)*, 135–36 (emphasis mine). The translation is adapted from Tu, "Hsiung Shih-li's Quest," 266–67. A similar claim to having reached enlightenment independently of book learning is made by Xiong in his preface to the *Treatise on Consciousness-Only*, traditionally dated to 1930. On this, see Sang, *Xiong Shili's Understanding of Reality and Function*, 233. Ng Yu-kwan points out that after his purported enlightenment, Xiong "felt that he could understand them [various texts of the Buddhist and Confucian traditions] individually and also, all of a sudden, he could comprehend them clearly as a whole, integrating them altogether. At that point, he felt consciously that he had grasped the essence of Confucianism, Buddhism, and Daoism." Ng, "Xiong Shili's Metaphysical Theory," 222.

86. Makeham, "Translator's Introduction," lxviii. Tu Weiming contends that insofar as it took the form of system, Xiong's philosophy differs from that of Wang Yangming. See Tu, "Hsiung Shih-li's Quest," 257.

87. Makeham, "Translator's Introduction," lxviii, n.110. On this topic, see also Makeham, "Role of Masters Studies," 73–101.

88. Xiong, *Shili yuyao*, 178. The English translation is adapted from Wu, "Xiong Shili," 151. On the all-inclusive nature of the syncretism of the *New Treatise* and Xiong's philosophy more generally, see other comments made by Xiong and reported in Sang, *Xiong Shili's Understanding of Reality and Function*, 223–24.

89. Makeham, "Translator's Introduction," xix, n.31. For Xiong's quote, see Xiong, *Xiong Shili quanji*, vol. 8, 423. Yu Jiyuan also argues that Xiong "synthesized several main doctrines of Confucianism and integrated them into a coherent system in order to show that the cultivation of virtue has an ontological and cosmological foundation." Yu, "Xiong Shili's Metaphysics of Virtue," 142. I discuss these issues in Philippe Major, "The Politics of Writing Chinese Philosophy: Xiong Shili's *New Treatise on the Uniqueness of Consciousness* and the 'Crystallization of Oriental Philosophy,'" *Dao* 18, no. 2 (June 2019): 241–58.

90. While I agree with Yu Jiyuan that "Xiong's philosophical goal was not 'to comment on the six classics,' but for 'the six classics to comment for me,'" I am less convinced that Xiong "did not aim to be a faithful commentator, but saw himself as an original thinker who based his work on the ancient classics." The above

analysis suggests that Xiong did aim at being a faithful commentator of the truth of the Confucian tradition, although his goal was to systematize the core message of Confucianism rather than comment on each classic in a philological manner. See Yu, "Xiong Shili's Metaphysics of Virtue," 128. Nie Minyu 聂民玉 makes a similar claim in *Tiyong bu'er: Xiong Shili jingxue sixiang yanjiu* 体用不二: 熊十力经学思想研究 [The Nonduality of Reality and Functions: An Analysis of Xiong Shili's Study of the Classics] (Beijing: Remin, 2015), 10.

91. Amy Olberding, "Philosophical Exclusion and Conversational Practices," *Philosophy East & West* 67, no. 4 (2017): 1031 (emphasis in original). On this topic, see also Amy Olberding, "It's Not Them, It's You: A Case Study Concerning the Exclusion of Non-Western Philosophy," *Comparative Philosophy* 6, no. 2 (2015): 14–34.

Conclusion

1. This discussion is indebted to J. G. A. Pocock's insightful analysis of the political uses of tradition in "Time, Institutions and Actions: An Essay on Traditions and Their Understanding," in *Politics, Language, and Time: Essays on Political Thought and History* (Chicago: University of Chicago Press, 1989), 233–72.

2. A lengthy text Liang wrote in 1961 is revealing of the fraught relationship he had with Xiong. In it, Liang fiercely criticized Xiong Shili's philosophy on a number of fronts, highlighting in particular its lack of scientific tenor, its subjectivity, its lack of attention to the work of others, its overemphasis on the building of philosophical system and on ontology, and its overall superficiality. See Liang Shuming 梁漱溟, "Du Xiong zhu ge shu shu hou" 读熊著各书书后 [After Reading the Works of Xiong], in *Liang Shuming quanji*, vol. 7, 734–86. On the fraught relationship between Xiong and Liang, see Jing, *Xin ruxue yu ershi shiji Zhongguo sixiang*, 159–77.

3. Joseph R. Levenson, *Confucian China and Its Modern Fate, Volume 1: The Problem of Intellectual Continuity* (Berkeley: University of California Press, 1966), especially xiii–xix.

4. I describe what it means to think of May Fourth as a hegemonic project in the subsection "The antitradition of May Fourth" of the Introduction.

5. Kojève, *Notion of Authority*, 53 (emphases in original). This is why the movement to study history *objectively* that emanated out of the May Fourth Movement (Gu Jiegang, Hu Shi, etc.) challenged the authority of tradition by establishing a distance between the scholar and the past studied. In other words, it refused to make of the past a tradition that would authoritatively affect the present of the researcher. On this movement, and Gu Jiegang (顧頡剛; 1893–1980) in particular, see Laurence A. Schneider, *Ku Chieh-kang and China's New History: Nationalism and the Quest for Alternative Traditions* (Berkeley: University of California Press, 1971).

6. Kojève, *Notion of Authority*, 64.

7. Insofar as refraining to recognize the authority of the past is already in and of itself to challenge this authority, it matters very little whether the break from the past is real or imagined. What matters is that such break is *believed* to exist.

8. Besides the authorities of the past, the future, and eternity, Kojève also discusses the authority of the present, characterized in his study by the Hegelian relation between master and slave. On the association of each type of authority with a temporal marker, see Kojève, *The Notion of Authority*, 48–56.

9. Levenson, *Confucian China*, xviii.

10. This goes to show how it is the opacity of the classics, which results in great part from the passage of time, that makes them powerful sources of authority. Classics remain authoritative only to the extent that their meaning cannot be readily accessible; only to the extent that they open themselves up only to a chosen elite. It is also worth noting that classics are not the only texts that function as sources of authority because of their opacity (certain texts of Derrida spontaneously come to mind).

11. This goes the show the religious nature of the text's discourse on Confucianism, at least if we adopt a broader definition of "religion," such as that of Rodney L. Taylor: "Religion [. . .] involves a perception of, knowledge of, or insight into, that which constitutes the Absolute and, in addition, the ability to provide a means for the individual to engage in an ultimate transformation toward that which is regarded as the Absolute, the fulfillment of the relationship between the individual and the Absolute." In the case of *Eastern and Western Cultures*, Confucius serves as a stand-in for the Absolute, which can be embodied by contemporaries who learn to live their lives intuitively—through the help of the classics or, perhaps more easily, thought that of *Eastern and Western Cultures*. Rodney L. Taylor, "The Religious Character of the Confucian Tradition," *Philosophy East & West* 48, no. 1 (1998): 84

12. Chapter 3 makes the argument that although *Eastern and Western Cultures* does not explicitly state that Liang is a sage, its historical narrative and its depictions of Confucius do imply that he is.

13. Although Confucius had been able to foresee the future, he had remained silent on the proper path that would lead to this future, which involves the fulfilling of humanity's basic needs. The text does not explain how a sage such as Confucius could uphold an ideal without realizing that it was unfit for the time and without placing it within the proper historical metanarrative.

14. Laclau and Mouffe, *Hegemony and Socialist Strategy*, xiii.

15. Slavoj Žižek, "Class Struggle or Postmodernism? Yes, Please," in *Contingency, Hegemony, Universality*, 123–25.

16. Judith Butler, "Competing Universalities," in *Contingency, Hegemony, Universality*, 175–77.

17. The text's understanding of history as a plurilinear process, whereby the West, China, and India evolve along parallel pathways, only applies to the premodern period. In the modern period, the three pathways become three periods of an unilinear process of evolution that applies to humanity as a whole.

18. I discuss in the introduction the process by which May Fourth actors, in the late 1910s, projected the "modern West" onto the inevitable, emancipatory future of history in a first step before filling in the "modern West" with content that benefited them in a second step.

19. Of course, not all readers must have been inclined to accept that the historical model of *Eastern and Western Cultures* was rooted in an objective assessment of historical trends. Hu Shi, among others, criticized this historical model as pure fantasy. See Hu Shi 胡适, "Du Liang Shuming xiansheng de *Dongxi wenhua ji qi zhexue*" 读梁漱溟先生的《东西文化及其哲学》 [On Reading Liang Shuming's *Eastern and Western Cultures and Their Philosophies*], in *Hu Shi wenji* 胡适文集 [The Collected Works of Hu Shi], ed. Ouyang Zhesheng 欧阳哲生 (Beijing: Beijing daxue chubanshe, 1998), vol. 3, 185–86. For Liang Shuming's reply to Hu Shi's criticisms, see Liang Shuming 梁漱溟, "Da Hu ping *Dongxi wenhua ji qi zhexue*" 答胡评《东西文化及其哲学》 [Answering Hu's Critique of *Eastern and Western Cultures and Their Philosophies*], in *Liang Shuming quanji*, vol. 4, 738–56.

20. On the notion of empty signifier, see Laclau, *Emancipation(s)*, 36–46 and "Structure, History and the Political," in *Contingency, Hegemony, Universality*, 182–212.

Bibliography

Adler, Joseph A. *Reconstructing the Confucian Dao: Zhu Xi's Appropriation of Zhou Dunyi*. Albany: State University of New York Press, 2014.
Alitto, Guy S. *The Last Confucian: Liang Shu-ming and the Chinese Dilemma of Modernity*. Berkeley: University of California Press, 1986.
Ames, Roger T. "Achieving Personal Identity in Confucian Role Ethics: Tang Junyi on Human Nature *as* Conduct." *Oriens Extremus* 49 (2010): 143–66.
Ames, Roger T., and David L. Hall. *Thinking Through Confucius*. Albany: State University of New York Press, 1987.
An, Yanming. "Liang Shuming and Henri Bergson on Intuition: Cultural Context and the Evolution of Terms." *Philosophy East & West* 47, no. 3 (1997): 337–62.
Anderson, Perry. "The Antinomies of Antonio Gramsci." *New Left Review* 100 (1976): 5–78.
Arendt, Hannah. "Tradition and the Modern Age." In *Between Past and Future: Six Exercises in Political Thought*, 17–40. New York: The Viking Press, 1961.
——— . "What Is Authority?" In *Between Past and Future: Six Exercises in Political Thought*, 91–141. New York: The Viking Press, 1961.
Assis, Amit. "Author-ity." *Mafte'akh* 2 (2011): 1–28.
Aviv, Eyal. *Differentiating the Pearl from the Fish-Eye: Ouyang Jingwu and the Revival of Scholastic Buddhism*. Leiden: Brill, 2020.
Barthes, Roland. "The Death of the Author." In *Authorship: From Plato to Postmodernism: A Reader*, edited by Seán Burke, 125–30. Edinburgh: Edinburgh University Press, 1995.
Bourdieu, Pierre. *The Political Ontology of Martin Heidegger*. Translated by Peter Collier. Stanford: Stanford University Press, 1991.
——— . "Rites of Institution." In *Language and Symbolic Power*, edited by John B. Thompson, translated by Gino Raymond and Matthew Adamson, 117–26. Cambridge: Polity, 1991.
Bresciani, Umberto. *Reinventing Confucianism: The New Confucian Movement*. Taipei: Taipei Ricci Institute for Chinese Studies, 2001.

Brière, S. J. O. *Fifty Years of Chinese Philosophy, 1898–1950*. Translated by Laurence G. Thompson. Westport: Greenwood Press, 1979.

Burke, Seán. *The Death and Return of the Author: Criticism and Subjectivity in Barthes, Foucault and Derrida*. Edinburgh: Edinburgh University Press, 1998.

Butler, Judith. "Competing Universalities." In *Contingency, Hegemony, Universality: Contemporary Dialogues on the Left*, by Judith Butler, Ernesto Laclau, and Slavoj Žižek, 136–81. London: Verso, 2000.

Butler, Judith, Ernesto Laclau, and Slavoj Žižek. *Contingency, Hegemony, Universality: Contemporary Dialogues on the Left*. London: Verso, 2000.

Cao, Yueming 曹躍明. *Liang Shuming sixiang yanjiu* 梁漱溟思想研究 [Research in the Thought of Liang Shuming]. Tianjin: Tianjin remin chubanshe, 1995.

Chak, Chi-shing. "The Contemporary Neo-Confucian Rehabilitation: Xiong Shili and His Moral Metaphysics." PhD diss., University of California, 1990.

Chan, Alan. "Philosophical Hermeneutics and the *Analects*: The Paradigm of 'Tradition.'" *Philosophy East & West* 34, no. 4 (October 1984): 421–36.

Chan, N. Serina. *The Thought of Mou Zongsan*. Leiden: Brill, 2011.

Chan, Wing-tsit. *Religious Trends in Modern China*. New York: Columbia University Press, 1953.

———. *A Source Book in Chinese Philosophy*. Princeton: Princeton University Press, 1963.

Chang, Hao. *Chinese Intellectuals in Crisis: Search for Order and Meaning (1890–1911)*. Berkeley: University of California Press, 1987.

———. "New Confucianism and the Intellectual Crisis of Contemporary China." In *The Limits of Change: Essays on Conservative Alternatives in Republican China*, edited by Charlotte Furth, 276–302. Cambridge: Harvard University Press, 1976.

——— 張灝. "Zhongguo jindai sixiangshi de zhuanxing shidai" 中國近代思想史的轉型時代 [The Transitional Period of Modern Chinese Intellectual History]. *Ershiyi shiji* 二十一世紀 52 (April 1999): 29–39.

Chen, Duxiu 陈独秀. "Bo Kang Youwei *Gonghe pingyi*" 驳康有为《共和评议》 [Refuting Kang Youwei's *Impartial Words on Republicanism*]. In *Chen Duxiu zhuzuo xuanbian* 陈独秀著作选编 [Selected Works of Chen Duxiu], edited by Ren Jianshu 任建树, vol. 1, 388–404. Shanghai: Shanghai Renmin, 2009.

———. "Da peijian qingnian (kongjiao)" 答佩剑青年（孔教）[Answering the Sword-Bearing Youth (Confucianism)]. In *Chen Duxiu zhuzuo xuanbian* 陈独秀著作选编 [Selected Works of Chen Duxiu], edited by Ren Jianshu 任建树, vol. 1, 311–12. Shanghai: Shanghai Renmin, 2009.

———. "Dongxi minzu genben sixiang zhi chayi" 东西民族根本思想之差异 [The Differences in the Fundamental Thinking of Eastern and Western Peoples]. In *Chen Duxiu zhuzuo xuanbian* 陈独秀著作选编 [Selected Works of Chen Duxiu], edited by Ren Jianshu 任建树, vol. 1, 193–96. Shanghai: Shanghai Renmin, 2009.

———. "Falanxiren yu jinshi wenming" 法兰西人与近世文明 [The French and Modern Civilization]. In *Chen Duxiu zhuzuo xuanbian* 陈独秀著作选编 [Selected Works of Chen Duxiu], edited by Ren Jianshu 任建树, vol. 1, 164–65. Shanghai: Shanghai Renmin, 2009.

———. "Jinggao qingnian" 敬告青年 [Call to Youth]. In *Chen Duxiu zhuzuo xuanbian* 陈独秀著作选编 [Selected Works of Chen Duxiu], edited by Ren Jianshu 任建树, vol. 1, 158–63. Shanghai: Shanghai Renmin, 2009.

———. "Kelinde bei" 克林德碑 [The Von Ketteler Monument]. In *Chen Duxiu zhuzuo xuanbian* 陈独秀著作选编 [Selected Works of Chen Duxiu], edited by Ren Jianshu 任建树, vol. 1, 439–47. Shanghai: Shanghai Renmin, 2009.

———. "Kongzi zhi dao yu xiandai shenghuo" 孔子之道与现代生活 [The Way of Confucius and Modern Life]. In *Chen Duxiu zhuzuo xuanbian* 陈独秀著作选编 [Selected Works of Chen Duxiu], edited by Ren Jianshu 任建树, vol. 1, 264–69. Shanghai: Shanghai Renmin, 2009.

———. "Tiaohelun yu jiu daode" 调和论与旧道德 [The Reconciliation Theory and the Old Morality]. In *Chen Duxiu zhuzuo xuanbian* 陈独秀著作选编 [Selected Works of Chen Duxiu], edited by Ren Jianshu 任建树, vol. 2, 133–36. Shanghai: Shanghai Renmin, 2009.

———. "The Way of Confucius and Modern Life." In *Sources of Chinese Tradition*, edited by Wm. Theodore de Bary and Richard Lufrano, vol. 2, 353–56. New York: Columbia University Press, 2000.

———. "Wo zhi aiguozhuyi" 我之爱国主义 [My Patriotism]. In *Chen Duxiu zhuzuo xuanbian* 陈独秀著作选编 [Selected Works of Chen Duxiu], edited by Ren Jianshu 任建树, vol. 1, 231–36. Shanghai: Shanghai Renmin, 2009.

———. "Wuren zuihou zhi juewu" 吾人最后之觉悟 [Our Final Awakening]. In *Chen Duxiu zhuzuo xuanbian* 陈独秀著作选编 [Selected Works of Chen Duxiu], edited by Ren Jianshu 任建树, vol. 1, 201–04. Shanghai: Shanghai Renmin, 2009.

———. "Xianfa yu kongjiao" 宪法与孔教 [Constitution and Confucianism]. In *Chen Duxiu zhuzuo xuanbian* 陈独秀著作选编 [Selected Works of Chen Duxiu], edited by Ren Jianshu 任建树, vol. 1, 248–52. Shanghai: Shanghai Renmin, 2009.

———. "Yijiuyiliu nian" 一九一六年 [1916]. In *Chen Duxiu zhuzuo xuanbian* 陈独秀著作选编 [Selected Works of Chen Duxiu], edited by Ren Jianshu 任建树, vol. 1, 197–200. Shanghai: Shanghai Renmin, 2009.

———. "Zai lun kongjiao wenti" 再论孔教问题 [On the Issue of Confucianism Again]. In *Chen Duxiu zhuzuo xuanbian* 陈独秀著作选编 [Selected Works of Chen Duxiu], edited by Ren Jianshu 任建树, vol. 1, 278–80. Shanghai: Shanghai Renmin, 2009.

———. "Zai zhiwen *Dongfang zazhi* jizhe" 再质问东方杂志记者 [Further Questions for the Correspondents of *The Eastern Miscellany*]. In *Chen Duxiu zhuzuo xuanbian* 陈独秀著作选编 [Selected Works of Chen Duxiu], edited by Ren Jianshu 任建树, vol. 2, 39–48. Shanghai: Shanghai Renmin, 2009.

Chen, Lai 陈来. "Dui xin wenhua yundong de zai sikao: cong 'wusi' houqi de Liang Shuming shuoqi" 对新文化运动的再思考——从「五四」后期的梁漱溟说起 [Rethinking the New Culture Movement: On Liang Shuming in the Late Period of the May Fourth Movement]. *Nanchang daxue xuebao (rensheban)* 南昌大学学报 (人社版) 1 (2000): 1–5.

———. "Liang Shuming de *Dongxi wenhua ji qi zhexue* yu qi wenhua duoyuanzhuyi" 梁漱溟的《东西文化及其哲学》与其文化多元主义 [Liang Shuming's *Eastern and Western Cultures and Their Philosophies* and Its Cultural Pluralism]. In *Xiandai Zhongguo zhexue de zhuixun: xin lixue yu xin xinxue* 现代中国哲学的追寻——新理学与新心学 [*The Search for Modern Chinese Philosophy: New Cheng-Zhu Studies and New Lu-Wang Studies*], 3–40. Beijing: Renmin, 2001.

Chen, Yongjie 陈永杰. *Xiandai xin rujia zhijueguan kaocha: yi Liang Shuming, Feng Youlan, Xiong Shili, He Lin wei zhongxin* 现代新儒家直觉观考察——以梁漱溟、冯友兰、熊十力、贺麟为中心 [*An Examination into the Concept of Intuition in New Confucianism: The Cases of Liang Shuming, Feng Youlan, Xiong Shili, and He Lin*]. Shanghai: Dongfang chuban zhongxin, 2015.

Cheng, Zhongying 成中英. "Zonglun xiandai Zhongguo xin rujia zhexue de jieding yu pingjia wenti" 综论现代中国新儒家哲学的界定与评价问题 [A Comprehensive Discussion of the Issues of the Definition and Evaluation of Modern Chinese New Confucian Philosophy]. In *Xuanpu lunxueji: Xiong Shili shengping yu xueshu* 玄圃论学集: 熊十力生平与学术 [Collected Essays from Xuanpu: Xiong Shili's Life and Work], edited by Cao Yuetang 曹月堂. Beijing: Sanlian, 1990.

Chew, Matthew. "Academic Boundary Work in Non-Western Academies: A Comparative Analysis of the Philosophy Discipline in Modern China and Japan." *International Sociology* 20, no. 4 (December 2005): 530–59.

Ching, Julia. "Truth and Ideology: The Confucian Way (*Tao*) and Its Transmission (*Tao-T'ung*)." *Journal of History of Ideas* 35, no. 3 (1974): 371–88.

Chow, Kai-Wing, Hon Tze-ki, Ip Hung-yok, and Don. C. Price, eds. *Beyond the May Fourth Paradigm: In Search of Chinese Modernity*. Lanham: Lexington, 2008.

Chow, Tse-tsung. *The May Fourth Movement: Intellectual Revolution in Modern China*. Cambridge: Harvard University Press, 1960.

Chu, Hsi. *Learning to Be a Sage: Selections from the* Conversations of Master Chu, Arranged Topically. Translated with commentary by Daniel K. Gardner. Berkeley: University of California Press, 1990.

Ciaudo, Joseph. "Bergson's 'Intuition' in China and Its Confucian Fate (1915–1923): Some Remarks on *Zhijue* in Modern Chinese Philosophy." *Problemos* 35 (2016): 35–50.

———. "Introduction à la métaphysique bergsonienne en Chine: échos philosophiques et moralisation de l'intuition." *Noesis* 21 (2013): 293–328.

———. "Replacer Chen Duxiu dans son vocabulaire: *La nouvelle jeunesse* et le problème de la culture chinoise." *Oriens Extremus* 54 (2015): 23–57.

Cole, Alan. *Fathering Your Father: The Zen of Fabrication in Tang Buddhism*. Berkeley: University of California Press, 2009.

———. *Fetishizing Tradition: Desire and Reinvention in Buddhist and Christian Narratives*. Albany: State University of New York Press, 2015.
Csikszentmihalyi, Mark. *Material Virtue: Ethics and the Body in Early China*. Leiden: Brill, 2004.
Cuevas, Bryan J. "Rebirth." In *Encyclopedia of Buddhism*, edited by Robert E. Buswell, vol. 2, 712–14. New York: Macmillan Reference/Thomson/Gale, 2004.
Davies, Gloria. *Worrying about China: The Language of Chinese Critical Inquiry*. Cambridge: Harvard University Press, 2007.
de Bary, Wm. Theodore. *Neo-Confucian Orthodoxy and the Learning of the Mind-and-Heart*. New York: Columbia University Press, 1981.
de Certeau, Michel. *Histoire et psychanalyse, entre science et fiction*. Paris: Gallimard, 2002.
Defoort, Carine. "Five Visions of Yang Zhu Before He Became a Philosopher." *Asian Studies* 8, no. 2 (2020): 235–56.
———. "Unfounded and Unfollowed: Mencius's Portrayal of Yang Zhu and Mo Di." In *Having a Word with Angus Graham: At Twenty-Five Years into His Immortality*, edited by Carine Defoort and Roger T. Ames, 165–84. Albany: State University of New York Press, 2018.
Doleželová-Velingerová, Milena, and David Der-wei Wang. "Introduction." In *The Appropriation of Cultural Capital: China's May Fourth Project*, edited by Milena Doleželová-Velingerová and Oldřich Král, 1–27. Cambridge: Harvard University Press, 2001.
Duara, Prasenjit. *Rescuing History from the Nation: Questioning Narratives of Modern China*. Chicago: University of Chicago Press, 1996.
Dussel, Enrique. "Eurocentrism and Modernity (Introduction to the Frankfurt Lectures)." *Boundary 2* 20, no. 3 (Fall 1993): 65–76.
Fabian, Johannes. *Time and the Other: How Anthropology Makes Its Object*. New York: Columbia University Press, 1983.
Fang, Keli 方克立, and Cao Yueming 曹躍明. "Liang Shuming de feilixingzhuyi zhexue sixiang shuping" 梁漱溟的非理性主義哲學思想述評 [A Critique of Liang Shuming's Non-Rational Philosophical Thought]. In *Cong wusi dao xin wusi* 從五四到新五四 [From May Fourth to New May Fourth], edited by Yü Ying-shih 余英時 and Bao Zunxin 包遵信, 340–85. Taipei: Shibao wenhua, 1989.
Feigon, Lee. *Chen Duxiu: Founder of the Chinese Communist Party*. Princeton: Princeton University Press, 1983.
Forster, Elisabeth. *1919—The Year That Changed China*. Berlin: De Gruyter Oldenbourg, 2018.
Foucault, Michel. "What Is an Author?" In *Textual Strategies: Perspectives in Post-Structuralist Criticism*, edited by Josué V. Harari, 141–60. London: Methuen, 1979.
———. "What Is Enlightenment?" In *The Foucault Reader*, edited by Paul Rabinow, 32–50. New York: Pantheon Books, 1984.
Fröhlich, Thomas, and Axel Schneider, eds. *Chinese Visions of Progress, 1895 to 1949*. Leiden: Brill, 2020.

Fung, Edmund S. K. *The Intellectual Foundations of Chinese Modernity: Cultural and Political Thought in the Republican Era*. Cambridge: Cambridge University Press, 2010.

———. "Nationalism and Modernity: The Politics of Cultural Conservatism in Republican China." *Modern Asian Studies* 43, no. 3 (2009): 777–813.

Furth, Charlotte. "May Fourth in History." In *Reflections on the May Fourth Movement: A Symposium*, edited by Benjamin I. Schwartz, 59–68. Cambridge: Harvard University Press, 1972.

———. *Ting Wen-chiang: Science and China's New Culture*. Cambridge: Harvard University Press, 1970.

Gadamer, Hans-Georg. *Truth and Method*. Translated by Joel Weinsheimer and Donald G. Marshall. New York: Continuum, 2003.

Gardner, Daniel K. *Chu Hsi and the* Ta-hsueh*: Neo-Confucian Reflection on the Confucian Canon*. Cambridge: Harvard University Press, 1986.

Garfield, Jay L. *Empty Words: Buddhist Philosophy and Cross-Cultural Interpretation*. Oxford: Oxford University Press, 2002.

Gauchet, Marcel. *The Disenchantment of the World: A Political History of Religion*. Translated by Oscar Burge. Princeton: Princeton University Press, 1997.

Giddens, Anthony. *The Consequences of Modernity*. Cambridge: Polity Press, 1990.

Guo, Meihua 郭美华. *Xiong Shili bentilun zhexue yanjiu* 熊十力本体论哲学研究 [Research on the Ontological Philosophy of Xiong Shili]. Chengdu: Bashu, 2004.

Guo, Qiyong 郭齊勇. *Ruxue yu ruxueshi xinlun* 儒學與儒學史新論 [New Articles on Confucianism and Its History]. Taipei: Xuesheng shuju, 2002.

———. *Tiandi jian yige dushuren: Xiong Shili zhuan* 天地間一個讀書人: 熊十力傳 [A Scholar Between Heaven and Earth: A Biography of Xiong Shili]. Taipei: Yeqiang chubanshe, 1994.

———. "Wusi de lingyige bei ren hulüe de chuantong: wenhua baochengzhuyi de xingcheng, fazhan ji qi yiyi" 五四的另一个被人忽略的传统: 文化保成主义的形成、发展及其意义 [Another Forgotten Tradition of May Fourth: The Formation, Development, and Meaning of Cultural Conservatism]. Accessed April 16, 2022. https://www.aisixiang.com/data/30184.html.

———. *Xiong Shili yu Zhongguo chuantong wenhua* 熊十力與中國傳統文化 [Xiong Shili and Traditional Chinese Culture]. Hong Kong: Tiandi, 1988.

Guo, Qiyong 郭齐勇, and Gong Jianping 龚建平. *Liang Shuming zhexue sixiang* 梁漱溟哲学思想 [The Philosophical Thought of Liang Shuming]. Beijing: Peking University Press, 2011.

Habermas, Jürgen. *The Philosophical Discourse of Modernity: Twelve Lectures*. Translated by Frederick Lawrence. Cambridge: Polity Press, 1987.

Han, Yu 韓愈. "Shishuo" 師說 [On Teachers]. In *Han Yu wenji huijiao jianzhu* 韓愈文集彙校箋注 [Collected Writings of Han Yu: Compiled Recensions and Annotations], compiled and annotated by Liu Zhenlun 劉真倫 and Yue Zhen 岳珍, vol. 2, 139–46. Beijing: Zhonghua shuju, 2010.

Hanafin, John J. "The 'Last Buddhist': The Philosophy of Liang Shuming." In *New Confucianism: A Critical Examination*, edited by John Makeham, 187–218. New York: Palgrave, 2003.

Hartog, François. "Ouverture: Autorités et temps." In *Les Autorités: Dynamiques et mutations d'une figure de référence à l'Antiquité*, edited by Didier Foucault and Pascal Payen, 23–36. Grenoble: Éditions Jérôme Million, 2007.

———. *Regimes of Historicity: Presentism and Experiences of Time*. Translated by Saskia Brown. New York: Columbia University Press, 2015.

———. "Temps du monde, histoire, écriture de l'histoire." *L'inactuel* 12 (2004): 93–102.

Harvey, David. *The Condition of Postmodernity: An Enquiry into the Origins of Cultural Change*. Oxford: B. Blackwell, 1989.

Harvey, Peter. *An Introduction to Buddhism: Teachings, History and Practices*. New York: Cambridge University Press, 2013.

He, Lin 賀麟. *Dangdai Zhongguo zhexue* 當代中國哲學 [Contemporary Chinese Philosophy]. Taipei: Shidai shuju, 1974.

He, Xinquan 何信全. *Ruxue yu xiandai minzhu: dangdai xin rujia zhengzhi zhexue yanjiu* 儒學與現代民主———當代新儒家政治哲學研究 [Confucianism and Modern Democracy: Studies in the Political Philosophy of New Confucianism]. Taipei: Zhongyang yanjiuyuan Zhongguo wenzhe yanjiusuo, 2009.

Heelas, Paul, Scott Lash, and Paul Morris, eds. *Detraditionalization: Critical Reflections on Authority and Identity*. Cambridge: Blackwell, 1996.

Henderson, John B. *Scripture, Canon, and Commentary: A Comparison of Confucian and Western Exegesis*. Princeton: Princeton University Press, 1991.

Hon, Tze-ki. *The Allure of the Nation: The Cultural and Historical Debates in Late Qing and Republican China*. Leiden: Brill, 2015.

———. *Revolution as Restoration: Guocui xuebao and China's Path to Modernity, 1905–1911*. Leiden: Brill, 2013.

Hu, Shih. *The Development of the Logical Method in Ancient China*. Shanghai: The Oriental Book Company, 1922.

——— 胡适. "Du Liang Shuming xiansheng de *Dongxi wenhua ji qi zhexue*" 读梁漱溟先生的《东西文化及其哲学》 [On Reading Liang Shuming's *Eastern and Western Cultures and Their Philosophies*]. In *Hu Shi wenji* 胡适文集 [The Collected Works of Hu Shi], edited by Ouyang Zhesheng 欧阳哲生, vol. 3, 182–97. Beijing: Beijing daxue chubanshe, 1998.

Huang, Max Ko-wu 黃克武. "Hewei tianyan? Yan Fu 'tianyan zhi xue' de neihan yu yiyi" 何謂天演？嚴復「天演之學」的內涵與意義 [What Is *Tianyan*? The Meaning and Significance of Yan Fu's *Theory of Natural Evolution*]. *Zhongyang yanjiuyuan jindaishi yanjiusuo jikan* 中央研究院近代史研究所集刊 85 (September 2014): 129–87.

Huang, Yushun 黄玉顺. *Chaoyue zhishi yu jiazhi de jinzhang: "Kexue yu xuanxue lunzhan" de zhexue wenti* 超越知识与价值的紧张：「科学与玄学论战」的哲学问题 [Transcending the Tension Between Knowledge and Value: The

Philosophical Issue in the "Debate on Science and Metaphysics"]. Chengdu: Sichuan renmin chubanshe, 2002.
Jacobs, Struan. "Edward Shils' Theory of Tradition." *Philosophy of the Social Sciences* 37, no. 2 (June 2007): 139–62.
Jameson, Fredric. *A Singular Modernity: Essay on the Ontology of the Present*. London: Verso, 2002.
Jenco, Leigh K. *Changing Referents: Learning Across Space and Time in China and the West*. Oxford: Oxford University Press, 2015.
Jensen, Lionel M. *Manufacturing Confucianism: Chinese Traditions and Universal Civilization*. Durham: Duke University Press, 1997.
Jiang, Tao. "*Ālayavijñāna* and the Problematic of Continuity in the *Cheng Weishi Lun*." *Journal of Indian Philosophy* 33 (2005): 243–84.
———. "Incommensurability of Two Conceptions of Reality: Dependent Origination and Emptiness in Nāgārjuna's *MMK*." *Philosophy East & West* 64, no. 1 (January 2014): 25–48.
Jing, Haifeng 景海峰. *Xin ruxue yu ershi shiji Zhongguo sixiang* 新儒学与二十世纪中国思想 [New Confucianism and Twentieth-Century Chinese Thought]. Zhengzhou: Zhongzhou guji chubanshe, 2005.
———. *Xiong Shili* 熊十力 [Xiong Shili]. Taipei: Dongda, 1992.
Jullien, François. *Un sage est sans idée: ou l'autre de la philosophie*. Paris: Seuil, 1998.
Jung, Carl Gustav. *Mysterium Coniunctionis: An Inquiry into the Separation and Synthesis of Psychic Opposites in Alchemy*. Translated by R. F. C. Hull. In *The Collected Works of C. G. Jung*, 2nd ed., edited by Sir Herbert Read, Michael Fordham, Gerhard Adler, and William McGuire, vol. 14. Princeton: Princeton University Press, 1970.
Kojève, Alexandre. *The Notion of Authority (A Brief Presentation)*. Translated by Hager Weslati. London: Verso, 2014.
Koselleck, Reinhart. *Futures Past: On the Semantics of Historical Time*. Translated by Keith Tribe. New York: Columbia University Press, 2004.
Kwok, D. W. Y. *Scientism in Chinese Thought, 1900–1950*. New Haven: Yale University Press, 1965.
Laclau, Ernesto. *Emancipation(s)*. London: Verso, 1996.
———. "Structure, History and the Political." In *Contingency, Hegemony, Universality: Contemporary Dialogues on the Left*, by Judith Butler, Ernesto Laclau, and Slavoj Žižek, 182–212. London: Verso, 2000.
Laclau, Ernesto, and Chantal Mouffe. *Hegemony and Socialist Strategy: Towards a Radical Democratic Politics*. London: Verso, 2014.
Lau, D. C., trans. *The Analects*. London: Penguin, 1979.
Leclerc, Gérard. *Histoire de l'autorité. L'assignation des énoncés culturels et la généalogie de la croyance*. Paris: Presses Universitaires de France, 1996.
Lee, Leo Ou-fan. "Incomplete Modernity: Rethinking the May Fourth Intellectual Project." In *The Appropriation of Cultural Capital: China's May Fourth Project*,

edited by Milena Doleželová-Velingerová and Oldřich Král, 31–65. Cambridge: Harvard University Press, 2001.

———. "In Search of Modernity: Some Reflections on a New Mode of Consciousness in Twentieth-Century Chinese History and Literature." In *Ideas Across Cultures: Essays in Honor of Benjamin Schwartz*, edited by Merle Goldman and Paul A. Cohen, 109–35. Cambridge: Harvard University Press, 1990.

Lee, Ming-huei 李明輝. "Dangdai xin rujia de daotonglun" 當代新儒家的道統論 [The Discourse of the Genealogy of the Way in New Confucianism]. In *Dangdai ruxue zhi ziwo zhuanhua* 當代儒學之自我轉化 [*The Self-Transformation of Contemporary Confucianism*], 149–73. Taipei: Zhongyang yanjiuyuan Zhongguo wenzhe yanjiusuo, 1994.

Levenson, Joseph R. *Confucian China and Its Modern Fate, Volume 1: The Problem of Intellectual Continuity*. Berkeley: University of California Press, 1966.

———. "'History' and 'Value': The Tensions of Intellectual Choice in Modern China." In *Studies in Chinese Thought*, edited by Arthur F. Wright, 146–94. Chicago: University of Chicago Press, 1953.

Lewis, Mark Edward. *Writing and Authority in Early China*. Albany: State University of New York Press, 1999.

Li, Dazhao 李大釗. "Dongxi wenming genben zhi yidian" 東西文明根本之异点 [The Fundamental Differences Between Eastern and Western Civilizations]. In *Li Dazhao quanji* 李大釗全集 [The Complete Works of Li Dazhao], edited by The Chinese Li Dazhao Research Association, vol. 2, 211–24. Beijing: Renmin, 2006.

Li, Qingliang 李清良. "Lun Ma Yifu dui Xiong Shili *Xin weishi lun* zhi yingxiang" 論馬一浮對熊十力《新唯識論》之影響 [On the Influence of Ma Yifu on Xiong Shili's *New Treatise on the Uniqueness of Consciousness*]. *Taiwan Dongya wenming yanjiu xuekan* 臺灣東亞文明研究學刊 7, no. 1 (2010): 201–32.

Li, Yuanting 李淵庭, and Yan Binghua 閻秉華. *Liang Shuming nianpu* 梁漱溟年谱 [A Chronicle of Liang Shuming's Life]. Beijing: Shangwu yinshuguan, 2018.

Liang, Shuming. *Les cultures d'Orient et d'Occident et leurs philosophies*. Translated by Luo Shenyi. Paris: You Feng, 2011.

———. "The Cultures of the East and West and Their Philosophies." Translated by Andrew Covlin and Jinmei Yuan. *Dao* 1, no. 1 (2001): 107–27.

——— 梁漱溟. "Da Hu ping *Dongxi wenhua ji qi zhexue*" 答胡評《东西文化及其哲学》 [Answering Hu's Critique of *Eastern and Western Cultures and Their Philosophies*]. In *Liang Shuming quanji* 梁漱溟全集 [The Complete Works of Liang Shuming], edited by the Committee of the Academy of Chinese Culture, vol. 4, 738–56. Jinan: Shandong Remin, 1991.

——— 梁漱溟. *Dongxi wenhua ji qi zhexue* 东西文化及其哲学 [Eastern and Western Cultures and Their Philosophies]. In *Liang Shuming quanji* 梁漱溟全集 [The Complete Works of Liang Shuming], edited by the Committee of the Academy of Chinese Culture, vol. 1, 319–547. Jinan: Shandong Remin, 1989.

——— 梁漱溟. "*Dongxi wenhua ji qi zhexue* daoyan"《东西文化及其哲学》导言 [Preface to *Eastern and Western Cultures and Their Philosophies*]. In *Liang Shuming quanji* 梁漱溟全集 [The Complete Works of Liang Shuming], edited by the Committee of the Academy of Chinese Culture, vol. 1, 254–66. Jinan: Shandong Remin, 1989.

——— 梁漱溟. "Du Xiong zhu ge shu shu hou" 读熊著各书书后 [After Reading the Works of Xiong]. In *Liang Shuming quanji* 梁漱溟全集 [The Complete Works of Liang Shuming], edited by the Committee of the Academy of Chinese Culture, vol. 7, 734–86. Jinan: Shandong Remin, 1993.

——— 梁漱溟. "Meiguo xuezhe Ai Kai xiansheng fangtan jilu zhaiyao" 美国学者艾恺先生访谈记录摘要 [Summary of the Record of the Interview with American Scholar Guy S. Alitto]. In *Liang Shuming quanji* 梁漱溟全集 [The Complete Works of Liang Shuming], edited by the Committee of the Academy of Chinese Culture, vol. 8, 1137–78. Jinan: Shandong Remin, 1993.

——— 梁漱溟. "Wo de zixue xiaoshi" 我的自学小史 [A Brief History of My Self-Study]. In *Liang Shuming quanji* 梁漱溟全集 [The Complete Works of Liang Shuming], edited by the Committee of the Academy of Chinese Culture, vol. 2, 659–98. Jinan: Shandong Remin, 1989.

——— 梁漱溟. "Wo dui renlei xinli renshi qianhou zhuanbian butong" 我对人类心理认识前后转变不同 [On the Differences Between My Early and Late Understandings of Human Psychology]. In *Liang Shuming quanji* 梁漱溟全集 [The Complete Works of Liang Shuming], edited by the Committee of the Academy of Chinese Culture, vol. 7, 130–43. Jinan: Shandong Remin, 1993.

——— 梁漱溟. "Xianggang tuoxian ji Kuan Shu liang er" 香港脱险寄宽恕两兒 [Letter to My Two Sons [Pei]kuan and [Pei]shu upon My Escape from Hong Kong]. In *Liang Shuming quanji* 梁漱溟全集 [The Complete Works of Liang Shuming], edited by the Committee of the Academy of Chinese Culture, 2nd ed., vol. 6, 330–45. Jinan: Shandong Remin, 2005.

——— 梁漱溟. "Zishu" 自述 [Autobiography]. In *Liang Shuming quanji* 梁漱溟全集 [The Complete Works of Liang Shuming], edited by the Committee of the Academy of Chinese Culture, vol. 2, 1–34. Jinan: Shandong Remin, 1989.

——— 梁漱溟. "Zishu zaonian sixiang zhi zaizhuan zaibian" 自述早年思想之再转再变 [An Account of the Many Changes in My Early Thought]. In *Liang Shuming quanji* 梁漱溟全集 [The Complete Works of Liang Shuming], edited by the Committee of the Academy of Chinese Culture, vol. 7, 177–84. Jinan: Shandong Remin, 1993.

Liang, Shu Ming, and Guy S. Alitto. *Has Man a Future? Dialogues with the Last Confucian*. Heidelberg: Springer, 2013.

Lin, Anwu. "Liang Shuming and His Theory of the Reappearance of Three Cultural Periods: Analysis and Evaluation of Liang Shuming's *Eastern and Western*

Cultures and Their Philosophies." *Contemporary Chinese Thought* 40, no. 3 (2009): 16–38.

———— 林安梧. "Liang Shuming ji qi wenhua sanqi chongxian shuo: Liang zhu *Dongxi wenhua ji qi zhexue* de xingcha yu shitan" 梁漱溟及其文化三期重現說——梁著《東西文化及其哲學》的省察與試探 [Liang Shuming and His Theory of the Reappearance of Three Cultural Periods: Analysis and Evaluation of Liang Shuming's *Eastern and Western Cultures and Their Philosophies*]. In *Dangdai xin rujia zhexue shi lun* 當代新儒家哲學史論 [On the History of New Confucian Philosophy], 99–125. Taipei: Wenhai jijinhui, Mingwen, 1996.

Lin, Chen-kuo. "Hsiung Shih-li's Hermeneutics of Self: Making a Confucian Identity in Buddhist Words." *NCCU Philosophical Journal* 8 (2002): 69–90.

Lin, Shaoyang 林少阳. *Dingge yi wen: Qingji geming yu Zhang Taiyan "fugu" de xin wenhua yundong* 鼎革以文：清季革命与章太炎「复古」的新文化运动 [Revolution by Words: Late Qing Revolution and Zhang Taiyan's "Antiquarian" New Culture Movement]. Shanghai: Shanghai renmin, 2018.

Lin, Xiaoqing Diana. *Feng Youlan and Twentieth Century China: An Intellectual Biography*. Leiden: Brill, 2016.

Lin, Yü-sheng. *The Crisis of Chinese Consciousness: Radical Antitraditionalism in the May Fourth Era*. Madison: University of Wisconsin Press, 1979.

———— 林毓生. "Hu Shi yu Liang Shuming guanyu *Dongxi wenhua ji qi zhexue* de lunbian ji qi lishi hanyi" 胡適與梁漱溟關於《東西文化及其哲學》的論辯及其歷史涵義 [Hu Shi and Liang Shuming's Debate on *Eastern and Western Cultures and Their Philosophies* and Its Historical Significance]. In *Zhengzhi zhixu yu duoyuan shehui* 政治秩序與多元社會 [Political Order and Pluralistic Society], 303–24. Taipei: Lianjing chuban, 1989.

————. "Radical Iconoclasm in the May Fourth Period and the Future of Chinese Liberalism." In *Reflections on the May Fourth Movement: A Symposium*, edited by Benjamin I. Schwartz, 23–58. Cambridge: Harvard University Press, 1973.

Lincoln, Bruce. *Authority: Construction and Corrosion*. Chicago: University of Chicago Press, 1994.

Liu, Junping, and Qin Ping. "Contemporary Chinese Studies of Xiong Shili 熊十力." *Dao* 5, no. 1 (December 2005): 159–72.

Liu, Lydia H. *Translingual Practice: Literature, National Culture, and Translated Modernity—China, 1900–1937*. Stanford: Stanford University Press, 1995.

Liu, Shu-hsien. *Essentials of Contemporary Neo-Confucian Philosophy*. Westport: Praeger, 2003.

————. "Hsiung Shih-li's Theory of Causation." *Philosophy East & West* 19, no. 4 (1969): 399–407.

————. "Xiong Shili (Hsiung Shih-li)." In *Encyclopedia of Chinese Philosophy*, edited by Antonio S. Cua, 801–06. New York: Routledge, 2003.

Lu Xun. *Diary of a Madman, and Other Stories*. Translated by William A. Lyell. Honolulu: University of Hawai'i Press, 1990.

———— 鲁迅. *Kuangren riji* 狂人日记 [Diary of a Madman]. In *Lu Xun quanji* 鲁迅全集 [The Complete Works of Lu Xun], vol. 1, 444–56. Beijing: Renming wenxue, 2005.

Lusthaus, Dan. "Yogācāra School." In *Encyclopedia of Buddhism*, edited by Robert E. Buswell, vol. 2, 914–21. New York: Macmillan Reference/Thomson/Gale, 2004.

Lynch, Catherine. *Liang Shuming and the Populist Alternative in China*. Leiden: Brill, 2018.

Ma, Yong 马勇, ed. *Modai shuoru: mingren bixia de Liang Shuming, Liang Shuming bixia de mingren* 末代硕儒——名人笔下的梁漱溟 梁漱溟笔下的名人 [The Last Generation of Great Confucians: Liang Shuming in the Writings of Famous Intellectuals and Famous Intellectuals in the Writings of Liang Shuming]. Shanghai: Dongfang chuban zhongxin, 1998.

MacIntyre, Alasdair. *After Virtue*. Notre Dame: University of Notre Dame Press, 1981.

Major, Philippe. "The Confucian Atomistic Individual? Selfhood in Xiong Shili's *New Treatise on the Uniqueness of Consciousness*." *Philosophy East & West* 71, no. 4 (October 2021): 938–58.

————. "The Politics of Writing Chinese Philosophy: Xiong Shili's *New Treatise on the Uniqueness of Consciousness* and the 'Crystallization of Oriental Philosophy.'" *Dao* 18, no. 2 (June 2019): 241–58.

————. "Rethinking the Temporalization of Space in Early Republican China: Liang Shuming's *Eastern and Western Cultures and Their Philosophies*." *International Communication of Chinese Culture* 4, no. 2 (May 2017): 171–85.

————. "Review of *Xiong Shili's Understanding of Reality and Function, 1920–1937*, by Sang Yu." *Dao* 20, no. 1 (2021): 165–69.

————. "Textual Authority and Its Naturalization in Liang Shuming's *Dong-Xi wenhua ji qi zhexue*." *Monumenta Serica* 65, no. 1 (June 2017): 123–45.

————. "Tradition and Modernity in Liang Shuming's *Eastern and Western Cultures and Their Philosophies*." *Philosophy East & West* 68, no. 2 (April 2018): 460–76.

Makeham, John, ed. *The Awakening of Faith and New Confucian Philosophy*. Leiden: Brill, 2021.

————. "Disciplining Tradition in Modern China: Two Case Studies." *History and Theory* 51 (2012): 89–103.

————. "Introduction." In *Learning to Emulate the Wise: The Genesis of Chinese Philosophy as an Academic Discipline in Twentieth-Century China*, edited by John Makeham, 1–25. Hong Kong: The Chinese University of Hong Kong Press, 2012.

————, ed. *Learning to Emulate the Wise: The Genesis of Chinese Philosophy as an Academic Discipline in Twentieth-Century China*. Hong Kong: The Chinese University of Hong Kong Press, 2012.

———. *Lost Soul: "Confucianism" in Contemporary Chinese Academic Discourse.* Cambridge: Harvard University Asia Center, 2008.

———. "The New *Daotong*." In *New Confucianism: A Critical Examination*, edited by John Makeham, 55–78. New York: Palgrave, 2003.

———. "The Retrospective Creation of New Confucianism." In *New Confucianism: A Critical Examination*, edited by John Makeham, 25–53. New York: Palgrave, 2003.

———. "The Role of Masters Studies in the Early Formation of Chinese Philosophy as an Academic Discipline." In *Learning to Emulate the Wise: The Genesis of Chinese Philosophy as an Academic Discipline in Twentieth-Century China*, edited by John Makeham, 73–101. Hong Kong: The Chinese University of Hong Kong Press, 2012.

———. "The Significance of Xiong Shili's Interpretation of Dignāga's *Ālambanaparīkṣā* (Investigation of the Object)." *Journal of Chinese Philosophy* 40, no. 5 (2013): 205–25.

———. "Translator's Introduction." In *New Treatise on the Uniqueness of Consciousness*, i–lxviii. New Haven: Yale University Press, 2015.

———. "Xiong Shili's Critique of Yogācāra Thought in the Context of His Constructive Philosophy." In *Transforming Consciousness: Yogācāra Thought in Modern China*, edited by John Makeham, 242–82. Oxford: Oxford University Press, 2014.

———. "Xiong Shili's Understanding of the Relationship Between the Ontological and the Phenomenal." In *Chinese Metaphysics and Its Problems*, edited by Li Chenyang and Franklin Perkins, 207–23. Cambridge: Cambridge University Press, 2015.

Marincola, John. *Authority and Tradition in Ancient Historiography.* Cambridge: Cambridge University Press, 2004.

Meisner, Maurice. "Cultural Iconoclasm, Nationalism, and Internationalism in the May Fourth Movement." In *Reflections on the May Fourth Movement: A Symposium*, edited by Benjamin I. Schwartz, 14–22. Cambridge: Harvard University Press, 1972.

Meynard, Thierry. "Introducing Buddhism as Philosophy: The Cases of Liang Shuming, Xiong Shili, and Tang Yongtong." In *Learning to Emulate the Wise: The Genesis of Chinese Philosophy as an Academic Discipline in Twentieth-Century China*, edited by John Makeham, 187–216. Hong Kong: The Chinese University of Hong Kong Press, 2012.

———. "Is Liang Shuming Ultimately a Confucian or Buddhist?" *Dao* 6 (2007): 131–47.

———. "Liang Shuming and His Confucianized Version of Yogācāra." In *Transforming Consciousness: Yogācāra Thought in Modern China*, edited by John Makeham, 201–41. Oxford: Oxford University Press, 2014.

———. *The Religious Philosophy of Liang Shuming: The Hidden Buddhist*. Leiden: Brill, 2011.

Møllgaard, Eske J. *The Confucian Political Imagination*. Cham: Palgrave Macmillan, 2018.

Muller, Charles. "Bashi" 八識 [Eight Consciousnesses]. *Digital Dictionary of Buddhism*. Accessed April 16, 2022. http://www.buddhism-dict.net/cgi-bin/xpr-ddb.pl?q=八識.

———. "Cheng weishi lun" 成唯識論 [Demonstration of Consciousness-only]. *Digital Dictionary of Buddhism*. Accessed April 18, 2022. http://www.buddhism-dict.net/cgi-bin/xpr-ddb.pl?q=成唯識論.

———. "Qi shijian" 器世間 [Receptacle World]. *Digital Dictionary of Buddhism*. Accessed April 16, 2022. http://www.buddhism-dict.net/cgi-bin/xpr-ddb.pl?q=器世間.

Ng, Yu-kwan. "Xiong Shili's Metaphysical Theory about the Non-Separability of Substance and Function." In *New Confucianism: A Critical Examination*, edited by John Makeham, 220–51. New York: Palgrave, 2003.

Nie, Minyu 聶民玉. *Tiyong bu'er: Xiong Shili jingxue sixiang yanjiu* 体用不二：熊十力经学思想研究 [The Nonduality of Reality and Functions: An Analysis of Xiong Shili's Study of the Classics]. Beijing: Renmin, 2015.

Nylan, Michael. *The Five "Confucian" Classics*. New Haven: Yale University Press, 2001.

Olberding, Amy. "It's Not Them, It's You: A Case Study Concerning the Exclusion of Non-Western Philosophy." *Comparative Philosophy* 6, no. 2 (2015): 14–34.

———. "Philosophical Exclusion and Conversational Practices." *Philosophy East & West* 67, no. 4 (2017): 1023–38.

Payen, Pascal. "Introduction: Les Anciens en figures d'autorité." In *Les Autorités: Dynamiques et mutations d'une figure de référence à l'Antiquité*, edited by Didier Foucault and Pascal Payen, 7–22. Grenoble: Éditions Jérôme Million, 2007.

Peng, Hsiao-yen 彭小妍. "'Renshengguan' yu Ouya houqimeng lunshu" 「人生觀」與歐亞後啓蒙論述 ["Views of Life" and the Eurasian Post-Enlightenment Discourse]. In *Wenhua fanyi yu wenben mailuo: wanming yijiang de Zhongguo, Riben yu Xifang* 文化翻譯與文本脈絡——晚明以降的中國、日本與西方 [Cultural Translation and Textual Contexts: China, Japan, and the West Since the Late Ming], 221–67. Taipei: Zhongyang yanjiuyuan Zhongguo wenzhe yanjiusuo, 2013.

———. *Weiqing yu lixing de bianzheng: Wusi de fanqimeng* 唯情與理性的辯證：五四的反啟蒙 [Dialectics Between Affect and Reason: The May Fourth Counter-Enlightenment]. Taipei: Lianjing chuban, 2019.

Pocock, J. G. A. "Time, Institutions and Actions: An Essay on Traditions and Their Understanding." In *Politics, Language, and Time: Essays on Political Thought and History*, 233–72. Chicago: University of Chicago Press, 1989.

Puett, Michael. *The Ambivalence of Creation: Debates Concerning Innovation and Artifice in Early China*. Stanford: Stanford University Press, 2001.

Pusey, James Reeve. *China and Charles Darwin.* Cambridge: Harvard University Press, 1983.
Rescher, Nicholas. *Philosophical Textuality: Studies on Issues of Discourse in Philosophy.* Frankfurt: Ontos Verlag, 2010.
Revault d'Allonnes, Myriam. *Le pouvoir des commencements: Essai sur l'autorité.* Paris: Seuil, 2006.
Ricoeur, Paul. *Time and Narrative, Volume 3.* Translated by Kathleen Blamey and David Pellauer. Chicago: University of Chicago Press, 1988.
Rošker, Jana. *Searching for the Way: Theory of Knowledge in Pre-Modern and Modern China.* Hong Kong: The Chinese University of Hong Kong Press, 2008.
Roy, A. T. "Liang Shu-ming and Hu Shih on the Intuitional Interpretation of Confucianism." *Chung Chi Journal* 1, no. 2 (1962): 139–57.
Sang, Yu. "The Role of the *Treatise on Awakening Mahāyāna Faith* in the Development of Xiong Shili's *Ti-yong* Metaphysics." In *The Awakening of Faith and New Confucian Philosophy*, edited by John Makeham, 132–71. Leiden: Brill, 2021.
———. *Xiong Shili's Understanding of Reality and Function, 1920–1937.* Leiden: Brill, 2020.
Scanlon, Larry. *Narrative, Authority and Power: The Medieval Exemplum and the Chaucerian Tradition.* Cambridge: Cambridge University Press, 1994.
Schmithausen, Lambert. *Ālayavijñāna: On the Origin and the Early Development of a Central Concept of Yogācāra Philosophy.* Tokyo: The International Institute of Buddhist Studies, 1987.
Schneider, Laurence A. *Ku Chieh-kang and China's New History: Nationalism and the Quest for Alternative Traditions.* Berkeley: University of California Press, 1971.
Schwarcz, Vera. *The Chinese Enlightenment: Intellectuals and the Legacy of the May Fourth Movement of 1919.* Berkeley: University of California Press, 1986.
Schwartz, Benjamin I. "Notes on Conservatism in General and in China in Particular." In *The Limits of Change: Essays on Conservative Alternatives in Republican China*, edited by Charlotte Furth, 3–21. Cambridge: Harvard University Press, 1976.
Schwermann, Christian, and Raji C. Steineck, eds. *That Wonderful Composite Called Author: Authorship in East Asian Literatures from the Beginnings to the Seventeenth Century.* Leiden: Brill, 2014.
Scott, James C. *Seeing Like a State: How Certain Schemes to Improve the Human Condition Have Failed.* New Haven: Yale University Press, 1998.
Shen, Sung-chiao, and Sechin Y. S. Chien. "Turning Slaves into Citizens: Discourses of *Guomin* and the Construction of Chinese National Identity in the Late Qing Period." In *The Dignity of Nations: Equality, Competition, and Honor in East Asian Nationalism*, edited by Sechin Y. S. Chien and John Fitzgerald, 49–69. Hong Kong: Hong Kong University Press, 2006.
Shih, Shu-mei. *The Lure of the Modern: Writing Modernism in Semicolonial China, 1917–1937.* Berkeley: University of California Press, 2001.
Shils, Edward. *Tradition.* Chicago: University of Chicago Press, 1981.

Shimada, Kenji 島田虔次. *Shin Jukka tetsugaku ni tsuite: Yū Jūriki no tetsugaku* 新儒家哲学について：熊十力の哲学 [On New Confucian Philosophy: The Philosophy of Xiong Shili]. Kyoto: Tōhōsha, 1987.

Slingerland, Edward, trans. *Analects: With Selections from Traditional Commentaries.* Indianapolis: Hackett Publishing Company, 2003.

Tagawa, Shun'ei. *Living Yogācāra: An Introduction to Consciousness-Only Buddhism.* Translated by Charles Muller. Boston: Wisdom Publications, 2009.

Tan, Sor-hoon. "Balancing Conservatism and Innovation: The Pragmatic *Analects*." In *Dao Companion to the* Analects, edited by Amy Olberding, 335–54. Dordrecht: Springer, 2014.

———. "Contemporary Neo-Confucian Philosophy." In *History of Chinese Philosophy*, edited by Bo Mou, 540–70. Abingdon: Routledge, 2009.

———. "Three Corners for One: Creativity and Tradition in the *Analects*." In *Confucius Now: Contemporary Encounters with the* Analects, edited by David Jones, 59–79. Chicago: Open Court, 2008.

Taylor, Charles. *A Secular Age.* Cambridge: Belknap Press, 2007.

———. *Sources of the Self: The Making of Modern Identity.* Cambridge: Harvard University Press, 1989.

———. "Two Theories of Modernity." In *Alternative Modernities*, edited by Dilip Parameshwar Gaonkar, 172–96. Durham: Duke University Press, 2001.

Taylor, Peter. *Modernities.* Minneapolis: University of Minnesota Press, 1999.

Taylor, Rodney L. "The Religious Character of the Confucian Tradition." *Philosophy East & West* 48, no. 1 (1998): 80–107.

Thoraval, Joël. "Liang Shu Ming: Qu'était devenu le 'dernier Confucéen' sous le régime communiste?" *Bulletin de Sinologie* 52 (1989): 22–26; 53 (1989): 22–29.

———. "Sur la transformation de la pensée néo-confucéenne en discours philosophique moderne. Réflexions sur quelques apories du néo-confucianisme contemporain." *Extrême-Orient, Extrême-Occident* 27 (2005): 91–119.

Tillman, Hoyt Cleveland. *Confucian Discourse and Chu Hsi's Ascendancy.* Honolulu: University of Hawai'i Press, 1992.

———. "Reflections on Classifying 'Confucian' Lineages: Reinventions of Tradition in Song China." In *Rethinking Confucianism: Past and Present in China, Japan, Korea, and Vietnam*, edited by Benjamin A. Elman, John B. Duncan, and Herman Ooms, 33–64. Los Angeles: UCLA Asian Pacific Monograph Series, 2002.

———. "Zhu Xi's Prayers to the Spirit of Confucius and Claim to the Transmission of the Way." *Philosophy East & West* 54, no. 4 (2004): 489–513.

Tu, Wei-ming. *Confucian Thought: Selfhood as Creative Transformation.* Albany: State University of New York Press, 1985.

———. "Hsiung Shih-li's Quest for Authentic Existence." In *The Limits of Change: Essays on Conservative Alternatives in Republican China*, edited by Charlotte Furth, 242–75. Cambridge: Harvard University Press, 1976.

Van den Stock, Ady. *The Horizon of Modernity: Subjectivity and Social Structure in New Confucian Philosophy.* Leiden: Brill, 2016.

Van Slyke, Lyman P. "Liang Sou-ming and the Rural Reconstruction Movement." *The Journal of Asian Studies* 18, no. 4 (1959): 457–74.

Vandermeersch, Léon. "Préface." In Liang Shuming, *Les cultures d'Orient et d'Occident et leurs philosophies,* translated by Luo Shenyi, xi–xx. Paris: You Feng, 2011.

Waldron, William S. *The Buddhist Unconscious: The Ālaya-vijñāna in the Context of Indian Buddhist Thought.* London: Routledge Curzon, 2003.

Walliss, John. "The Problem of Tradition in the Work of Anthony Giddens." *Culture and Religion* 2, no. 1 (2001): 81–98.

Wang, Aihe. *Cosmology and Political Culture in Early China.* Cambridge: Cambridge University Press, 2000.

Wang, Fansen 王汎森. "Cong chuantong dao fan chuantong: liangge sixiang mailuo de fenxi" 從傳統到反傳統——兩個思想脈絡的分析 [From Traditionalism to Anti-Traditionalism: An Analysis of Two Intellectual Trends]. In *Cong wusi dao xin wusi* 從五四到新五四 [From May Fourth to New May Fourth], edited by Yü Ying-shih 余英時 and Bao Zunxin 包遵信, 242–67. Taipei: Shibao wenhua, 1989.

———. "Zhongguo jindai sixiang zhong de 'weilai'" 中國近代思想中的「未來」 [The "Future" in Modern Chinese Thought]. *Tansuo yu zhengming* 探索与争鸣 9 (2015): 64–71.

Wang, Hui. "The Fate of 'Mr. Science' in China: The Concept of Science and Its Application in Modern Chinese Thought." *Positions* 3, no. 1 (Spring 1995): 1–68.

———. *The Politics of Imagining Asia.* Edited by Theodore Huters. Cambridge: Harvard University Press, 2011.

——— 汪晖. *Xiandai Zhongguo sixiang de xingqi* 现代中国思想的兴起 [The Rise of Modern Chinese Thought]. Beijing: Sanlian, 2008.

Wang, Kun 王锟. *Kongzi yu ershi shiji Zhongguo sixiang* 孔子与二十世纪中国思想 [Confucius and Twentieth-Century Chinese Thought]. Jinan: Qilu Shushe, 2006.

Wang, Yuanyi 王遠義. "Ruxue yu makesizhuyi: xilun Liang Shuming de lishiguan" 儒學與馬克思主義：析論梁漱溟的歷史觀 [Confucianism and Marxism: An Analysis of Liang Shuming's View of History]. *Taida wenshizhe xuebao* 臺大文史哲學報 56 (2002): 145–95.

Wang, Zhongjiang 王中江. "Xiong Shili de 'benxin' jinhua lun" 熊十力的「本心」进化论 [On the Evolution of the "Inherent Mind" in Xiong Shili]. *Tianjin shehui kexue* 天津社会科学 2 (2011): 126–33.

Wang, Zongyu 王宗昱. *Liang Shuming* 梁漱溟 [Liang Shuming]. Taipei: Dongda, 1992.

———. "Shi rujia, haishi fojia: fang Liang Shuming xianshen" 是儒家，還是佛家：訪梁漱溟先生 [Confucian or Buddhist? A Discussion with Mr. Liang Shuming]. *Wenxing* 文星 115 (1988): 67–69.

Weber, Ralph. "Authority: Of German Rhinos and Chinese Tigers." In *Comparative Philosophy Without Borders*, edited by Arindam Chakrabarti and Ralph Weber, 143–74. New York: Bloomsbury Academic, 2016.

Wesołowski, Zbigniew. "Understanding the Foreign (the West) as a Remedy for Regaining One's Own Cultural Identity (China): Liang Shuming's (1893–1988) Cultural Thought." *Monumenta Serica* 53 (2005): 361–99.

Williams, Paul. *Mahāyāna Buddhism: The Doctrinal Foundations*. London: Routledge, 2009.

Wilson, Thomas A. "Genealogy and History in Neo-Confucian Sectarian Uses of the Confucian Past." *Modern China* 20, no. 1 (1994): 3–33.

———. *Genealogy of the Way: The Construction and Uses of the Confucian Tradition in Late Imperial China*. Stanford: Stanford University Press, 1995.

Wu, Chan-liang 吳展良. "Liang Shuming de shengsheng sixiang ji qi dui Xifang lixingzhuyi de pipan (1915–1923)" 梁漱溟的生生思想及其對西方理性主義的批判 (1915–1923) [Liang Shuming's Generative Thought and Its Critique of Western Rationalism (1915–1923)]. In *Zhongguo xiandai xueren de xueshu xingge yu siwei fangshi lunji* 中國現代學人的學術性格與思維方式論集 [A Collection of Articles on the Academic Nature and Mode of Thinking of Modern Chinese Scholars], 183–238. Taipei: Wunan, 2000.

———. "Western Rationalism and the Chinese Mind: Counter-Enlightenment and Philosophy of Life in China, 1915–1927." PhD diss., Yale University, 1993.

Wu, Longcan. "Xiong Shili: A Founder of Contemporary New Confucianism." *Confucian Academy* 3, no. 1 (2016): 148–59.

Xiong, Shili. *New Treatise on the Uniqueness of Consciousness*. Translated by John Makeham. New Haven: Yale University Press, 2015.

——— 熊十力. *Shili yuyao* 十力语要 [Important Remarks of Shili]. In *Xiong Shili quanji* 熊十力全集 [The Complete Works of Xiong Shili], edited by Xiao Shafu 蕭萐父, vol. 4, 1–554. Wuhan: Hebei Jiaoyu chubanshe, 2001.

——— 熊十力. *Shili yuyao chuxu* 十力语要初续 [First Sequel to the Important Remarks of Shili]. In *Xiong Shili quanji* 熊十力全集 [The Complete Works of Xiong Shili], edited by Xiao Shafu 蕭萐父, vol. 5, 1–287. Wuhan: Hebei Jiaoyu chubanshe, 2001.

——— 熊十力. *Xinshu* 心书 [Book of the Mind]. In *Xiong Shili quanji* 熊十力全集 [The Complete Works of Xiong Shili], edited by Xiao Shafu 蕭萐父, vol. 1, 1–42. Wuhan: Hebei Jiaoyu chubanshe, 2001.

——— 熊十力. *Xin weishi lun* 新唯識論 [New Treatise on the Uniqueness of Consciousness]. Taipei: Taiwan xuesheng shuju, 1985.

——— 熊十力. *Xin weishi lun (wenyanwen ben)* 新唯识论 (文言文本) [New Treatise on the Uniqueness of Consciousness: Classical Chinese Edition]. In *Xiong Shili quanji* 熊十力全集 [The Complete Works of Xiong Shili], edited by Xiao Shafu 蕭萐父, vol. 2, 1–149. Wuhan: Hebei Jiaoyu chubanshe, 2001.

——— 熊十力. *Xin weishi lun (yutiwen ben)* 新唯识论 (语体文本) [New Treatise on the Uniqueness of Consciousness: Vernacular Edition]. In *Xiong Shili quanji*

熊十力全集 [The Complete Works of Xiong Shili], edited by Xiao Shafu 蕭 萐父, vol. 3, 1–549. Wuhan: Hebei Jiaoyu chubanshe, 2001.

Yang, Zhende 楊貞德. *Zhuanxiang ziwo: jindai Zhongguo zhengzhi sixiang shang de geren* 轉向自我：近代中國政治思想上的個人 [Turning Toward the Self: The Individual in Modern Chinese Political Thought]. Taipei: Zhongyang yanjiuyuan Zhongguo wenzhe yanjiusuo, 2009.

Yu, Jiyuan. "Xiong Shili's Metaphysics of Virtue." In *Contemporary Chinese Philosophy*, edited by Chung-Ying Cheng and Nicholas Bunnin, 127–46. Malden: Blackwell Publishers, 2002.

Yü, Ying-shih. "Neither Renaissance nor Enlightenment: A Historian's Reflections on the May Fourth Movement." In *The Appropriation of Cultural Capital: China's May Fourth Project*, edited by Milena Doleželová-Velingerová and Oldřich Král, 299–324. Cambridge: Harvard University Press, 2001.

——— 余英時. "Qian Mu yu xin rujia" 錢穆與新儒家 [Qian Mu and New Confucianism]. In *You ji feng chui shuishang lin: Qian Mu yu xiandai Zhongguo xueshu* 猶記風吹水上鱗—錢穆與現代中國學術 [Like Recording the Wind Blowing over Shimmering Water: Qian Mu and Modern Chinese Scholarship], 31–98. Taipei: Sanmin shuju, 1991.

———. "The Radicalization of China in the Twentieth Century." *Daedalus* 122, no. 2 (1993): 125–50.

———. "Some Preliminary Observations on the Rise of Qing Confucian Intellectualism." In *Chinese History and Culture, Volume 2, Seventeenth Century Through Twentieth Century*, edited by Josephine Chiu-Duke and Michael S. Duke, 1–39. New York: Columbia University Press, 2016.

——— 余英時. "Wusi yundong yu Zhongguo chuantong" 五四運動與中國傳統 [The May Fourth Movement and Chinese Traditions]. In *Shixue yu chuantong* 史學與傳統 [Historiography and Tradition], 93–107. Taipei: Shibao wenhua, 1982.

——— 余英時. *Zhongguo jindai sixiangshi shang de Hu Shi* 中國近代思想史上的胡適 [Hu Shi in Modern Chinese Intellectual History]. Taipei: Lianjing chuban, 1984.

——— 余英時. "Zhongguo jindai sixiangshi shang de jijin yu baoshou" 中國近代思想史上的激進與保守 [Radicalism and Conservatism in Modern Chinese Intellectual History]. In *You ji feng chui shuishang lin: Qian Mu yu xiandai Zhongguo xueshu* 猶記風吹水上鱗—錢穆與現代中國學術 [Like Recording the Wind Blowing over Shimmering Water: Qian Mu and Modern Chinese Scholarship], 199–242. Taipei: Sanmin shuju, 1991.

Zhang, Wei. *What Is Enlightenment: Can China Answer Kant's Question?* Albany: State University of New York Press, 2010.

Zhang, Wenru. "Liang Shuming and Buddhist Studies," translated by Jaroslaw Duraj. *Contemporary Chinese Thought* 40, no. 3 (2009): 67–90.

Zheng, Dahua 鄭大華. *Liang Shuming yu xiandai xin ruxue* 梁漱溟與現代新儒學 [Liang Shuming and New Confucianism]. Taipei: Wenjin, 1993.

Zheng, Jiadong 鄭家棟. "Dangdai xin rujia de daotonglun" 當代新儒家的道統論 [The Discourse of the Genealogy of the Way in New Confucianism]. In *Dangdai xin ruxue lunheng* 當代新儒學論衡 [A Critical Evaluation of New Confucianism], 1–37. Taipei: Guiguan, 1995.

———. *Xiandai xin ruxue gailun* 现代新儒学概论 [A General Account of New Confucianism]. Nanning: Guangxi renmin chubanshe, 1990.

Žižek, Slavoj. "Class Struggle or Postmodernism? Yes, Please." In *Contingency, Hegemony, Universality: Contemporary Dialogues on the Left*, by Judith Butler, Ernesto Laclau, and Slavoj Žižek, 90–135. London: Verso, 2000.

Index

absolute truth, 74–75, 140–42, 144. *See also* truth
action and thought, 50
agency, 25, 41, 45–46, 48, 86, 199n87
agricultural metaphors, 75–76
alienation, 65, 67
Alitto, Guy S., 108–09, 202, 206, 223n6, 228nn62–63
Analects (*Lunyu* 論語): commentarial tradition, 227n52; Confucius in, 1, 102, 105, 107, 225n27; intuitive spirit in, 111–14, 119; metaphysical issues, 225n23; mind in, 155–56; and resoluteness, 52; as source of authority, 24
anthropocentrism, 34
antidelusions, 74
anti-intellectualism, 21, 133–34
antitraditions: as term, 3; Confucianism as, 57, 83, 97, 104, 129, 181; discursive power of, 95; as emancipatory, 167; genealogy of the way (*daotong* 道統) as, 125; and hegemony, 95, 166; and historicity, 20–23, 32, 120, 126–28, 130; iconoclastic potential of, 130; and legitimacy, 127; of May Fourth, 11–15, 192n52; of modernity, 7–11, 93, 95; ouroboric, 173; politics of, 4, 174; and traditions, 32

antitraditions-as-value, 33
apophatic mode of explanation (*zhequan* 遮詮), 142, 148, 161
Arendt, Hannah, 186n18, 186n22
Asaṅga, 147, 151–53, 157, 200n89, 236n56, 237n64
atomization, 63, 78–79, 82, 86, 92, 134, 223n8
authenticity, 26, 115, 174, 200nn91–92
authoritarianism, 186n22
authority: contemporary vs. past, 114–15; of *dao*, 3; discursive techniques, 121; and *Eastern and Western Cultures*, 121, 127; of eternity, 169–73; and genealogy of the way, 155; and (trans)historicity, 159–60; Kojève on, 120, 168–69, 187n27, 229n75; literary, 187n25; and May Fourth hegemonic group, 168; and nature, 103; and reader, 120–23, 139; of reason, 90; rejection of, 172; of sages and masters, 108, 129, 141, 149; social dialectics of, 6–7, 9–10, 120–21, 186n20; sociality of, 120; and temporality, 165, 171; of texts, 70, 99, 120–23; of tradition, 4–7, 18, 97–98, 100, 126, 187n27, 241n7; and Yogācāra tradition, 150–53; zones of, 165

263

autonomy, 63, 78–79, 90–93; and colonialism, 91; and emancipation, 86–87; heteronomy to, 90; and May Fourth intellectuals, 62; and modernity vs. premodernity, 90; in *New Treatise*, 86–87, 91–93; and oppression, 94; and philosophical language, 177; and teleology, 90

awakening (*jue* 覺), 70, 74–79, 92, 134; from fragmentation to oneness, 141; and language, 142; Xiong Shili's, 156–57

The Awakening of Mahāyāna Faith (*Dasheng qixin lun* 大乘起信論), 60, 152, 161

Barthes, Roland, 24, 199n85

benxin (本心). *See* inherent mind

Bergson, Henri, 37, 109, 206n37, 217n44, 225n25, 226n37, 237n64

blue, perception of color, 66

Bodhisattvas, 49, 135, 137, 156

the body: attachment to, 65, 71; birth of, 66–67, 69, 71, 85; Cartesian images of, 91–92; matter and, 70; mind's enslavement to, 70; and the past, 72; rejection of, 222n2

Bolshevik revolution, 14, 31

Bourdieu, Pierre, 150, 162

Buddhism: terminology, 205n19, 209n67; apophatic explanation, 142; conflation with Indian culture, 37, 55; vs. Confucianism, 153, 158–59; desire, 109; as emancipatory end of history, 50; enlightenment in, 74, 87; ideals (as culture), 38; Indian, 55, 152; instantaneous arising and ceasing, 70; karmic power in, 66; in modern Confucian texts, 199n89; Sinitic, 152; and suffering, 49; and teleology of history, 54; as tradition, 55; two truths theory, 140, 144, 146–48; will as turning from desire in, 35

Butler, Judith, 174

capitalism, 36, 210n80

causality, 50, 71–72, 80, 148

ceyin zhi xin (惻隱之心). *See* heart of compassion

Changes (*Yijing* 易經): change in, 42, 60, 70, 105; Confucius in, 225n29; metaphysics of, 107; (re)production in, 218n61; terminology, 217n44, 227n54, 238n83; textual sources, 156; universe in, 71–72; virtue in, 155; Xiong Shili's reading of, 156–57, 218n63, 218n65, 238n76

Chang Hao (張灝), 189n36, 193n57, 235n48

Chan Wing-tsit (陳榮捷), 71–72, 210n76, 218n61

Chen Baisha (陳白沙), 119

Chen Duxiu (陳獨秀), 12–14, 30, 32, 35, 42, 87–88, 109, 115, 190n38, 190n42, 191n48, 197n80

Cheng Hao (程顥), 98, 153, 156

Cheng weishi lun (成唯識論). *See Demonstration of Consciousness-only*

Cheng Yi (程頤), 98

Chen Huanzhang (陳煥章), 116

China: authority of text in, 98; cultural ideals, 102; equated with Confucianism, 55; and futurity, 60, 87–88; as historically stagnant, 39–40, 44; individuality in, 41; modernity's metanarrative in, 11; national issues (in *New Treatise*), 62; and teleological history, 51

China Institute of Inner Learning (*Zhina neixue yuan* 支那內學院), 61, 236n61

Chinese culture: Confucius's role in, 103, 211n89; in *Eastern and*

Western Cultures, 89; equated with Confucius, 90; harmony in, 38; historical development, 55; and historical model (in *Eastern and Western Cultures*), 39; ideal of, 51; metaphors for, 57; revival of, 38; scientific value in, 42; and socialism and psychology, 38; as traditions-as-history, 38; universality of, 89; value in, 88; and Western culture, 14, 30, 35, 51–52, 57, 109

Chinese philosophy, 61

Christianity, 35, 116, 205n23

chuang (創). *See* creativity

civilization, 30–31

classic, as term, 223n4

cognitive objects: and birth of the body, 67; and consciousness, 77, 153, 156, 237n68; as external, 237n68; and Fundamental Reality, 76; and mental associates, 66; and the mind, 65, 79; and potentiality, 47

Cole, Alan, 19–20

collective emancipation, 84, 86

colonialism, 9–10, 36, 87, 91, 94

color, 66

commentaries, 114, 118, 124–25, 230n84

Confucian family system, 13, 30, 41, 62

Confucian iconoclasm, 15–20; historical context, 4; ouroboric aspects, 19; as project, 23; as reaction to May Fourth, 3; sources of, 22; and universality, 180–81

Confucianism: terminology, 200n90; anti-intellectualist, 133; as antitradition, 57, 83, 97, 104, 129, 181; authority of, 97–98; vs. Buddhism, 153, 158–59; vs. Christianity, 116; conversions to, 31; essentialist understandings of, 199n87; ethical codes, 41–42; histories of, 117; ideals (as culture), 38; and May Fourth, 16; non-cartesian readings of, 222n2; orthodoxy, 116, 125; and power relations, 26; reauthorization of, 181; religion (status as), 20; Republican-era scholarship on, 31–32; returns to origins, 195n73; and social hierarchy, 41; sociopolitical dimensions, 163; as tradition, 55, 153–57; traditionalism of, 1; transmission of, 171. *See also* modern Confucianism; Neo-Confucianism; New Confucianism

Confucius: authority of, 53, 97, 122, 238n76; gathering past culture, 103; ideal of, 38, 55, 105; intuition of, 102; living spirit of, 106; as master weaver, 108; misinterpretations of, 115–16; naturalizing, 100–104; philosophy of human life (*rensheng zhexue* 人生哲學), 39; quotes misattributed to, 107; spirit-ideal of, 114, 227n53; spirit of, 50–53; as a tradition, 172; transcendence for, 53

consciousness, 46, 147; vs. cognitive objects, 156; as continuously arising and ceasing, 71; Dharmapāla's conceptualization of, 148; eight consciousnesses, 47, 147–48, 151, 215n31; self-animation of, 70–71; and spirit, 209n65; uniqueness of, 237n68; unity of, 148

conservatism, 8, 14, 27, 29, 54–55, 201n93, 202n1

constant transformation (*hengzhuan* 恆轉), 68–69

continuous renewal, 73

contraction (*xi* 翕), 68–69, 217n45

conventional truth, 74–75, 140–41, 144–45, 147, 178

cooking, 110–11, 170
cost-benefit analysis (*jijiao lihai* 計較利害), 104, 108
"Counsels of Yu the Great" (*Dayu mo* 大禹謨), 124, 230n88
creativity (*chuang* 創), 71–72, 76
Csikszentmihalyi, Mark, 201n92
cultural differences, 34
cultural incompatibility, 30, 35
cultural pluralism, 33–36
Cultural Revolution, 185n11, 194n67, 197n80
cultural synthesis, 30, 51
cultures: defined, 34, 38; anthropomorphization of, 35; -as-artifice, 103; culture-as-nature, 103–04; globalization of, 33; homogenization of, 33, 40; pluralism, 33–36; will of, 35

Dai Zhen (戴震), 39, 118
da jietuo (大解脫). *See* great liberation
dao (道): and anti-intellectual Confucianism (Yü Ying-shih), 133–34; authority of, 3; deviation from, 101; intuition of, 21; Liang Shuming on, 117, 124; and nature, 100, 103; and philosophical systems, 159; sages embodying, 97–98; terminology, 104; transmission of, 125, 155, 228n63
daotong (道統). *See* genealogy of the way
Dasheng qixin lun (大乘起信論). *See The Awakening of Mahāyāna Faith*
datong (大同). *See* great harmony
Davies, Gloria, 197n80
Dayu mo (大禹謨). *See* "Counsels of Yu the Great"
death of the author, 24–26, 93, 199n85, 231n91
degeneration, 69, 84–85, 119

delusions, 74, 82
democracy, 1, 13, 34–35, 40–41, 44, 51–52, 88
Demonstration of Consciousness-only (*Cheng weishi lun* 成唯識論), 147, 152, 235n42, 239n83
denial, discursive strategies of, 150, 162, 178
Descartes, René, 91–92
desire: and the body, 65; in Buddhism, 109; in Chinese vs. Western culture, compared, 34–35; for enlightenment, 74; fulfilment of, 45; and resoluteness, 52; in Indian culture, 37; and metanarrative, 50; renunciation of, 49, 135; and seeds, 47
despotism, 13, 30, 40–41
determinism, 44–46, 50–51, 53, 56–57, 73, 170, 172, 208n63
Dewey, John, 37
Dharmapāla, 144, 146–52, 235n42, 235n46
diligent sincerity (*dun* 敦), 69
discernment (*hui* 慧), 76–77, 144, 147, 160–61, 234n34, 234nn34–35
discourses, 32–33, 148, 162
discursive techniques: overview, 7; acultural understanding of modernity (Taylor), 10; and authority, 121; of Chen Duxiu, 13; commenting on classics, 108–09; in *Eastern and Western Cultures*, 144, 175–76; genealogy of the way (*daotong* 道統), 109, 125; historical, 127; iconoclastic, 128; legitimacy of, 123; in *New Treatise*, 136–38, 178; performativity of, 135; synecdoche, 55; unilinear metanarrative of modernity, 10; the West as partially imagined other, 40; and Yogācāra tradition, 151

disinterestedness, 61, 63, 122, 145, 152, 162, 178
Doctrine of the Mean (*Zhongyong* 中庸), 101, 107, 123–25, 155
Documents (*Shujing* 書經), 124
Dongxi wenhua ji qi zhexue (東西文化及其哲學). See *Eastern and Western Cultures and Their Philosophies*
Dong Zhongshu (董仲舒), 125
doubt, 92
dun (敦). *See* diligent sincerity
Dussel, Enrique, 185n15
Du Yaquan (杜亞泉), 13, 30

Eastern and Western Cultures and Their Philosophies (*Dongxi wenhua ji qi zhexue* 東西文化及其哲學), 24; author as sage in, 99; and authority, 121, 127; classics in, 107–10, 156; Confucian authority in, 170; Confucianism in, 119; Confucius as authority in, 121–22, 127; cultural typology in, 33–36, 40; Eastern culture in, 83–84; future (authority of) in, 171–72; genealogy in, 125–26; and hermeneutics, 124–26; historical context, 29–32, 53–54, 56–57, 85, 98; historical metanarrative in, 36–39; historical traditions in, 84; history in, 56; history of Confucianism in, 117–19; iconoclasm of, 120; matter in, 85; May Fourth in, 129, 175–76; as mediating intellectual oppositions, 32; metanarrative in, 98, 171; modernity as caesura in, 39–44; naturalization of sage in, 100–04; naturalization rhetoric in, 122–23; and Neo-Confucianism, 123, 126; vs. *New Treatise*, 81, 93–94; and preservation of Confucius's spirit, 105; publication history, 196n78, 203n11; reception of, 29, 196n78, 202n1; self and non-self in, 86; on sinicization of Western culture, 37–38; spirit and matter in, 44–50; spirit of Confucius in, 50–53; syncretism in, 60; teleological history in, 88; tradition-as-history in, 41; tradition in, 55, 97; transcendence in, 47; transhistoricity in, 133–34; on the West, 40; Western thought in, 109. *See also* Liang Shuming
Eastern cultures, 33–35, 38, 43–44, 89, 207n57
emancipation, 44, 48; antitraditions as, 167; and atomization process, 82; and autonomy, 86–87; collective, 84; discourses of, 84; individual, 84; and mind, 64; of the present, 70; and teleological history, 86–87; and tradition, 17, 83; traditional frameworks of, 85
emotions, 65, 215n25
enlightenment: and autonomy, 87; vs. book learning, 239n85; and conventional truth, 145; desire for, 74; and fundamental wisdom, 234n37; in *New Treatise*, 84, 177; and Reality, 233n25; soteriological passage to, 70; and temporality, 75; vs. unenlightenment, 218n54
the Enlightenment, 40, 87, 90, 187n26, 193n59, 223n8
eternal return, 64–67
eternity, 128–29, 169–73
ethics, 41–42, 62–63, 75, 102, 180
Eucken, Rudolf Christoph, 37
Eurocentrism, 4, 22, 35–36, 39, 54, 180
evolution, 45–46, 73–75, 191n46
existential issues, 36–37, 50
expansion (*pi* 闢), 68–69, 217n45

Fabian, Johannes, 189n33

faith, 122, 182, 232n22
the fall, 65–66, 214n22
feeling, 66, 100–01, 112–13
Feng Youlan (馮友蘭), 194n64, 196n78, 222n4
filial piety (*xiao* 孝), 111, 113
fishing, 110–11, 170
Forster, Elisabeth, 190n38
Foucault, Michel, 94
fragmentation, 67–68, 70, 79, 141
freedom, 45, 50–51, 70–72, 79, 85
functions (*yong* 用): and Fundamental Reality (*shiti* 實體) or Reality (*ti* 體), 68, 70, 72, 74, 79–80, 143, 149–50, 216n42; scholarship on, 81
Fundamental Reality (*shiti* 實體), 68–69, 72, 79; and absolute truth, 141; access to, 72; as constant change, 143; as discursive technique, 135; and functions, 68, 70, 72, 74, 79–80, 143, 149–50, 216n42; and language, 82, 149, 151; nonduality of Reality and functions, 68, 143, 216n41; oneness of, 74, 77, 92; as signifier, 143–44; as unchanging, 143
fundamental wisdom (*xuanxue* 玄學), 138, 141–42, 145, 147, 232n15, 234n37
Fung, Edmund S. K., 201n93
futurity, 13, 15, 38, 94, 175, 196n78

gang (剛). *See* resoluteness
Gardner, Daniel K., 124, 230n85
Gauchet, Marcel, 185n15
gender, 123
genealogy of the way (*daotong* 道統), 198n82; as antitradition, 125; and authority, 155; in *Eastern and Western Cultures*, 115–20, 228n63; logic of, 194n63; in *New Treatise*, 154–55; origins of, 97–98; and reactivation of *dao*, 21; texts discussing, 15; Zhu Xi's, 125–26, 223n2
Germany, 150
Giddens, Anthony, 185n12
globalization, 33, 37, 40
gnosis, 138, 141, 177
God, 24
government, 186n22
great harmony (*datong* 大同), 115
great liberation (*da jietuo* 大解脫), 79
guild socialism, 37–38
Guo Qiyong (郭齊勇), 197n79, 218n63

Habermas, Jürgen, 5, 8–9, 188n28
habits, 65–66, 79–81, 101–02, 108
habituated mind (*xixin* 習心), 64–65, 67, 69, 74, 81, 161
habituated tendencies (*xiqi* 習氣), 65–67, 70, 73–75, 80–81, 215n29, 215n35, 216n38; and the past, 148; as shared, 81–82, 221n95
Hanafin, John J., 199n89
Han dynasty, 97, 106
Han exegesis, 106, 117, 123–25, 230n84
Han Yu (韓愈), 97, 117, 224n16
harmony, 37–38, 40, 52
Hartog, François, 186n16, 189n32
heart of compassion (*ceyin zhi xin* 惻隱之心), 112–13
heart of shame (*xiuwu zhi xin* 羞惡之心), 112–13
heaven (*tian* 天): and antitraditions, 128; flowing principle of heaven (*tianli liuxing* 天理流行), 107; and intuition, 101, 115; and naturalization discourses, 123; and sage, 104, 111, 130, 173

hegemony: contestations of, 190n40; counter-hegemonic operations, 15, 174–78; and discourse, 11; and May Fourth, 11–15, 190n38; and sagehood, 178–82
Heidegger, Martin, 150
He Lin (賀麟), 211n83
Henderson, John B., 186n17, 211n90, 231n92
hermeneutics, 6, 18, 106, 123–27; of immediacy, 111–12, 114; unmediated, 156
heteronomy, 87, 90–91, 94, 174, 177
historical antitraditions, 21–22, 32, 99–100, 126–27
historical determinism, 45–46
historical materialism, 46–47
historicity and transhistoricity, 127, 159–60
history: and determinism, 50; and human liberty, 10; and literary authority, 187n25; metanarratives of, 29, 32, 36–39, 87–88; modern vs. premodern, 40; 1916 as splitting, 14; objective study of, 240n5; and philosophy of life of Confucius, 39; as plurilinear process, 242n17; predeterminism, 44–46; progressive, 39; and spirit, 56; teleological, 117, 207n44, 210n78; telos of, 49, 209n72; and value, 194n64
Hon Tze-ki, 184n5, 201n93
Huayan Buddhism, 60, 220
hui (慧). *See* discernment
humaneness (*ren* 仁), 62, 69, 105, 112, 119
humanity, 36–38, 40, 44, 46–49, 74, 196n78
human nature (*xing* 性), 64, 67, 100, 104; alienation from, 65; moral vs. psycho-physical, 156; self-nature (*zixing* 自性), 77
hunting, 110–11, 170
Hu Shi (胡適), 30, 60, 87–88, 109–10, 116, 129, 190n38, 204n14, 213n8, 224n5, 242n19

iconoclasm: defined, 19; antitraditions reproduced by, 95; and criticism, 144–46; discursive techniques, 128; in *Eastern and Western Cultures*, 85, 122; as hegemonic discursive device, 164; and idealism, 85; in *New Treatise*, 85, 134, 162, 173; in *New Youth*, 31; sociohistorical contexts of, 167; spirit vs. history within, 129; and teachers, 125; textual, 19; and tradition-as-history, 17; and truth, 145, 147
idealism, 39, 48, 69, 85, 123, 217n46, 222n2, 229n76
immediacy, 111–12, 114
imperialism, 9, 11, 36, 87, 94
impermanence, 205n22, 219n69, 226n37
Indian culture, 34–35, 37–38, 55, 222n5
individual emancipation, 3, 17, 84
individualism, 62, 91–92
individuality, 41–42, 57, 124, 177
industrialization, 36
inherent mind (*benxin* 本心), 60, 65–67, 74–75, 81, 86, 92, 119; as term, 161; atomization of, 134; origins of, 64; and spatiality, 79; and temporality, 79; and universe, 68
instantaneous arising and ceasing (*chana shengmie* 剎那生滅), 70–72, 218n61, 220n77
interpersonal relationships, 36–38, 48

intuition (*zhijue* 直覺), 38, 100–01, 103–04; and Confucius, 102, 105; as cultural ideal, 227n53; vs. habit, 101–02; and humaneness (*ren* 仁), 112–13; as natural way of life, 103; in philosophy, 109; vs. rationality (*lizhi* 理智), 89, 101; as reading method, 106–08; and reason, 115; and sense-making, 111
irony, 139

Jacobs, Struan, 195n72
James, William, 37
Japan, 30, 60–61, 87, 94
Jenco, Leigh K., 191n44
Jensen, Lionel M., 199n87, 201n92
jijiao lihai (計較利害). *See* cost-benefit analysis
Jinan, 31
Jing Haifeng (景海峰), 232n22
Jullien, François, 225n21
Jung, Carl, 195n69

Kang Youwei (康有為), 13, 115–16, 118, 129–30, 195n73, 228n63, 230n82
kaojuxue (考據學). *See* Qing philology
kataphatic mode of explanation (*biaoquan* 表詮), 148, 161
Kojève, Alexandre, 120, 168–69, 187n27, 229n75, 241n8
Kongzi (孔子), 201n92. *See also* Confucius
Koselleck, Reinhart, 189n32
Kropotkin, Peter, 37

Laclau, Ernesto, 174, 190n40, 190n43
language: and absolute truth, 141–42; and awakening (*jue* 覺), 142; classical Chinese, 138; descriptive language, 69; explanation (apophatic mode of), 142; and Fundamental Reality (*shiti* 實體), 82, 149, 151; habits shaped by, 81; metaphors, 75–76; neologisms, 105; of *New Treatise*, 60, 69, 75; and Oneness, 70, 143; philosophical, 177; prescriptive language, 69; and temporality, 137–38; translingual practice, 22
Laozi (老子), 115
learning, 75–78, 114, 134
Leclerc, Gérard, 188n28
Lee, Leo Ou-fan, 192n50
Levenson, Joseph R., 167–68, 194n64
Leys, Simon, 185n11
li (禮). *See* rituals
Liang Qichao (梁啟超), 31–32, 62, 118
Liang Shuming (梁漱溟): authority as author, 121–22, 128, 173, 176, 180, 225n27, 228n62; and genealogy of the way (*daotong* 道統), 117; lectures by, 31; and May Fourth discourse, 93; as mediating figure (politically), 31–32; narrative of thought, 50; and tradition, 133; understanding of classics, 108–09, 114; and Xiong Shili, 240n2. *See also Eastern and Western Cultures*
liberalism, 14, 60, 91
liberation, 40, 79, 85–86
liberty, 3, 5, 10, 22, 87, 175, 182
Li Dazhao (李大釗), 30, 109, 129
Liezi (列子), 117
life (*sheng* 生), 71–72, 105, 107
Liji (禮記). *See Record of Rites*
Lin Anwu (林安梧), 205n27
Lin Shaoyang (林少陽), 184n5
Lin Yü-sheng (林毓生), 183n4, 190n37, 192n52, 197n80, 202n1
Liu, Lydia H., 22, 91
Liu Shu-hsien, 233n25
liyue (禮樂). *See* ritual and music

lizhi (理智). *See* rationality
Lunyu (論語). *See Analects*
Luo Changpei (羅常培), 31, 203n11
Lu Xiangshan (陸象山), 125, 153, 156
Lu Xun (魯迅), 57, 128
Lynch, Catherine, 31, 202n2, 204n14, 207n44, 211n82, 225n20

Madhyamaka, 60, 148
Makeham, John, 60–61, 147, 152, 157–58, 159, 183n3, 193n61, 197n79, 198n82, 199n89, 214n18, 220n78, 232n10, 235n40, 237n64
mandate of heaven (*tianming* 天命), 45–46, 100–01, 187n22, 208n63
Marincola, John, 187n25
marriage, 174
Marxism, 14, 46, 60, 202n2
materialism, 69, 217n46
material needs, 34, 36–37, 48–49, 51–52
matter: and the body, 70; and contraction and expansion, 68–69; in *Eastern and Western Cultures*, 85; idealistic struggle against, 48; and mind, 69; and the past, 84–85; and spirit, 44–50; spiritualization of, 49
May Fourth: as term, 183n4; antitradition of, 11–15, 192n52; and authority, 168; and Confucianism, 16; discursive milieu of, 129; and Eastern vs. Western cultures debates, 32; factions, 94; futurity in discourse, 175–76; and hegemony, 11–15, 190n38; and individualism, 62, 91; and Liang Shuming, 93; and modernity, 12, 88; modern West in, 40; in *New Treatise*, 64; and Orientalism, 89; political context, 14, 30; success (evaluating), 14–15; and teleological history, 88, 90, 169; in texts, 100; and tradition, 88, 169–70; and West, 13; and Xiong Shili, 93
Ma Yifu (馬一浮), 213n9
mechanization, 36
medicine, 41
Meisner, Maurice, 197n80
Mencius (*Mengzi* 孟子): allusions to, 220n83; and *Eastern and Western Cultures*, 119; and inherent mind (*benxin* 本心), 60; and intuition, 113; and *New Treatise*, 75–76, 156; quotes attributed to Confucius, 107; mentioned, 226n42
Mencius (Mengzi 孟子), 97–98, 107, 124–25, 136, 154–55, 222n1, 228n62, 231n89, 238n75
mental associates (*xinsuo* 心所), 65–70, 73, 75–77, 79, 136, 147–48, 216nn36–37; in *New Treatise*, 67; and sensory experience, 77
metacommentaries, 111, 134–35, 138, 152, 177
metanarratives: Eurocentric, 54; of history, 29, 32, 36–39, 87–88; of modernity, 10, 30, 50, 54; of tradition, 33, 54
metaphysics: as term, 232n15; anthropocentric, 34; Chinese, 41–42; conceptual discussions, 144; of constant transformation, 105; in *Eastern and Western Cultures*, 46–47; and flow of universe, 45; in *New Treatise*, 68, 141, 158
Meynard, Thierry, 49–50, 199n89, 202n3, 208n63, 209n65, 209n72, 212n5, 213n7, 222n5, 231n93
mind (*xin* 心): atomization of, 82; and contraction and expansion, 69; and emancipation, 64; evolution of, 75; and external factors, 82; habituation of, 65; and matter, 69; oneness of, 67–70; and self-cultivation,

mind *(continued)*
  155; theory of, 152; -to-mind transmission, 223n2; and traditions, 64; and the universe, 68, 79. *See also* habituated mind; inherent mind
mind-universe, 59, 63–64, 68, 80–81, 84, 86, 147, 163. *See also* universe
mixin (迷信). *See* superstitions
modern Confucianism: iconoclasm of, 1–5, 15–16, 19, 24–26, 168, 182, 200n90; terminology, 200n90
modernity: acultural understandings of (Taylor), 10; antitraditions of, 7–11, 93, 95; authoritative sources, 109; and authority of tradition, 169; as caesura, 39–44; dialectics of, 9; discourse of, 93–94; in *Eastern and Western Cultures,* 29; as emancipated from past, 44; framework of, 50; historical emergence of, 10; historical time of, 8; and May Fourth, 12, 88; metanarratives of, 10, 30, 50, 54; and power relations, 26; vs. premodernity, 5, 90; telos of, 50; universal, 61
Møllgaard, Eske J., 184n6, 195n71, 210n77, 222n1
monarchy, 29–30, 90
monism, 68, 235n48
morality, 31, 62
Mouffe, Chantal, 174, 190n40
mourning, 112
Mou Zongsan (牟宗三), 15, 62–63, 198n82
movement, 71
Mozi (墨子), 116
museums, 5

Nanjing decade, 160
nationalism, 62–63, 234n39
nature, 104; vs. artifice, 103; as authority, 103; domination of (by the West), 34, 36; naturalization discourse, 119, 122–23, 128, 176
Neo-Confucianism, 4, 15, 21, 97–98, 118, 123–27, 154–55
the new (*xin* 新), 72
New Confucianism, 1–3, 15, 24; terminology, 200n90
New Culture Movement, 29
newness, 159
New Treatise on the Uniqueness of Consciousness (*Xin weishi lun* 新唯識論), 24, 59; anti-intellectualism in, 134; authority of, 159–60, 173; autocommentaries in, 137–38, 177; and autonomy, 87, 91–93; Buddhist sources in, 152–53; classics in, 135–38, 156–57; Confucianism tradition in, 153–57; contemporary issues in, 60–64; counter-hegemonic operations in, 177–78; critiques by, 69; delusion of tradition in, 72–75; discursive figures in, 151–52; dual positioning of, 139–44; vs. *Eastern and Western Cultures,* 81, 93–94; emancipation in, 86; freedom from past in, 70–72; genealogy of the way in, 154–55; historical context, 59–60, 85; iconoclasm in, 134, 162, 164, 173; influences on, 152; (un)learning in, 75–78; as means to truth, 173; metacommentaries in, 135, 177; mind-universe in, 86; and New Confucianism, 198n82; as new theory, 159; objecthood in, 92; oneness of mind in, 67–70; ontology of mind-universe, 59, 84; philosophical system in, 60, 61–62, 63, 157–58, 159–60, 163; publication history, 212n2, 232n16; rejection of teleology, 73; as response to May Fourth, 64; self-cultivation in, 64–67; soteriology of, 180;

textual authority in, 140; tradition in, 64, 84, 170–71; truth in, 145–46; vocabulary borrowing in, 161; and Yogācāra tradition, 150–51, 153–54. *See also* Xiong Shili
New Youth (*Xin qingnian* 新青年), 24, 30–31, 115
Ng Yu-kwan, 213n14
Nie Shuangjiang (聶雙江), 119
nominal discourses, 149–50
nonduality, 68, 143, 216n41, 220n84
noumenal vs. the phenomenal, 70
Nylan, Michael, 232n11

objectification, 142
objects, 71, 92, 101, 153
Odes (*Shijing* 詩經), 239n83
Olberding, Amy, 163
one-many polarity, 70
Oneness: of absolute truth, 141; fragmentation to, 70; of Fundamental Reality, 77; and judging discourse, 149; and language, 143; language of, 70; of mind, 67–70; of reality, 74, 92; rhetoric of, 164; and the self, 78–79, 85; transhistoricity of, 160; and the universe, 70, 85, 135, 141
ontology: of discourses, 148–50; of mind-universe, 63; monist, 68, 235n48; of traditions, 80, 84; for Xiong Shili, 218n63
ordinary people, 139–40, 145–46, 160
Orientalism, 89, 92
origins, 84; iconoclastic potential, 84; perceived deviations from, 119
orthodoxy (*zhengtong* 正統), 104
otherness, 78, 86, 94
ouroboric antitraditions, 173
ouroboric tradition, 161
Ouyang Jingwu (歐陽竟無), 61, 152

participation, 50, 62
particularity vs. universality, 174, 179
passivity, 62
the past: and the body, 72; freedom from, 70–72, 91; and habituated tendencies, 148; iconoclastic readings of, 84; inheritances of, 67; Kojève on, 168–69; and matter, 84–85; and the mind's habits, 65–66; and the present, 72, 74–75, 85; and self-cultivation, 67; as temporal marker of liberty, 175; transcending, 97
Payen, Pascal, 6
Peking University, 31, 54, 61, 107, 208n58
perception of color, 66
perfection, 74
performativity, 82, 109–15, 134
phenomena, 68, 70, 72
philosophical systems, 60–63, 68
philosophy: Chinese, 61; of culture, 212n93, 226n39; language of, 177; of life, 111; in *New Treatise*, 145; philosophical systems, 60–63, 68, 157–60, 163; syncretic, 157; Western, 60, 109, 150; Western and Chinese contrasted, 37, 163
pi (闢). *See* expansion
Pocock, J. G. A., 240n1
political discourse, 87
polysemy, 108
possession, 65
potentiality, 76, 124
precociousness (*zaoshou* 早熟), 39
predeterminism, 44–45, 50
premodernity, 40, 90
prescriptive language, 69
the present, 70, 72, 74–75, 85
present self (*xianzai de wo* 現在的我), 46–48
preservation, 5, 54, 105, 157

previous self (*qianci de wo* 前此的我/ *yicheng de wo* 已成的我), 46–47
print capitalism, 14
private morality, 62
private possession, 65
progress in premodern period, 40
psychology, 37–38
public morality, 62

qianci de wo (前此的我). *See* previous self
Qing empire, 2, 14, 29, 114–15, 118
Qing philology (*kaojuxue* 考據學), 18, 114–15, 118, 133, 156, 177

rationality (*lizhi* 理智), 102, 110–11, 129; detrimental effects of, 210n80; vs. intuition, 89, 144; in *New Treatise*, 234n34; Western conceptions of, 38, 52, 101, 116
Reality (*ti* 體). *See* Fundamental Reality
reason, 90, 93, 101, 115
recognition, 139, 151, 155
Record of Rites (*Liji* 禮記), 111, 115
religious narratives, 19, 185n15
ren (仁). *See* humaneness
Renaissance, 40
Republican period, 60
resoluteness (*gang* 剛), 51–53, 114
Revault d'Allonnes, Myriam, 188n28
revivalism, 55
revolutions, 14, 29–31, 62, 184n5
Ricoeur, Paul, 186n19
ritual and music (*liyue* 禮樂), 163
rituals (*li* 禮), 16, 42
ruism, as term, 200n92
ruler (*zhuzai* 主宰), 69
Russell, Bertrand, 37, 226n37

sages and masters: authority of, 108, 129, 141, 149; authors self-presenting as, 99, 160; and canonization, 97; claims to sagehood, 180; and Confucian iconoclasm, 178; and hegemony, 178–82; intuition of, 111, 122; intuitive spirit, 108; mirroring, 104–09; naturalization of, 100–04, 176; and natural realm, 104; in *New Treatise*, 155–56; performance of, 109–15, 134; as subject, 179; teachings of, 78, 82; texts claims to sageliness, 127; textual transmission, 134; universality as figure, 179, 182
salvation, 62–63
saṃsāra, 37
sangang wuchang 三綱五常. *See* three bonds and five relationships
Sang Yu, 81, 152
scholar-officials, 12
Schopenhauer, Arthur, 109
science, 42, 51–52, 60, 88
Scientism, 189n36
Scott, James C., 188n30
seeds, 65, 148
the self: and non-self, 65, 67, 79, 85–86, 93; notions of, 46–47; and oneness, 78–79, 85; and the past, 168–69; realization by, 77; traditions of, 80, 84; and the universe, 49
self-animation (*zidong* 自動), 70–71
self-consciousness, 62
self-creativity, 76
self-cultivation, 63–67, 69, 72, 74–76, 79; and authority of text, 139; and habituated tendencies, 80; as metacommentary, 134; and mind, 155; *New Treatise* as guide for, 136; as process of atomization, 223n8; as reactivation of origin, 152; and tradition, 70
self-nature, 77

self-recognition, 76
self-renewal, 80
self-sufficiency, 78
sensory experience, 77
Shandong, 30–31. *See also* Jinan
Shen Cheng (申根), 52
shendu (慎獨). *See* vigilance in solitude
sheng (生). *See* life
shi (士). *See* scholar-officials
Shih Shu-mei, 188n30
Shils, Edward, 3, 185n10
shiti (實體). *See* Fundamental Reality
Shujing (書經). See *Documents*
Shun (舜), 124
sinicization, 37–38
Sino-Japanese war, first, 11
Slingerland, Edward, 227n52
social capital, 139
social Darwinism, 11–12, 30, 87, 191n46
social hierarchies, 41
soteriology, 60, 63, 65, 69, 79–80, 135, 180
spatiality: concept of, 71; and inherent mind, 79; in *New Treatise*, 59, 63; of *New Treatise*, 61; and temporality, 10, 40, 43, 56, 189n33
spirit: and consciousness (*yishi* 意識), 209n65; and history, 56; and intuition, 105; and matter, 44–50; teleology and, 85; thirstiness of, 48; tradition-as-value as, 56
spiritualization, 48–49
subjecthood, 17, 179–80, 187n26
subject-object relations, 57, 65–66, 78, 92, 101, 142, 144
suffering, 37, 49
superstitions (*mixin* 迷信), 41–42, 92
Supreme Change (*taiyi* 太易), 68
syncretism, 60, 157, 213n7

taiyi (太易). *See* Supreme Change

Taizhou school (*Taizhou xuepai* 泰州學派), 39, 118
Tang Junyi (唐君毅), 158–59, 198n81
Taylor, Charles, 10
Taylor, Peter, 185n12
tea, 47–48
teleological history, 87–90, 117; and China, 51; and emancipation, 86–87; May Fourth model of, 90, 169; and rejection of future, 94; second phase of, 172; uses of, 88
teleology: and autonomy, 90; in *Eastern and Western Cultures*, 86; and history, 49, 54, 56; of modernity, 50; spirit and, 85; and universe's transformation, 73; and the West, 32, 35, 40, 44, 88
temporality: atemporality, 169; and authority, 165; of Chinese vs. Western culture, 89–90; and genealogy, 155; and inherent mind, 79; and language, 138; of modernity, 8; in *New Treatise*, 59, 63; of *New Treatise*, 61; and spatiality, 10, 40, 43, 56, 189n33; between texts, 137; timelessness, 165
terminology, 32–33
textiles, 85–86, 95, 108, 185n14
texts: authority of, 4–7, 70, 120–23, 155; and authority of sages, 104; and authority of tradition, 97–99; canonization of, 97; discursive techniques, 121; hermeneutics, 106; iconoclasm of, 19; and May Fourth hegemonic group, 168; oneness of, 70; performativity of, 82; polysemy, 108; proofs in, 113; -reader relationship, 136; reading methods, 123–27, 136–37, 229n81; situatedness of, 134; spatio-temporality of, 56; and tradition, 154; transmission of, 134; validity

texts (continued)
  of readings, 115; as woven with tradition, 85–86
thirstiness, 47–48
Thoraval, Joël, 208n59
thought and action, 50
thought-instants, 71
three bonds and five relationships (sangang wuchang 三綱五常), 13, 16, 41, 163
Three Kingdoms period, 117
tian (天). See heaven
tianming (天命). See mandate of heaven
tianren heyi (天人合一). See union of heaven and human
Tillman, Hoyt Cleveland, 125, 230nn86–87
tiyong (體用) polarity, 68, 143, 234n33
traditionalism, 29, 109
traditions: defined, 2–3, 204n15; and agency, 25; and antitraditions, 32; -as-history, 17, 32–33, 38–39, 41–42, 44, 48, 53, 114, 116–20, 122, 206n38; -as-value, 17, 19, 38, 52–53, 56, 90, 126, 206n38; authority of, 4–7, 97–98, 126, 187n27; Buddhism as, 55; Confucianism as, 55, 153–57; continuity of, 20–21, 195n72; delusion of, 72–75; and democracy, 88; and discursivity, 166; in *Eastern and Western Cultures*, 55, 81, 97; and emancipation, 17; freedom from, 85; historical, 32, 222n3; Kojève on, 168–69; legitimacy of, 61; and mind's liberation, 64; and modernity, 5; monopolization of, 93–95; in *New Treatise*, 64, 81, 84; ontology of, 80, 84; origins of, 80–81; ouroboric, 161; and preservation, 1–2, 54; reauthorization of, 100; and science, 88; of the self, 80, 84; and self-cultivation, 70; as shared, 81–82; subject-object relations, 57; subsumption of, 157–59; survival of, 61; temporality of, 186n19; texts as transmitted through, 154; transformation of, 166; transhistoricity of, 165; universality embodied through, 182; value of, 164; as weaving through texts, 85–86; and Western culture, 89
transcendence, 47, 53
transformation, 68–69, 105, 136
transhistoricity, 46, 48, 122, 127, 130; and authority of tradition, 165; direct access to truth, 7; in *Eastern and Western Cultures*, 133–34; historical "proofs" of, 151; and historicity, 127, 159–60; monopolization of, 165–66; and tradition's value, 130
Treaty of Versailles, 30
truth: absolute vs. conventional, 74–75, 140–41; conventional, 161; and iconoclasm, 145, 147; monopolization by elites, 9, 185n15; and Neo-Confucianism, 154–55; in *New Treatise*, 145–46; and rationality (lizhi 理智), 144; as relative, 145; scientific, 196n77; transhistorical, 100; two truths theory, 140, 144, 146–48
Tu Weiming, 222n2

unconditional freedom (xuan jie 懸解), 79
unilinear history, 39, 86–88
union of heaven and human (tianren heyi 天人合一), 38

universality, 22; of Chinese culture, 89; and Chinese identity, 180; and Confucian iconoclasm, 180–81; of futurity, 15; individual's access to, 87; vs. particularity, 174, 179; of sages, 179; of Western knowledge (claimed), 168

universal modernity, 61

the universe: creative flow of, 72; and inherent mind (*benxin* 本心), 68; life force of, 65; life-universe, 34; metaphysical flow, 45; metaphysics of, 34; and mind, 68, 79; oneness and, 70, 85, 141; and the self, 49; telos of, 73; transformations of, 34. *See also* mind-universe

utilitarianism, 50

utopia, 115

value, 170, 194n64

Vasubandhu, 147, 151, 157

vigilance in solitude (*shendu* 慎獨), 78

Wang Aihe, 187n22

Wang Gen (王艮), 39, 118

Wang Hui (汪暉), 8, 191n48

Wang Yangming (王陽明), 4, 39, 153, 156, 161

Wang Zhong (汪中), 117

Weber, Max, 101

Wei-Jin period, 117

weishi (唯識), 153, 237n68

the West: as birthplace of teleological history, 40; forward-oriented will of, 34, 36, 40; as imaginary other, 40; and May Fourth, 13; teleology, 44

Western culture: globalization of, 37; harmony (lack of), 40; and material needs, 48; telos of, 88; and tradition, 89; universality of, 130; as utilitarianism, 50

Western philosophy, 60, 109, 150

Whitman, Walt, 85

the will (*yiyu* 意欲), 35, 45–46, 54, 109, 129–30; of Chinese culture, 36–37; forward-oriented, 34, 36; of Indian culture, 34–35; and rationality, 38; as turning from desire, 37; of Western culture, 34

Wilson, Thomas A., 125, 223n2, 231n90

wisdom (*zhi* 智), 67, 74, 76–77, 138; vs. discernment, 144–45, 160–61; as method, 144–45; in *New Treatise*, 146. *See also* fundamental wisdom

the world, 34, 48–50, 101

World War I, 31

Wuchang Uprising, 213n14

wuxing (五行), 41

Wu Yu (吳虞), 115

xi (翕). *See* contraction

xianzai de wo (現在的我). *See* present self

xiao (孝). *See* filial piety

xin (心). *See* mind

xin (新). *See* the new

xing (性). *See* human nature

Xinhai Revolution, 29–30

Xin qingnian 新青年. *See New Youth*

xinsuo (心所). *See* mental associates

Xin weishi lun (新唯識論). *See New Treatise on the Uniqueness of Consciousness*

Xiong Shili (熊十力): as author, 137–38, 177, 232n10, 239n90; biographical details, 236n61; *Book of the Mind* (*Xinshu* 心書), 62; letters by, 62–63, 158–59; and Liang Shuming, 240n2; and May Fourth discourse, 93; ontology, 218n63; personal awakening of, 135–36,

Xiong Shili *(continued)*
  156–57; and sages of past, 155. See also *New Treatise*
xiqi (習氣). *See* habituated tendencies
xiuwu zhi xin (羞惡之心). *See* heart of shame
xixin (習心). *See* habituated mind
xuan jie (懸解). *See* unconditional freedom
xuanxue (玄學). *See* fundamental wisdom
Xuanzang (玄奘), 147
Xunzi (荀子), 117, 125

Yan Fu (嚴復), 191n46, 217n44
Yang Zhu (楊朱), 116; as chapter of the *Liezi*, 117
Yan Hui (顏回), 124–25
Yao (堯), 124
yicheng de wo (已成的我). *See* previous self
Yijing (易經). See *Changes*
yinyang (陰陽), 41, 72, 219n66
yiyu (意欲). *See* the will
Yogācāra, 47, 59, 146–53; conception of consciousness, 141; in *New Treatise*, 160, 162; seeds in, 65; terminology, 60, 161; wisdom in, 200n89; Xiong Shili's study of, 61. See also *weishi*
yong (用). *See* functions

Yu (禹), 124
Yuan Shikai (袁世凱), 30
Yu Jiyuan, 219n68
Yü Ying-shih (余英時), 15, 21, 133, 184n5, 193n55

Zai Wo (宰我), 112, 170
zaoshou (早熟). *See* precociousness
Zeng Shen (曾參), 124–25
Zhang Xun (張勳), 30
Zhang Zai (張載), 156, 228n62
Zheng Jiadong (鄭家棟), 194n63, 228n63
zhengtong (正統). *See* orthodoxy
zhequan (遮詮). *See* apophatic mode of explanation
zhi (智). *See* wisdom
zhijue (直覺), as neologism, 225n25. *See also* intuition
Zhongyong (中庸). See *Doctrine of the Mean*
Zhou Dunyi (周敦頤), 98, 124
Zhuangzi (莊子), 79, 221n93, 235n41, 239n83
Zhu Xi (朱熹), 21, 97–98, 118, 123–26, 154, 223n2
zhuzai (主宰). *See* ruler
zidong (自動). *See* self-animation
Zisi (子思), 107, 124–25
Žižek, Slavoj, 174

www.ingramcontent.com/pod-product-compliance
Lightning Source LLC
Chambersburg PA
CBHW030528230426
43665CB00010B/805